Reconceptualising Agency and Childhood

By regarding children as actors and conducting empirical research on children's agency, Childhood Studies have gained significant influence on a wide range of different academic disciplines. This has made agency one of the key concepts of Childhood Studies, with articles on the subject featured in handbooks and encyclopaedias.

Reconceptualising Agency and Childhood is the first collection devoted to the central concept of agency in Childhood Studies. With contributions from experts in the field, the chapters cover theoretical, practical, historical, transnational and institutional dimensions of agency, rekindling discussion and introducing fundamental and contemporary sociological perspectives to the field of research. Particular attention is paid to connecting agency in the social sciences with Childhood Studies, considering both the theoretical foundations and the practice of research into agency. Empirical case studies are also explored, which focus upon child protection, schools and childcare at a variety of institutions worldwide.

This book is an essential reference for students and scholars of Childhood Studies, and is also relevant to Sociology, Social Work, Education, Early Childhood Education and Care (ECEC) and Geography.

Florian Esser is a lecturer in the Department of Social Pedagogy and Organisation Studies at the University of Hildesheim, Germany.

Meike S. Baader is Professor for General Educational Science at the University of Hildesheim, Germany.

Tanja Betz is Professor for Childhood Studies and Elementary and Primary Education in the Department of Educational Sciences at Goethe University Frankfurt, Germany.

Beatrice Hungerland is Professor of Childhood Studies at the Magdeburg-Stendal University of Applied Sciences, Germany.

Routledge Research in Education

Reconceptualising Agency and Childhood

New perspectives in Childhood Studies

Edited by Florian Esser, Meike S. Baader, Tanja Betz and Beatrice Hungerland

Routledge
Taylor & Francis Group
LONDON AND NEW YORK

First published 2016 by Routledge

2 Park Square, Milton Park, Abingdon, Oxfordshire OX14 4RN
711 Third Avenue, New York, NY 10017

Routledge is an imprint of the Taylor & Francis Group, an informa business

First issued in paperback 2017

Copyright © 2016 Florian Esser, Meike S. Baader, Tanja Betz and Beatrice Hungerland

British Library Cataloguing in Publication Data
A catalogue record for this book is available from the British Library

Library of Congress Cataloguing in Publication Data
Names: Esser, Florian, editor.
Title: Reconceptualising agency and childhood : new perspectives in childhood studies / edited by Floran Esser, Meike S. Baader, Tanja Betz, and Beatrice Hungerland.
Description: New York, NY : Routledge, 2016.
Identifiers: LCCN 2015036971| ISBN 9781138854192 (hardback) | ISBN 9781315722245 (ebook)
Subjects: LCSH: Children—Study and teaching. | Children—Social conditions. | Child psychology. | Children—Services for.
Classification: LCC HQ767.85 .R435 2016 | DDC 305.23—dc23
LC record available at http://lccn.loc.gov/2015036971

ISBN: 978-1-138-85419-2 (hbk)
ISBN: 978-0-8153-5990-6 (pbk)

Typeset in Galliard
by diacriTech, Chennai

Contents

Notes on contributors

Timo Ackermann is a PhD student in the Department of Social Pedagogy and Organisation Studies at the University of Hildesheim, Germany. His research interests are: Child Protection, Decision Making, Welfare Organisations and Organisational Change. His publications include *Kinder im Kinderschutz. Zur Partizipation von Kindern und Jugendlichen im Hilfeprozess. Eine explorative Studie* [*Children in child protection. About the participation of children and juveniles in the process of care. An explorative study*] (Köln: NZFH, 2013; together with R. Wolff, U. Flick, T. Ackermann, K. Biesel, F. Brandhorst, S. Heinitz, M. Patschke and P. Robin).

Priscilla Alderson is Professor Emerita of Childhood Studies, University College London Institute of Education. Her work includes books and papers on children's rights, competence, wisdom and decision making and the ethics of research with children (details are available at www.ioe.ac.uk/ ssru). Her latest book is *The Politics of Childhoods Real and Imagined: An Introduction to Critical Realism and Childhood Studies* (London: Routledge, November 2015).

Meike S. Baader is Professor for General Educational Science at the University of Hildesheim, Germany. Her research foci are: Childhood, Youth and Family in Modern Societies; Gender Studies; History of Education; Paedophilia and Social Sciences (1960–2000); and Discourses on Motherhood. She edited with co-editors F. Esser and W. Schröer *Kindheiten in der Moderne. Eine Geschichte der Sorge* [Childhood in the Modern Era. A History of Care] (Frankfurt/M.: Campus, 2013). Recently she published "Modernizing early childhood education: the role of German women's movements after 1848 and 1968" (in H. Willekens, K. Scheiwe, & K. Nawrotzki [Eds.], *The Development of Early Childhood Education in Europe and North America: Historical and Comparative Perspectives* [pp. 217-234]. Houndmills: Palgrave Macmillan, 2015).

Tanja Betz is Professor for Childhood Studies and Elementary and Primary Education in the Department of Educational Sciences at Goethe University Frankfurt, Germany. In her research, she focusses on actors (children, parents and professional staff) and institutions of childhood (primary schools, families, ECEC) and how they re-produce or overcome social inequalities. Her publications include *Kindheit und Profession. Konturen und Befunde eines Forschungsfeldes* [*Childhood and profession. Outlines and Findings of a Research Area*] (Weinheim, Basel: Beltz Juventa, 2014; co-editor Peter Cloos); and a paper on "Risks in early childhood. Reconstructing notions of risk in political reports on children and childhood in Germany", *Child Indicators Research*, 2013.

Sabine Bollig is a post-doctoral researcher in the research unit INSIDE at the University of Luxembourg, Grand-Duché du Luxembourg. Her work focusses on the practical and discursive formation of early childhood in medical and educational settings and children's position and practices in day care, mainly explored by ethnographic methods. Her recent book publications include *MultiPluriTrans in Educational Ethnography. Approaching the Multimodality, Plurality and Translocality of Educational Realities* (Bielefeld: transcript, 2015; co-edited by M. -S. Honig, S. Neumann, and C. Seele).

Frederick de Moll is a research associate in the Department of Educational Sciences at Goethe University, Frankfurt, Germany. His primary areas of interest are social inequality in early and middle childhood and the ways in which social class affects parenting styles and children's out-of-school lives. Recently, he has published a paper on "Inequality in pre-school education and care in Germany: an analysis by social class and immigrant status" (*International Studies in Sociology of Education*, 2014; co-authored by Tanja Betz).

Claudia Dreke is Professor for Social Education and Sociological Perspectives on Childhood, Department of Humanities at the Magdeburg-Stendal University of Applied Sciences, Germany. Her research interests include children's and adults' agency and (re-)production of social inequalities in educational institutions. Recently, she published "Bewegung im sozialen Raum? Schulische Sozialisation und künftige soziale Platzierungen von Kindern aus der Sicht von Lehrkräften in Italien und Deutschland" ["Movements in Social Space? Socialization in Schools and the Children's Future as Imagined by School Teachers in Italy and Germany"].

Torsten Eckermann is a research associate at the Department of Educational Sciences at the University of Kassel. His current research areas are children's peer culture, doing and undoing differences in the primary school, cooperative learning and children's play. Recently, he has published a paper on "Das Spiel mit der Geschlechterdifferenz – aufs Spiel gesetzte Grenzen? Geschlechterkonstruktionen beim Pausenspiel von Grundschulkindern aus praxistheoretischer Perspektive" ["Playing with gender differences – playing with gender boundaries? The social construction of gender among children and their peers on elementary school playgrounds from a practice-theoretical perspective"] (GENDER – Zeitschrift für Geschlecht, Kultur und Gesellschaft, 2015).

Florian Esser is a lecturer in the Department of Social Pedagogy and Organisation Studies at the University of Hildesheim, Germany. His work mainly focusses on children's agency and bodies in welfare organisations and on social pedagogy and the history of childhood. His latest publications include *Das Kind als Hybrid. Empirische Kinderforschung (1896–1914)* [*The Child as a Hybrid. Empirical Child Study (1896–1914)*] (Weinheim: Beltz Juventa, 2013) and "Fabricating the developing child in institutions of education. A historical approach to documentation." *Children & Society*, 29(3) 2015, 174–183.

Friederike Heinzel is Professor of Educational Studies with a focus on primary school education at the University of Kassel, Germany. Her main research fields are the linkage between childhood and primary school research, social interaction in primary school education, research methods in childhood studies, and case study work in teachers' education. Her most relevant publication in childhood studies is *Methoden der Kindheitsforschung. Ein Überblick über Forschungszugänge zur kindlichen Perspektive* [*Methods of Childhood Studies. An overview on research approaches to the perspectives of children*] (2nd ed.; Weinheim & München: Juventa, 2012).

Beatrice Hungerland is Professor of Childhood Studies at the Magdeburg-Stendal University of Applied Sciences, Germany. Her main academic fields are sociology of childhood, childhood research, working children and children's rights. She also teaches Childhood Studies in the International master course M.A. Childhood Studies and Children's Rights (MACR) at the Freie Universität Berlin, Germany. In 2014, she edited (together with Helga Kelle) an issue of *Zeitschrift für Soziologie der Erziehung und Sozialisation* with the main topic: "Children as actors – agency and childhood" (*ZSE*, 34. Jg. 2014, H. 3).

Laura B. Kayser is a research associate and PhD student in the Department of Educational Sciences at Goethe University, Frankfurt, Germany. Her main interests are childhood and social inequality studies (especially Bourdieu) as well as qualitative research and research with children. In her PhD project she examines the meaning of social inequality and generational relations in the context of children's in- and out-of-school lives from children's perspectives. Recently, she has published a paper on "Parents' classed orientations as a starting point for inequality-sensitive parent-teacher cooperation" (*Zeitschrift für Grundschulforschung* [*Journal for Primary School Research*], 2015, co-authored by Tanja Betz).

Helga Kelle is Professor of General Educational Science at Bielefeld University, Germany. Her fields of research are (early) childhood studies, theories of education, methods and methodology of qualitative research, and practice analyses of developmental diagnostics. Her recent co-edited publications include the Special Issue 2015 of *Children & Society* on "Documentation in childhood", co-edited with Maarit Alasuutari.

Günter Mey is Professor of Developmental Psychology at the Magdeburg-Stendal University of Applied Sciences, Germany. He is also director of the Institute for Qualitative Research at the International Academy Berlin, Germany. He is editor of the international open access journal *Forum Qualitative Forschung/ Forum: Qualitative Social Research*. He has edited several books, including two handbooks on qualitative research (Springer VS, KSV), two volumes on Grounded Theory Methodology (HSR, Springer VS) and volumes on psychological perspectives on intergenerational relations and the understanding of society (both Psychosozial Verlag); he has also published numerous articles related to qualitative methods and childhood research. In 2015, he directed the documentary film *In Search of Martha Muchow* and edited the volume *The Life Space of the Urban Child. Perspectives on Martha Muchow's Classic Study* (New Brunswick & London: Transaction Publisher, co-edited with Hartmut Gunther).

David Oswell is Professor and Head of the Department of Sociology, Goldsmiths College, University of London. His research has been theoretically engaged with the relations between representations of children and childhood, manifestations of agency, and accumulations of power and authority in institutions and infrastructures. Empirically, his research has considered historical formations of children and childhood in radio and television, as well as contemporary figurations of the child in governmental discourse and practice regarding Internet and broadcast media. His book publications include: *Television, Childhood and the Home: A History of the Making of the Child Television Audience in Britain* (Oxford: Clarendon Press, 2002), *Culture and Society* (London: SAGE Publications, 2006), *Cultural Theory: Volumes 1–4* (London: SAGE Publications, 2010) and *The Agency of Children: From Family to Global Human Rights* (Cambridge: Cambridge University Press, 2013).

Samantha Punch is Professor of Sociology at the School of Applied Social Science, the University of Stirling, Scotland. Her research interests include siblings and birth order, childhoods and youth transitions in Latin America, rural livelihoods in China, Vietnam and India and children's food practices in Scotland. Her book publications include *Children and Young People's Relationships: Learning across Majority and Minority Worlds* (London: Routledge, 2013).

Eberhard Raithelhuber is Assistant Professor at the Department of Educational Science at the University of Salzburg, Austria. During the last ten years, he has published on transitions in the life course, agency in social theory, transnationalism and migration, social support and social intervention, youth and young adults, regional development and networks, social policy, citizenship and democracy. His book publications include *Übergänge und agency: Eine sozialtheoretische Reflexion des Lebenslaufkonzepts [Transitions and Agency. A Reflection of the Life Course Approach from the Perspective of Social Theory]* (Opladen: Budrich UniPress, 2011).

Pierrine Robin is a lecturer in the Department of Social Sciences at the University Paris Est Créteil in Paris. Her work mainly focusses on children's agency in care. Her publications include *Beiträge zur Qualitätsentwicklung im Kinderschutz, Kinder im Kinderschutz – Zur Partizipation von Kindern und Jugendlichen im Hilfeprozess – Eine explorative Studie* (Köln: NZFH, 2013, together with R. Wolff, U. Flick, T. Ackermann, K. Biesel, F. Brandhorst, S. Heinitz, M. Patschke and P. Robin).

Hia Sen is Assistant Professor at the Presidency University Kolkata, India. Her specialisation is in the area of Sociology of Childhood. She has been particularly concerned with the lived experiences of childhood among the middle classes in contemporary India and on how childhoods in different social-historical contexts are conceptualised as a specific biographical phase. Her publications include *"Time-Out" in the Land of Apu: Childhoods, Bildungsmoratorium and the Urban Middle Classes of West Bengal* (Berlin: Springer Verlag, 2014).

Spyros Spyrou is Associate Professor in the Department of Social and Behavioral Sciences at the European University Cyprus and Director of the Center for the Study of Childhood and Adolescence. His current work mainly focusses on children's identities, borders, qualitative research methodology and knowledge production. He has recently co-edited with Miranda Christou *Children and Borders* (Houndmills: Palgrave Macmillan, 2014).

Hanne Warming is Professor of Sociology, Childhood and Social Work, and head of the research group "Changing Societies: Citizenship, Participation and Power", at the Department of Society and Globalisation, Roskilde University, Denmark. Her research interests are on childhood, child welfare, children's everyday lives, perspectives, participation and lived citizenship, and how sociological theories can inform/be informed by – and need re-construction for the purpose of – childhood studies. She has led substantial research projects funded by a range of funders including the Danish Council for Independent Research: Social Sciences (FSE), The Danish Ministry of Social Affairs, The Egmont Foundation and the Obel Foundation. Likewise, she has participated in various international and comparative research projects, including "Social Services – a comparative Nordic study" (1994–1996), "Squaring the Welfare Circle in Europe" (1994–95), "Cost Action 19: Children's Welfare" (2001–2006) and the EU Child Participation Study (2013).

Anne Wihstutz is Professor of Sociology at Berlin Protestant University of Applied Sciences, Germany. She is currently also the equal opportunities commissioner of Berlin Protestant University of Applied Sciences. Her fields of research cover care work, recognition theories, citizenship studies and children's rights. Her book publications include *Verantwortung und Anerkennung. Qualitative Studie zur Bedeutung von Arbeit für Kinder* [*Responsibility and*

Recognition. Qualitative Study on the Meaning of Work to Children] (Münster, Berlin: LiT, 2009).

Tamaki Yoshida researched physical punishment in two primary schools in Tanzania for her PhD at UCL Institute of Education. She has worked at the Japanese embassy in Dar es Salam. Her areas of interest are children's agency, international development and critical realism.

Reconceptualising agency and childhood

An introduction

Florian Esser, Meike S. Baader, Tanja Betz and Beatrice Hungerland

Agency is, without question, one of the key concepts, possibly *the* key concept of Childhood Studies (James & James, 2012, p. 3). And yet the present volume is, after David Oswell's comprehensive monograph on children's agency (Oswell, 2013), the first to explicitly and systematically focus on this key concept, its use in Childhood Studies and its significance for the (further) development of this branch of research. There are several reasons for this interest in a more systematic engagement with the concept of agency, first and foremost the fact that agency has a major influence on research activities in Childhood Studies and beyond. However, the inclusion of agency in Childhood Studies is associated with conflicting interests (Renner, 2015, p. 304). These will be explored from a critical and interdisciplinary perspective in this volume. Critical theoretical and empirical questions on the robustness of this concept will also require attention. The present volume thus offers a comprehensive overview of the debate about the concept of agency in Childhood Studies, bringing together various strands of theory from the debate about childhood agency, which also display national and transnational differences. The aim here is to reconceptualise agency so that its considerable potential can continue to be utilised for future research and theory development on children and childhood, both nationally and internationally. Elements of theory from the wider social theory debate, gender studies, postcolonial studies and historical research are included here, in order to offer an interdisciplinary and transdisciplinary view of the broad spectrum of relevant questions, approaches and developments.

Children as actors: agency in Childhood Studies

The significance of agency as a key concept for Childhood Studies goes back to the original aspiration of this area of research: to appreciate children's active contribution to the shaping of their social worlds and to society, and to theoretically conceptualise and empirically analyse this contribution. This was explained, for example, by Allison James and Alan Prout, who formulated the following influential statement in the foreword to their 1990 publication, *Constructing and Reconstructing Childhood*: "Children are and must be seen as active in the construction and determination of their own social lives, the lives of those around them and of the societies in which they live. Children are not just the passive subjects of social structures and processes" (Prout & James, 1990, p. 8).

Some years later, Allison James, Chris Jenks and Alan Prout (1998) used a new term to convey the same meaning: "childhood agency". This term remains well established to this day. In the current second edition of *Key Concepts in Childhood Studies*, published in 2012, the section entitled "Agency" contains the following comment: "The idea that children can be seen as independent *social actors* is core to the development of the new paradigm of the study of children and young people" (James & James, 2012, p. 3). And of course there is also a prominently positioned article on agency in the *Palgrave Handbook of Childhood Studies* – in Section 1, among the "Concepts of Childhood Studies" (James, 2009). This leads to the question of how this concept was able to become such an obvious and omnipresent element of Childhood Studies. Why did agency become so central for the paradigmatic shift to which the proponents of Childhood Studies laid claim? The following interconnected factors may be seen as crucial for the popularity and centrality of the concept of agency within Childhood Studies:

1   One source of inspiration – roughly from the late 1980s – was academia, and the academic study of children. The now almost dogmatic insistence on agency and its constitutive importance for Childhood Studies can be seen as the result of a critical reaction to nearly all the previous discussions of children and childhood in academic research, which had been criticised as adult-centred (Burman, 1994; Turmel, 2008, p. 307; Stainton Rogers & Stainton Rogers, 1992). Psychology, sociology and the academic disciplines of education and social work were accused of instrumentalising children and childhood, and of only being interested in the process of growing up or in the state of adulthood. Whether they were theories of socialisation in sociology, developmental theories in psychology or theoretical approaches in the field of educational science, they were all (according to these criticisms) based on a developmental paradigm that regarded children purely as future adults and considered the successful transition to adulthood to be its goal. Childhood, according to the critics, was thus reduced to a phase in life and a transitory state on the way to adulthood, and children's current thinking and acting receded into the background, while their learning and preparation for adulthood were treated as more important. This applies, for example, to the perspectives of the "scholarisation" and "pedagogisation" of childhood. The new aspect of "New Childhood Studies" was the claim that "childhood and children's social relationships and cultures are worthy of study in their own right and not just in respect to their social construction by adults" (Prout & James, 1990, p. 8). The idea was that childhood

would become an independent focus of research in the social sciences and that children themselves would become statistical units, e.g. in social reporting (Sgritta, 2005). The conclusion was that public and political attention had previously focused more on family and processes of "familialisation" than on children. It was therefore necessary to build up a separate reporting system and indicators relating to the living conditions of children, a system that is now nationally and internationally established (for more about the beginnings, see Qvortrup et al., 1994; Betz, 2008, 2010a, 2010b; UNICEF, 2010). Within these reporting systems, within child indicator research and beyond, the focus on the actor was emphasised (Betz, 2008, p. 46; Fattore, Mason & Watson, 2012). Here children were integrated into the research by means of quantitative, standardised and mostly representative methods, but also increasingly by qualitative methods (Fattore et al., 2012). In the course of these changes, children also became research subjects in a narrower sense in other branches of research (Hungerland, 2015; for example in developmental psychology, see Mey, 2005, and in this volume). James (2007) summed up this general aspiration with this concise phrase: "giving voice to children's voices". This insistence on taking children into account in social research, but also in social reporting, helped to establish the field of Childhood Studies in scholarship and research.

2 Second, however, agency was related to not only how children and childhood should be represented in the social sciences, but also how they behaved as actors in their own lives. This was supposed to simultaneously draw attention to political processes and the political agenda, which had not previously focused on children as a separate group with their own interests and needs. The central positioning of the agency concept in Childhood Studies was also intended as a contribution to the social emancipation of children (Betz, 2008, p. 63). Childhood Studies discovered children as a "minority group", which, due to its marginalised social position, lacked opportunities for articulation – and not (only) skills related to development or socialisation – in an adult-dominated society (James, Jenks, & Prout, 1998, p. 210). Children often go unseen and unheard, and have relatively few visible opportunities to influence society. This is evident, for example, in their limited rights, in their status as semi-citizens, and in the fact that they do not have the right to vote, as well as in their exclusion from paid employment, the trend towards "decommodification", and compulsory schooling, etc. The thesis, still convincing today, is that the marginalised social position of children should not be attributed to the fact that they lack the skills required for participation, but to their systematic exclusion from opportunities for participation and active involvement. This is justified with their lack of physical and mental maturity: On the one hand, they are seen as vulnerable, and excluded for their own protection; and on the other hand, the idea of the *Bildungsmoratorium* or *pädagogisches Moratorium* (the

extension or prolongation of education) not only exempts children from paid employment, but simultaneously excludes them from this social sphere. This line of argument – the systematic linking of childhood and adulthood with their respective freedoms but also restrictions – is partly based on references to feminism. According to feminist theory, unjust, hierarchical gender orders and the "unequal" generational order are theoretically and empirically connected (Alanen, 1992, pp. 26ff.), and produce societies that have a powerful impact on the acting and being of adults and children. From this perspective, perceiving children as actors and reconstructing their agency meant carrying out research on their expressivity, their relative independence and their rebelliousness towards structures established by adults. Such research could take place, for example, in educational institutions, in families, or in children's cultures created by children. Furthermore, these largely politically motivated developments were concerned with "giving children a voice", by questioning them and listening to their views in the "here and now" about "relevant" matters (mostly from an adult point of view), and allowing their well-being and agency to be expressed. This interlinking of research objects and political concerns is, for example, characteristic of the international "child indicators movement" (Ben-Arieh, 2008, 2010); here Betz (2013) speaks of the "amalgamation of research and politics" (p. 639). The children's rights movement also displays a close link between child-related (practice-based) research and political concerns (Stoecklin, 2013).

The insight that children are, within the generational power structure, structurally disadvantaged in relation to adults and thus have the status of a social minority, has found its way from Childhood Studies into socio-political practice aimed at improving the position of children in society. Since the adoption of the UN Convention on the Rights of the Child (CRC 1989), children all over the world have been accorded the status of subjects having rights. This means that they are no longer the objects of arbitrary action by adults, but can exercise their rights, and can insist on the observation of these rights themselves (Liebel, 2007, p. 209). The United Nations Convention sees children as having rights and obligations, and as such, no fundamental limits are placed on their agency. At the same time, the law limits children's agency by defining them as "minors" who are dependent on adults and who have special limitations and duties, but also rights to protection. Research based on the rights of children claims to take the subject or actor status of children seriously and support it by using participatory research methods that allow children to be "co-researchers", partaking in the interpretation and use of the data collected (Liebel, 2008; Kellett, 2005). The aim of such practice-based research projects is to enable children to explore their environment independently, to understand and question it and thus ultimately to actively co-create and change it. Child-based, subject-oriented research claims to give children a chance to express themselves in their own language and form (Honig, 1999). The idea is that this will not only generate insights into the effects of social phenomena on children as a group, but will also express appreciation and recognition for children's utterances and needs (Hungerland, 2015).

Both the representation of children in the context of social research and their position as social actors have been influenced by two interconnecting factors. From a scholarly perspective, the aim was to adequately represent the agency of children, while from a political perspective, this more accurate representation was expected to help improve children's situation. In terms of the history of science, this interlinking of an analytical and an emancipatory focus can be explained by the fact that international and transnational stimuli from the "new social movements" that have emerged since the 1970s, such as the women's movement, various movements to liberalise education and child-raising and the children's rights movement, have been transferred into academia (Baader, 2014). The above-mentioned close connection between criticism of the gender order and criticism of the generational order in the social sciences was not first formed in the context of these sciences, but had already been formulated early on by the new women's movement, for example in Shulamit Firestone's international bestseller of 1970, *The Dialectic of Sex* (Baader, 2015a). Another work that broke new ground with regard to children's position in society, their rights and their voices, and thus with regard to academic and political "interest in the child", was published by the historian Philipp Ariès in 1962. This study, which attracted international attention, made the epistemically important observation that the understanding of childhood had changed within society, and was therefore not an anthropological constant. Ariès wrote the history of childhood in the modern age as a history of the loss of "childhood agency", and thus provided key stimuli for a social constructivist perspective on childhood.

A key concept on trial

Now, however, around 25 years after the first edition of *Constructing and Reconstructing Childhood* (James & Prout, 1990) was published, childhood agency as an established concept, or even a paradigm, is once again becoming a focus of attention. Some of this attention has been critical. This is because the last few years have revealed not only the potential of the agency concept (in particular, its significant contribution to the establishment and international dissemination of Childhood Studies), but also – and partly as a result of this – its side effects or limitations. These have then become an object of debate.

To a certain degree, the research can be divided into micro-sociological actor-based research from the perspective of *children*, which is often politically and pedagogically motivated, and more discursive or macro-sociological research on the social production of *childhood* by an adult-dominated society – in which children and childhood are suppressed, marginalised and regulated. In the German research, this is often marked linguistically with a differentiation into child studies

(*Kinderforschung*) and Childhood Studies (*Kindheitsforschung*) (Honig, Leu, & Nissen, 1996; Hengst & Zeiher, 2005). This could be described as a meeting between a world from above and a world from below, offering a representation of what Fuchs (2001, p. 25) has described critically as the "Great Divide" of the social sciences. This divide runs between the micro-level and the macro-level, between subject and object, between action and structure. For Childhood Studies, it also runs, in simplified terms, between a more structure-based Scandinavian tradition and a more ethnographic, actor-oriented Anglo-Saxon tradition. The German debate in Childhood Studies is shaped both by structure-oriented and actor-oriented approaches. In an international comparison of the different national or regional forms taken by New Childhood Studies, Hengst (2003) underlines the fact that the German debate, due to the establishment of a micro-sociological approach in sociology, was not able to reject the concept of socialisation as vehemently as the Anglo-Scandinavian discourse had (James, 2013).

An additional factor is that a large proportion of the existing research is based on a concept of the "child as actor", which is ultimately substantialist and anthropological, while there are fewer articles examining the talk of the child as actor from a (de-)constructivist perspective (see Betz, 2013). In the dominant ontological discussion about the child, the image of the "child as a deficient being", the "child as a developmental being" or the "child as a vulnerable being" (Baader, 2015b) is "simply" countered – often within the framework of modernisation theory – with the image of the "child as actor", which is marked as a "modern" perspective on children and childhood (Esser, 2013, pp. 18–21). This also applies to the self-characterisation within the child indicators movement, where it is asserted that the political and academic agenda no longer focuses or should no longer focus on the perspective of the adults, but on that of the children ("from an adult to a child perspective": Ben-Arieh, 2008, 2010; for a critical view see Betz, 2013). There is also a certain tension in research related to children's rights: between the assumption of a fundamental actor status, a special legal position and the practices of resource provision by adults. Often the reality of action research projects with children, in which they are supposed to be given space to exercise their agency, shows that the decisions about the initiative and the conditions for participation depend on what adults are prepared to allow (Hungerland, 2015).

Thus, thanks to an anthropological premise – that the child simply "is" an actor – the connection to the social conditions of childhood, which should play a defining role in Childhood Studies, is often lost (Honig, 2009). A substantialist concept of the actor and the child is based on a de-historicised, de-socialised, individual-centred idea of action. Action becomes, simply, a human capability. The difference between children and adults also becomes blurred: In the end, they are all competent actors, whose natural "agency" is waiting to be discovered during the research process (Punch, 2002, p. 321), or may come to light via political participation projects. Furthermore, this interpretation makes it difficult to define the specific features of Childhood Studies with reference to the "child as actor". For at least 3,000 years, children have been seen as having actor status, and this has proven to have a critical role in shaping modern thinking about children (Bradley, 2013). Educators have always been happy to evoke the child's status as actor when seeking to distinguish their own pedagogical programmes and ideas from the established concepts of childhood and the generational order. Moreover, the fixed and exaggerated assumption of children's agency conveys the expectation that children should show agency – in the expected form (Bordonaro & Payne, 2012). This, however, makes it difficult, particularly in the initiatives and debates relating to children's rights, to allow any form of children's "agency" that runs counter to the adult perspective. This is shown, for example, by Twum-Danso Imoh (2013), in her interviews with children who experience physical violence by adults and interpret this as an expression of love and concern. The assumption of agency also creates the expectation that (adult) researchers have to enable and "uncover" this agency on the part of children. This means that one of the tasks in the research process is to detect this agency and make it "public": "If children are social actors then they have a part to play in their own representation, to have their voices heard and to be positioned as the subjects rather the objects of research" (Fattore et al., 2012, p. 430). This ultimately means, however, that the only "real" form of Childhood Studies is (qualitative) research with children. Furthermore, if children are, during the research process, expected to show agency (or a particular form of agency corresponding to the public/political discourse), this reproduces the problem of the "instrumentalisation of children", which Childhood Studies had set out to combat.

A further point of criticism raised in Childhood Studies is not only that the concept of children's agency has not been sufficiently developed theoretically but, more importantly, that it exists alongside but largely unconnected to another key theoretical concept, that of "generational ordering" (e.g. Bühler-Niederberger, 2011; Alanen, 2009). Generational ordering has, in recent years, proven to be a productive concept, and one that is in many respects theoretically compatible with childhood agency. It relates to the on-going social construction of the complementary categories of children and adults, and makes it possible to analyse the discourses and practices in which different positions, forms of authority, responsibilities and access to resources are distributed across the generations. Processes of generational ordering are seen as a core element of social order, allowing childhood to be developed and constantly re-produced as a social marker of differentiation, and also giving opportunities to examine adulthood.

A number of works in Childhood Studies subscribe to both of these concepts, and yet the lack of theoretical connection between the concepts of childhood agency and generational ordering means that their findings are seen as lacking theoretical foundation and being of little use for social analysis (Bühler-Niederberger, 2011, p. 199). The concepts therefore need to be systematically analysed and positioned in relationship to one another. A precondition for this is that child agency has to be developed theoretically as a relational concept in order to be able to connect it to the concept of generational ordering: thus the discourses and practices of generational ordering present themselves as the condition for children's agency, which is made possible and limited by generational ordering. At the same time, however, the actions of children also have a reproductive or transformative effect on the generational order. Within the sociology of childhood, it is hoped that the theoretical linking of the two concepts of agency and generational ordering will help to overcome the dualism of structure and agency. This also links in with the fundamental question of Childhood Studies, which attempts to explain children's capacity to act within their individual positioning as children in different social contexts (Hungerland & Kelle, 2014).

Reconceptualising agency and childhood I: new paths in the theoretical conceptualisation of agency (Section I)

As a result of these developments, Prout's critical comment that "the 'agency' in 'children's agency' remains inadequately theorised" (Prout, 2000, p. 16) has led, around 15 years later, to a debate about an appropriate reconceptualisation of agency (Esser, 2016). This theoretical reflection makes up the first section of the present volume, "Theoretical perspectives".

The first impetus for theoretical reflection on agency in Childhood Studies has mainly empirical foundations. Its starting point is specific analyses in which Childhood Studies scholars have attempted to reconstruct children's agency but have failed (Jensen, 2014; Muftee, 2015; Klocker, 2007). Their research has to do with children outside the Western world who do not possess the social capacity to act and create, which has normally been associated with agency in Childhood Studies. An alternative term used here is "thin agency", to reflect this capacity to act within narrow limits.

These and other empirically based approaches (Bühler-Niederberger & Schwittek, 2014; Polvere, 2014) are ultimately aimed at a "modelling" of agency. In other words, a Western concept of agency, which takes an autonomously acting subject as its starting point, is modified or modelled for non-Western childhoods or for the lives of children in total institutions. Bordonaro and Payne (2012, p. 366) take a fundamentally critical view of such attempts. They argue that such modifications still perpetuate a Western ideal of "thick agency", or the autonomous capacity for action. This is an idea that they call into question, however – not just for children outside the Western world, but also for children in Western societies. In line with proponents of feminist theories, they fundamentally reject a worldview in which the masculine and autonomous subject is treated as the gold standard. Cockburn (2013, p. 14) also observes that "all people, including adults, are interlinked, interdependent and reliant on others". A theory of agency that does not wish to simply transfer fictions of Western autonomy from the adult male subject to children must therefore not denigrate dependency and the need for care, and thus the vulnerability of humans and children. *Anne Wihstutz* follows this line of enquiry in her chapter, taking feminist theories of care as her starting point and relating these to Childhood Studies.

Both feminist theories of care as well as certain strands within Social Theory share the aspiration to locate agency in social relations and interdependency instead of independence and autonomy. Relational social theories, as discussed most notably in the contributions of *David Oswell, Florian Esser* and *Eberhard Raithelhuber*, are based on the assumption that agency is not inherent in individual entities but that these entities themselves and their agency are originally produced in relationships (Sørensen, 2013, pp. 117f.). Agency is therefore not a quality that children possess by nature; instead, it is produced in conjunction with a whole network of different human and non-human actors, and is distributed among these. A similar impetus to decentralise agency is found in practice theories, as *Sabine Bollig* and *Helga Kelle* discuss in their chapter. Here, agency is inherent in the practices in which actors participate. Subsequent chapters in the book pick up these fundamental theoretical perspectives, along with further perspectives on the agency concept, including ones based on social theory. These theoretical perspectives are then given more concrete form in relation to research practice, the historical and transnational perspective and children's agency in the institution of childhood.

Reconceptualising agency and childhood II: effects on research practice (Section II)

Since the beginnings of New Childhood Studies, the vehemently posited claim to regard children as actors has linked the theoretical foundations of this branch of scholarship with its practical research orientation. This has occurred in the framework of a mainly qualitative, actor-based research profile, especially in situations where children's agency was particularly important. Perceiving children as actors has always been associated with a methodological aspiration: the aim was to give children, who had previously been condemned to silence, a voice, and to formulate reality from their perspective (James, 2007; for a critical view, see Honig, 1999). In many cases, Childhood Studies scholars have focused their efforts on reconstructing agency by documenting the utterances of children, with a strong emphasis on authenticity (Spyrou, 2011). The importance of ethnographic approaches in Childhood Studies also springs from the need to get as close as possible to children's everyday lives and experiences.

The second section of the book, "Children as actors in research", will examine the frequent tendency to equate agency with authenticity in research practice (Komulainen, 2007). *Spyros Spyrou*, for example, criticises an overly substantialist understanding of "the" voice of children. As an alternative, he advocates a reflexive approach, which is also open to silent and ambiguous aspects of verbal utterances. The approach outlined by *Hanne Warming* is also reflexive;

she argues that the research process should include reflecting on the institutionally formed identity positions of children and researchers, from which agency arises, and dealing with these in a playful way. *Priscilla Alderson* and *Tamaki Yoshida* emphasise the fact that their approach is inspired by the "critical realism" of philosophy, and not sociology. They thus provide a counterweight to the relational and practice-theory-based approaches presented in Section I. Alderson and Yoshida stress, however, that they also take existing social realities as their starting point. Here, they distinguish between different forms of power: first, a power that suppresses "agency", and second, a form of power that enables it. Agency-related research that is not based on a substantialist concept of agency can also be expanded to include quantitative approaches, although there is as yet little research on this (cf. de Moll & Betz, Section V).

Contexts of agency in Childhood Studies: reconceptualising agency and childhood: historical, transnational and institution-based approaches (Sections III–V)

As shown in Sections I and II, then, agency has been challenged and reconceptualised in Childhood Studies with regard to both theory and research practice. The necessary stimuli for this do not come solely from importing relevant theoretical discussions from other contexts into Childhood Studies. Instead it is findings from various areas of research within Childhood Studies that have inspired doubts about the theoretical *and* empirical adequacy of a model of agency based on autonomous and substantialist actors. In particular, research on childhoods from historical, transnational and institutional perspectives offer the relevant stimuli for a critical reconceptualisation of agency.

Historical traditions of agency (Section III)

In the section on "Agency in historical perspective", *Meike S. Baader* gives insights into how agency, as an important feature of children and childhood, can be traced back in historical-systematic terms at least as far as the Romantic period. It becomes clear where exactly these substantialist and anthropological assumptions come from, in which philosophical and pedagogical contexts they arose, how they are connected with debates about the Christian religion and how they are transformed, but at the same time preserved, in discourses about childhood in the modern age. *Günther Mey* evokes Martha Muchow's study on "life space" (*Lebensraum*), an important German work on agency from the 1920s, now also published in English (Muchow & Muchow, 2015), while *Beatrice Hungerland* investigates various agency concepts since the 1950s, which manifest themselves in the context of different ideas of generational order. These three chapters call into question the historical self-understanding of Childhood Studies, the conviction that it was the "New Sociology of Childhood" that first introduced the idea of children's agency into the academic discourse on childhood, in the form of a paradigmatic shift (Ryan, 2008). On the contrary, children's agency has long been inscribed – in various ways – into academic, popular and political discourses about childhood. Historical Childhood Studies, however, can not only reconstruct the fact *that* a concept of children's agency existed before the "New Sociology of Childhood", but can also answer the empirically interesting question of *how* agency has been ascribed to and inscribed onto children at different times, and what consequences this has for childhood in each case.

Transnational and majority world perspectives of agency (Section IV)

Besides insights into the historical situatedness and changeability of agency and childhood, it is insights from (post-)colonial and transnational studies that have done the most to challenge universalist assumptions about "global" human agency. Here, the idea of autonomous and individual agency has been unmasked as a Western concept for the appropriation and exploitation of the world. At the same time, these research contexts have generated important theoretical and empirical stimuli for the further development of the concept of agency. These are especially helpful in situations where Childhood Studies scholars are operating outside the so-called "Western world".

Samantha Punch questions why there continues to be a gap between the academic discourse of childhood agency and the arenas of policy and practice. She suggests that our understanding of children's agency could be enhanced by engaging in cross-cultural dialogue between the so-called majority and minority worlds. Another majority world perspective is offered by *Hia Sen*. She uses the concept of the "subaltern" to consider how the idea of children's agency might be translated into her Indian research context. Last, *Laura B. Kayser* takes the example of a children's rights project, also located in India, to show how the children perceive themselves as members of a marginalised social group and engage with the contextual boundaries of the generational order from this social position. The chapters in this section do not only raise the issue of the adequacy of a Western understanding of agency for the so-called "majority worlds" and refine this understanding for post-colonial and non-Western contexts. They can also be understood on a much more fundamental level as a critical questioning and reconceptualisation of agency in the majority *and* minority worlds.

Agency in institutions of childhood (Section V)

A third field of research whose activities have led to a critical reconceptualisation of agency is concerned with the effects of the institutionalisation of childhood (Zeiher, 2009). Earlier proponents of Childhood Studies did observe children's agency in institutions, but mostly at times and in places where adults were as little involved as possible (for a very early example, see Opie & Opie, 1959). They assumed that agency had the greatest possible scope to develop in such situations, and that children's "productive" (and not reproductive) contribution to world-making could be observed here. If agency was identified in generational relationships, this was generally a matter of resistance on the part of children, whose agency was restricted by adults, who, in turn, represented institutions (Esser, 2016). If, however, agency is regarded as relational and socially produced, then it never develops in opposition to social relationships, but always within them. An institutionalised childhood, then, gives rise to certain questions: not just whether institutions restrict agency, but also, more importantly, how institutions of childhood and children (co-)produce agency and therefore reproduce social and thus generational orders. *Claudia Dreke* examines these questions for children's day-care, Timo *Ackermann* and *Pierrine Robin* for the institution of child protection, and *Thorsten Eckermann* and *Friederike Heinzel* for the primary school system. Lastly, Frederick *de Moll* and *Tanja Betz* investigate to what extent the production of unequal agency can be ascribed not only to the institution of "school" or children's dispositions towards school and their out-of-school practices, but also to their social class affiliation and their status as children. The chapter not only constructs a link between different social institutions, but its quantitative approach also challenges the largely implicit assumption that research on agency requires qualitative research designs.

Conclusion

This volume assembles contributions on agency from a range of different social theories, research methods, times, localities, institutions and disciplines. The individual chapters resort to ontologies from relational and post-structuralist approaches to critical realism; the deployed research methodologies reach from qualitative to quantitative designs; the chapters cover a time range from the nineteenth century until today, the second decade of the twenty-first century; they investigate children's agency between highly institutionalised settings and peer activities; and their authors come from as different disciplines as psychology and sociology; some more engaged in applied sciences, others more interested in basic research. Addressing agency from these manifold perspectives, the individual chapters – not unsurprisingly – come to quite different conceptions of agency. This is not regarded as a deficit or disadvantage. Presenting the on-going academic and professional debate on agency in a piecemeal fashion like this does not aim to achieve a perpetual and singular concept of agency. Instead, *Reconceptualising Agency and Childhood* shows that agency is a dynamic and highly debated concept, which – exactly because of this – has the potential to work as a key concept of Childhood Studies in the years to come.

References

Alanen, L. (1992). *Modern Childhood? Exploring the 'Child Question' in Sociology.* Jyväskylä: Kasvatustieteiden Tutkimuslaitos.

Alanen, L. (2009). Generational order. In J. Qvortrup, W. A. Corsaro & M. -S. Honig (Eds.), *The Palgrave Handbook of Childhood Studies* (pp. 159–174). London: Palgrave Macmillan.

Baader, M. S. (2014). Die reflexive Kindheit [The Reflexive Childhood]. In M. S. Baader, F. Esser & W. Schröer (Eds.), *Kindheiten in der Moderne: Eine Geschichte der Sorge [Childhoods in the Modern Era: A History of Care]* (pp. 414–455). Frankfurt/M., New York: Campus.

Baader, M. S. (2015a). Vulnerable Kinder in der Moderne in erziehungs- und emotionsgeschichtlicher Perspektive [Vulnerable Children in the Modern Era from the Perspective of a History of Education and Emotion]. In S. Andresen, C. Koch & J. König (Eds.), *Vulnerable Kinder: Interdisziplinäre Annäherungen [Vulnerable Children: Interdisciplinary Approaches]* (pp. 79–102). Wiesbaden: Springer VS.

Baader, M. S. (2015b). Modernizing early childhood education: the role of German women's movements after 1848 and 1968. In H. Willekens, K. Scheiwe & K. Nawrotzki (Eds.), *The Development of Early Childhood Education in Europe and North America: Historical and Comparative Perspectives* (pp. 217–234). Houndmills, New York: Palgrave Macmillan.

Ben-Arieh, A. (2008). The child indicators movement: past, present and future. *Child Indicators Research, 1*(1), 3–16.

Ben-Arieh, A. (2010). From child welfare to children well-being. The child indicators perspective. In S. B. Kamerman, A. Ben-Arieh & S. Phipps (Eds.), *From Child Welfare to Child Well-Being. An International Perspective on Knowledge in the Service of Policy Making* (pp. 9–22). Dordrecht: Springer.

Betz, T. (2008). *Ungleiche Kindheiten. Theoretische und empirische Analysen zur Sozialberichterstattung über Kinder [Unequal Childhoods. Theoretical and Empirical Studies on Child Indicators]*. Weinheim: Juventa.

Betz, T. (2010a). Informed child policy on the basis of standardised children's surveys. *Forum 21. European Journal on Child and Youth Research, 12*(4), 1–6. Retrieved from www.coe.int/t/dg4/youth/Source/Resources/Forum21/II_Issue_No4/II_No4_Children_surveys_en.pdf (accessed 30 July 2015).

Betz, T. (2010b). Modern children and their well-being. Dismantling an ideal. In S. Andresen, I. Diehm, U. Sander & H. Ziegler (Eds.), *Children and the Good Life. New Challenges for Research on Children* (pp. 13–28). Dordrecht: Springer.

Betz, T. (2013). Counting what counts. How children are represented in national and international reporting systems. *Child Indicators Research, 6*(4), 637–657.

Bordonaro, L. I. & Payne, R. (2012). Ambiguous agency. Critical perspectives on social interventions with children and youth in Africa. *Children's Geographies, 10*(4), 365–372.

Bradley, K. (2013). Images of childhood in classical antiquity. In P. S. Fass. (Ed.), *The Routledge History of Childhood in the Western World* (pp. 17–39). London, New York: Routledge.

Bühler-Niederberger, D. (2011). *Lebensphase Kindheit: Theoretische Ansätze, Akteure und Handlungsräume [Childhood as a phase of life: Theoretical approaches, actors and arenas of actions]*. Weinheim, Munich: Juventa.

Bühler-Niederberger, D. & Schwittek, J. (2014). Young children in Kyrgyzstan: agency in tight hierarchical structures. *Childhood, 21*(4), 502–516.

Burman, E. (1994). *Deconstructing Developmental Psychology*. London, New York: Routledge.

Cockburn, T. (2013). *Rethinking Children's Citizenship*. Basingstoke, Hampshire, UK: Palgrave Macmillan.

Esser, F. (2013). *Das Kind als Hybrid: Empirische Kinderforschung (1896–1914)* [*The Child as a Hybrid. Empirical Child Study (1896–1914)*]. Weinheim, Munich: Beltz Juventa.

Esser, F. (2016). Children's agency and welfare organizations from an intergenerational perspective. In S. Punch & R. Vanderbeck (Eds.), *Families, Intergenerationality and Peer Group Relations (forthcoming)*. Dordrecht: Springer.

Fattore, T. Mason, J. & Watson, E. (2012). Locating the child centrally as subject in research: towards a child interpretation of well-being. *Child Indicators Research*, *5*(3), 423–435.

Fuchs, S. (2001). Beyond agency. *Sociological Theory*, *19*(1), 24–40.

Hengst, H. (2003). Ein internationales Phänomen. Die neue soziologische Kindheitsforschung [An international phenomenon. The new sociology of childhood]. In B. Orth, Th. Schwietring & J. Weiß (Eds.), *Soziologische Forschung. Stand und Perspektiven. Ein Handbuch* [*Sociological Research. State of the Art and Perspectives. A Handbook*] (pp. 195–213). Opladen: Leske & Budrich.

Hengst, H. & Zeiher, H. (Eds.) (2005). *Kindheit soziologisch* [*Childhood sociologically*]. Wiesbaden: Springer VS.

Honig, M. -S. (1999). Forschung "vom Kinde aus"? Perspektivität in der Kindheitsforschung [Childhood "from the Child's Point of View"? Perspectivity in Childhood Studies]. In M. -S. Honig, A. Lange & H. R. Leu (Eds.), *Aus der Perspektive von Kindern? Zur Methodologie der Kindheitsforschung* [*From the Children's Point of View? The Methodology of Childhood Studies*] (pp. 33–50). Weinheim, Munich: Beltz Juventa.

Honig, M. -S. (2009). How is the child constituted in Childhood Studies? In J. Qvortrup, W. A. Corsaro & M. -S. Honig (Eds.), *The Palgrave Handbook of Childhood Studies* (pp. 62–77). Basingstoke, Hampshire, UK: Palgrave Macmillan.

Honig, M. -S., Leu, H. R. & Nissen, U. (1996). Kindheit als Sozialisationsphase und als kulturelles Muster: Zur Strukturierung eines Forschungsfeldes [Childhood as a Time of Socialisation and as a Cultural Pattern: The Structurisation of a Field of Research]. In M. -S. Honig, H. R. Leu & U. Nissen (Eds.), *Kinder und Kindheit: soziokulturelle Muster – sozialisationstheoretische Perspektiven* [*Children and Childhood: Socio-cultural Patterns - Socialisation Theories*] (pp. 9–29). Weinheim: Juventa.

Hungerland, B. (2015). Children as actors in Muchow's life space study and its implications for "new" Childhood Studies. In G. Mey & H. Günther (Eds.), *The Life Space of the Urban Child: Perspectives on Martha Muchow's Classic Study* (pp. 249–264). New Brunswick, London: Transaction Publishers.

Hungerland, B. & Kelle, H. (2014). Kinder als Akteure – Agency und Kindheit: Einführung in den Themenschwerpunkt [Children as Actors - Agency and Childhood: Introduction to the Special Issue]. *Zeitschrift für Soziologie der Erziehung und Sozialisation*, *34*(3), 227–232.

James, A. (2007). Giving voice to children's voices: practices and problems, pitfalls and potentials. *American Anthropologist*, *109*(2), 261–272.

James, A. (2009). Agency. In J. Qvortrup, W. A. Corsaro & M. -S. Honig (Eds.), *The Palgrave Handbook of Childhood Studies* (pp. 34–45). Basingstoke, Hampshire, UK: Palgrave Macmillan.

James, A. (2013). *Socialising Children*. Basingstoke, UK: Palgrave.

James, A. & James, A. (2012). *Key Concepts in Childhood Studies* (2nd ed.). Los Angeles: Sage Publications.

James, A. & Prout, A. (Eds.). (1990). *Constructing and Reconstructing Childhood: Contemporary Issues in the Sociological Study of Childhood*. London, New York: The Falmer Press.

James, A. Jenks, C. & Prout, A. (1998). *Theorizing Childhood*. Cambridge: Polity Press.

Jensen, K. B. (2014). Space-time geography of female live-in child domestic workers in Dhaka, Bangladesh. *Children's Geographies, 12*(2), 154–169.

Kellett, M. (2005). *How to Develop Children as Researchers*. London: Sage.

Klocker, N. (2007). An example of "thin" agency: child domestic workers in Tanzania. In R. Panell, S. Punch & E. Robson (Eds.), *Global Perspectives on Rural Childhood and Youth: Young Rural Lives* (pp. 83–94). New York: Routledge.

Komulainen, S. (2007). The ambiguity of the child's "*voice*" in social research. *Childhood, 14*(1), 11–28.

Liebel, M. (2007). *Wozu Kinderrechte. Grundlagen und Perspektiven* [*Why Children's Rights? Basics and Approaches*]. Weinheim: Juventa.

Liebel, M. (2008). Forschende Kinder [Children as Researchers]. In *Neue Praxis. Zeitschrift für Sozialarbeit, Sozialpädagogik und Sozialpolitik*, 38 Jg. H. 3, 239–251.

Mey, G. (Ed.) (2005). *Handbuch Qualitative Entwicklungspsychologie. Positionen und Verfahren* [*Handbook of Qualitative Developmental Psychology. Positions and Methods*]. Cologne: Kölner Studien Verlag.

Muchow, M. & Muchow, H. H. (2015 [1935]). The life space of the urban child. In G. Mey & H. Günther (Eds.), *The Life Space of the Urban Child: Perspectives on Martha Muchow's Classic Study* (pp. 61–146). Brunswick: Transaction Publisher.

Muftee, M. (2015). Children's agency in resettlement: a study of Swedish cultural orientation programs in Kenya and Sudan. *Children's Geographies, 13*(2), 131–148.

Opie, I. & Opie, P. (1959). *The Lore and Language of Schoolchildren*. Oxford: Oxford University Press.

Oswell, D. (2013). *The Agency of Children: From Family to Global Human Rights*. Cambridge: Cambridge University Press.

Polvere, L. (2014). Agency in institutionalised youth: a critical inquiry. *Children & Society, 28*(3), 182–193.

Prout, A. (2000). Childhood bodies. Construction, agency and hybridity. In A. Prout (Ed.), *The Body, Childhood and Society* (pp. 1–18). Houndmills, UK: Macmillan.

Prout, A. & James, A. (1990). A new paradigm for the sociology of childhood? Provenance, promise and problems. In A. James & A. Prout (Eds.), *Constructing and Reconstructing Childhood. Contemporary Issues in the Sociological Study of Childhood* (pp. 7–34). London/New York/Philadelphia: RoutledgeFalmer.

Punch, S. (2002). Research with children: the same or different from research with adults? *Childhood, 9*(3), 321–341.

Qvortrup, J. Bardy, M., Sgritta, G. & Wintersberger, H. (Eds.) (1994). *Childhood Matters: Social Theory, Practice and Politics*. Aldershot, UK: Avebury.

Renner, K. J. (2015). The ambiguous role of agency in Childhood Studies. *Child, special issue of WSQ, 43*(1/2), 304–307.

Ryan, P. J. (2008). How new is the "new" social study of childhood? The myth of a paradigm shift. *Journal of Interdisciplinary History, 38*(4), 553–576.

Sgritta, G. B. (2005). Kindheitssoziologie und Statistik. Eine generationale Perspektive [Sociology of Childhood and Statistics. A Generational Approach]. In H. Hengst & H. Zeiher (Eds.), *Kindheit soziologisch [Childhood sociologically]* (pp. 49–64). Wiesbaden: VS.

Sørensen, E. (2013). Human presence: Towards a posthumanist approach to experience. *Subjectivity, 6*(1), 112–129.

Spyrou, S. (2011). The limits of children's voices: from authenticity to critical, reflexive representation. *Childhood, 18*(2), 151–165.

Stainton Rogers, R. & Stainton Rogers, W. (1992). *Stories of Childhood: Shifting Agendas of Child Concern.* Hassocks: Harvester.

Stoecklin, D. (2013). Theories of action in the field of child participation: in search of explicit frameworks. *Childhood, 20*(4), 443–457.

Turmel, A. (2008). *A Historical Sociology of Childhood: Developmental Thinking, Categorization and Graphic Visualization.* Cambridge: Cambridge University Press.

Twum-Danso Imoh, A. (2013). Children's perceptions of physical punishment in Ghana and the implications for children's rights. *Childhood, 20*(4), 472–486.

UNICEF (2010). *The Children Left Behind. A League Table of Inequality in Child Well-Being in the World's Rich Nations.* Innocenti Report Card 9. Florence: UNICEF Innocenti Research Centre.

United Nations General Assembly (CRC) (1989). *Convention on the Rights of the Child.* Retrieved from UN Office of the High Commissioner for Human Rights website: www.ohchr.org/en/professionalinterest/pages/crc.aspx (accessed 15 October 2015).

Zeiher, H. (2009). Institutionalization as a secular trend. In J. Qvortrup, W. A. Corsaro & M. -S. Honig (Eds.), *The Palgrave Handbook of Childhood Studies* (pp. 127–139). Basingstoke, Hampshire, UK: Palgrave Macmillan.

Section I

Theoretical perspectives

Chapter 1

Re-aligning children's agency and re-socialising children in Childhood Studies

David Oswell

In Childhood Studies, in contrast to strands of thinking that have foregrounded a political emphasis on "child-centredness" (e.g. reference to standpoint theory [Alanen, 1994]) and a theoretical emphasis on the reflexive agency of children in the context of social structure (James and Prout, 1990; James et al., 1998), there has been a line of thinking that has stressed the distributed, ontologically heterogeneous, and dependent capacities of children (Lee, 2001; Oswell, 2013; Prout, 2005). In the first line of thinking, children's agency is often discussed in the context of a sociological problematic concerning agency and structure, often resting on the theoretical premises of Anthony Giddens' social theory; in the second, agency is often understood as distributed across "actor-networks" or "assemblages" in the context of "post-social" theories derived from Bruno Latour or Gilles Deleuze. In much of the literature in the field, the distinctions between these two lines of thinking are often not made evident. However, where the differences are made evident, discussion often centres on the distinction between human-centred and post-humanist epistemologies of children's agency. This chapter will frame these two lines of thinking about children and childhood in the context of broader shifts in sociological understanding concerning the ontology of agency, the questioning of the scalar attributions of structure (macro) and agency (micro), and a methodological shift of focus from ethnography and discourse analysis (James and Prout, 1990) to what is often seen as a more "object-centred" focus on devices, descriptions, liveness and invention (Marres, 2012; Back and Puwar, 2012; Lury and Wakeford, 2013). In doing so, the intention is to refocus discussion on the question of children as a complex social collectivity and to offer a line of thinking fit for understanding the place of children within an ontologically complex, interconnected, multi-mediated social world.

If there was ever a singular form of children's agency, it is clear now that agency as a topic of social theory and empirical investigation is plural. Across the disciplines of anthropology, sociology, history, literary studies, social psychology, media, cultural studies and others that might be seen to comprise

Childhood Studies, there are different and differently accented models of accounting for the activeness and interactions of children. Sometimes "agency" is foregrounded as a particular conceptual idea, sometimes it is not. I make no attempt to capture this diversity. Rather, in this chapter I want to consider two major strands of thinking within Childhood Studies that are often merged and muddied, yet provide two very distinct ways of considering the agency of children. These two strands can be broadly considered in terms of, on the one hand, a notion of agency that adopts a child-centred epistemological and political standpoint (Alanen, 1994) aligned with a theory of the child as a reflexive self in the context of social structure that is made and remade (James & Prout, 1990; James, Jenks, & Prout, 1998) and, on the other, an understanding of the distributed, ontologically heterogeneous and dependent capacities of children (Lee, 2001; Oswell, 2013; Prout, 2005). In the first line of thinking, children's agency is often discussed in the context of a sociological problematic concerning agency and structure, often resting on the theoretical premises of Anthony Giddens' social theory (see also Raithelhuber in this volume); in the second, agency is often understood as distributed across "actor-networks" or across "assemblages" in the context of "post social" theories derived from Bruno Latour or Gilles Deleuze (see also Esser in this volume). This chapter will frame these two lines of thinking about children and childhood in the context of broader shifts in sociological understanding concerning the political ontology of agency, the questioning of the scalar attributions of structure (macro) and agency (micro), and a methodological shift of focus from ethnography and discourse analysis (see James & Prout, 1990) to what is often seen as a more "object-centred" focus on devices, descriptions, liveness and invention (see Marres, 2012; Back & Puwar, 2012; Lury & Wakeford, 2013). In doing so, the intention is to refocus discussion on the question of children as a complex social collectivity and to offer a line of thinking fit for understanding the place of children within an ontologically complex, interconnected, multi-mediated social world.

One "new paradigm", two problematics

At a moment when Childhood Studies was forming as a field of study – at least, that is, as a field of study as we currently know it, although the empirically informed understandings of children and childhood were rich and textured – two clear but related problematics are visible. The first problematic was articulated in Allison James and Allan Prout's opening chapters in the edited collection on *Constructing and Reconstructing Childhood*, which was originally published in 1990. In many ways this was a founding statement for the "new paradigm" of Childhood Studies. The main contours of this intervention will be familiar to many: childhood is a social construction; childhood is a variable of social analysis and is always articulated with other social variables, such as class, gender, sexuality, disability, "race" and ethnicity; children should be studied in their own right, not as dependent on a framing relationship with and by adults; children are active in the construction of their social lives; ethnography is a privileged method for the social investigation of children; and childhood is a social phenomenon that is both constructed and reconstructed, such that children are actively engaged in the double hermeneutic of this construction and reconstruction (Prout & James, 1990, pp. 8–9). The emphasis is on social construction, on the particularity of that social construction inasmuch as any childhood is formed through particular articulations with other social variables and contexts, and on children as reflexively active and having capacity in the construction and reconstruction of their social lives. As such, it provides (a) a theoretical understanding of the ontology of the child, which it offers (in one form at least) through Giddens' structuration theory; (b) a clear direction regarding the politics of children, inasmuch as children's agency is seen to be an articulation from the perspective and position of their experience, through their voice, and in the context of a structural inequality (and any politics of Childhood Studies was seen to need to align itself with and support that positionality); and (c) a broad-reaching methodological orientation, insofar as the construction of children and childhood is understood through interpretative, qualitative and ethnographic sociology and anthropology. The writings associated with this problematic are paradigmatic and programmatic with regard to the *theoretical*, the *political* and the *methodological*.

Giddens' social theory provided Childhood Studies with a means for analysing the double (re)construction of childhood, such that children were themselves seen to be reflexive and agentic subjects, who could both interpret social settings and act in relation to those settings with a view to the achievement of their intentions: "Every act which contributes to the reproduction of a structure is also an act of production, and as such may initiate change by altering the structure at the same time as it reproduces it" (Giddens, 1979, p. 69, quoted in Prout & James, 1990, p. 28). Prout and James provide a Giddensian inflection to what Jens Qvortrup earlier referred to in terms of the need to emphasise children as social beings, rather than social becomings (Qvortrup, 1985; see also Jenks, 1996). The focus on this double hermeneutic draws attention to the process of construction as a process instantiated in the present. A critique of a model of childhood predicated on the notions of "growth", "development" and "socialisation" (Alanen, 1988; Jenks, 1982) was argued on the basis that children's lives actually have a "degree of autonomy" from any conditions of linearity (Alanen, 1988, p. 60). The determination of social structure, but also the power of agency to change that structure, are instantiated in the present time. A theory of the being-ness of children, of their ontology, is understood as a form of *political ontology*, inasmuch as a statement about what children are is also a statement about their capacity to change the organisation of the social world in which they live. This strong ontological claim is articulated with a strong *methodological* claim regarding not only how we might, but how we should investigate the beingness of children: namely, the agentic presentness of children is understood in terms of children's lived experience, which can be empirically investigated through ethnographic and qualitative methods (Alanen, 1988, p. 60).

Moreover, even when empirical investigations favour an understanding of the constitution of competence in relations of social interaction (in contrast to the residual individualism of Giddens' model), there is still an emphasis on these interactions in conditions of co-presence (Hutchby & Moran-Ellis, 1998). Even in research that draws on different theoretical resources to consider the agentic subjectivity of children in their everyday lives, such as in Berry Mayall's (2002) or Leena Alanen's (2000) research, there is still an engagement with the problematic of the self-presence of children as a social group. A standpoint epistemology that draws from Sandra Harding and Dorothy Smith frames the relationality of generational difference, child (and childhood) and adult (and adulthood), within a singular perspective that is both political and ontological. Moreover, even when there is a concern to factor the history of children's lives, such history is often considered only inasmuch as "the past influences the present" (Mayall, 2002, p. 39) and, in doing so, the self-present subjectivity of children is left unquestioned.

Amidst the emergence of this "new paradigm" are research and writings that methodologically sit happily with it, but in fact come from a very different and antithetical theoretical heritage, one that would question the political alignment of experience, authenticity and voice. This second problematic appears in its more theoretical guise not only in Prout's single-authored book, *The Future of Childhood* (2005), but also in different forms in the work of Nicholas Lee (2001), André Turmel (2008), and Claudia Castañeda (2002). In its more theoretical guise, it is influenced by Foucauldian ideas of power and knowledge, actor-network theory's approach to materiality and semiosis, Deleuzian ideas of becoming and connection, and post-structuralist understandings of subjectivity. But inasmuch as this problematic never discloses itself fully as a new paradigm, at least in any programmatic form, it is better to refer to this as an "infra-paradigm", one that ghosts and has a phantasmatic presence. That this infra-paradigm could sit so happily with, and not thoroughly problematise, the politics of voice, authenticity and experience perhaps suggests either that the theoretical labour of post-Foucauldian and actor-network analysis was not taken seriously or that the politics of voice, authenticity and experience was itself gestural and not aligned with a systematically formed theoretical architecture. Suffice it to say that methodologically there was a confluence with the "new paradigm" because much of the second problematic was empirical in focus, in the first instance not explicitly theoretical, and largely emerged from an interest with science, technology, medicine and the body (see Mayall, 2013). To a large extent, this infra-paradigm is never foregrounded as antithetical to the "new paradigm", and writers, such as and most notably Alan Prout, are seen to sit in both paradigms, not least because the infra-paradigm is never presented as a paradigm. Prout's research into children in medical settings draws on theoretical ideas from post-Foucauldian and actor-network theory, but is also positioned alongside the very differently theoretically positioned research of Pia Christensen (1998, 2000). We might typify this infra-paradigm less through its theoretical or political formation than through its methodological orientation. There is a methodological emphasis on the axiom of "no *a priori*" inasmuch as the patterns of social association, which are often presumed to be social structure, cannot be presumed before empirical investigation. The axiom of "no *a priori*" means that no assumptions can be made beforehand either but also about who or what acts *as* an actor (human or non-human). Thus Prout, sympathetic to Alanen's notion of "generational ordering" or "generationing" as a performative, is insistent that this is a process, not a finished product; it is open-ended and emergent, not closed, and it is heterogeneous with regard to its materiality (Prout, 2005, p. 78). Turmel, in his history of the devices and technologies through which children have been measured, assessed and judged in the context of "normal development", also explicitly frames his historical sociology in a way that downplays the theoretical as a point of differentiation from other sociologies of childhood. He frames the central sociological question as follows: "What is childhood from a sociological standpoint if it is no longer either a residue of social theory or a peripheral phenomenon of adult society?" (Turmel, 2008, p. 306). The point, then, is not to mark out an actor-network approach to children and childhood from a Giddensian approach in terms of the different and competing theories, but rather to contest a theoretical approach *per se*. This move (which is resonant with an ethnomethodological orientation) is central to the longstanding antipathy between science and technology studies and the history and philosophy of science (see Lynch, 1997). But it is more broadly a form of empirical (rather than empiricist) sociology that, for example, allows Turmel to focus on the particular "inscription devices" through which children, as a collectivity, become visible as a social phenomenon. Turmel explicitly draws on actor-network methodologies and more broadly on science and technology studies to consider this (e.g. Latour & Woolgar, 1986). He is not interested in the "idea of childhood" as "the Hegelian pure idea – produced by philosophers" (Turmel, 2008, p. 3).

Inasmuch as the infra-paradigm does not emphasise any theoretical antagonism toward the "new paradigm" (due to its deflation of "the philosophical" within the horizon of empirical devices, statements, technologies and socio-historical settings), nor any political antagonism (due to its understanding of children and childhood not as a perspective to be championed but as a field of empirical enquiry), it is able often to sit happily side-by-side and below them. There has been no "bust-up" along the fault lines of humanism against anti-humanism, or theoretical (and political) posturing with regard to the veridicality of philosophical positions. Given the prevalence of such battles across the social and cultural sciences over the last 25 years, it is certainly strange that Childhood Studies has not similarly been poisoned. That is to its good, but the question now is whether such a confluence can be maintained in the sociological conditions of the contemporary or whether the cracks will begin to show. I consider this question in the context of three sociological trends, or at least major questions, regarding ontology, scale and methodology.

From strong to weak ontology

As argued above, against the philosophical mode of the time, Childhood Studies founded itself very deliberately on a "metaphysics of presence" (see Derrida, 1982). The alignment of the centred child subject (as both agentic and reflexive) with experience and authenticity of experience, and with clarity of voice (as organised political speech), rests on a notion that the agency of the child and children centres on their being and acting in the present. James and Prout (1990), in the conclusion to their edited collection, are critical, as are many other writers in the field, of constructions of children and childhood in terms of a nostalgic past, a vision of the future society, and as being locked outside of time. The past, the future and the timelessness of children and childhood have provided the dominant forms through which children are conceptualised and imagined with regard to their temporalisation: "the 'present' of childhood is systematically down-played" the "present is continuously banished to the past, the future or out of time altogether" (James & Prout, 1990, p. 220). This formulation does more than simply provide the basis for a critique (and understanding) of age-based constructions of generational difference and transition or developmentalist models of child socialisation as a linear and normalising process or welfarist and other constructions of the child as the future saviour of humanity or notions of childhood innocence (see also Baader in this volume). As argued above, this formulation is a statement about the ontology of children "as beings-in-the-present" (James & Prout, 1990, p. 232), about their mode of existence ("childhood as a continuously experienced and created social phenomenon" [James & Prout, 1990, p. 231]) and thus also about the extension of their capacity ("[c]hildren can thus be thought through as active beings in a social world at all points in their growth and development" [James & Prout, 1990, p. 233]).

As argued above, this can be understood in strong programmatic terms as a statement of the political ontology of childhood, but it can also be understood, conversely, from the position of the second infra-paradigm. The "new paradigm" can be re-interpreted in terms of how all ontologies are themselves embedded within accounts of the world and how there are multiple ontologies embedded in multiple accounts (see Mol, 2002). These ontologies are always situated (Haraway, 1988). In this sense, the ontological claims of the "new paradigm" must be understood as weak claims. Children are present in the present, but there is much more to say than this. Children have "presence", but such presence is supported and infrastructured, itself situated in claims and counter-claims. Moreover, if the claims are ontologically weak, then two modes of thinking open up: first, as the political philosopher Jane Bennett has argued, it means we do not have to think of ontology from the point of view of "a traditional metaphysician"; we can emphasise "the necessarily speculative and contestable character of [our] onto-story" (Bennett, 2001, p. 160 ff.); but also, second, we are able to be more ontologically generous with regard to our understanding of the child-self, the social and the world; we are open to considering the onto-logical richness of those relations in a way that both disperses agency across the human and non-human and construes those associations as vibrant, enchanted and sociologically interested and interesting. In that sense, the work of Latour, Callon, Barad, Haraway, Deleuze and others (often headed in terms of "the turn to ontology" [Woolgar & Lezaun, 2013] or "the new materialism"), all become sources of provocation for testing the empirical and the experiential. But equally, so do Giddens, Bourdieu and others. In that sense, the claim to weak ontology becomes an invitation to think of the ontological worlds of children in the context of the experimental.

In the purview of such weak ontologies, children's agency (children as "active", "participative" and politically demonstrative) is less something that can be or needs to be asserted, and more something to be explored (see Prout, 2005, p. 65). Moreover, when the ontological world of children is opened up, what "counts", what is "counted" and what is "accounted for" itself becomes open. The various methodological turns to the visual (Knowles, 2014; Pink, 2007), the auditory and sonic (Back, 2007), the sensory (Pink, 2009) and the material-ity and object-ness of the world (Marres, 2012) in their different ways signal a sociological interest in social relations that are not only mediated by voice, text or the symbolic. Moreover, the innovations from science and technology studies and from sociologies of the environment and animals (Latour, 2004; Massumi, 2014) suggest a richness with regard to what now counts as the ontological. The problematic, then, is not one that starkly contrasts structure against agency, but one that considers how children's agency might be assembled and infrastructured within and across a range of devices, materialities, technologies and other sentient bodies. It is an understanding of a children's agency, as Lee (2001) argued, that is very much dependent and unfinished.

Scalar attributes and scaling

The shape of Childhood Studies as an interdisciplinary space has to a large extent been formed and moulded through "structure" and "agency" understood as spatial but also scalar categories, inasmuch as the former refers to "macro" social categories and processes and the latter to "micro" ones. Moreover, since Ariès in the 1960s, an understanding of a foundational differentiation between children and adults has been formulated according to both a spatial and scalar differentiation between "adulthood" and "childhood" (see Oswell, 2013). Thus, Chris Jenks (1982, p. 10) states that:

> the child cannot be imagined except in relation to a conception of the adult, but interestingly it becomes impossible to produce a well defined sense of the adult and his society without first positing the child. From this may be distilled two elements that appear common to all approaches to childhood. First, a belief that *the child instances difference and particularity,* and secondly, following from the former, a desire to account for the integration of that difference into *a more broadly conceived sense of order and universality that comprises adult society* (my italics).

This packaging of children into a Euclidean modelling of space is certainly open to questioning.

Monika Krause (2013) has recently argued for a strategy of recombination regarding the categories of "micro" and "macro". She argues that this scalar distribution only began as a sociological debate in the early 1960s, when "micro-sociologists", thus named, positioned themselves and responded against the perceived "macro-focus of the dominant schools in post-war sociology in the United States" (p. 142). Ever since, the distinction has been formative in the organisation of conferences, undergraduate curriculum, empirical research and social theoretical discussion. She argues that the distinction was less a theoretical specification than a polemical articulation, often not defined or only vaguely so. In a second wave of the debate in the 1980s, the concern was less about contesting the dominance of macro-sociology than about "bridging the gap between" the two sociologies. From this second wave, Krause mentions Jeffrey Alexander, Randall Collins, Stephen Fuchs, Karin Knorr-Cetina, Aaron Cicourel, Nicos Mouzelis, George Ritzer and Norbert Wiley, but we might also add Anthony Giddens as a key protagonist for "bridging the gap" from UK sociology and social theory, and Pierre Bourdieu from France. In this context, agency, individual, lifeworld, the everyday, local, discursive and symbolic interaction and meaning and meaning-making are all seen as attributes of the micro-sociological in contrast to structure, the collective, system, monumental, global, statistical and objectivity, which are seen as attributes of the macro-sociological. Alongside "gap bridging", which implies a distance that needs to be corrected, Krause also looks at "recombination" insofar as this strategy is concerned with releasing "aspects of the distinction [...] from their association with one side of the divide" and reassessing them in a more fluid mix (Krause, 2013, p. 145). In Childhood Studies, Prout (2005) has forcefully argued for an understanding of childhood in conditions of hybridity and Lee (2001) for the status of childhood as ambivalent.

Whereas Krause seeks to open up and disaggregate, as an epistemological exercise, the attributes of the categories of "micro" and "macro", work within actor-network theory has sought to consider how scale is itself produced within sociological settings. Latour's investigation and analysis of mapping, measuring, writing and travel, in the context of early European imperial pursuits, is one example of this. This analysis frames his more pronounced theoretical statements about globalisation in the 1990s and 2000s (e.g. Latour, 2005). Another example is Albena Yaneva's research on architectural practice and the processes of scaling. Observing how architects in the Netherlands and New York use different methods and devices to scale projects, Yaneva considers the processes of "scaling up", "scaling down" and "jumping", not in the sense of a proportional model of the relation between models and the real world, nor through mathematical modelling, nor through a phenomenological method in which scale is understood from a subjective perspective, but rather as a "rhythmic conduit" inasmuch as the conduit is "an ordered variation in a series of moves performed with different intensities and speeds" (Yaneva, 2005, p. 870). Architects can zoom in, stand back, build bigger or smaller, adapt lighting and texture. Modelscopes (like elongated microscopes) are used alongside models and computer diagrams. Architects jump from scale to scale without reference to any objective scaling measure: "small and large models exist together, guiding the architects from one to the other, and crystallizing in a circuit … [T]here is no stable distinction between small and large, real and virtual" (Yaneva, 2005, p. 886). In her writing with Latour, she is critical of a notion of scaling that is reducible to Euclidean space. On the contrary, scaling is the rhythmic ordering through which scaled space is made. There are not just two or even three dimensions. It is through understanding the architectural drawing and modelling in particular practices that we can understand how space is conceptualised and made. There is no external space, no external measure "within which" all other spatialisation and modelling are understood and measured. For the architects, as for Yaneva and Latour, "[i]t would be simply inappropriate to limit to *three dimensions* an activity that, by definition, means piling on more and more dimensions every time" (Latour & Yaneva, 2008). Spatial and scalar practices are constructive of space and scale (see Massey, 2005).

Such an understanding offers a way of problematising any micro/macro divide. It suggests a multiplicity of scales to be empirically investigated and mapped. And yet, we cannot be naive to the fact that Yaneva, as with Latour in his studies, seems to focus on the local settings, on conditions of co-presence. What they observe are practices that seem to be discretely contained. They observe sociological settings. Yaneva is clear that, following Bruno Latour and Steve Woolgar (1986), Mike Lynch (1997) and Karin Knorr-Cetina (1999), who empirically observe the laboratory setting, she will study the architectural office "in the same way" (Yaneva, 2005, p. 869). But I think that this does not demonstrate an ascendency of the micro and the local as the place where things and worlds are really made, the place where agency really happens. On the contrary, what, for example, Latour and Woolgar are clear to show is that inscription devices (namely, those machines that make, describe and account for the world) are not local as such, but they have a scalar complexity. It is not simply micro actors making up the macro, or local actors making up the global. In actor-network theory there is a deconstruction of that notion of scale. Latour and Woolgar do not hold the laboratory as a unitary dimensional space; it is not Euclidean or Cartesian, for example. Rather, what they observe is that actors (whether humans or diagrams or test tubes) do not have a singular scale. On the contrary, Latour and Woolgar refer to how "a 'bioassay for TRF' counts as *one* inscription device even though it takes five individuals three weeks to operate and occupies several rooms in the laboratory" (Latour & Woolgar, 1986, p. 89). Some of what they look at is small, some big, some happening in the moment, some over much longer periods of time. Their observation of the laboratory is not in that sense phenomenological. Just as any ontology is weak, so too is any procedure for scaling partial and situated, but in such a manner that the setting is itself unstable and not settled in terms of its scalar attributes.

Methodological opportunities

As many have argued, sociology is "facing an unprecedented challenge and opportunity" (see Back & Puwar, 2012, p. 6). The privileged position of the sociologist, armed with ethnographic, survey and interview methods, documenting, mapping and listening to the social within the bounded groups of the locality or nation, is now questioned and recontextualised in relation to a surfeit of data. Data is made available in both its raw and manufactured (already analysed and coded) forms (see Marres, 2012a). Data is "live", in "real time", instantaneous, continuous, perpetual, insidious, complex and enormous in quantity. The array of devices that now deliver data is huge, from mobile phones to sophisticated algorithms processing transactions. Those able to access those devices and data are both heavily circumscribed (inasmuch as much governmental and commercial data is available to very few) and yet also readily used and made meaningful by huge numbers of ordinary people (e.g. Facebook data, Instagram, Twitter). In such an environment, the position of the sociologist is certainly much less secure (Savage & Burrows, 2007). But this insecurity is no less an opportunity for the sociologist of children and childhood.

I am not suggesting that this moment of questioning should provide an opportunity to throw out research that relies on interview and ethnographic observation. Rather, this is an opportunity to investigate the range of different methods that might be available now (from visual and acoustic sociologies (Back, 2007) to social media methods (Marres, 2012a; Murthy, 2013) to new experimental and mobile methods (e.g. walking the city [Back, 2012]), but also to explore the range of methods that have been deployed over time and outside of the normal centres of science and research in the study of children and childhood. This is an opportunity to consider psychology and paediatrics not through a lens critical of development and linear progression, but rather as sites for the *inven-tion* of methods and as *resources* for making children and childhood observable. The historical research of not only Turmel (2008) but also David Armstrong (1979) is significant here. But what is needed is not that theory provides an epistemological blinker, or an easy shadow against which to box and spar, but rather that method is understood with regard to the techniques and devices through which children and their relation to the world is disclosed. Moreover, any genealogical investigation of methods and devices would not be limited to the social sciences; the arts and humanities and natural and medical sciences would also avail themselves as archival reserves. Childhood Studies has often been too quick to dismiss some disciplines rather than others. As part of the rapproche-ment that Prout (2005, pp. 91–92) and others (Alanen, 2012) talk about, the conversation would not settle on theory, but on method. For example, if we can foreclose and reduce the investigation so as, in the first instance, to hold off any theoretical judgement and only to consider the use of particular methods, then we might notice, naively, the similarities between Charles Darwin's observations of his children and Berry Mayall's ethnographic investigations of children in class-room settings (Darwin, 1877; Mayall, 2002). A genealogy of particular methods and devices might reveal a history less prejudiced than one constricted through theoretical judgement.

Les Back, in his discussion of what a "live" and living sociology might look like, talks about a reassessment of the tools of sociology in order to redis-cover a sociology that is "imbued with vitality", that describes societies that "breathe and feel", that includes portraits and human voices and that is fresh and embodied (Back, 2007, p. 165). But Back understands this vitality in the context of a reassessment of the sociological craft, a reinvention of "the nature of observation and measurement", and a sociological world that is mediated and re-mediated through "multimedia techniques and new informational technolo-gies". For Back, these are opportunities for thinking about the "interactivity" of sociological research and the possibilities for new forms of iteration and iter-ability (Back, 2007, p. 165). The voices that are made audible are disclosed in a sociological world that is rich not only in terms of what counts as data, but also in the vibrancy, recalcitrance and agency of that data (see Latour, 2004). The explosion of techniques and methods brings with it a surfeit of what counts as data and an assemblage of senses and technology regarding the observing and describing of that material. Thus, visual sociology (Pink, 2007), sensory sociology (Pink, 2009) and an object-centred sociology (Marres, 2009) help to grasp the thickness of the medium or the substance through which social rela-tions are assembled and arranged, but are in themselves inadequate to grasp that thickness.

Back talks about the need to move on from a minimalist social science writ-ing, a form of *"thin description* or *flat sociology* bereft of vitalism or life or [...] any beauty". He calls for a "literary sociology" that is thick and detailed and open to the ephemeral performances, the quirkiness, the patterns and sta-bilities of social life (Back, 2007, p. 164). The new technologies and devices through which children and their lives are disclosed are means of description, ways of describing the world (see Oswell, 2013). They present a para-sociality (Horton & Wohl, 1956) that is graphic and resonant. The presentation of data is not representational; rather, it is real and virtual. It is a form of authenticity or intimacy with the lives of children that is not clouded by any presupposition that the sociologist can simply and transparently represent their voices and their interests. Of course, it was precisely that problem, that dilemma, that faced Qvortrup when he was considering the "modest demand" of *accounting for* and *accounting with* children: "[i]f we seriously mean to improve life conditions for children we must, as a minimum precondition, establish reporting systems in which they are heard themselves as well as reported by others" (Qvortrup, 1990, p. 94). For Qvortrup, it was important that children, as a collectivity, were not ignored in statistical data; it meant that Childhood Studies could not simply forego quantitative analysis; the forms of modelling and the categories of analysis within that modelling are significant. And yet for Qvortrup this modest demand is constantly met with the problem of representation, namely that chil-dren "are most often represented by other agencies which means, at the same time, other interests" (Qvortrup, 1990, p. 95). The sociologist's task is not to solve the problem and to settle scores, but to document and make available the different and irreducible "interests" and "voices" in such ways that underscore such irreducibility and lack of transparency as sociologically interesting, if not politically difficult.

Conclusion

In returning to that foundational moment of Childhood Studies, at least as a fantasy of origins, my intention has been to suggest that a problematic cen-tred on a political ontology of children's agency was doubled and ghosted by one whose orientation was tempered by a deliberate ontological naivety, a methodological orientation happy to consider, without prejudice, the varied and multi-dimensional ontological conditions of existence for children's lives. Although these two problematics could rest happily together (one subtended by the other, one declaring itself "the new paradigm", the other nameless), the current questions we ask about the nature of the social, I argue, present "the new paradigm" in a new light, one that is demonstrably not insistent on a strong ontology with regard to children's agency, one that recognises the entangled and messy nature of that complex. I suggest that the questions we ask about the social now require that we reconsider not just how we scale the social and how we think about agency within that scaling, but also how we situate our investigations with regard to methods and devices for disclosing the social. In doing so, I suggest that any understanding of the relationality of children and childhood (Alanen, 2000) must be understood in the context of a radical contingency (see Oswell, 2013; Prout, 2005), one open to the situatedness of any ontology (Haraway, 1988).

References

Alanen, L. (1988). Rethinking childhood. *Acta Sociologica, 31*(53), 53–67.
Alanen, L. (1994). Gender and generation: feminism and the "Child Question". In J. Qvortrup, M. Bardy, G. Sgritta & H. Wintersberger (Eds.), *Childhood Matters: Social Theory, Practice and Politics* (pp. 27–42). Aldershot: Avebury.
Alanen, L. (2000). From sociologies of childhood to generational analysis. Paper delivered to *Childhood and Social Theory* Colloquium, University of Keele.
Alanen, L. (2012). Disciplinarity, interdisciplinarity and childhood studies. *Childhood, 19*(4), 419–422.
Armstrong, D. (1979). Child development and medical ontology. *Social Science and Medicine, 13,* 9–12.
Back, L. (2007). *The Art of Listening.* Oxford: Berg.
Back, L. (2012). Live sociology: social research and its futures. *Sociological Review, 60*(S1), 18–39.
Back, L. & Puwar, N. (2012). A manifesto for live methods: provocations and capacities. *Sociological Review, 60*(S1), 6–17.
Bennett, J. (2001). *The Enchantment of Modern Life: Attachments, Crossings, and Ethics.* Princeton: Princeton University Press.
Castañeda, C. (2002). *Figurations: Child, Bodies, Worlds.* Durham: Duke University Press.
Christensen, P. (1998). Difference and similarity: how children's competence is constituted in illness and its treatment. In I. Hutchby & J. Moran-Ellis (Eds.), *Children and Social Competence: Arenas of Action* (pp. 187–201). London: Falmer Press.
Christensen, P. (2000). Childhood and the cultural constitution of vulnerable bodies. In A. Prout (Ed.), *The Body, Childhood and Society* (pp. 38–59). London: Macmillan.
Darwin, C. (1877). A biographical sketch of an infant. *Mind, 2*(7), 285–294.
Derrida, J. (1982). *Margins of Philosophy.* Chicago: University of Chicago Press.
Giddens, A. (1979). *Central Problems in Social Theory: Action, Structure and Contradiction in Social Analysis.* London: Macmillan.
Haraway, D. (1988). Situated knowledges: the science question in feminism and the privilege of partial perspective. *Feminist Studies, 14*(3), 575–599.
Horton, D. & Wohl, R. (1956). Mass communication and parasocial interaction: observations on intimacy at a distance. *Psychiatry, 19,* 215–229.
Hutchby, I. & Moran-Ellis, J. (Eds.) (1998). *Children and Social Competence: Arenas of Action.* London: Falmer Press.
James, A. & Prout, A. (1990). *Constructing and Reconstructing Childhood: Contemporary Issues in the Sociological Study of Childhood.* Basingstoke, UK: Falmer Press.
James, A., Jenks, C. & Prout, A. (1998). *Theorizing Childhood.* Cambridge: Polity Press.
Jenks, C. (1982). *The Sociology of Childhood: Essential Readings.* London: Basford Academic and Educational Press.
Jenks, C. (1996). *Childhood.* London: Routledge.

Knorr-Cetina, K. (1999). *Epistemic Cultures: How the Sciences Make Knowledge.* Cambridge: Harvard University Press.

Knowles, C. (2014). *Flip-Flop: A Journey through Globalisation's Backroads.* London: Pluto Press.

Krause, M. (2013). Recombining micro/macro: the grammar of theoretical innovation. *European Journal of Social Theory, 16*(2), 139–152.

Latour, B. (2004). *Politics of Nature: How to Bring the Sciences into Nature.* Cambridge: Harvard University Press.

Latour, B. (2005) *Reassembling the Social: An Introduction to Actor-Network Theory.* Oxford: Oxford University Press.

Latour, B. & Woolgar, S. (1986). *Laboratory Life: The Construction of Scientific Facts.* Princeton: Princeton University Press.

Latour, B. & Yaneva, A. (2008). "Give me a gun and I will make all buildings move": An ANT's view of architecture. In R. Geiser (Ed.), *Explorations in Architecture: Teaching, Design, Research* (pp. 80–89). Basel: Birkhäuser.

Lee, N. (2001). *Childhood and Society: Growing Up in an Age of Uncertainty.* Milton Keynes: Open University Press.

Lury, C. & N. Wakeford (2013). *Inventive Methods: The Happening of the Social.* London: Routledge.

Lynch, M. (1997). *Scientific Practice and Ordinary Action: Ethnomethodology and Social Studies of Science.* Cambridge: Cambridge University Press.

Marres, N. (2009). Testing the powers of engagement: green living experiments, the ontological turn and the undoability of involvement. *European Journal of Social Theory, 12*(1), 117–133.

Marres, N. (2012). *Material Participation: Technology, the Environment and Everyday Publics.* London: Palgrave Macmillan.

Marres, N. (2012a). The redistribution of methods: on intervention in digital social research, broadly conceived. *Sociological Review, 60,* 139–165.

Massey, D. (2005). *For Space.* London: Sage Publications.

Massumi, B. (2014). *What Animals Teach Us about Politics.* Durham: Duke University Press.

Mayall, B. (2002). *Towards a Sociology for Childhood: Thinking from Children's Lives.* Milton Keynes: Open University Press.

Mayall, B. (2013). *A History of the Sociology of Childhood.* London: Institute of Education Press.

Mol, A. (2002). *The Body Multiple: Ontology in Medical Practice.* Durham: Duke University Press.

Murthy, D. (2013). *Twitter: Social Communication in the Twitter Age.* Cambridge: Polity Press.

Oswell, D. (2013). *The Agency of Children: From Family to Global Human Rights.* Cambridge: Cambridge University Press.

Pink, S. (2007). *Doing Visual Ethnography.* London: Sage Publications.

Pink, S. (2009). *Doing Sensory Ethnography.* London: Sage Publications.

Prout, A. (Ed.) (2000). *The Body, Childhood and Society.* London: Macmillan.

Prout, A. (2005). *The Future of Childhood.* London: Routledge Falmer.

Prout, A. & James, A. (1990). A new paradigm for the sociology of childhood? Provenance, promise and problems. In A. James & A. Prout (Eds.), *Constructing and Reconstructing Childhood. Contemporary Issues in the Sociological Study of Childhood* (pp. 7–34). London: Routledge Falmer.

Qvortrup, J. (1985). Placing children in the division of labour. In P. Close & R. Collins (Eds.), *Family and Economy in Modern Society* (pp. 129–145). London: Macmillan.

Qvortrup, J. (1990). A voice for children in statistical and social accounting: a plea for children's right to be heard. In A. James & A. Prout (Eds.), *Constructing and Reconstructing Childhood: Contemporary Issues in the Sociological Study of Childhood* (pp. 78–98). Basingstoke: Falmer Press.

Savage, M. & Burrows, R. (2007). The coming crisis of empirical sociology. *Sociology*, *41*(5), 885–899.

Turmel, A. (2008). *A Historical Sociology of Childhood: Developmental Thinking, Categorization and Graphic Visualization*. Cambridge: Cambridge University Press.

Woolgar, S. & Lezaun, J. (2013). The wrong bin bag: a turn to ontology in science and technology studies. *Social Studies of Science*, *43*(3), 321–340.

Yaneva, A. (2005). Scaling up and down: extraction trials in architectural design. *Social Studies of Science*, *35*(6), 867–894.

Chapter 2

Children as participants in practices

The challenges of practice theories to an actor-centred sociology of childhood

Sabine Bollig and Helga Kelle

This chapter examines how new practice theories might provide more advanced theoretical and analytical perspectives for the study of childhood in the social sciences. It moves away from common conceptions of agency with reference to the dichotomy of structure and agency and reflects on the relationship of sociality, agency and actors as conceived in recent practice theories. In the main section, three key aspects of those theories are introduced and discussed: (1) the corporeality and material/mental structure of practices; (2) the role of artefacts and objects in the performance and reproduction of practices; and (3) the practice theory shift in perspective from intentionally acting human actors to multiple participants of practice and to agency as a feature and effect of practices. The concluding sections discuss the challenges which these practice theory reflections pose to childhood studies: To the extent that agency is conceptualised not only as a (biographically) incorporated characteristic of children as individuals but as a feature of practices in which children are involved as participants, it is understood to depend on situations and to be more variable, context-sensitive and complex than has been recognised in the field of childhood studies in the past. Practice theories are thus shown to open up new, differentiated heuristic perspectives for the field of Childhood Studies, which in turn challenge the adult-centrist approach of practice theories.

Certainly one of the major achievements of the "new social studies of childhood" is that they have contributed to the wide acceptance of the idea that children are social and societal actors. Although reflecting on children's autonomy has a long tradition in theories of education and socialisation (Honig, 1999; see also Baader in this volume), it is the sociological perspective that has laid emphasis on children as members of a distinct social group who have to be studied in their own right, and who are "active in the construction of their own lives, the lives of those around them and of the societies in which they live" (Prout & James, 1990, p. 8, cited in James, 2009, p. 40). While the main objective in Childhood Studies was initially to show that children actively participate in shaping their current living conditions, and thus that they must be regarded *a priori* as actors, today the focus, as Prout (2000) puts it, is more on decentralising agency and on providing empirical evidence to show that sometimes children do exercise their agency – that is, their actions have certain effects on their relationships – and other times they do not. What Prout outlines here is essentially a kind of differential agency research that focuses on the heterogeneous resources, practices and contexts that establish the variability of children's agency rather than simply taking the assumption that children are actors as a general premise.

With considerable input from a wide debate on agency within the social sciences at large (Barnes, 2000; Caldwell, 2012), this differential view on children's agency has brought about an increase in the number and range of theoretical, methodological and empirical approaches in Childhood Studies, for example in regard to collectivistic understandings of agency (Corsaro, 2005) or with emphasis on the discourses and heterogeneous networks and assemblages in which children receive agentic positions – or not (Oswell, 2013; Prout, 2000). A considerable number of those approaches to agency pose a challenge to traditional concepts of children's agency in the sociology of childhood that draw on Giddens' (1984) social theory of structuration. Oswell (2013) notes that Giddens' theory, with its dichotomous understanding of "structure" and "agency" (and their interdependence) at first provided considerable inspiration for putting Childhood Studies on a firm praxeological foundation. As such, it has informed the widely accepted view that children's agency is limited by the structures of the generational order to exercising agency *as* children (Alanen & Mayall, 2001; Bühler-Niederberger, 2011; Honig, 2009). Depending on the specific perspective that researchers in the field of Childhood Studies took when theorising on childhood (based on Giddens' work), their analytical focus was either on the question of reproduction caused by social structures (and thus more on "structure") or on the question of children's own capacities to reflect, deal with and change the situations in which they are involved (and thus more on "agency") (see Vandenbroeck & Bouverne-De Bie, 2006).

However, according to Oswell (2013), it is precisely because of this dichotomous view that Giddens' conceptualisation of agency is now considered outdated. Because the more recent social theories emphasise the "fracturing of subjectivity and its constructed and performative nature" (p. 62), the field of Childhood Studies is expected to elaborate new models of children's agency according to what we may call post-modern or post-structural approaches to it. This chapter, therefore, focuses on practice theory perspectives on agency to identify the challenges they pose to actor-centred research on childhood, and it does so along two nexuses: the nexus between agency concepts and practice theories, and the nexus between practice theories and research on childhood. In the following, we will first show, in three steps, how practice theories refer to the actor concept, and detail what criticism practice theories have levelled at (traditional) action theories. We conclude the chapter with a discussion of the implications such a concept of agency has for Childhood Studies.

Practices and their actors: the relationship of sociality, agency and actors in practice theories

A fundamental characteristic of recent theory programmes that have emerged in the wake of what has become known as the "practice turn" (Schatzki, Knorr-Cetina, & Savigny, 2001) is that they all have fundamentally redefined the social (see Reckwitz, 2002; Schmidt, 2012; Shove, Pantzar, & Watson, 2012). These theories conceptualise the social as a web of differently interconnected, situated and embodied practices that must be regarded as "a temporally unfolding and spatially dispersed nexus of doings and sayings" (Schatzki, 1996, p. 89). Thus, the traditional distinction between micro-theories and macro-theories is overcome by focusing on the question of the reproduction and transformation of social orders caused during the actual performance of assembled bundles of practices. As a result, the traditional theories of the subject and of action are confronted with a perspective that "places the focus not on forms of consciousness, ideas, values, norms, communication, or systems of signs and symbols, but rather on social practices in their situatedness, their material embeddedness in bodies and artefacts, and their dependence on practical skills and implicit knowledge" (Schmidt, 2012, p. 24*).

Accordingly, the practice theory perspective on the social is focused neither on actors' capacities nor on the social's determination by structures. In line with the fundamental practice theory assumption that the social is determined primarily by informality, temporality, materiality and performativity, the "place of the social" is instead regarded as the observable enactment of practised orders itself.

At first glance, it may seem reasonable to speak of *the* practice theories, considering that fundamental assumptions are shared by all such theories, but there are significant differences between the various practical and analytical approaches. For example, Giddens and Bourdieu, two social theorists who made major contributions during the first phase of the practice turn, have been criticised for some time for overemphasising the structural dimension of society by using the dichotomies "structure"/"agency" and "practice"/"field", respectively (see, e.g., Caldwell, 2012). More recent approaches, such as Schatzki's social-site ontology, dissolve the structural dimension and put in its place an understanding of fluid arrangements and networks that take the form of interlinked social performances that occur in spatially dispersed and temporally unfolded, materially situated and interconnected contexts.

In the three sections that follow, we shall present theoretical and systematic reflections on the status of (human) actors and their agency in practice theories. We identify three elements of practice theory that are of particular interest: the material/mental structure of practices, the embeddedness of practices in artefacts and objects and agency as both a feature and an effect of practices.

The material/mental structure of practices

One aspect with which more recent practice theories are concerned is the material/mental structure of practices. This aspect addresses the idea that the body and the consciousness each contribute to practices in their own specific way. The fact that the body is considered to be of vital importance in this becomes immediately apparent in Schatzki's definition of practices as nexuses of "*bodily* doings and sayings" (Schatzki, 1996, emphasis added). Reckwitz (2003, p. 290) points out that this involves aspects of incorporation and aspects of performance. "Inwardly", the performance of a practice necessarily requires the incorporation of knowledge. In this respect, bodies are storage containers for practices that have been performed in the past, the large majority of which can only be performed again because the body "remembers" how to perform them. This knowledge remains largely implicit and bound to the performance of practices; it is "known" by actors primarily through their physical participation.

The boundedness of practices to the body ensures not only their performability but also their outward social understandability, in the sense that these movements and activities can be identified as a skilful performance both by the individual who is performing them and by the individual's social environment. The reason for this is that bodily movements are symbols to express mental characteristics such as intentions, objectives and strategies. However, this is not to say that there is an actual correspondence relationship of any kind between mental processes and bodily expressions. On the contrary, as Schatzki (2001) emphasises, individuals develop an understanding of agency and action coordination through social practices by *ascribing* this expression to bodily activities. These ascriptions are mental acts and patterns of understanding and, as such, are socially regulated; they have no social existence until they are expressed and become manifest in the form of practices on the basis of social identification criteria. This means that practice theories are not concerned with the ways in which mental processes structure practices; rather, they focus on "how mental performances and mental states become registered, ratified, confirmed, and observable in practices; how they manifest themselves in the form of bodily doings and sayings; and how they contribute to practices" (Schmidt, 2012, p. 12*).

To facilitate the understanding of practices and of the actors who perform them, it should first be noted that the practical consciousness, or wisdom, of individuals plays a central role in the performance of practices – for only to individuals with such skills can something make sense. However, because the meaningful combination of individual acts into a nexus occurs in the practices themselves, it is not until the bodily performance is actually carried out that a social interrelation between patterns of behaviour and patterns of understanding materialises, "where understanding is structured and intelligibility (*Verständlichkeit* and *Bedeuten*) articulated (*gegliedert*)" (Schatzki, 1996, p. 12, German terms in original). In practice theory, "individuals feature as the *carriers* or hosts of a practice [… and] understandings, know-how, meanings and purposes are not taken to be personal attributes" (Shove, Pantzar, & Watson, 2012, p. 7, original emphasis), but instead are regarded as elements and qualities of a practice in which the individuals participate. In other words, the acting subject or the competent actor is replaced with a concept of *participation in practices*. Later in the chapter, we will discuss what implications a participatory perspective such as this has for the question of agency; that is, the potential to act differently and to influence practices. First, however, we shall turn our attention to another contributor to practices: artefacts and objects.

The embeddedness of practices in artefacts and objects

The special interest of practice theories in the material also becomes apparent in that artefacts and objects are ascribed indispensable capacities that are needed for the performance of practices.

Perhaps the most radical perspective of all in the family of practice theories is actor-network theory (ANT), which fundamentally symmetrises the actions of human and nonhuman actors (see Latour, 2005; Law & Hassard, 1999). In this model, all entities of practices – which include humans, objects, spaces and even discourses – are treated as equal "actants" of the social, whose potential for action ("actantiality") derives from their ability to communicate with other actants and to transform one another within networks. In fact, Latour prefers the term "actants" because he believes it is a more appropriate term for a relational understanding of agency.

The interest of ANT in the fluid chains of translation in which social action emerges and reproduces itself locally in the form of the capacities of an ensemble of actors/actants (see Latour, 2005) is compatible with what might be called a "flat" understanding of the social, which is also a characteristic of the other practice theories. However, the symmetrisation of human and nonhuman actors has drawn fierce criticism, especially from advocates of practice theory perspectives, for blurring or dissolving the boundaries of the term "actor" and for using the term "action" in an ultimately intentionalist sense. Some authors have also noted that it is impossible for ANT to assign any systematic place to the bodily, which plays a central role in practice theories (see, for example, Hirschauer, 2004; Schatzki, 2002). For this very reason, Schmidt (2012) consigns ANT to the fringes of the field of practice theories, noting that it can conceptualise practices only as the "interlinking of acts" because it ascribes equal capacity to act to artefacts/objects and humans. On the contrary, conceptualising practices as conglomerates of acts in which meaning is produced and articulated is nothing less than one of the defining characteristics of practice theories, and that is something, as Schmidt highlights, that artefacts cannot do on their own: They make possible, restrict and transform practices, but they do not make their acts observable and intelligible for others. Or, "to put it more precisely using a concept from ethnomethodology, artefacts do not themselves confer *accountability* upon their acts", meaning that ANT ignores the fact that objects never contribute to the identification of a social occurrence in which they participate "as this social occurrence or that, and thus to actualize it meaningfully" on their own but only through interaction with human participants (p. 69*, original emphasis).

Schatzki (2002, 2010), taking a similar view on the relationship of practices, humans and objects, distinguishes between practices and material arrangements, and establishes a relationship between them using concepts from order theory. He considers orders not as structures but as socio-material arrangements that are produced as a result of practices, which in turn provide the settings and tools needed to perform and contextualise practices. Empirically, objects and practices are thus extremely closely interwoven, even if theory does not position objects in practices in the same way as it positions human actors.

In opposition to social-theoretical differentiations such as those described above, Hirschauer (2004) proposes using the fluidity and malleability of the very term "practice" more fully in order to create new opportunities for analytic description. Hirschauer advocates a "participatory perspective" (p. 74*) that avoids any sort of reification of actors while at the same time considering them as being "inevitably *included* in the performance of social phenomena" (p. 89*, original emphasis). Such an analytic conception of individuals, bodies, artefacts and consciousness as "*participants* in social processes" (p. 74*, original emphasis) would be less concerned with the status or with the motivations and options of action of each individual actor/actant and more concerned with the contributions the practices require of and receive from each participant: "from the body, special abilities and positions; from objects, specific fits and suitabilities; from persons, the mobilization of the knowledge needed in a given context and the development of appropriate motivations and emotions" (p. 89*).

Agency as a feature and an effect of practices

A participatory perspective as described thus views the relationship between actors and practices from the opposite end: The focus is shifted away from the question of how practices are produced, regulated or initiated to the question of how specific participants in practices become actors as the practices are being performed. These practices also provide the subject positions required for their performance. However, it is important to note that actor qualities do not simply inscribe themselves into the human participants through habituation. It is true that social practices often take the form of habits and routines, but this should not be taken to mean that they can be considered to be mere performances of the same unchanging practice (Shove, Pantzar & Watson, 2012). Placing too much emphasis on routine in this way would make it impossible to give appropriate consideration to social change or to agency, that is, the potential of individual human participants to change practices. In order to shed more light on the actor concept of practice theories, it is also necessary to draw attention to the tension between routinisation and crisis that characterises practices (see Reckwitz, 2002). To unravel this tension analytically, we can build on Schatzki's (1996, 2002) distinction between "dispersed" and "integrative" practices, for it not only allows us to explain how actors are "infiltrated" into practices and how webs of practices disperse in space and time, but it can also be used to show how the potential for change arises from the very practices themselves.

According to Schatzki (1996, pp. 91–93), "dispersed practices" are those practices that are dispersed among spatiotemporal arrangements and are characteristic of many fields of practice. Like other types of practice, they consist of routinised sets of "doings and sayings", but because they are less complex and less specific, they function and can be found in a wide variety of social fields. Examples of dispersed practices include the practices of waiting, greeting, and helping, which, as customs in the sense intended by Wittgenstein, become understandable through practical reference to themselves. As these practices are being performed, they are identified as specific practices by the participants involved, and thus elicit a response from the repertoire of customs connected to these practices.

"Integrative practices", on the other hand, are specific to the contexts in which they are performed and are constituted by a specific connection of nexuses of doings and sayings. This connection is not merely the result of the practical, incorporated meaning; rather, this implicit meaning must be regarded just as a preliminary organising element of integrative practices. Other organising elements include explicit "rules" in the sense of a "knowing-that", as well as "general understandings" and "teleo-affective structures", the last of which refer to the bodily/emotional and mental orientation to tasks, norms, and purposes and ends. This orientation plays a central role in the actor concept in that it embeds hierarchies of purposes and ends and regulates what activities are generally considered to be, and can be regarded as, "proper" or "acceptable". However, it is not a characteristic of individuals either; rather, it "is carried by the practice" (Schatzki, 1996, p. 93) in which the individual actors then get enmeshed and redefine these teleo-affective structures as their "individual interests" (Reckwitz, 2003, p. 293*).

This distinction between dispersed and integrative practices makes it clear why Schatzki refers to practice as "a temporally unfolding and spatially dispersed nexus of doings and sayings": It is a distinction that brings the ability of practices to be dispersed among various different contexts to the foreground, while at the same time also organising themselves in a specific way in each context. For integrative practices do not merely consist of dispersed practices; rather, they transform them depending on the specific circumstances of a given situation. For this reason, the individual actors do not necessarily have to participate in the entire practice from beginning to end, nor do they necessarily have to have all of the abilities required for performing a practice. Thus, the distinction between dispersed and integrative practices allows us to explain not only how actors are "infiltrated" into practices, but also how they "find" actor and subject positions there, which in turn enable them to act further (which can also mean to act creatively). However, just because the decentralisation of the human actors is emphasised here does not mean that motivations for action were deliberately ignored in practice theories; in fact, they are themselves considered from a praxeological perspective – namely, as a characteristic of practices rather than as something separate from or preceding them.

Another reason that agency, as an empirical phenomenon, arises from the practices themselves is that these practices are never static and never occur in isolated form; rather, they are constantly involved in processes of becoming interconnected, merged and integrated with other practices into ensembles. As a result, human participants always participate in a multitude of practices that provide not only a multitude of actor positions but also heterogeneous and, possibly, even conflicting forms of practical knowledge, which the actors incorporate as they perform the practices. So, because "every agent carries out a multitude of different social practices, the individual is the unique crossing point of practices, of bodily-mental routines" (Reckwitz, 2002, p. 256).

The practice theory understanding of agency thus emerges in connection with a concept of human participants who participate in practices as subjects, with subjects being understood as the crossing points of behavioural and knowledge complexes of different social practices (Reckwitz, 2002, p. 256). Thus, if we conceptualise subjects here as "a more or less loosely connected bundle of different forms of practical knowledge" (Reckwitz, 2003, p. 296*), then it is the heterogeneity and, in some cases, the irreconcilability of these forms of practical knowledge that has the potential to make the understanding and the behaviour of individuals, as well as the transformation of practices, unpredictable. And this is a potential that is present in every practice because they are always assembled with other practices. Agency, understood as the capacity of actors to change situations, thus refers to "a potential that is determined not by a pre-practical autonomy of the subjects but by the contextuality, temporality, and agonality of the practices" (Reckwitz, 2003, p. 297*). To put it succinctly, it is precisely because the actor status of human participants emerges in a flow of practices, the choice of which depends on the specific circumstances of a given situation, that the human participants, as actors, have the capacity to change the practical contexts in which they are involved.

Children as participants in practices: challenges to an actor-centred sociology of childhood

With regard to the question of children's agency, we might say with reference to practice theories that everyone who is involved in practices must be regarded as a participant. However, those who participate in practice gain a specific understanding of themselves as actors – and thus as subjects – only through their participation in practice, and their potential capacity to act depends not only on how specific subject positions are assigned to each individual actor in the distributed and collectivised performance of practices. This means that children's situated agency is not conceptualised merely as having its roots in the social order category "childhood", that is, in their actorship *as* children (see Bühler-Niederberger, 2011). Rather, children continuously participate in the production of actor positions in their daily lives: In every practice in which they participate, they produce self-positioning actively and with considerable situational variability.

In this final section, we shall discuss, in four systematic steps, the challenges the practice theory reflections presented above pose to childhood theory and research.

Children's agency beyond peer cultures

Defining the subject as a bundle of behavioural and knowledge complexes is also – and above all – a provocation that challenges concepts of the independent nature of children's worlds and in particular the focus on the "actual practice of agency in children's peer cultures" – as opposed to adults' cultures – as prominently advocated by Corsaro (2005, p. 246). This perspective on the independent nature of children's cultures can be understood to suggest that children's agency (whether conceptualised as individual or as collective agency) primarily emerges as a result of the separation of children's and adults' practice spheres. From the practice theory perspective, we would instead suggest considering the differential forms of children's agency as an effect of encounters between different practice ensembles, their choreography and their interconnection. Various ethnographic studies conducted in the context of schools, for example, have provided evidence that peer culture and teaching culture cannot be considered independently of each other because there is constant interaction between them (see, for example, Huf, 2013).

Children as participants in practices of doing generation

The question of children's capacity to act *as* children, on the other hand, implies the question of how generational order is enacted in practices; that is, how the distinction between children and adults is implicitly or explicitly drawn (Honig, 2009). The challenge to differential agency research, then, is to conceptualise the contributions children make, and what effects and what scope for shaping practices they have, as participants in practices. One of the most important aspects in this context is that the practice theory conceptualisation of the social as something that "is suspended in a mesh of practices and orders" (Schatzki, 2002, p. xxi) is formulated as an alternative to the traditional concept of structure. Therefore, structures, such as generational orders, can only be understood as meshes and arrangements of bundles of practices that unfold in the form of emergent phenomena in the reproduction and interlinking of practices. Thus, we cannot simply assume that children are positioned *as* children in practices that involve adults (in their role *as* adults); rather, we must analyse the fluid interlinkages of practices of differentiation, which sometimes position children as children, but sometimes do not.

Accordingly, the generational order must be analysed both as a medium and as an effect of *specific* practices, with a particular focus on the situated distribution of power within practices that may not necessarily be predetermined by a structurally asymmetrical balance of power between adults and children. For example, Hengst (2013), writing about consumption and media worlds, notes that generational differentiations do not necessarily have a bearing on all practice contexts of a child, even if differentiations interact with practices in specific ways (which, we should add, must also be specifically analysed).

Children as participants in socio-material practices

Another challenge to the field of Childhood Studies are the practice theory assumptions that practices are embedded in material artefacts and objects, and that the performance of practices in socio-material arrangements is a necessary condition for the emergence of social order. According to Prout (2000, p. 17), children's agency must be regarded as an "effect" that is "brought about by the assembly of heterogeneous materials". In emphasising that children's agency is produced as a result of the interconnections and translations of a set of various different discursive, biological and technological resources, Prout draws primarily on actor-network theory in the sense intended by Latour. If this perspective is taken, the specific socio-material arrangements in which childhood is constituted must become the focus of attention, such as the worlds of childcare and educational institutions, which provide socio-material arrangements with specific pedagogical purposes in mind (Lenz Taguchi, 2010). A number of recent studies have drawn attention to how objects and artefacts are actively involved in the practices of testing, diagnosing and teaching children and therefore are crucial for the practical construction of "the normal", "developing", "learning" and the "child at risk" (Sørensen, 2009; Kelle, 2010; Kontopodis, 2007). These studies show that different socio-material and interactional arrangements provide children with very different resources, and that there are different limitations to their self-positioning as a result. In testing situations, for instance, children incorporate and adopt the logic of the test either by qualifying their accomplishments during the test ("I didn't do too well in this one") or by exceeding the expectations inherent in tests ("I can also say this in Russian"), which means that tests have a significant influence on children's performance as well, in that they appear to force them to assume particular actor positions and to exhibit situated forms of agency (Kelle & Schweda, 2014). However, these studies focus mainly on materials that use some sort of childhood-related "scripts" – such as educational objects, toys or testing materials – and thus focus primarily on the question of how children are shaped as actors in their actual implementation. Questions that receive less attention in these studies are how the embeddedness of children and artefacts in socio-material practices brings out agentic positions and subjectivities in encounters with less instrumental "materials" such as natural environments, or how those practices are reinforced and changed by the interplay of particular contributions of children and non-human participants in those practices themselves.

Young children as participants in practices: challenges of Childhood Studies to practice theories

One aspect that is particularly interesting to Childhood Studies and takes a differential perspective to approach the agency concept is the continuum that runs between participation and agency. The question is: What minimum competencies do the participants need in what practices in order to be considered to be actors? With regard to Schatzki's central category of description, "nexus of doings and sayings", we might say that not all practices necessarily involve "sayings"; after all, there are also silent practices, and few, if anyone, would deny that actors who do not (yet) speak have the status of actors. Research that focuses on the study of the situated productions of actor status and agency can draw on pertinent examples of practices that involve very young children (infants) (e.g. Kelle & Jancsó, 2010), which show what practical productions as actors are virtually expected of young children if the practices in which they are involved require individuals who have knowledge and are able to develop emotions and motivations. However, it is precisely because these abilities are often expected in practices that involve young children, despite their inability to meet this expectation, that the development of such abilities is stimulated in a step-by-step process of socialisation: The children are involved and addressed over and over again, thus causing them to start taking the initiative and assuming their role as actors. This means that children are expected to exhibit ritual competencies of participating in – or "playing along" with – practices even before they can intellectually grasp many of the situations with which they are confronted (cf. Cahill, 1987). The notion of "playing along" appears to be closely related to Bühler-Niederberger's (2011) concepts of "complicity" (*Komplizenschaft*) and "competent docility" (*kompetente Gefügigkeit*): all these concepts imply the ritualisation of practices. At the same time, the connotative dimension of "playing along" is more complex: Rather than referring to children's efforts to rise to adults' expectations, it refers to the flexibility and negotiability of that which is accepted as competent playing along by each participant. By continuously participating in various different practice ensembles, children not only shape their agency with situational variability at any given time, but they also accumulate practical knowledge about context-dependent, variable scopes from which they can draw when participating in practices in the future.

However, if there were too great an emphasis on the assumption that children are initially and residually incompetent, and that this incompetency is gradually overcome through the development of competencies in the process of socialisation, then this would lead us back to the source of the criticism that Childhood Studies have levelled at socialisation theory and research in recent years. The practice theory reflections allow for rather different childhood theory conclusions to be drawn: If agency is conceptualised not just as a characteristic of children as individuals which is incorporated (and which must be incorporated in the life course and in the process of socialisation) but also as a feature and an effect of practices, then agency is also conceptualised in a more situationally variable, more context-sensitive and more complex way than would be possible by relying exclusively on the notion of a gradual development of competencies. For Childhood Studies this means, among other things, that consideration must be given to the question of how children's participation in a variety of very different practice ensembles is connected to the potential for upsetting and challenging routines, which in turn provides the potential for the development of more complex capacities to act.

Finally, the purpose of these reflections is to show not only that practice theories pose a challenge to childhood research but that, reversely, Childhood Studies also pose a challenge to the further development of practice theories: In some respects, practice theories suffer from an inherently adultist bias whose deconstruction would be down to childhood sociology.

Note

* All citations marked with an asterisk have been translated from the original German.

References

Alanen, L. & Mayall, B. (eds.) (2001). *Conceptualizing Child-Adult Relations.* London and New York: RoutledgeFalmer.

Barnes, B. (2000). *Understanding Agency: Social Theory and Responsible Action.* London and Thousand Oaks, CA: Sage Publications.

Bühler-Niederberger, D. (2010). Introduction: childhood sociology – defining the state of the art and ensuring reflection, *Current Sociology, 58*(2), 155–64.

Bühler-Niederberger, D. (2011). *Lebensphase Kindheit: Theoretische Ansätze, Akteure und Handlungsräume [Childhood as a phase of life: theoretical approaches, actors and fields of action].* Weinheim, Munich: Juventa.

Cahill, S. E. (1987). Children and civility: ceremonial deviance and the acquisition of ritual competence, *Social Psychology Quarterly, 50*(4), 312–21.

Caldwell, R. (2012). Reclaiming agency, recovering change? An exploration of the practice theory of Theodore Schatzki, *Journal for the Theory of Social Behaviour, 42*(3), 283–303.

Corsaro, W. A. (2005). Collective action and agency in young children's peer cultures, in J. Qvortrup (ed.), *Studies in Modern Childhood: Society, Agency, Culture,* pp. 231–47. Houndmills, UK; New York: Palgrave Macmillan.

Giddens, A. (1984). *The Constitution of Society: Outline of the Theory of Structuration.* Cambridge: Polity Press.

Hengst, H. (2013). *Kindheit im 21. Jahrhundert: Differenzielle Zeitgenossenschaft [Childhood in the 21st century: differential contemporaneity].* Weinheim and Basel: Beltz Juventa.

Hirschauer, S. (2004). Praktiken und ihre Körper: Über materielle Partizipanden des Tuns [Practices and their bodies: on material participants of action], in K. H. Hörning & J. Reuter (eds.), *Doing Culture: Neue Positionen zum Verhältnis von Kultur und sozialer Praxis [New views on the relation of culture and social praxis],* pp. 73–91. Bielefeld, Germany: Transcript.

Honig, M. -S. (1999). *Entwurf einer Theorie der Kindheit [Concept of a theory of childhood].* Frankfurt/M.: Suhrkamp.

Honig, M. -S. (2009). How is the child constituted in childhood studies?, in J. Qvortrup, W. A. Corsaro & M. -S. Honig (eds.), *The Palgrave Handbook of Childhood Studies*, pp. 62–77. Houndmills, UK; New York: Palgrave Macmillan.

Huf, C. (2013). Children's agency during transition to formal schooling, *Ethnography and Education*, 8(1), 61–76.

James, A. (2009). Agency, in J. Qvortrup, G. Valentine, W. A. Corsaro & M. -S. Honig (eds.), *The Palgrave Handbook of Childhood Studies*, pp. 34–45. Houndmills, UK; New York: Palgrave Macmillan.

Kelle, H. (ed.) (2010). *Kinder unter Beobachtung: Kulturanalytische Studien zur pädiatrischen Entwicklungsdiagnostik [Children under surveillance. Culture-analytical studies on paediatric development diagnostics]*. Opladen, Germany; Farmington Hills, MI: Budrich.

Kelle, H. & Jancsó, J. (2010). Kinder als Mitwirkende in medizinischen Vorsorgeuntersuchungen: Zur Enkulturation in entwicklungsdiagnostische Verfahren [Children as participants in medical check-ups], in F. Heinzel & A. Panagiotopoulou (eds.), *Qualitative Bildungsforschung im Elementar- und Primarbereich: Bedingungen und Kontexte kindlicher Lern- und Entwicklungsprozesse [Qualitative research in elementary and primary education: conditions and contexts of child learning and developmental processes]*, pp. 132–50. Baltmannsweiler, Germany: Schneider Hohengehren.

Kelle, H. & Schweda, A. (2014). Interactional complexity and child performative knowledge in language assessments for entry to school, in A. Rasmussen, J. Gustafsson & B. Jeffrey (eds.), *Performativity in Education: An International Collection of Ethnographic Research on Learners' Experiences*, pp. 213–38. Painswick, UK: E&E Publishing.

Kontopodis, M. (2007). Human development as semiotic-material ordering: sketching a relational developmental psychology, *Critical Social Studies*, 9(1), 5–20.

Latour, B. (2005). *Reassembling the Social: An Introduction to Actor-Network-Theory*. Oxford, New York: Oxford University Press.

Law, J. & Hassard, J. (1999). *Actor Network Theory and After*. Oxford, Malden: Blackwell.

Lenz Taguchi, H. (2010). *Going Beyond the Theory/Practice Divide in Early Childhood Education: Introducing an Intra-active Pedagogy*. Abingdon, UK; New York: Routledge.

Oswell, D. (2013). *The Agency of Children: From Family to Global Human Rights*. Cambridge, New York: Cambridge University Press.

Prout, A. & James, A. (1990). A new paradigm for the sociology of childhood? Provenance, promise and problems, in A. James & A. Prout (eds.), *Constructing and Reconstructing Childhood. Contemporary Issues in the Sociological Study of Childhood*, pp. 7–34. London: Routledge Falmer.

Prout, A. (2000). Childhood bodies, construction, agency and hybridity, in A. Prout (ed.), *The Body, Childhood and Society*, pp. 1–18. Houndmills, UK: Macmillan.

Reckwitz, A. (2002). Toward a theory of social practices: a development in culturalist theorizing, *European Journal of Social Theory*, 5(2), 243–63.

Reckwitz, A. (2003). Grundelemente einer Theorie sozialer Praktiken: Eine sozialtheoretische Perspektive [Basic elements of a theory of social practices: a social-theoretical perspective]. *Zeitschrift für Soziologie*, 32(4), 282–301.

Schatzki, T. R. (2010). Materiality and social life. *Nature and Culture*, 5(2), 123–149.

Schatzki, T. R. (1996). *Social Practices: A Wittgensteinian Approach to Human Activity and the Social*. Cambridge, New York: Cambridge University Press.

Schatzki, T. R. (2001). Practice mind-ed orders, in T. R. Schatzki, K. Knorr-Cetina and E. v. Savigny (eds.), *The Practice Turn in Contemporary Theory*, pp. 42–55. London, New York: Routledge.

Schatzki, T. R. (2002). *The Site of the Social: A Philosophical Account of the Constitution of Social Life and Change*. University Park: Pennsylvania State University Press.

Schatzki, T. R., Knorr-Cetina, K. & Savigny, E. v. (eds.) (2001). *The Practice Turn in Contemporary Theory*. London, New York: Routledge.

Schmidt, R. (2012). *Soziologie der Praktiken: Konzeptionelle Studien und empirische Analysen* [*Sociology of practices: conceptual studies and empirical analyses*]. Berlin: Suhrkamp.

Shove, E., Pantzar, M. & Watson, M. (2012). *The Dynamics of Social Practice. Everyday Life and How It Changes*. London; Thousand Oaks, CA: Sage Publications.

Sørensen, E. (2009). *The Materiality of Learning: Technology and Knowledge in Educational Practice*. Learning in Doing series. New York: Cambridge University Press.

Vandenbroeck, M. & Bouverne-De Bie, M. (2006). Children's agency and educational norms: a tensed negotiation, *Childhood*, *13*(1), 127–43.

Chapter 3

Neither "thick" nor "thin"

Reconceptualising agency and childhood relationally

Florian Esser

This chapter deals with a substantialist understanding of agency, which predominates in Childhood Studies. In the recent past, this key concept has come up against its limits within empirical research, and alternatives have thus been developed, which claim that children have a "thin" agency. Continuing in this vein but also challenging this view, this chapter aims to create a definition, based on relational social theories, of what childhood is and what agency thus means for children in different social contexts. Systematically and empirically, it will be shown that first, the social world is made up of both human and non-human actors; second, identities are produced situationally, in relation to these different actors; and third, children, like all other social actors, have different identities in different social networks. A relational understanding of this kind can reconstruct agency outside of the classic dualisms of personality and society, child and adult, action and structure, and so on.

Even though Childhood Studies has now become an interdisciplinary project, some important debates on fundamental matters go back to sociological discussion. In the 1980s and 1990s, Childhood Studies was seen as the New Sociology of Childhood, distancing itself with a critical stance from existing conceptualisations of children and childhood in the social sciences. The representatives of this new paradigm accused the dominant socialisation theories of primarily defining childhood in terms of the skills that children need to acquire as future adults, and thus as equal members of society (for example, James & James, 2004; Uprichard, 2008). In Childhood Studies, this kind of model was opposed by the assumption that the child is a social actor. Socialisation theories, or at least traditional ones based on structural functionalism, deal with the internalisation of values and norms, as well as the development of the skills required to ensure the subject's agency within a given society. In Childhood Studies, by contrast, it was assumed that children already possessed social "actancy". Focusing on agency, a reconstruction was undertaken of how children act *against* existing social structures, changing them and thus becoming social actors (for criticism on this, see Esser, 2009, p. 12f.).

This chapter attempts a critical revision of this understanding of agency in Childhood Studies. It criticises the fact that by simply reversing the logic of socialisation theories based on structural functionalism, the two conflicting fronts that are the cause of criticism are reproduced: "the" children are set up in opposition to "the" adult society. Instead of starting out from a dualist view, with children vs. adults, agency vs. socialisation, action vs. structure and actor vs. society, thinking should be based on a relational understanding of social processes. This has not yet been systematically introduced into Childhood Studies, though it holds both critical and analytical potential when answering the question of what social capacity and opportunities to act children possess.

Relational approaches allow agency itself to be "socialised". Drawing on relational social theories allows the discussion on children's agency to be continued alongside, and complementing, conventional understandings of socialisation. This chapter develops an approach using reflections from social theory to understand children as social actors without reproducing dichotomies of action and structure. Instead of choosing to define agency in terms of their anthropological status as beings who are not fully developed (for criticism on this, see Woodhead, 2009, p. 56) or defining them in terms of their social status as members of society with limited skills, this chapter starts out from their social status as the "child" (Honig, 2009). Children act on the basis of the possibilities, wishes, aims and cultural practices that they can have as children. A "child" is thus not defined by its social incompleteness, which it can only overcome by developing into an adult through individual maturing, socialisation and education. Children *are* already social beings, which, however, are given a special social status qua being children (Warming, 2006).

Starting out from a critical reception of conventional notions in Childhood Studies, the first chapter explains the basic understanding of agency in the context of relational social theories. The second chapter lays out three central aspects of agency with regard to childhood by systematic, empirical means, following on from arguments sketched out within network theory. Finally, the conclusion assesses the value of relational approaches towards agency with regard to Childhood Studies.

Agency as a key term in Childhood Studies

Since the 1980s, it has been a constantly recurring credo of Childhood Studies not only to see children as future members of society, but also to view them and the lives they live as independent subjects of research. Although agency thus became one of the central terms in Childhood Studies in the social sciences, the statement made by Prout back in 2000 is still largely true: "the 'agency' in 'children's agency' remains inadequately theorized" (p. 16). The reason for this should not be sought in the idea of agency being a theoretically little-elaborated term. On the contrary, social theorists and cultural scientists have been debating for many years over the discussion sparked by Anthony Giddens, also in the 1980s (Giddens, 1984; for an overview, see also Raithelhuber, 2008 or Passoth, Peuker & Schillmeier, 2012).

These debates touch on the fundamental questions surrounding the relationship between action and structure, subject and object, social change and social stability, etc. However, these discussions and their findings have as yet had hardly any influence on Childhood Studies: It "needs to be said that much of the writing on children's agency draws on a particular rendition of the relation between agency and structure which largely ignores the huge wealth of writing more broadly within sociology on this topic" (Oswell, 2013, p. 38). Accordingly, research today is still dominated by an understanding of childhood, which says that children possess a pre-social, natural agency that is systematically destroyed and corrupted by social force (for a critical view of this, see Baader, 2004; Esser, 2016). *Here*, agency always comes across as positive and does not need to be portrayed any further as a problem (again, for a critical view, see Tisdall & Punch, 2012, p. 256). From this point of view, agency is something that attaches itself to children and can (and should) blossom whenever social aspects appear especially "weak".

Empirical studies thus often reconstructed agency in places such as the playground, where adults are less often physically present, or hardly ever intervene on children's interaction (Esser, 2009, p. 12ff.). While structuralist/functionalist socialisation theories dealt with how children internalise the values and norms they use to achieve agency within a given society, and to be included in that society, agency analyses in Childhood Studies were frequently about providing evidence of "natural", pre-social agency that children could use in opposition to existing social structures (Esser, 2009, p. 12f.).

Accordingly, agency analyses have come up against their limits whenever the social appears to be "strong", constraining children (Esser, 2016). In studies on childhood in "total institutions" (Goffman, 1973), exploitative working conditions or transnational programmes accompanying resettlements, the authors were able to find little of the agency that children were meant to possess as effective social actors. On the contrary, the children they researched seemed to have a very limited range of possible courses of action. Logically, the authors then asked, from a critical point of view, whether the Western, liberal assumption that children possess agency, as a capacity to act independently, really applies to all children. As an alternative, they argued that there are children who, rather than possessing this "thick agency", only have a "thin agency" (e.g. see Jensen, 2014; Muftee, 2015). As easy as it may be to follow the criticism of a substantialising the concept of agency, the solution of assuming that children have a "thin agency" is difficult from a theoretical perspective. Bordonaro and Payen (2012), for example, put forward the criticism that even the concept of thick and thin agency carries along with it the norms of a Western model of actorship: There are, after all, some privileged children who have achieved the goal of "thick" agency, and others who have to make do with a "thin" agency.

The following thus attempts to counter this kind of dualist understanding by presenting a relational approach that on one hand aspires to "socialise" agency, while on the other aims to overcome its position opposing structure (see also Bollig & Kelle, Oswell and Raithelhuber in this volume). Agency theory "aims not just to sidestep the 'structure and agency' problem, but to build on grounds of concepts that eliminate that problem" (White, 2008, p. 15; on this, see also Latour, 1999a, p. 16). For relational social theories, the social is flat (Latour, 2005, pp. 165–172), that is there are not two orders or mechanisms within a dichotomous social reality – no Coleman Bathtubs and no secret structures that might pull social actors' strings. Instead, relational social theories assume that the social can be explained by means of relationships, i.e. ties. Seen from the point of view of social theory, the main focus is not on identical actors who form relationships with other actors through their actions. Instead, the key point is the relationships *between* these actors, which cannot, however, ever be seen as a fixed, regulated structure. In this interpretation it is the dynamic, situational ties that define the actors, and not the reverse (Fuchs, 2001, p. 251).

With relation to children and childhood, this means that children never have any capacity or potential to act at the pre-social stage; this always comes about through the social relationships in which children are integrated. The question is thus: What agency comes with childhood, and what positions as actors does this give children *as children* (Honig, 2013, p. 144) in different contexts? Formulated in this way, agency is thus always first related to childhood as a social construction. Second, in empirical terms, agency always has to be analysed in terms of concrete relationships; in other words, it is a social phenomenon. Children are not viewed as identical actors; they are understood in their social relationality. Seen thus, agency is therefore not a pre-social anthropological property, but an effect of social relationships. Oswell (2013) speaks of "a sense of agency which is both dispersed, or distributed but also fractured, or disarticulated" (p. 62). This is also a way to put an end to the romantic dichotomy according to which the adult is a representative of a conservative structure and children act as rebellious, fresh newcomers (see Bühler-Niederberger & Schwittek, 2014 or de Moll & Betz in this volume for other alternatives). Instead, agency must be related to social contexts and "their" childhoods. Childhood would then be a prerequisite *and* result of positionings that take place based on a categorisation as a child.

Relational agency perspectives and network theories

Such an understanding of agency can be developed with particular ease using the model of the network, which plays a central role in relational social theories. The first aspect of a network is that it is defined by means of various nodes, linked to one another by relationships (ties). While social network analysis (SNA) has usually started out from the nodes, i.e. the actors, who had relationships with other actors, relational theories turn that attitude around: It is not the actors who define their relationships; instead, the nodes can only be defined through the different ties in which they are caught up. This is what gives them their position, their specific properties and opportunities within the network: "The nodes themselves 'have' no agency" (Fuchs, 2001, p. 256) – they gain agency through their relationships.

In relational sociology, network analysis perspectives are linked particularly to the names Bruno Latour, Harrison White and Stephan Fuchs. Drawing upon the theories developed by these protagonists, three different aspects of children's social capacity and potential to act are picked out below from a relational point of view and a more detailed empirical examination is undertaken, based on work from Childhood Studies.

Human and non-human entities: actor-network theory

The first thing that stands out about a network-analysis understanding of relational social theories is a certain type of empiricism: It is only by observing who, or what, in a network can become an actor that the question can be answered of who or what possesses what agency. This idea is connected most strongly to Latour and the *Science and Technology Studies* (STS) (a classic: Latour & Woolgar, 1979/1986). In their laboratory studies, the representatives of *Science and Technology Studies* showed how scientific insights are not produced by researcher subjects as independent observers of an objectively existing reality. Instead, the objects of knowledge production themselves start to interact with the researchers and become actors in the process of gaining insight. Things can thus by all means be equally valid nodes – actors – in the framework of what Latour famously termed the "actor network" (Latour, 1999a, p. 16) or the "collective" (Latour, 1999b, p. 303). In this spirit, children also only gain agency through interacting with a whole range of other entities or "actants", which can take a variety of forms, such as material objects, institutions and legal regulations, subjects or documents.

This perspective leads to mixtures of the natural and cultural spheres, mixtures that change the status not only of things but also of people (Latour, 1993). Hybrid subjects are produced (Esser, 2013a; Haraway, 1991) whose agency comes about through interplay with material worlds and is distributed among those worlds (Knorr-Cetina, 2001, p. 527ff.). Actor-network theory (ANT) and its understanding of agency were adopted in various contexts in Childhood Studies (e.g. see Bollig & Kelle in this volume). In his historical analyses, for example, André Turmel (2008) was able to describe the development of the concept of a normal child during the twentieth century as an interplay between different "actors", including graphs, tables and diagrams. He describes the resulting collective of childhood as an actor network. In this context, Turmel argues in favour of an anti-essentialist understanding of agency: "A child's agency is not the property of a subject, but rather is derived from a distributed network of subjects, bodies, materials, texts and technologies; namely childhood as heterogeneous and complex" (Turmel, 2008, p. 34; see also Esser, 2015).

Bernard Place (2000), too, uses ANT to carry out a physical analysis of children in an intensive care ward: He analyses a "technomorphic body" (Place, 2000, p. 179) in which heterogeneous elements (such as the heart, blood pressure, oxygen mask and incubator) are made up of different spheres and "dealt with" as a network by the medical staff and carers. For Place, again, the child as an actor is not the smallest social particle that makes up societies: The child is embedded in a whole network of different objects, people and practices, within which agency is produced. The fact that agency is not a human capacity opposed to society but is socially produced and distributed amongst different human and non-human actors does not mean that questions of inequalities in power are denied. They are just addressed differently. ANT "decodes the ordering techniques of those who would be powerful. It shows how they translate, conceal and profit from the networks which make them up" (Law, 1994, p. 105).

Going beyond existing studies, ANT promises further, as yet untapped potential for a "new wave" of Childhood Studies, as described by Ryan. Though Kraftl complains that too few studies enter into a heuristic going beyond biosocial dualisms (Kraftl, 2013, p. 17), at least the necessary theoretical food for thought appears to be available (Lee & Motzkau, 2011).

The contouring of identities in social relationships

Relational sociological theories thus assume that people (and things) are not self-identical actors. ANT offers insights into the concept that it takes a whole network of human and non-human actors for them to stabilise. The next step is to ask the question of what shape children can take as nodes, i.e. actors, in social networks. For this purpose it is worth examining Harrison C. White's sociological considerations. White is one of the forefathers of modern, quantitative social network analysis (SNA). At the same time, with his main theoretical work "Identity and Control", a second, fully revised version of which was published in 2008, he is seen as one of the progenitors of relational sociology.

For White, identities arise from attempts to achieve control: "Identities emerge from turbulence seeking control within social footings that can mitigate uncertainty" (White, 2008, p. 17). In White's theory, it is again the webs of relationships that produce possible identities. These identities, i.e. the nodes in the network, are not necessarily human subjects. On the contrary: "people" are just one special example of nodes within a network. "Subsequently, identities and ties may string and profile under some circumstances [...] into what you and I think of as persons" (White, 2008, p. xviii). White thus interprets the term "identity" radically differently than the psychological/philosophical tradition in which it originated, and in which it is generally used. According to his anti-humanist understanding, "identity" does not first and foremost mean a person's individual identity; in fact, that is an effect and result of certain setups within the network, rather than vice versa. Accordingly, White believes that identities that, for example, are related to socialisation processes (for the classic view of this, see Mead, 1934), are higher-sense identities formed by various first-sense identities connecting (White, 2008, p. 17).

The second key term is "control". For White, control does not mean gaining dominance over other identities or relationships; he sees networks as dynamic, but not in the shape of individual nodes being able to control other nodes or the network itself. To this extent, though relational agency theories hold the potential to explain social change and movement, they are not based on a voluntarism that would see individual nodes as able to change the entire system. Instead, stability in fact results from the network.

Bühler-Niederberger and Schwittek (2014) offer a very coherent criticism of theories that always attest to agency when children can be made responsible for social change, but are not analytically open enough to deal with children's contribution to social reproduction. Relational theories may offer a solution to this problem by not defining agency through the effects of individuals' actions on a superordinate structure. In this light, it makes no difference whether agency changes or reproduces the system, whether it is "thick" or "thin". In terms of the subject of children's capacity and potential to act, relational theories thus assume that the "child" itself is one possible identity in the network. This allows for certain positionings within the network that produce certain opportunities for control.

This point, too, can in turn be further elucidated based on empirical work from Childhood Studies. One constantly recurring question is that of how to ascribe agency to children in Childhood Studies when, due to the dominant balance of power in an adult-centric society, they are often powerless and vulnerable (Tisdall & Punch, 2012, p. 256). The advantage of relational theories is that this question can be phrased differently, namely, without reproducing any dichotomy between action and structure. Instead of children, as competent actors, being contrasted with structures that corrupt and limit children's "natural" agency, it is about relationships *between* actors with different properties and agencies.

In her classic study, for example, Jenny Kitzinger (1997) uses biographical interviews to describe how a girl who was exposed to sexualised violence from her father managed to avoid some of her weekend visits to him by faking illnesses and arranging accidents. Christensen (2000, p. 57), meanwhile, was able to show how, for children, *illness* is closely related to the fact that, in modern Western societies, childhood is seen as a stage in life that is characterised by vulnerability. The girl in Kitzinger's research was not able to defend herself against the attacks by her father in direct interaction with him, as his daughter, but she was at least able to use her vulnerability as a characteristic of childhood (produced in social relations) to fall ill, and thus get away from her father to some extent. In one way, as a child, she was thus in a position of powerlessness and vulnerability; at the same time, however, she was able to use precisely that position to show that as a child in need of protection, she had a right to be cared for at home by her mother when ill. Thus, a specific identity as an actor, which is made possible inside a network, results in a certain form of agency for this child, an agency that, analytically, also involves weakness.

This example shows that there is not just a simple dichotomy: on one hand, adult power, standing for the structure of a patriarchal family, and on the other, a child's vulnerability and helplessness. At the same time, however, the power and powerlessness that children experience, in view of generational and other social hierarchies, play a crucial role when it comes to agency, especially from the point of view of relational network analysis. For this reason, questions of identity and control can and must continue to be asked, as questions of power (Law, 1994, p. 105). Subjective capability to act and autonomy cannot simply be assumed to exist. Instead, questions are asked about the social conditions behind opportunities to act arising from certain positions. At the same time, the example also shows how physical and, at the same time, embodied agency is.

The spread of identities and networks

The social has thus far been described on the basis of networks made up of human and non-human, individual and collective actors. "Child" – used so far in the singular – describes a possible position and identity as an actor, which gives rise to agency in relation to other actors or identities (see also Eckermann & Heinzel in this volume). However, this is not always the same positioning within *one* network and, equally, not always the same agency. James and Prout (1996) criticise developmental psychology and socialisation theory for having made precisely that assumption: that "the child at home, in the street and at school is in all respects the same child" (p. 50). According to James and Prout's critique, the child is neither an anthropological universal, as classic developmental psychology would argue, nor a social one as some theories of socialisation would assume.

Here, too, relational approaches offer potential for explanation, in that they do not presume that subjects always have the same identity: "Subjectivity seems also to be a circulating capacity, something that is partially gained or lost by hooking up to certain bodies of practice" (Latour, 1999a, p. 23). Even if certain actors – whether they are children, states or human rights – occur in a particularly stable, fixed form, this too comes from the interplay between the network and actor, not from the actor alone: "Fixed and stable nodes, which seem to self-sufficiently exist in themselves, are *made* fixed and stable by becoming embedded in a cluster of relations, where they lose some of their former degrees of freedom to gain more identity or self-similarity" (Fuchs, 2001, p. 254, original emphasis).

Yet this does not mean that individual children are always assigned the same identity of the "child" in their everyday lives. After all, relational network theories vehemently reject this kind of classic structural argumentation. Their position as a child within an existing social structure does not, therefore, tie them to one particular point: "Even as children, we mix with different groups while intermixing our living in different realms" (White, 2008, p. 11). According to White, social reality is characterised by constantly switching between different network domains, by "netdom switches" (p. 2). Thus, a human or non-human being never has just one identity but instead switches between different netdoms. This means that children belong to different networks, in which generational hierarchies (among other things) play a role but are not the only determining factors. Their sex, age, social stratum or cultural background in a network may also be of importance. Which of these points might be relevant when defining their identity depends, however, on specific ties.

The relationship between different netdoms and agency can also be described in concrete empirical terms – in this case with the help of my own study on *doing family* in family-like groups in homes (Esser, 2013b). To fulfil their social pedagogical task, these child and youth welfare organisations rely upon the existence of a "whole", fully rounded child. Unlike other pedagogical institutions, such as day-care centres, schools or sports associations, children's residential care must aim not to be functionally limited to certain tasks or fields of life. However, this "whole" child did not simply come into existence through children being taken into a group within a home, but instead had to be produced, by mobilising a whole series of different actors. This included, for example, weekly schedules, which gave the organisation a view of the child as a complete entity even if the child was currently not physically present. This allowed children to be addressed as members of a residential group, which children could use to draw conclusions on their everyday rights to organising their free time. For example, one girl pointed at her weekly schedule, complaining to a staff member that it was too empty and provided her with too few activities. The social pedagogue took this demand seriously and arranged additional extracurricular education and leisure activities for the girl, of the kind that currently characterise other childhoods within a family (Vincent & Ball, 2007).

The roundedness that this produced was, however, manufactured *within* the netdom of the residential group. At the same time, the children were also involved in other netdoms, such as that of their family of origin. The children had to switch between these netdoms. Sometimes the different identities stood next to one another relatively unproblematically; at other times, however, conflicts arose that the various actors had to deal with. This took place, for example, if both families claimed the distinction of *exclusively* offering "their" child a place of care and protection.

For children, as a result, the fact that they are children means they do not have one fixed identity as "a child". The actor positions that they can assume in different network domains – in different netdoms – are always determined in part by the fact that they are children. The task faced by empirical research is to reconstruct the positionings and agency that accompany childhood. This connects with analyses that are based on theories of intersectionality and interdependency; these emphasise the fact that agency does not result merely from whether individuals are assigned to the categories of "child" or "adult". Instead, studies of this kind show that a range of different categories (such as sex, ethnicity or status level) may be relevant when identities emerge within relationships (Konstantoni, 2012).

Conclusion: the value of relational perspectives for Childhood Studies

This chapter started out from an understanding of agency as a "capacity of individuals to act independently" (James & James, 2012, p. 3) – an understanding that is widespread but also heavily contested in Childhood Studies. Criticism was voiced over the idea that a voluntaristic or substantialist understanding of agency would lead to reification. Children are declared social actors and empirical research is said to give evidence for their pre-existing yet undocumented agency. Together with other approaches in Childhood Studies (for an overview, see Esser, 2016), relational approaches address the issue of agency differently. If agency is positioned in social interdependence, rather than in individual independence, this leads to a question that may lead empirical research an alternative way: What agency does childhood involve and what actorship are children allotted as children in different contexts? Understood in this way, agency cannot be separated from childhood, as an element of the generational hierarchy that defines that agency, and is itself defined through that agency. Second, in empirical terms it can be said to be a *social* phenomenon: not a human characteristic but an effect of social relationships. To this extent, it can also only be empirically defined within those relationships. As a consequence, third, this renders redundant the dualism according to which adults stand for the rigidity of the existing social structure and children for the pre-social power that produces social change.

At the same time, however, this does not make questions of power, powerlessness or control redundant. Contrary to the neo-liberal postulate that individuals are always capable of acting with personal responsibility, from the point of view of the social sciences, the question needs to be asked of the social conditions that make possible the different expressions of self-determination (Scherr, 2013, p. 237). Relational approaches to agency offer a wider view on what courses and ranges of action these relationships open up for the different actors, i.e. such outlooks are sensitive to the balances of power *and* the potential for enablement that inhabit these structures. Simultaneously, among other things, they can also fathom out the role played by institutions of childhood with regard to agency.

Put in terms of systems theory, agency is thus not only a second-order but also a third-order observation problem. In other words, it is not just a question of observation by science; the subject must also be brought up, through self-reflection, of how science carries out such observations during research. Childhood Studies has to ask what kinds of childhood it helps produce (see also Warming in this volume). For a long time, in Childhood Studies, the agency perspective was linked to the thought that the children's authentic voices should be heard (e.g. see the classic work by Opie & Opie, 1959; also James, 2007; Wyness, 2013). However, if the logical consequences of the outlined relational network approach are thought all the way through, i.e. self-reflectively, then agency, too, is produced through scientific practice. It, too, is thus a laboratory or a netdom in which agency and actors come about through their mobilisation in relationships. Research will not be able to solve this dilemma, but it must at least give up on any unreflected pretence to authenticity and observe itself as it produces agency (Spyrou, 2011).

In summary, relational approaches thus offer several kinds of potential to enrich the discussion about the reconceptualisation of agency in Childhood Studies. The variants described above that are based on network thinking, especially, offer an outlook grounded in interdependency rather than independence, allowing different human and non-human actors to be involved heuristically in producing agency, actors who can, in turn, take on different identities. Moreover, they provide a theoretical framework that, on the one hand, on an analytical level, establishes few norms while at the same time proving sensitive to questions related to theories of power, and can examine Childhood Studies in a self-reflective manner as an actor in the production of agency.

References

Baader, M. S. (2004). Der romantische Kindheitsmythos und seine Kontinuität in der Pädagogik und in der Kindheitsforschung [The romantic myth of childhood and its continuity within pedagogy and childhood studies]. *Zeitschrift für Erziehungswissenschaft*, *7*(3), 416–430.

Bordonaro, L. I. & Payne, R. (2012). Ambiguous agency: critical perspectives on social interventions with children and youth in Africa. *Children's Geographies*, *10*(4), 365–372.

Bühler-Niederberger, D. & Schwittek, J. (2014). Young children in Kyrgyzstan: agency in tight hierarchical structures. *Childhood*, *21*(4), 502–516.

Christensen, P. H. (2000). Childhood and the cultural constitution of vulnerable bodies. In A. Prout (Ed.), *The Body, Childhood and Society* (pp. 38–59). Houndmills, UK: Macmillan.

Esser, F. (2009). *Kinderwelten - Gegenwelten? Pädagogische Impulse aus der Neuen Kindheitsforschung* [*Children's worlds - Counter worlds? Pedagogical stimuli from Childhood Studies*]. Baltmannsweiler: Schneider Hohengehren.

Esser, F. (2013a). *Das Kind als Hybrid: Empirische Kinderforschung (1896–1914)* [*The Child as a Hybrid. Empirical Child Study (1896–1914)*]. Weinheim, Munich: Beltz Juventa.

Esser, F. (2013b). Familienkindheit als sozialpädagogische Herstellungsleistung: Ethnographische Betrachtungen zu 'familienähnlichen' Formen der Heimerziehung [Family childhood as construction of social pedagogy. Ethnography of 'family like' residential child care units]. *Diskurs Kindheits- und Jugendforschung*, *8*(2), 163–176.

Esser, F. (2015). Fabricating the developing child in institutions of education: a historical approach to documentation. *Children & Society*, *29*(3), 174–183.

Esser, F. (2016). Children's agency and welfare organizations from an intergenerational perspective. In S. Punch & R. Vanderbeck (Eds.), *Families, Intergenerationality and Peer Group Relations* (forthcoming). Dordrecht: Springer.

Fuchs, S. (2001). *Against Essentialism: A Theory of Culture and Society*. Cambridge: Harvard University Press.

Giddens, A. (1984). *The Constitution of Society: Outline of the Theory of Structuration*. Cambridge: Polity.

Goffman, E. (1973). *Asylums. Essays on the social situation of mental patients and other inmates*. Middlesex: Penguin Books.

Haraway, D. J. (1991). A cyborg manifesto: science, technology, and socialist-feminism in the late twentieth century. In D. Haraway (Ed.), *Simians, Cyborgs and Women* (pp. 149–181). New York: Routledge.

Honig, M.-S. (2009). How is the child constituted in childhood studies? In J. Qvortrup, W. A. Corsaro & M.-S. Honig (Eds.), *The Palgrave Handbook of Childhood Studies* (pp. 62–77). Basingstoke, Hampshire: Palgrave Macmillan.

Honig, M.-S. (2013). Kindheiten [Childhoods]. In A. Scherr (Ed.), *Soziologische Basics: Eine Einführung für pädagogische und soziale Berufe* [*Sociological Basics: An introduction for educational and social professions*] (2nd extended and updated ed., pp. 143–148). Wiesbaden: Springer VS.

James, A. (2007). Giving voice to children's voices: practices and problems, pitfalls and potentials. *American Anthropologist, 109*(2), 261–272.

James, A. & James, A. (2004). *Construction Childhood: Theory, Policy and Social Practice*. Basingstoke: Palgrave Macmillian.

James, A. & James, A. (2012). *Key Concepts in Childhood Studies* (2nd ed.). Los Angeles: Sage Publications.

James, A. & Prout, A. (1996). Strategies and structures. Towards a new perspective on children's experiences of family life. In J. Brannen & M. O'Brien (Eds.), *Children in Families. Research and Policy* (pp. 41–52). London: Falmer Press.

Jensen, K. B. (2014). Space-time geography of female live-in child domestic workers in Dhaka, Bangladesh. *Children's Geographies, 12*(2), 154–169.

Kitzinger, J. (1997). Who are you kidding? Children, power, and the struggle against sexual abuse. In A. James & A. Prout (Eds.), *Constructing and Reconstructing Childhood. Contemporary Issues in the Sociological Study of Childhood*. (2nd ed., pp. 165–189). London, Philadelphia: Routledge/Falmer.

Knorr-Cetina, K. (2001). Postsocial relations. Theorizing sociality in a postsocial environment. In G. Ritzer & B. Smart (Eds.), *Handbook of Social Theory* (pp. 520–537). London: Sage Publications.

Konstantoni, K. (2012). Children's peer relationships and social identities: exploring cases of young children's agency and complex interdependencies from the Minority World. *Children's Geographies, 10*(3), 337–346.

Kraftl, P. (2013). Beyond "voice", beyond "agency", beyond "politics"? Hybrid childhoods and some critical reflections on children's emotional geographies. *Emotion, Space and Society, 9*, 13–23.

Latour, B. (1993). *We Have Never Been Modern*. New York: Harvester Wheatsheaf.

Latour, B. (1999a). On recalling ANT. In J. Law & J. Hassard (Eds.), *Actor Network Theory and After* (pp. 15–25). Oxford: Blackwell.

Latour, B. (1999b). *Pandora's Hope: Essays on the Reality of Science Studies*. Cambridge: Harvard University Press.

Latour, B. (2005). *Reassembling the Social: An introduction to Actor-Network-Theory*. Oxford: Oxford University Press.

Latour, B. & Woolgar, S. (1979/1986). *Laboratory Life: The Construction of Scientific Facts*. Princeton, NJ: Princeton University Press.

Law, J. (1994). *Organizing Modernity*. Oxford: Blackwell.

Lee, N. & Motzkau, J. (2011). Navigating the bio-politics of childhood. *Childhood, 18*(1), 7–19.

Mead, G. H. (1934). *Mind, Self, and Society: From the Standpoint of a Social Behaviorist*. Chicago: University of Chicago Press.

Muftee, M. (2015). Children's agency in resettlement: a study of Swedish cultural orientation programs in Kenya and Sudan. *Children's Geographies, 13*(2), 131–148.

Opie, I. & Opie, P. (1959). *The Lore and Language of Schoolchildren*. Oxford: Oxford University Press.

Oswell, D. (2013). *The Agency of Children: From Family to Global Human Rights*. Cambridge: Cambridge University Press.

Passoth, J.-H., Peuker, B. & Schillmeier, M. (Eds.). (2012). *Agency without Actors? New Approaches to Collective Action*. London, New York: Routledge.

Place, B. (2000). Constructing the bodies of ill children in the intensive care unit. In A. Prout (Ed.), *The Body, Childhood and Society* (pp. 172–194). Houndmills: Macmillan.

Prout, A. (2000). Childhood bodies: construction, agency and hybridity. In A. Prout (Ed.), *The Body, Childhood and Society* (pp. 1–18). Houndmills: Macmillan.

Raithelhuber, E. (2008). Von Akteuren und *agency*. Eine sozialtheoretische Einordnung der *structure/agency*-Debatte [Of Actors and Agency. The structure/agency debate in the context of Social Theory]. In H. G. Homfeldt, W. Schröer & C. Schweppe (Eds.), *Vom Adressaten zum Akteur: Soziale Arbeit und Agency* [*From Client to Actor. Social Work and agency*] (pp. 17–45). Opladen, Germany; Farmington Hills, MI: Barbara Budrich.

Scherr, A. (2013). Agency - ein Theorie- und Forschungsprogramm für die Soziale Arbeit? [Agency - a theory and research perspective for Social Work?] In G. Graßhoff (Ed.), *Adressaten, Nutzer, Agency: Akteursbezogene Forschungsperspektiven in der Sozialen Arbeit* [*Clients, users, agency: Actor centred research perspectives in Social Work*] (pp. 229–242). Wiesbaden: Springer VS.

Spyrou, S. (2011). The limits of children's voices. From authenticity to critical, reflexive representation. *Childhood, 18*(2), 151–165.

Tisdall, E. K. M. & Punch, S. (2012). Not so "new"? Looking critically at childhood studies. *Children's Geographies, 10*(3), 249–264.

Turmel, A. (2008). *A Historical Sociology of Childhood. Developmental Thinking, Categorization and Graphic Visualization*. Cambridge: Cambridge University Press.

Uprichard, E. (2008). Children as "being and becomings": children, childhood and temporality. *Children & Society, 22*(4), 303–313.

Vincent, C., & Ball, S. J. (2007). "Making up" the middle class child: families, activities and class dispositions. *Sociology, 41*(6), 1061–1077.

Warming, H. (2006). "How can you know? You're not a foster child": dilemmas and possibilities of giving voice to children in foster care. *Children, Youth and Environments, 16*(2), 28–50.

White, H. C. (2008). *Identity and Control: How Social Formations Emerge* (2nd ed.). Princeton: Princeton University Press.

Woodhead, M. (2009). Child development and the development of childhood. In J. Qvortrup, W. A. Corsaro & M.-S. Honig (Eds.), *The Palgrave Handbook of Childhood Studies* (pp. 46–61). Basingstoke, Hampshire: Palgrave Macmillan.

Wyness, M. G. (2013). Children's participation and intergenerational dialogue. Bringing adults back into the analysis. *Childhood, 20*(4), 429–442.

Chapter 4

Children's agency

Contributions from feminist and ethic of care theories to sociology of childhood

Anne Wihstutz

The chapter focusses on children's agency from a feminist ethic of care perspective. Drawing on the works of difference-centred theorists, agency is discussed as embedded in specific historic, social and economic conditions, whereby social actors are depicted as participating in various relationships at one time. Starting from this point and drawing on theoretical works of feminist ethics of care (Tronto, 1993), care relations between children and parents are discussed as interdependent. A perspective on responsiveness is the focal point of this study. This approach opens up a one-sided and vertical understanding of children's dependence and adults' independence, yielding a structural understanding of reciprocity. By examining specific care relationships involving children as young carers, the value of a perspective based on an ethic of care in childhood sociology regarding children's agency is illustrated.

Children's ability to participate in society is determined by their status as not yet fully incorporated members of society who do not (yet) possess equal rights. This has serious consequences for their identity and the recognition of their capacity for agency. Modernity's model of childhood conceptualises the child as a developing, dependent being, whose task is to be trained in specialised institutions. Childhood as a specific phase is therefore conceived as a space of protection, care and preparation, in which the child is free from responsibility for others, from the burden of generating income, but also free from the rights afforded by political participation. From a legal perspective the child is constructed as a "minor", and thus different from adults. By means of the "institutionalized, juristically regulated chronologisation of childhood" (Mierendorff, 2010, p. 24), the relationship between adults and children is fixed as a hierarchical one.

From these opening reflections, the current chapter aims to contribute to the expansion of a concept of children's agency. It differentiates epistemic and empirical dimensions with reference to children's perspectives (Honig, 1999) and places in question those dichotomies founded on the binary oppositions between children and adults or actors and structures, instead focusing on interdependent and reciprocal conditions of dependence and independence. In this context, relational theories are of particular interest. The chapter thus responds to the criticism voiced in the discipline of childhood sociology that the physical, material and emotional dependencies of children are not sufficiently reflected in the concept of agency (Prout, 2005). This criticism is directed towards, respectively, the insufficient consideration of the social conditioning of children's lives, the absence of contextualisation and the limited recognition of childhood's structuring by generational hierarchies. In this chapter, through the application of difference-centred theoretical approaches, children are understood as differently equal members of society. This concept of difference is then developed from an ethical care perspective founded on the human need for care.

The analysis of concrete relationships of care will lead to the development of an expanded concept of children's agency. In attempting to make a feminist ethic of care productive in this context, my starting point is that of moral conflicts in relationships of care. I make links to empirical parent-child relationships such as those between caring children and their care-dependent parents. Through this care ethic perspective, dependency and need come to the fore. Relationships of care are described as being embedded within power relationships. As a result, we can discuss specific actions in specific situations by real people. The understanding of ethics underpinning this chapter emerges in reflection upon conflicts and reveals itself in actions (Conradi, 2001, p. 166, footnote 42).

In the first part of the chapter, I discuss theoretical concepts of agency in terms of their significance to care theories. In the second part of the chapter, these theories are then applied to empirical works on young carers and their families. Through an ethical consideration of the phenomenon of young carers, children's agency is understood in a new or expanded light from the perspective of responsiveness and interdependence.

A relational understanding of agency

The question of a two-way dependency of structure and actor is fundamental to sociological debate. The sociology of childhood understands childhood as constitutive for social structure. A sociology of children, by contrast, focuses on the level of interaction between social actors. Within this context, children are mostly conceptualised as endowed with agency per se (Prout, 2005; James & James, 2012). Critics bemoan the fact that such a subject-oriented approach always already imagines children as agentic. As a result, an ontologisation of children is paradoxically promoted by that new form of child research, which had accused approaches founded in developmental psychology and socialisation theory of precisely that same failing (Esser, 2008).

Lee (2001) identifies a dualistic model of agency and structure in those discussions of childhood sociology, which presume a separation between beings and becomings. By emphasising the status of children as "beings in their own right", for Prout and others the new sociology of childhood runs the risk of "endorsing the myth of the autonomous and independent person"

(Prout, 2005, p. 66) by following a concept of an autonomous subject, liberated from all interdependencies, something which it sought to criticise from the very start. According to Lee (2001), there is no longer any such thing as a "complete" (being) adult that is to be contrasted with a "developing" (becoming) child. On the basis of the breakdown of traditional patterns of life, Lee argues that adults re-invent themselves within the new production of familial forms, that they re-form themselves throughout their lives and learn to adapt to new developments (technological, etc.). Adults are in this way as much "becomings" as children are "beings", without their specific rights to be recognised as persons with their own needs and interests being placed in question (Prout, 2005).

If we follow this premise, then we must consider the engagement of the individual with her social and material environment as a lifelong process of transformation. The human being is bound in different relationship frameworks, which exist synchronously and in parallel to one another, are interwoven and are generated, reproduced and transformed by specific conditions. Such an approach is necessarily concerned with interdependencies and demands that we interrogate how people are embedded into their different social relationships (Martin & Dennis, 2010, cited in James & James, 2012, p. 5). The starting point is then a relational and dynamic connection between social actors and specific contexts. The latter are understood as both given and as undergoing transformations. The question of a person's agency is not to be answered without consideration of the specific contexts and power structures (see also Punch in this volume).

Participation as "other "–"different" forms of participation?

Inspired by difference-centred approaches such as the pedagogics of the oppressed; post-colonial studies; feminist, transgender, queer and anti-racist theories, my argument now turns to the question of power and participation. It is difference-centred theories that focus their analysis on the mechanisms of social inclusion and exclusion (for an overview, see Moosa-Mitha, 2005, p. 370ff). Common to them is an analysis of hegemonic discourses and normative institutional practices that prevent individuals and groups from participating in society on an equal basis, since they are ascribed the status of being "different". A central topic of difference-centred theoretical approaches is what could be called the everyday struggle for participation as citizens who are embedded in multiple complex relationships and as such have specific socio-economic, historical and racist or sexist experiences that shape their struggle for equal rights, social participation and belonging.

In theories founded on race or gender critiques, the concept of agency refers to the agency of participation, insofar as participation is not only understood as outcome-driven or externally situated, materialised action.[1] Difference-centred theorists understand agency as the expression of a dialectical relationship between the individual sense of self and collective action. The self in the sense of difference-centred theoretical approaches is "a responsive one, showing agency in interacting with its own lived reality" (Moosa-Mitha, 2005, p. 375). Moosa-Mitha understands agency as something always standing "in relation", as the expression of personal needs and situational interpretations in relationships marked by difference. Moreover, agency is not thought of as synonymous with positively evaluated actions or limited to conformity with minority world notions of childhood (see above).

On the basis of her own ethnographic work with former sexually exploited children, Moosa-Mitha develops the concept of children as differently equal and thus introduces the perspective of "other", different everyday life realities into the debate about citizenship (Moosa-Mitha, 2005). Within the context of theorising children's agency, children's participation is understood as the expression of their specific analysis of and reflection on their life realities. Since agency is not connected to externally recognisable transformations, the concept, if understood in this way, could contribute to the recognition of the complex ways in which children's agency is expressed in their varied relationships (Moosa-Mitha, 2005).

As a result, ethical questions can be addressed regarding the concept of agency. From an ethical perspective, there is interest in how social actors reflect upon their own activities. They interpret a situation and their actions from their own specific perspective.

In the following, I seek to outline the perspective of an ethical consideration of children's participation in social relationships in more detail. Ethical theory is of special interest to the debate on children's agency because it focuses on moral dilemma. Due to its emphasis on power relationships, my argument is limited to feminist elaborations on care ethics. An ethic of care places the focus on specific practices, attitudes and activities of care, responsibility and concern.

A feminist ethic of care

A feminist care ethic asks the question of what constitutes a good life, with particular reference to the possibilities of participation and belonging.

Care as praxis: actions and attitudes

Tronto (1993) understands care as an all-encompassing human activity. This includes "everything that we do to maintain, continue, and repair our 'world' so that we can live in it as well as possible. That world includes our bodies, our selves, and our environment, all of which we seek to interweave in a complex, life-sustaining web" (Tronto, 1993, p. 103).

According to Tronto, care is understood as a specific function of socio-political culture (Tronto, 1993). The activities of care are culturally determined. She explains this by pointing out that very few societies would share the Western conception of care that implies that only the biological mother is responsible for her child. Care, in Tronto's terms, encompasses dimensions of practice and disposition. The development of an ethic of care is founded on the analysis of society where care is reduced to a lesser importance. Looking at the distribution of rewards such as money and prestige, care figures low. "Care is devalued as work in our society" (Tronto, 1993, p. 117). Through a connection with privacy, emotion, and the needy, those who engage in care practically experience devaluation. According to Tronto, neediness is conceived as a threat to autonomy. "Those who have more needs than us appear to be less autonomous, and hence less powerful and less capable" (Tronto, 1993, p. 120). By "us", she refers to the concept of the autonomous, independent adult, who is considered not-needy. Following Tronto (1993) and Conradi (2001), care is therefore understood in a feminist ethics as a socio-historically conditioned form of social praxis, and as a social praxis it is determined by conditions that are themselves mutable (Conradi, 2001, p. 50).

Considering care from an ethical perspective means enhancing its status, valorising care as a form of praxis and discussing it anew in terms of fair participation in society. Since the feminist ethic of care takes into account the framework of relationships, the position of the individual within these contexts and the material and social determinations of such, the focus is directed towards concrete dependencies and power structures. From Tronto's perspective, care is not bound to a specific gender (Conradi, 2001, p. 19); rather, it fundamentally presumes that every person in the course of their life is dependent on the help of others. The need for help emerges and changes over time. It can arise in certain situations, and is thus to be thought of as context-dependent. Agency can be lost in certain circumstances, and it can be experienced and regained in others. Something similar applies to the acceptance of assistance. Help cannot be accepted under all circumstances, for example if the dignity or self-esteem of the affected person would be injured as a result (Spies, 2013, p. 68). Against the background of vulnerability, an imbalance arises between those who give help and those who accept it. Relationships of care are embedded in asymmetrical structural relations. Tronto develops an ethic of care from the analysis of societies organised into gender hierarchies (Tronto, 1993).

Ethical premises

In naming the premises of an ethic of care, we can list knowledge of fundamental human physical and mental vulnerability as well as the embedding of the praxis of care in asymmetrical relationships. At its core is an assumption about a general relation to others. Community and society are conceptualised such that the individual in need will receive help, and that he or she responds to others' need for support. A fundamental starting point is thus neither an immediately reciprocal relationship nor a utilitarian orientation. "The social community/society [sic] is understood as a network of relationships and connections in which every individual is bound as provider and recipient" (Großmaß, 2006, p. 331*)[2]. In connection with the core premise of the vulnerability or neediness and dependence of every human being, "an ethics of care starts with people *as* they *are* and *where* they are, taking account of their positionality and standpoints, the relationships between them and the responsibilities that are assigned and assumed within these relationships" (Monchinski, 2010, p. 48, emphasis in original).

Seeking recourse to an ethical perspective is also productive for the sociological debate on children's agency because in doing so, normative assumptions about the specific child-adult relationship as outlined for modernity's model of childhood can be critically questioned. In the following my theoretical elaborations on agency and care will be applied to the phenomenon of young carers. An observation of the phenomenon of young carers from an ethical perspective appears illuminating, since in this case children and parents have developed relationships of attentiveness and responsibility towards one another, which are often considered child-inappropriate, as will be discussed below. On the basis of empirical observations (Metzing, 2007; Dearden & Becker, 2004; Jones et al., 2002), questions are raised regarding the motivation and reflections of the social actors involved.

Young carers: the agency of children[3]

Children as caregivers[4] (and heads of household, breadwinners, etc.; for an overview, see Payne, 2012) have been categorised as children "out of place" (Boyden, 1990; Nieuwenhuys, 1998) and as a social problem because of their agency (Payne, 2012). The definition of child-headed households (CHHs) offered by Payne (2012), "in which adults or guardians are either absent or not fully functioning in terms of providing for the material and emotional needs of children" (p. 399), could cover families of young carers, too, to the extent that these not only care for but also provide for emotional needs in *lieu* of parents. Coming from the AIDS and orphan crisis debates, child-headed households are typically portrayed "as social problems in which expressions of agency run contrary to the mainstream moral and social order in society" (Payne, 2012, p. 401). In these debates, children with such responsibilities are depicted both as a risk to themselves and to wider society. Their agency is considered as extraordinary and in terms of "coping" with situations of loss. Such children therefore count as highly vulnerable, as children "at risk".

It is not my point to argue against the severe situations of constraint that children face when shouldering responsibilities usually faced by adults. There is enough empirical data to underpin the argument of constraint and precarity. In particular, it is the generational position and the age of the child that prove challenging because children are not granted access to the social, material and practical resources often available to adults in the same community (Payne, 2012; Evans & Becker, 2007).

My point in this chapter is to shift the focus onto the self-reflection of the children involved in these particular family arrangements of care. Therefore, in the following I will develop my argument by looking at the reflections on everyday life arrangements developed by young caregiving children and their families. My elaborations draw mainly on the qualitative study by Metzing (2007) on "children and young people as carers for chronically ill relatives"[5]. In her qualitative study, Metzing (2007)[6] examines the construction of familial care arrangements and the factors that influence the ways in which children provide help. The study focuses on the experience of children within the situation of chronic illness and examines how children experience and shape familial care in the role of carers.

Children and young people as carers for relatives

Metzing identifies two phenomena as key results of her study. First, she establishes that for children and young people, the most important issue is that everyday family life is maintained. They therefore develop a range of strategies that enable them to participate in care, in each case dependent on intervening conditions and their own motivations (Metzing, 2007, p. 85). Children "fill in the gaps" that chronic illness creates and are prepared to respond immediately to the situation. They are ready to give up planned intentions, and "deviate from their course" if the situation demands it. They continually evaluate their actions and adapt their activities correspondingly. In order to avoid external intervention, children prevent outsiders from gaining insight into their involvement in the management of the situation provoked by chronic illness within the family: They do not talk about it.

Metzing's second key insight is that it is important for the families that, in spite of the illness, they wish to be able "to continue living as normal" (Metzing, 2007, p. 179*). As much as the children may wish the chronically ill family member to be restored to good health, their concrete wishes are directed towards having a normal everyday life with the situation created by the illness. For the children (and their families), it is crucial that the reality of their lives is perceived and taken into account as normal by their environment[7]. They would like to have someone with whom they can talk about their experiences, as well as getting information about the illness and its possible consequences, and also sources of further assistance. Beyond this, they would like to have non-bureaucratic and flexible help on an everyday level, as well as time for their own issues; in other words, they would like to be able to allow themselves respite from the demands and responsibilities of caring. Finally, the families frequently experience financial hardship as a consequence of the illness, and as a result, they formulate a desire for financial assistance (Metzing, 2007, p. 139ff.).

Societies' generational structure in welfare regimes of the Global north describes parent-child relationships in such a way that parents take on responsibility for the care, supervision and education of their children. In the care praxis of children who are looking after needy parents this normative perspective on the parent-child relationship, which is also legally codified, may be reversed: Through their participation in the care arrangements, children and parents develop a relationship in which in specific ways and in specific situations, children take on responsibility for a parent. Depending on the situation, they experience themselves as invested with power, and the father or mother as in need of help (Jones et al., 2002). In their own individual ways, children involve themselves in the work of helping, offering palliative care, support, encouragement and similar things in caring for a relative. Through their involvement in such activities, they develop an ethical position, i.e. they take over responsibility based on a specific attitude to the situation and the relationship which I would like to designate as "responsiveness". They recognise that their family member requires help, but without fundamentally placing the parent-child relationship – in other words, the differences between children and adults – in question (Miller, 2005; Jones et al., 2002; Wihstutz, 2011). This care arrangement functions because, for their part, parents are able to recognise children's agency in these circumstances and can rely on their support.

Against the context of the social status of children as "underage" and unequally treated members of society, such a care arrangement must be questioned in terms of the potential for violence it harbours. The asymmetry between parents and children is not reversed, but within this care arrangement, the caregiving child can end up in a too-demanding position, both because he or she is emotionally and psychically dependent on the care of his or her parents and because the child does not have the same rights, legally, as those that adults have at their disposal[8].

From an ethical perspective, it is more of interest of how the children involved (and parents) reflect on their status and take up their own attitude or ethical position towards that situation.

Young carers: ethical observations on care

The particular relationships between parents and children that emerge when children take on responsibility for the support of a chronically ill parent demands from those involved an attitude of attentiveness, a concept coined by Tronto and glossed by Conradi as an awareness of others and their concerns (Conradi, 2001[9]). The asymmetry of vulnerability recognises the dissimilarities of those involved.

The appreciation of vulnerability is the fundamental basis for an action grounded in ethical principles of care, which orients itself around the other (and his or her well-being). The point of reference is always the enabling of and respect for the dignity of those who receive help and support as well as of those who act as caregivers.

From the feminist ethical perspective, care as praxis can be divided into four phases (Großmaß, 2006, pp. 331f.): "*caring about*" (1) describes an initial phase, in which the needs of the other are perceived for the first time. If the needs of the other have been perceived, then the question of one's own position with regard to those needs arises. Tronto describes this phase as *"taking care of"* (2). Empirical studies of young carers point to the connection between a lack of adequate external support and the engagement of children in the care of their relatives (Metzing, 2007; Aldridge, 2008; Dearden & Becker, 2004; Jones et al., 2002). This form of support, *"care giving"* (3) by children encompasses physical, medical-therapeutic assistance, mediating, supervisory and protective assistance, and the provision of emergency help, as well as emotional support (Metzing, 2007). Metzing recognises in this "emotional support" children's capacity to respond sensitively to their parents' moods, even if the latter are attempting to disguise their own emotional state. She explains this capacity through the "profound need" that the children feel to "ease the burden, to want to help" (Metzing, 2007, p. 98). From the ethical perspective, it is important that the offered help is indeed accepted as helpful by the person in need (*"care receiving"* (4))[10] (Großmaß, 2006, p. 331). By distinguishing these four phases for analytical purposes, it can be shown how far the praxis of care contributes to balancing out existing asymmetries in any particular relationship constellation.

Children and parents are repeatedly confronted with the demands of normative orientations required by a traditional "good" parent-child relationship. In face of these, families with chronic illness and with children involved in care need to figure out how to make appropriate and correct decisions, derived from their specific experiences.

Viewing the relationship between children and parents as one of care allows us to discuss care from the perspective of its potential for violence as well as possible strategies for empowerment[11]. From an ethical angle, the question of agency is significant – concerning agency in the practice of care as enabling both the caregiver and care recipient. Conradi terms this "empowered caring" (Conradi, 2001, p. 54), which from a position of power helps expand or open up agency. In this way, empowerment is also conceivable in relationships of care and dependency and can help balance out asymmetric relationships.

Seen within the context of the young carer, we have to ask which asymmetric relationships need to be rebalanced, since vulnerability lies not only with the care receiver, in this case, the ill parent. Empirical studies on young carers indicate that the involvement of children in familial care arrangements can lead to a strengthening of their agency (e.g. Metzing, 2007; Jones et al., 2002). Children understand themselves and are understood by their relatives as competent actors in this care arrangement. At the same time, the asymmetry between parents and children is not nullified.

These experiences can be quite ambivalent, as is demonstrated by the following quotation from a 14-year-old girl whose mother is severely traumatised: "My siblings are still small, and I cannot say, 'all right, I can't go on.

I'm letting everything drop'. I must, I have to be there (!) for them. Because, that's where the strength comes from. And I mean, I have to help them, my mother and my father" (Metzing, 2007, p. 88*).

For those parents who are reliant on support, depending on the help of their children is also bound up with ambivalent feelings. Payne also speaks of mixed feelings parents experience, of pride and guilt for depending on their children (Payne, 2012). Parents do not find it easy to make such demands of their children and do notice how their children are competent in the sense of dealing with the situation in an empathetic and reflective way.

Due to a specific normative understanding of good childhood and good parenthood, alongside dealing with this chronic illness-related crisis situation, there is something particularly explosive in the fact that neither children nor parents can turn to outsiders for advice. Both the parents and children fear that they could be torn apart as a family if the children's involvement became general knowledge. Left to their own devices in this, it becomes difficult for those involved to develop an alternative perception of the situation and their own place within it. Reflection on the state of affairs remains a matter purely of intra-family concern.

Under the aspect of responsiveness, from a perspective based on feminist ethics of care, the ambivalence embedded in these parent-child relationships can be brought to light. The orientation of responsiveness within the parent-child relationship is not constructed in opposition to the desire to defend free space for one's own needs. Rather, responsiveness refers to the attitude by which contradictory interests and needs can be recognised and balanced out. This denotes an understanding of the process that comprehends the framework of relations within which care takes place as dynamic and thus subject to change.

It is through the feminist ethical care perspective that we can understand children's involvement in family care arrangements as an expression of their agency.

Conclusion

From the feminist perspective of an ethic of care, the concepts of interrelation, responsiveness and praxis (understood as attitude and action) can be employed to develop the conceptual depth of childhood agency. Agency can then be understood as the expression of a specific relational interpretation of social conditions, in which children position themselves as belonging participants.

The premise of an ethic of care – that care relationships are embedded in asymmetric situations that contain the potential for violence – renders this perspective significant for any discussion of childhood agency. From the viewpoint of an ethic of care, one can ask how to balance out these asymmetries through the participation of children by looking at concrete processes of negotiation.

As discussed with reference to young carers, this ethical perspective allows us to consider the attempts by the social actors to reflect upon their interpretations of neediness in the context of societies' handling of vulnerability and predominant conceptions of parent-child relationships. The self-positioning of children within the framework of relationships of dependency and neediness can be understood as an act of ethical grounding. The consideration of care arrangements discussed in the foregoing from a feminist ethical perspective paves the way for analysis of the ways in which children position themselves as agentic.

A sociology of childhood that takes up a care perspective does not seek to ascribe a subject status to children that would see them as independent, self-sufficient individuals. Rather, its aim is to draw attention to interdependent, relational frameworks, moral considerations and other similar aspects that influence children's agency.

I have pointed to the significance of historically sedimented, specifically social and economic influences on agency by individuals and groups structurally positioned and socially perceived as different by reference to difference-centred approaches, and outlined the significance of context and power relations for the perception of agency. In conclusion, I discussed the phenomenon of caring children from the perspective of an ethic of care, and suggested ways in which such an extended concept of children's agency can be made productive for further work.

On the basis of questions that were originally formulated to address the praxis of social work (Großmaß, 2006, pp. 334f.), in closing, I will delineate some aspects of how a care perspective on children's agency could be carried over into the conceptualisation of what it means to be a child, or to be an adult. Through an ethic of care, we can see children and parents afresh through their social practices (care of) and their attitudes rooted in those practices (care for and care about). As the example of young carers and their families has highlighted, being vulnerable is interpreted specifically in each situation. This throws up the question of what constitutes vulnerability in children and adults. On what is it based? What is the basis for an acceptance of vulnerability that sees adults' vulnerability as different from that of children? Differentiation of this kind leads us to ask whether children who are conceptualised as vulnerable can respond to the vulnerability of adults with a sense of empowerment.

Due to the prevailing understanding of vulnerability or neediness, as I have explicated it specifically for child-parent care arrangements, it is possible for neither children nor adults to look for support from another instance. On the basis of this, one has to ask: Under what conditions would it be possible to think about ways of supporting parents and children that recognise the realities of family life and support the involvement of children in terms of their agency? Precisely this final aspect is crucial for the question of agency, since both children's and adults' interests need recognition. Finally, in every set of relations, one has to ask how help *and* recognition can be brought to the fore in both praxis and attitude.

These considerations start from an orientation around a "culture of attentiveness" (Conradi, 2001), which includes the immediate environment of those involved and general polity as such. By bringing the perspective of an ethic of care into the concept of (children's) agency, we can take into account children's self-perception and self-positioning in their interaction with social conditions and can reflect on this from a perspective of responsiveness as the expression of interdependent relationships between children and their social context.

Notes

1 In situations determined by racism and sexism, participation can mean, especially in the everyday life of Black women, that they free themselves from the ascribed status of inferiority through their own self-perception. Such participation can be interpreted both as a visible, open act of participation as well as an internally directed act of resistance, unfolding emancipatory and transformative effects (Moosa-Mitha, 2005).
2 All citations marked with an asterisk have been translated by the author.
3 See Wihstutz (2009) for a discussion of the concept of "vulnerable and needy parents" in connection with children taking on responsibility within the family.
4 "Caregivers" is used synonymously to "young carers". The former has been criticised for implying a one-sided view on parent-child relationships (Miller, 2005; Jones et al., 2002; Evans & Becker, 2007). In this chapter, "care" is referred to as attitude and activity (Tronto, 1993) thereby the term "young carer" is used in its broadest sense.
5 In the framework of an exploratory study, semi-structured interviews were conducted with 34 families over the course of 16 months. In 81 interviews overall, 41 children between the ages of 4½ and 19 years, as well as 41 parents, of whom two were grandparents, were involved (Metzing, 2007).
6 This study is not only the first comprehensive study to focus on the realities of young caring children and youth and their families in Germany (Metzing, 2007), but also major policy papers refer to it to support their argument on the existence of young carers in Germany and in Austria, respectively (SVR, 2014; Weinberger, 2011).
7 This finding is similar to the empirical findings of Payne (2012), in her study with children heading households in rural and urban Zambia. The children in her study consider their varied good and bad experiences of responsibility "to be part of their everyday life, the norm rather than exception" (Payne, 2012, p. 404).
8 Paediatric and psychiatric studies refer to the concept of "parentification" in connection with children who are involved as carers. This relates to the taking-on by children of tasks and roles that are usually associated with adults (Hooper et al., 2011). The role reversal is described as being not appropriate for the child and being allotted to the child by the parents, with serious and long-lasting consequences for the child's development (Stangl, 2010).
9 Tronto (1993, pp. 127f.) differentiates an attitude of care according to four ethical aspects: *attentiveness, responsibility, competence* and *responsiveness.*
10 According to Conradi, this reaction, or acceptance of help by the *care-receiving* person, taking into account the needs of the caregiver, is expressed by Tronto through the term *responsiveness* (Conradi, 2001, p. 225).
11 Work on young carers document how caregiving can be cause for pride and heightened self-esteem in young people (Robson, 2004; Robson & Ansell, 2000).

References

Aldridge, J. (2008). All work and no play? Understanding the needs of children with caring responsibilities. *Children & Society*, 22, 253–264.
Boyden, J. (1990). A comparative perspective on the globalisation of childhood. In A. James & A. Prout (Eds.), *Constructing and Reconstructing Childhood: Contemporary Issues in the Sociological Study of Childhood* (pp. 190–225). London: Falmer Press.

Bühler-Niederberger, D. (2005). *Kindheit und die Ordnung der Verhältnisse: Von der gesellschaftlichen Macht der Unschuld und dem kreativen Individuum* [*Childhood and the arrangement of conditions: About the social power of innocence and the creative individual*]. Weinheim, Munich: Juventa.

Cockburn, T. (2010). Children, the feminist ethic of care and childhood studies: is this the way to the good life? In S. Andresen, I. Diehm, U. Sander & H. Ziegler (Eds.), *Children and the Good Life, Children's Well-Being: Indicators and Research* (pp. 29–39). Heidelberg: Springer.

Cockburn, T. (2007). Reconstructing children's agency: boundaries of rights and care. In C. Beckett, O. Heathcote & M. Macey (Eds.), *Negotiating Boundaries: Identities, Sexualities, Diversities* (pp. 155–166). Newcastle: Cambridge Scholars Press.

Conradi, E. (2001). *Take Care: Grundlagen einer Ethik der Achtsamkeit* [*Take Care: Foundations of an Ethics of Carefulness*]. Frankfurt/M.: Campus.

Dearden, C. & Becker, S. (2004). Young carers in the UK: the 2004 report. London: Carers UK.

Esser, F. (2008). Agency und generationale Differenz: Einige Implikationen der Kindheitsforschung für die Sozialpädagogik [Agency and generational difference: a few implications of childhood studies for social paedagogy]. In H. -G. Homfeldt, W. Schröer & C. Schweppe (Eds.), *Vom Adressaten zum Akteur: Soziale Arbeit und Agency* [*From Recipient to Actor: Social Work and Agency*] (pp. 133–154). Opladen, Germany; Farmington Hills, MI: Verlag Barbara Budrich.

Evans, R. & Becker, S. (2009). *Children Caring for Parents with HIV and AIDS: Global Issues and Policy Responses*. Bristol: The Policy Press.

Großmaß, R. (2006). Die Bedeutung der Care-Ethik für die Soziale Arbeit [The meaning of care ethics in social work, ergänzt von A.Wihstutz]. In S. Dungs, U. Gerber, H. Schmidt & R. Zitt (Eds.), *Soziale Arbeit und Ethik im 21. Jahrhundert: Ein Handbuch* [*Social work and ethics in the 21st century: a handbook*] (pp. 319–339). Leipzig: Evangelische Verlagsanstalt.

Honig, M. -S. (1999). Forschung "vom Kinde aus"? Perspektivität in der Kindheitsforschung [Childhood "from the Child's Point of View"? Perspectivity in Childhood Studies]. In M. -S. Honig, A. Lange & H. R Leu (Eds.), *Aus der Perspektive von Kindern? Zur Methodologie der Kindheitsforschung* [*From the Children's Point of View? The Methodology of Childhood Studies*] (pp. 33–50). Weinheim, Munich: Juventa.

Hooper, L., DeCoster, J., White, N. & Voltz, M. (2011). Characterizing the magnitude of the relation between self-reported childhood parentification and adult psychopathology. *Journal of Clinical Psychology, 67*(10), 1028–1043.

James, A. & James, A. (2012). *Key Concepts in Childhood Studies* (2nd ed.). Los Angeles, London: Sage Publications.

Jones, A., Jeyasingham, D. & Rajasoorya S. (2002). *Invisible Families: The Strengths and Needs of Black Families in Which Young People Have Caring Responsibilities*. Bristol: The Policy Press.

Lee, N. (2001). *Childhood and Society: Growing Up in an Age of Uncertainty*. Buckingham: Open University Press.

Metzing, S. (2007). *Kinder und Jugendliche als pflegende Angehörige: Erleben und Gestalten familialer Pflege* [*Children and adolescents as caring relatives: experiencing and shaping of family care*]. Bern: Hans Huber.

Mierendorff, J. (2010). *Kindheit und Wohlfahrtsstaat: Entstehung, Wandel und Kontinuität des Musters moderner Kindheit* [*Childhood and welfare state: Origins, change and continuities of modern childhood patterns*]. Weinheim: Juventa.

Miller, P. (2005). Useful and priceless children in contemporary welfare states. *Social Politics*, *12*(1), 3–41.

Monchinski, T. (2010). *Education in Hope: Critical Pedagogies and the Ethic of Care.* New York: Peter Lang.

Moosa-Mitha, M. (2005). A difference-centred alternative to theorization of children's citizenship rights. *Citizenship Studies*, *9*(4), 369–388.

Nieuwenhuys, O. (1998). Global childhood and the politics of contempt. *Alternatives*, *23*(3), 124–145.

Payne, R. (2012). "Extraordinary survivors" or "ordinary lives"? Embracing "everyday agency" in social interventions with child-headed households in Zambia. *Children's Geographies*, *10*(4), 399–411.

Prout, A. (2005). *The Future of Childhood.* London, New York: Routledge Falmer.

Robson, E. (2004). Children at work in rural northern Nigeria: patterns of age, space and gender. *Journal of Rural Studies*, 20, 193–210.

Robson, E. & Ansell, N. (2000). Young carers in southern Africa: exploring stories from Zimbabwean secondary school students. In S. Halloway & G. Valentine (Eds.), *Children's Geographies* (pp. 174–193). London: Routledge.

Sachverständigenrat zur Begutachtung der Entwicklung im Gesundheitswesen (SVR). (2014). Bedarfsgerechte Versorgung – Perspektiven für ländliche Regionen und ausgewählte Leistungsbereiche [Needs-based provision – perspectives for rural regions and selected performance ranges]. Retrieved from www.svr-gesundheit. de/fileadmin/user_upload/Gutachten/2014/SVR-Gutachten_2014_ Langfassung.pdf (accessed 18 October 2015).

Spies, A. (2013). Care in Kooperation: Vernetzte Betreuungsformen als Ausdruck kommunaler Bildungsverantwortung [Care-Arrangements in networks as a means of municipal educational responsibility]. In M. A. Wolf, E. Dietrich-Daum, E. Fleischer & M. Heidegger (Eds.), *Child Care: Kulturen, Konzepte und Politiken der Fremdbetreuung von Kindern [Child care: cultures, concepts and politics of extra-familiar child care]* (pp. 66–79). Weinheim, Basel: Beltz Juventa.

Stangl, W. (2010). *Parentifizierung: Lexikon für Psychologie und Pädagogik [Parentification: Encyclopedia for Psychology and pedagogics].* Retrieved from http://lexikon.stangl.eu/1172/parentifizierung/ (accessed 13 September 2013).

Tronto, J. (1993). *Moral Boundaries: A Political Argument for an Ethic of Care.* New York, London: Routledge.

Weinberger, M. (2011). Young Carers- Kinder und Jugendliche als pflegende Angehörige. Unpublished BA thesis. Institut für Pflegewissenschaft. Medizinische Universität Graz. Retrieved from www.ig-pflege.at/downloads/news/2010/ Bakkalaureatsarbeit_Young_Carers.pdf (accessed 7 July 2014).

Wihstutz, A. (2011). Working vulnerability: agency of caring children and children's rights. *Childhood*, *18*(4), 447–459.

Wihstutz, A. (2009). *Verantwortung und Anerkennung: Qualitative Studie zur Bedeutung von Arbeit für Kinder [Responsibility and recognition: a qualitative study on the meaning of work for children].* Munich: LIT.

Chapter 5

Meanings of children's agency

When and where does agency begin and end?

Priscilla Alderson and Tamaki Yoshida

Agency may be doubted or seen as displaced or defused away from the individual and merging into social contexts. However, critical realism does the groundwork of unravelling problems to provide a firmer theoretical basis for social research. This chapter summarises some key concepts in critical realism, which help to validate real agency. Most of the examples are drawn from research in two primary schools in urban Tanzania.

To analyse agency, we will draw on concepts from critical realism (CR). Bhaskar (1998, 2008a) has developed this philosophy since the 1970s with Archer (2003), Porpora (1998), Sayer (2000) and others. "Critical" denotes the Marxist tradition, and "realism" refers to the central understanding of enduring, independent, already present social reality, which we can discover but do not invent or construct. One example of CR concepts is the separation of two kinds of power. CR contrasts coercive power2 that oppresses agency versus creative emancipating power1 that extends free agency. The difference is vital because power is usually reduced to power2, which is feared as inevitably oppressive, and this may be seen as the only way for adults to control children, and to stop them from having dangerous power. Instead, power1 is promoted when adults and children fulfil their human agency by protesting against injustice and working together for peace and freedom (Bhaskar, 2008b).

CR is accused of being too abstract, too laden with jargon and simply an unhelpful, unnecessary, alternative sociology. Replies to these and other criticisms could more than fill this chapter. We will briefly say here that CR is not a sociology. It is a philosophy that works to unravel and resolve serious problems and provide a firmer basis for understanding and analysis in social science and Childhood Studies (Alderson, 2016). We aim to avoid jargon wherever possible, except when there is a unique term for a specific concept. We also aim to avoid abstractions unless they can explain practical problems more clearly. If you are not yet familiar with CR, we do hope you will decide to look at this chapter and that you find it useful.

CR concepts will be reviewed in the following sections: agency and structure; four planar social being; knowing and being; the pull-push power of absence;

difference versus change; closed and open systems; natural necessity; and the possibility of naturalism. Most of our examples come from a PhD study of physical punishment in two primary schools in urban Tanzania. The research included observations, interviews with children, teachers and parents, group sessions and photographs, and some children kept diaries and made drawings and maps.

Agency and structure

Social research tends to ignore or deny children's agency in two main ways. Quantitative surveys emphasise social structures, contexts and variables that seem to shape and often determine children's lives (for example, Hansen et al., 2010). In contrast, qualitative, interpretive methods that emphasise social contexts can "decentre" individuals' agency. Agency may then appear to be "an effect brought about by the assembly of heterogeneous materials" and diverse resources "through which children's agency is (or is not) produced" (Prout, 2000, p. 17). There is ambiguity here about how and by whom children and/or their agency are produced, and Prout's use of actor network theory, which places people and objects on a similar level of agency, overlooks conscious human agency. Oswell's erudite analysis of agency concludes that "the individual child" myth, which "few believe", falsely sees children as possessing capacities individually. Instead, Oswell contends, "agency circulates around children" impersonally, and exists "only by virtue of their relationship with others" as facets of each local situation. "Agency neither starts nor finishes with any individual agent." It is orchestrated within narrative structures, character is not "real" and there is no single author but always multiple authors of agency. Agency is never a property and is always relational, in-between, dispersed (Oswell, 2013, pp. 264–270). While acknowledging these complexities, CR takes each child to be a distinct, conscious, embodied individual, possessing real though limited agency.

The possibility of individual agency may be denied if it seems to merge too much into the social context. Yet this denial mistakenly assumes all or nothing: Agency is either pure and separate from all context, or is lost in social contingencies. The reality lies between the extremes. Agency and structure can only exist in relation to each other, as separate but interacting, partly overlapping entities. Without the values and resources from structures that enable us to make sense of experience, agency would be either empty or else chaotically, meaninglessly overwhelmed. Porpora (1998, 2007) reviewed four concepts of social structures theorised in social science. First, structures are mainly created by individual agents through countless behaviours aggregated over time. However, this model is unrealistically dominated by seemingly free agents. If childhood is one such structure, it is hard to explain how or why children and adults "construct" certain types of childhood and not others, especially when the types are oppressive.

Second, structures are law-like regularities that govern, determine and explain somewhat mechanistic social behaviours. This model is favoured in quantitative surveys, in structural functionalism and in biology-led child development. Yet it takes too little account of agency and diversity. Model one assumes overly free, voluntary agency, and model two assumes overly determining structures.

Third, structures are seen as rules and resources on which agents can draw, such as in Giddens's (1979) structuration theory. Like Goldilocks, Porpora is still not satisfied, and he believes this model is too virtual, static, random and agency-dominated.

Porpora's fourth and preferred model is social structures seen as systems of human relations among social positions. Rather than being underlying or external rules to be invoked, structures such as childhood, the family, the school and the economy exist as powerful and enduring systems and positions in and through social relations. Over time, structures far precede and far outlast individual agents, who do not construct them. Yet agents constantly reproduce and resist, modify and interact with structures, and are shaped and reshaped by them through social processes in time and space.

Social structures, unlike natural ones, can only operate through human agency. However, structures cannot be reduced to agents' conceptions of them or to agents' activities. Agents draw on a range of structures and may choose between them. For example, religion, education, culture, history, biology and economics all present different, often conflicting, versions of childhood, which agents consciously or subconsciously adopt or reject. Margaret Archer (2003) analysed in great detail the time sequences during which (adult) agents draw on and then reflect and relate to structures through their internal conversations and later act on them. Children's knowledge, judgement, foresight, freedom of choice, control and agency are all very limited, but so too are adults' capacities. At all ages, human agency is constantly constrained by structures and by other agents, by resources and chance, as shown by the limited agency of the supposedly most powerful person in the world, the American president.

In the study of Tanzanian schools, contradictions were observed when children's actual competent agency was denied or overlooked, and they were held to be essentially irresponsible and immature. Yet children were also often held to be entirely responsible for their own agency and easily able to behave suitably if they wished. Children who misbehaved were blamed, while all the difficulties and barriers around them were often ignored. For many, the long school day continued with paid tuition until 4 or 5 p.m. and some stayed on to do self-study. High standards were demanded. One girl reported that students had to arrive at school at 6:30 a.m. "Then sweep for 30 minutes, and water flowers and clean toilets. Bad behaviour is to be late" (Yoshida, 2011, p. 176). Yet many of the teachers, and adults generally, were relaxed about being an hour or two late themselves, and teachers sometimes missed whole lessons. Research by Mizen and Ofosu-Kusi (2010) in Ghana, and by Alphonce Omolo (2015) in Kenya, shows how children's self-reliant agency similarly keeps knocking against very hard contexts and discrimination against children. Honwana saw the restricted yet resourceful and courageous agency of child soldiers in spatial terms. When they seem least powerful and lacking control and resources, they resist through tactical and "interstitial" agency. Young soldiers in Mozambique, "by virtue of this borderland condition … are able to be mobile and grab opportunities the moment they arise" (Honwana, 2005, pp. 49–50).

Porpora's fourth model can be compared to a river (agency), which reshapes the land (structures) around it, but the land also shapes the course and speed of the river. The image suggests that each child cannot have just any type of childhood; the type is highly organised by nature and society before the child is born, and much has to be accepted or can only be altered with great difficulty. Yet within those natural and social structural constraints, there is scope for choice and change, as the child, like the river, moves forward. Rather than static, spatial concepts about fixed edges between them, structure and agency can be seen as dynamic processes interacting across porous shifting boundaries and changing over time.

Four planes of social being

CR analyses all human life on four interacting planes of social being to help researchers to adopt comprehensive and also coherently organised views of children's rich, complex lives. The four planes are bodies in nature, interpersonal relations, social structures and inner being. The Tanzanian study vividly illustrated the importance of interrelating all four social planes in Childhood Studies.

On plane one, bodies in material relations with nature are essential bases for personal and physical agency. Children express all their agency through their speaking, acting body, and through their bodies, children may be deprived, constrained, punished, shamed, confined and excluded. The research topic of physical punishment especially opens up ethnography to exploring children's embodied physical-mental pain and trauma. Children were punished in the belief that fear, pain and shame would deter them from doing wrong, overriding their present agency in the hope of developing their future agency as responsible citizens.

Chris, George and Shabani (all names have been changed) talked about severe physical pain when they had to kneel on the concrete floor for long periods, or they had to go around the whole school, to be jeered at by other children, in a squat position until their legs felt "dead". They would be unable to walk home, or bend over in the toilet (Yoshida, 2011, pp. 167–168).

Attention to bodies also crucially turns to the very crowded hot classrooms with around 100 children cramped together. The researcher (T. Y.) still remembers discomfort and tiredness caused by sitting on dawati (a long desk with a bench attached to it) with students for several hours in the two schools, observing rote-learning lessons most of the time. In the classrooms with parts of the ceiling plaster coming off and no lighting, darkness during rain or heavy clouds made both students and teachers unable to read and write comfortably. Rain sometimes poured in through the windows (Yoshida, 2011, p. 166). Restless bodies show discomfort, boredom and inattention. Children were also punished through their partly physical-hormonal-social emotions, such as fear and shame, that were amplified by memories of past punishments. "The body 'remembers' pains and pleasures" (Archer, 2003, p. 202).

Shame also relates to plane two, interpersonal relations. When relating to other children and to adults, those who had been punished reacted with distress and contrition, or they tried to laugh and hide their shame. Adults preferred to blame irrational childhood, instead of seeing how children's reactions could be explained by the boring rote-learning, often exacerbated by hunger, lack of adequate seating, lighting and textbooks. Any complaints or resistance from students could result in negative adult-child relationships, and could be regarded as proof of children's inability to understand the adults' well-meant intentions towards them. Children's protests, be it against increased bus fares, strict school rules or physical punishment, are also often taken to prove their "needs" to be nurtured, rather than their reasonable agency (Yoshida, 2011, p. 170). Teachers were themselves professionally and financially constrained, and some were frustrated that they could not show more care for the children. Other teachers assumed that poor students misbehave, and this could seem to justify control through physical and emotional punishment.

Children's agency is also expressed through varying interpersonal interactions, in humour, friendship, loyalty, kindness, politeness, respect, ingenuity, skill and reliability, or ridicule, anger and violence. Subtle or blatant, overt or implied, children's changing and combined behaviours show their highly attuned, expressive, social competencies and awareness of others. The socially constructed nature of childhood reproduces, and is reproduced by, practices of inequity and domination. For example, silence is a sign of children's active respect for adults, not merely of incompetent, passive childhood. Challenging adults' authority in particular is regarded as difficult by children and "bad" by adults, so that children often actively and consciously "practised" silence (Yoshida, 2011, p. 152).

Interpersonal relations tend to be physical. For instance, during crowded journeys on the city minibuses, young children sit on strangers' laps, showing an ease about physical contact that is not usual in many other cultures. The friendly routines, such as hugs, handshakes, holding hands while talking together, friendly slaps, which go with the greetings "my brother" and "my sister", bind communities and extended families warmly together. Most city dwellers and workers, including school children who live far from their schools, use the city minibuses. These minibuses are overcrowded, hot and uncomfortable during rush hour, with women with washbasins filled with bananas, mangoes and doughnuts, popular as breakfast. Most people push forward when they try to board a crowded bus, although once they are on the bus, they can be very friendly and helpful.

The third plane of social being is social structures, often of oppression and violence that restrict children's fulfilled, competent agency. Hard-pressed families are under great pressure to pay for termly exams, and they rely on children not to fail. Those who fail annual exams have to repeat the year, sometimes several times. There is lack of knowledge, skill and time to help with problems such as dyslexia, so children tend to be blamed for their learning difficulties. The great shortage of staff and other resources mentioned earlier is often determined by the World Bank and other international agencies and donor countries. Precious funding is lost through inefficient and corrupt administration. Besides the weak law banning physical punishment in schools, there is lack of inspection and enforcement. The harder present living conditions become, the more hope is invested in educating children, often in punitive ways.

Social structures that shape agency, such as neocolonial legacies and neoliberal economic policies, tend to seem absent and invisible. It is therefore harder to detect and analyse them in observed ethnographies. Yet if these oppressive structures are ignored, students' failures can be wrongly blamed on them or on their teachers as if they are wholly free agents. For example, some children who were punished for their inattention during lessons said they usually do not have breakfast, or even lunch, and they only have one meal a day. Others have to wake up very early to help with the housework.

While explaining his sense of responsibility for his ageing parents, Brandon repeatedly spoke of children who "can't do anything for them" (the parents) now, dismissing all his present caring work (Yoshida, 2011, pp. 158–159). Both children and adults talked about "future" responsibilities, illustrating how powerful beliefs about competent adulthood and dependent childhood structured intergenerational relationships in a disconnected sequence of linear developmental stages: The small person now cannot contribute; only the future big person can.

Punishment is used not only to correct perceived wrongdoing, but is more endemic, structured into child-adult relations in every culture and country. The general school discipline exerted through children's bodies could be punitive. Teachers often repeatedly asked groups of students to stand up and sit down on the ground until they all did this properly, "not easy especially for hot, hungry, listless, and sometimes ill children" (Yoshida, 2011, p. 175). Children who complied were punished again and again along with noncompliers, until everyone complied.

The fourth plane of social being addresses personal inner being and also political concern about present social problems and hopes of better futures through agency and structures that work towards freedom and the good life in the good society. Human rights provide detailed maps of a good society. The school study shows that it is crucial to see children's rights well beyond Article 12 and the right to express a view, into which children's rights are far too often reduced. In the UN (1989) Convention's main 42 Articles, rights are a living, embodied reality. They are honoured when children and adults have an adequate standard of living, food and clean water, clothing and shelter, freedom of (embodied) expression, free association and privacy, protection from neglect and abuse, and respect for each child's worth and dignity. Alternatively, rights are violated when necessities and physical and mental freedom are withheld, and when bodies are punished, confined and humiliated. Children in the school study have high hopes of education opening up new futures, but they know that much of their future agency depends on world economies and employment.

Bhaskar (1998, 2008b) argues that real agency is influenced by resources and structures but not determined by them. The model of Tanzanian childhood relates to Tanzanian adulthood. The powers adults "can draw upon depend partly on their relations to one another, and to relevant parts of the context, such as educational institutions" (Sayer, 2000, p. 13). Many children in the two schools live with their extended family or their elder sibling(s) after one or both of their parents die, or after they move, to live nearer to a better school. One boy (aged 11), who lived with his grandparents, felt there was discrimination against orphans. He wrote in his diary for the research (in 2007):

> My mum left this world in 2006, and my dad … I don't like living without my parents … I pray every day … [but] sometimes I have to sleep with empty stomach, no food for the whole day … but there is no money to go to hospital when I am ill. (Yoshida, 2011, p. 139)

Children's lives exist on all four interacting planes of social being. Hunger and lack of material care (plane one), discrimination, disrespect, loneliness and emotional strain (plane two) and structures of childhood, national policies and international economics (plane three) can all have negative effects on plane four, children's inner being and agency, their education, health, bodily integrity and moral status (Ainsworth et al., 2005; Beegle et al., 2009). In Africa, the absolute number of people living on less than $2 a day has doubled since 1981 (Seery & Caistor-Arendar, 2014).

Thinking and being

CR separates the reality and being (of people, objects, events) from our thinking and knowing about them (Bhaskar, 1998). Intransitive reality (a school, a city) exists before we each encounter it and form our transitive perceptions about it. We discover reality and do not invent it, although we may invent our reactions and beliefs, perceptions and memories.

To collapse real things (living children) into thoughts (concepts of childhood) is termed the epistemic fallacy, when being (ontology) is reduced into thinking (epistemology). Theories of children's dependence and inadequacy can shape events, such as actual behaviours and interactions, but there is still a difference between the thought and the deed. Pain is both a real, physiological, biochemical, neural reaction and a felt, perceived experience, when pain may be increased or reduced by thoughts and emotions. Kneeling on a concrete floor for hours can be made worse by anxiety, stress, shame, uncertainty and helplessness – for instance, not knowing how long the punishment will last.

Adults may be so concerned with thoughts (models of the deficient versus the ideal child, forms of moral education, hope of forming future adults) that they overlook physical being. They regard shame or embarrassment as an essential part of punishment in learning "how to control the body" and how to correct the childishness they perceive in the child's mind. Yet the children concerned are highly aware of physical realty. Hassani (aged 13) described physical and emotional pain caused by the punishment of having to hop up and down repeatedly in front of younger classes for making a mistake. He experienced real physical loss of control over his own body through pain and humiliation (Yoshida, 2011, pp. 167–168). As with structure and agency, there is no definite dividing line between intransitive being in actual bodies and behaviours versus transitive thoughts, but there are differences. CR is concerned to avoid collapsing bodies into beliefs, and assuming that our physical lives are wholly constructed through our personal experiences and perceptions. Similarly, Childhood Studies show how childhood is a set of beliefs separate from real children and their living agency and competencies.

Many students say they do feel respected and listened to by adults, but others primarily experience non-recognition or coercion. They learn to be "well-behaved" by embodying docile compliance. Their freedom from physical and mental pain is achieved through instrumental or what may be labelled "rational", "adult-like" decisions, by their choice to be rule-following agents in the presence of adult power over them. They weigh up one choice over another. In this way they tend not to see their compliance as entirely meaningless; it is a form of agency. Silence, too, can be an embodied agency (Yoshida, 2011, pp. 152–154, 177).

Absence

Absence tends to be ignored in research, which concentrates on presence and evidence. Yet absence is central to CR. Absence is the almost infinite otherness, everything that has been lost into the past, besides all the infinite potential waiting in the future, of which only a tiny part will ever be realised. Absence is all that we might have been or known or done, but have not. It is a great causal power, a vacuum that absorbs almost all around it, and is therefore a prime mover: pushing and pulling everything forward into new times and spaces. To act is to change things by absenting or removing a present condition or constraint and forming a so-far-absent new condition (Bhaskar, 2008b).

Everything is partly defined by what it is not. Childhood agency is largely defined as incomplete because of the supposed absence of adult competencies. Students often talked about nonrecognition of their agency, either directly by referring to their right to be heard, or indirectly in the negating, omitting or marginalising of their agency. Moreover, a sense of "lack", "negation" and "absence" was sometimes felt and expressed by children in terms of their "future" responsibilities, informed by powerful traditions in child-adult relations. For example, Saida (age 14) wrote in her diary:

> …At our home. We like doing work very hard. Usually, each of us has to do some kind of work, and when we finish with our work you feel very good about your environment. Without our parents we aren't going to work. They [parents] raise us, provide for us, and protect us from illness. It means that

parents are expected to take some time off from work, when we [children] are around. So this is why we share work at home among children ... But one day my younger sibling, who was asked to run an errand to our neighbour, refused and ran away. (Yoshida, 2011, p. 141)

Saida is responsible and she seems to enjoy the work at home to help her parents. However, she notes a lack of willingness in that she and her siblings would not do the work without their parents. In noting her younger sister's resistance to work, she perhaps suggests the lesser moral status of the younger one.

To recognise the void and empty space of absence is essential because a world too tightly packed for movement (physical or mental) cannot change, and has no room for alternatives, new possibilities or transformations. The agency of childhood (and adulthood) involves becoming and be going, leaving and absenting former spaces to enter new future ones. Absence is also central to splits and gaps, lacks and needs in present schools and childhoods and potential new openings into future so-far-absent improvements.

Difference and change

Difference involves, for example, one child leaving a room and another entering it, so that a different child is there. However, an example of transforming change is when a child learns to read and the same child has new skills, independence, agency and a new identity and status as "a reader". Difference does not involve this real causal change and emergence of new identities, relationships and activities that nevertheless exist within the same changing person – or school or city. Whereas change combines with continuity, difference does not. Difference marks the child as other, someone who will one day be a different person, an adult. Change sees the same person lasting yet being transformed over a lifetime. Many similarities and equalities between children and adults can then be appreciated. Developmental psychology divides childhood into separate, scarcely connected stages, each with a different status and problems of being in stages towards adulthood. Children in the study said they could contribute to their family only "when" they grew up, "later" and "after" studying very hard and becoming adults, not while being a child. There are clear disconnections in the sequence of linear developmental stages, past, present and future. This model denies how children are already competent contributors (Yoshida, 2011, pp. 156–160). Children and adults use age as one of the most important markers of their different identities, a real influence on their lives (Nieuwenhuys, 2004).

Closed and open systems

School students' progress is often discussed as if it occurs within a closed system of a single overriding force: The student is taught and then memorises, understands and repeats the lesson, within the closed teaching-learning system. Yet in social life there are always many competing and conflicting forces and influences within open systems: the students' home life, health, ability, the type of school and teaching, the state of the toilets that might stop parents from allowing their daughters to attend school, all the other students, their aspirations and future employment opportunities, the education policies at local, national and international levels, and so on.

Some forces promote and celebrate children's agency. Others at the same time constrain and underestimate students' capacities so that their agency may take resisting and subversive forms. When interviewed, the Tanzanian teachers spoke of different influences and causes of children's problems and misbehaviours. Poverty may be said to cause bad, "uncivilised" and unsophisticated behaviours among local children, not found in more affluent areas of the city (Yoshida, 2011, p. 159). Although students also associated misbehaviours with poverty, they tended to explain causes more in terms of personal relationships with their family members or teachers. "Your father is alcoholic ... The father doesn't care about the child's outcomes ... Everyday they [family members] come back home anytime they want ... and they have nothing to talk about." "Teachers can be strict, and children can be scared of the teachers. That's why children become truants." Awareness of open systems avoids simplistic thinking, which blames individuals and proposes standard remedies. Instead, social life and change are seen to be highly complex and multi-layered.

Natural necessity

Natural necessity is the underlying causal reality that drives many of the ways in which children and adults behave. It works through physical, historical, social, political and economic structures and powers. Natural necessity also works through three levels: the empirical, the actual and the real.

The empirical level involves observers' experiences and perceptions, such as researchers' reports, statistics or conclusions. There were children's accounts and diaries during the school study, and the researcher's observations. Second, the actual level concerns events, people and objects that actually exist or occur, for example an episode of punishment. Most research works on these two descriptive levels.

However, this is rather like observing falling objects and recording the patterns of falling to see if there are "constant conjunctions" that explain how and why the objects fall. Maybe the power of falling is in the objects themselves or, by analogy, children's achievements are entirely through their own efforts. Maybe the objects influence one another's falling – or succeeding, such as when children are set to compete against one another.

CR also searches for deeper, real, explanatory causes, which are invisible and are only seen in their effects (Bhaskar, 1998). These are like gravity, which is taken to be the true explanation for falling objects, even though gravity itself cannot be seen or proven.

With physical punishment, adults are often unwilling to use it, and they know it seldom works to deter or reform misbehaviour. Yet many feel compelled to use punishment. Their agency, actions and beliefs could be seen as symptoms more than causes. The underlying explanations and causes for physical punishment systems include the pressures on teachers: to maintain order in very large classes of uncomfortable children; to prevent classes from becoming still more disorderly; to instil fear and obedience in the children; to prevent children from thinking they can win in the power2 battle for control over the class; to keep the respect of the parents and of teacher colleagues; to prevent complaints; to avoid being dismissed; and to maintain the actual and symbolic adult status of being a firm, not a weak, teacher.

When physical punishment is the norm, very few teachers are strong and skilful enough to succeed without using it, and to counter these real underlying causal influences with very limited resources. Attempts to change systems usually fail because they involve only the empirical and actual levels. To succeed, they have to address real, causal, natural necessity too.

The possibility of naturalism

Scientism assumes that methods in the natural and social sciences are identical. Reductionism assumes that the subjects-objects of social and natural science research are identical, such as when children's behaviour is observed as if they are animals, but their human motives and views are ignored. However, naturalism assumes that there can be an essential unity but not uniformity of methods between the natural and social sciences, because they are more alike than is usually believed (Bhaskar, 1998).

Interpretive researchers tend to consider that naturalism, the use of empirical, positivist and natural science methods in social science is inappropriate and naive. Social beliefs and behaviours are so contingent and transient, existing in the changing relations and perceptions of unpredictable agents, within invisible social structures and values. Whereas natural science deals with solid things, social science is about ideas.

However, CR contends that social and natural science both deal with things and ideas, solid bodies, specific actions, and also imaginative interpretations and unproven theories, such as gravity or evolution, which are only known in their effects. Social life is not wholly irregular and unpredictable. Deeper trends show some predictable consistencies, such as historical patterns in the use of physical punishment.

Naturalism accepts that social structures and agency really exist. For example, although social structures or systems of human rights can only operate through human agency, they have an enduring existence. There are long-standing, universal standards of justice against tyranny, theft and murder. Modern human rights can be seen as contemporary versions of how we understand and practise these ancient realties. Children's agency is fleetingly exercised, observed and interpreted, but it is also real in three main ways that are accepted in natural science: the abstract concept of agency is an unseen, causal, explanatory power like gravity; it is known in its effects that keep changing the world (such as when a child sweeps a school yard or sows some seeds), dealing with real objects and enduring ideas; and third, the effects can be observed and often measured. The possibility of naturalism can give social researchers greater confidence in the reality of their observations and analyses.

Conclusion

We have treated agency mainly in terms of children's practical, conscious responses in schools. We have not addressed other vital areas along a spectrum of children's agency stretching from babies' pre-fully-conscious physical-emotional-social agency (Alderson et al., 2005) to children's very different additionally rational agency, such as when they consciously make complex, stressful personal decisions and give informed, voluntary consent to high-risk surgery (Alderson, 2007) or when they are active child soldiers (Honwana, 2005). We have said little about the unjust constraining structures of neo-colonial global economics that enforce under-funding and under-resourcing in Tanzanian schools. Students' and teachers' agency then often appears as hope and courage when coping with problems.

Agency may be seen as ambivalent, intended or inadvertent, rational or foolish, cautious or risky, compliant or resistant, individual or collective, partly autonomous and partly heteronomous, chosen yet constrained, effective and ineffective, creative and destructive, competent and incompetent. An act may be viewed very differently from different perspectives. Critical realist analysis concludes that agency and the surrounding social structures take many forms, interact and overlap. Yet the conscious, embodied, individual agent also exists, partly separate from the surrounding structures and relationships that form, enable and constrain agency. Only the human agent can enact agency.

Even if the inner impulse of conscious agency, like the unconscious moving power of gravity, cannot be seen or proven, agency is "real" in at least two crucial ways. It has real effects when agents act and make changes. Second, most aspects of human social life (being a child, a student, a parent, an author) depend on assuming that we are each the same, sustained-though-changing, morally conscious individual agent throughout life (unless dementia sets in, but dementia proves how much we rely on that "normal" continuity). To deny unseen agency sets up untenable theory/practice contradictions. Authors who deny personal agency cannot claim to be named authors or protest about plagiarism. Such contradictions can only be resolved by accepting the reality of individual agency in theory and practice.

Based on our research (Yoshida, 2011), we suggest that agency involves (1) physical/verbal activity by the unique embodied agent with (2) thought and conscious decision-making, purpose and motive within (3) often very powerful and more or less enabling power1 or constraining power2 social relationships and structures. These factors evoke varying reactions in the agent from voluntary/ willing cooperation to active resistance. There is (4) some moral awareness about need and desire, harm and benefit to self and others (though awareness does not dictate action, many still decide to cause harm but agents do so consciously). And (5) time, space, resources and opportunity enhance and restrict limited human agency. However, inadequate resources do not preclude agency, they may generate it: hungry children may be active workers and soldiers. Finally, (6) agency tends to affect others and cause change.

CR has many other concepts that serve as useful tools for social research. So far, few childhood researchers have used them, and there is scope for much innovative work. Our introductory summaries are debated at great length by critical realists, who offer robust, practical ways for research to describe and understand the world, to validate knowledge and to address moral questions such as justice between generations and nations. Ruth Levitas (2010) and others contend that working towards more just societies is a central task for sociology, and childhood researchers are uniquely able to work with and for children and young people as agents towards this goal.

References

Ainsworth, M., Beegle, K. & Koda, G. (2005). The impact of adult mortality and parental deaths on primary schooling in north-western Tanzania. *Journal of Development Studies*, 41(3), 412–439.

Alderson, P. (2007). Competent children? Minors' consent to health care treatment and research. *Social Science and Medicine*, 65, 2272–2283.

Alderson, P. (2013). *Childhoods Real and Imagined*, Volume 1: *An Introduction to Critical Realism CR and Childhood Studies*. London: Routledge.

Alderson, P. (2016). *The Politics of Childhoods Real and Imagined*, Volume 2. London: Routledge.

Alderson, P., Hawthorne, J. & Killen, M. (2005). The participation rights of premature babies. *International Journal of Children's Rights*, 13, 31–50.

Archer, M. (2003). *Structure, Agency and the Internal Conversation*. Cambridge: Cambridge University Press.

Beegle, K., De Weerdt, J. & Dercon, S. (2009). The intergenerational impact of the African orphans crisis: a cohort study from an HIV/AIDS affected area. *International Journal of Epidemiology*, 38(2), 561–568.

Bhaskar, R. (1998). *The Possibility of Naturalism* (3rd ed.). Abingdon: Routledge.

Bhaskar, R. (2008a). *A Realist Theory of Science*. London: Routledge.

Bhaskar, R. (2008b). *Dialectic: The Pulse of Freedom*. London: Routledge.

Giddens, A. (1979). *Central Problems in Social Theory*. Basingstoke: Macmillan.

Hansen, K., Joshi, H. & Dex, S. (Eds.). (2010). *Children of the 21st Century: The First Five Years*. Bristol: Policy.

Honwana, A. (2005). Innocent and guilty: child soldiers as interstitial and tactical agents. In A. Honwana & F. De Boeck (Eds.), *Makers and Breakers: Children and Youth in Post-Colonial Africa* (pp. 31–52). Oxford: James Curry.

Levitas, R. (2010). Back to the future: Wells, sociology, utopia and method. *Sociological Review*, 58, 530–547.

Mizen, P. & Ofosu-Kusi, Y. (2010). Asking, giving, receiving: friendship as survival strategy among Accra's street children. *Childhood, 17*(4), 441–454.

Nieuwenhuys, O. (2004). *Children's Lifeworlds: Gender, Welfare, and Labour in the Developing World*. London: Routledge.

Omolo, A. (2015). *Violence against Children in Kenya: An Ecological Model of Risk Factors and Consequences, Responses and Projects*. Munich: Waxmann.

Oswell, D. (2013). *The Agency of Children: From Family to Global Human Rights*. Cambridge: Cambridge University Press.

Porpora, D. (1998). Four concepts of social structure. In M. Archer, R. Bhaskar, A. Collier, A. Lawson & A. Norrie (Eds.), *Critical Realism Essential Readings* (pp. 339–355). Abingdon: Routledge.

Porpora, D. (2007). Social structure. In M. Hartwig (Ed.), *Dictionary of Critical Realism CR* (pp. 422–425). London: Routledge.

Prout, A. (2000). *The Body, Childhood and Society*. Basingstoke: Palgrave Macmillian.

Sayer, A. (2000). *Realism and Social Science*. London: Sage Publications.

Seery, E. & Caistor-Arendar, A. (2014). *Even It Up: Time to End Extreme Inequality*. Oxford: Oxfam.

UN – United Nations General Assembly (1989). Convention on the rights of the child. Retrieved from UN Office of the High Commissioner for Human Rights, www.ohchr.org/en/professionalinterest/pages/crc.aspx (accessed 19 October 2015).

Yoshida, T. (2011). *Corporal Punishment of Children: A Critical Realist Account of Experiences from Two Primary Schools in Urban Tanzania*. PhD thesis. London: Institute of Education.

Chapter 6

Extending agency

The merit of relational approaches for Childhood Studies

Eberhard Raithelhuber

Current discussions on the concept of agency in the inter- and multidisciplinary field of Childhood Studies are a reaction to the deficits revealed in the way the New Sociology of Childhood has viewed agency: as an attempt to gain a more nuanced, differentiated understanding of agency on both an empirical and a theoretical level. My intention here is to contribute to the current reconceptualisation of agency, but not in the sense of providing a better or more nuanced understanding of individual or human agency. Quite the contrary, I argue for a different understanding of agency as social and collective, which allows for different sensitivities and methodologies in research on childhood. I will bring into play selected contributions on agency in the social theory and social anthropology of the last two decades that share a relational/relativistic approach towards the social. The core argument that I want to push forward is that a relational conception of agency can be one productive reaction towards the claim by Prout and others that we need to reflect on existing understandings of agency in the field, all the time striving for a qualitatively different approach toward agency. This perspective turns away from predominantly intentional and cognitive understandings of agency. Hence, agents are not substantialised agents, but often consist of overlapping entities or fabrics, which are complex and in motion. Consequently, agency can be seen as a realised, situated and permuted capacity, which can be accomplished through the combination of various interconnected "persons" and "things".

The presentation of children as "agentic social beings" and the idea of "children's agency" were core notions within the emerging field of the (New) Sociology of Childhood in the 1980s and 1990s. They still resonate powerfully in much of today's work. Indeed, this strong idea, in its dual aspect both as a normative assertion and as a call for an empirical and conceptual reorientation in the study of childhood (Alanen, 2010, p. 5) has inspired manifold queries. On the one hand, the powerful seed of "children's agency", most present in the so-called New Childhood Paradigm, has been nurtured by countless empirical contributions. One way or the other, many of these publications employ the term "agency" to exemplify the social construction of childhood and, in doing so, to testify to children's contribution to it as active social agents. On the other hand, scholars have also been critical in their reviews of the idea and concept of agency in Childhood Studies, in particular within the last decade. This reflects the growth of empirical research as well as the vast expansion of Childhood Studies into an interdisciplinary space with differentiated, multiple approaches.

It is probably fair to say that the Sociology of Childhood is now at a stage at which the established, mainstream understandings of agency are scrambled. Not only has children's agency become a "troubled idea" (Oswell, 2013, p. 7), but agency has also been accused of being one of the mantras in Childhood Studies (Tisdall & Punch, 2012, p. 255). Now, the idea has started to be investigated more profoundly. My intention here is to contribute to the current re-conceptualisation of agency, but not in the sense of providing a better or more nuanced understanding of individual or human agency. Quite the contrary: I argue for a different understanding of agency as social and collective, which allows for different sensitivities and methodologies in research on childhood, something that I will nevertheless only be able to hint at in this contribution. To open up conventional thinking, I employ a strategy of extending agency. I will bring into play selected contributions on agency in the social theory and social anthropology of the last two decades that share a relational/relativistic approach towards the social. I will very briefly recall some aspects of how agency was seen in the 1980s and 1990s in Childhood Studies, most prominently represented in the New Childhood Paradigm, when this development was very much influenced by the debate on a dualistic understanding and mediation of "(social) structure/agency" (see also Oswell, 2013, pp. 37–50). Then I will sketch out some conceptual contributions and recent reactions towards identified deficits in Childhood Studies. The intention of this is not to provide an overall review of the existing literature. Rather, the objective is to exemplify some critical aspects that, on the one hand, still remain unresolved and, on the other hand, are starting points for an extension of existing notions of agency in Childhood Studies. To move towards this extension I will then step back in history, recalling that the introduction of the concept of agency in Childhood Studies in the 1980s was closely linked to wider developments in the field of social theory. Within these discussions on agency, a number of recent contributions, which can be grouped under the label "relativistic/relational approaches", offer interesting perspectives for the future orientation of research.

The conventional understanding of agency in Childhood Studies and recent reactions

There is no doubt that within the last two to three decades, agency has become a prominent concept in countless fields of social science, amongst them Childhood Studies. This development in the social studies of childhood is most visible in the so-called "new childhood paradigm" (James & Prout, 1990). It is well known that this perspective claims to give voice to children and, likewise, acknowledges children's agency. Hence, children are denoted as "social actors" and "children's agency" becomes a core idea (Prout, 2008, p. 29). Inseparably from this claim, the new paradigm, which still resonates in many current contributions, draws attention to the fact that structural and socio-cultural conditions of childhood in modern society block, handicap or distort this fundamental capacity (Qvortrup, Corsaro, & Honig, 2009, p. 4). In short, what I call the conventional understanding of agency, deeply rooted in modernist sociology (Prout, 2011, p. 6), has a twofold nature. First, it states that children "have" or "possess" agency (e.g. in James, 2009, p. 42ff.; see also Mayall, 2002, pp. 33f.; Corsaro, 2005), thus being able to bring about change or to make a difference. Second, studies following this line of thought want to prove this "new" perspective and empirically investigate how individual children can express agency in the context of constraining and enabling conditions. This conventional understanding of agency joins the line of dualisms that characterise Western, Euro-centric perceptions of the world and about the world. It rests on fundamental divisions and oppositions, such as mind and body, individual and society, micro and macro, human and non-human, and so on. Thus, many contributions in the New Sociology of Childhood and, in particular, protagonists of the New Childhood Paradigm tend to display individualistic or even naturalistic conceptualisations of agency. They share a humanist account of agency that can be called a "capacity concept of agency" (Passoth, Peuker, & Schillmeier, 2012, p. 1) and that is widespread in sociological theory.

In recent years, a number of contributions have identified some weak points of this depiction, for example, going against a simple definition of agency as "the capacity of individuals to act independently" (James & James, 2012, p. 3). Some have tried to go beyond a mere critique, offering propositions for varying degrees of modification. For example, Bühler-Niederberger and Schwittek (2014) claimed that a conventional understanding of agency only considers agency in cases where children challenge or alter existing structures, i.e. where they make a difference to the existing order of the social. They presented the results of a study that takes children's agency into account as something that can also serve to solidify existing structures. Thus, partly leaning on Anselm Strauss, they start out from the assumption that ordering the social has to be understood as an on-going process to which every participant contributes through his or her active involvement (Bühler-Niederberger & Schwittek, 2014, p. 505). Hence, this implies that things and orders are not only altered by human activity, but also have to be kept stable or durable through that activity. At first sight, one might easily agree with their claim. Nevertheless, the criticism I would like to make is that this contribution does not provide any deeper understanding of agency, i.e. with regard to its production or form of existence that goes beyond conventional understanding. Their understanding of agency remains somehow individualistic, humanist and cognitive, though taking note of current contributions inspired by relational social theory (e.g. Oswell, 2013). To take another recent contribution, Larkins has presented an interesting paper arguing for "a fuller framework for understanding children's social and political agency in citizenship" (Larkins, 2014, p. 10). Partly leaning on Isin's ideas about Acts of citizenship (Isin, 2008), she claims that the Act comes first and that the actor is a consequence of this mobilisation. Although Isin is not primarily concerned with the concept of agency, his enactment approach does not start out from the idea that agency is something existing or residing within an actor-body or a pre-established agent (Isin, 2009, p. 383; Raithelhuber, 2015). In my reading of Isin, agency (political or otherwise) and agenthood both are a secondary product of enactment and an attribution within a complex milieu that is disturbed. Thus, they are not something that is "exercised" by children or is essentially "theirs", as Larkins suggests (2014, pp. 9, 13). Larkins does not deliver any information about the quality or constitution of this assumed agency, e.g. by asking how it can be that an agency of this kind is brought about and becomes manifest in that very situation. To turn to a third example, Konstantoni (2012) has presented a study based on Prout's critique of a much-too-strong notion of the autonomous, independent child and its agency (Prout, 2005). Nevertheless, her idea about interdependency seems to take the actor (or the individual) as a primary existing entity and a given. Only from that starting point does she examine connections, relations and their dynamics. Within this picture, the understanding of agency remains ensnared in the binarity or dualism of structure/agency, whereas structure is conceived as enabling and constraining factors. Hence, Konstantoni does not consider that agency itself might be a product of negotiation by different actors (including humans and things).

These three references are only some examples of a trait in the much broader discussion. In contrast, other recent contributions to agency in Childhood Studies already display a relational/relativistic understanding of agency. This is most visible in current empirical and conceptual contributions on embodiment and artefacts in Childhood Studies. They show that agency is slightly losing its exclusively "human" character. To take an example, Prout (2008, p. 33) refers to the work of Ogilvie-Whyte (2003), arguing that children's agency partly has to be understood as an effect of their interrelationship with artefacts. It is noteworthy that Ogilvie-Whyte (2003) employs aspects of a symmetrical sociology, which Latour has outlined (Latour, 2005). Hence, we can say that the understanding of agency in Prout's work already somehow conceptually extends beyond the conventional understanding. In this respect, the work by Woodyer (2008) on embodied practice and children's geographies is very promising. On the one hand, she discusses the significance of anti-dualist, anti-representational approaches for research on childhood. On the other hand, she takes up the relational/materialist concept of heterogeneous, hybrid geographies proposed by Whatmore (2002). This implies a de-centred understanding of agency as social agency and as a precarious achievement. Hence, Woodyer argues that the social and the material interact and gear into each other in messy ways. This allows her to start out from the connections between different, heterogeneous elements of relational configurations, i.e. the socio-material assemblages (Woodyer, 2008, p. 358f.). Once again, the connection to ANT stands out; here, it is enriched by references to non-representational theory (Thrift, 1996, p. 24). References to the work of Gell (1998) are also striking (see below).

To sum up, current discussions on the concept of agency in the inter- and multidisciplinary field of Childhood Studies are a reaction to the deficits revealed in the view of agency in "early" New Childhood Studies, trying to gain a more nuanced, differentiated understanding of agency on both an empirical and a theoretical level. While some take up new ideas on agency from the on-going discussions in social theory, for example those leaning on a relational/relativistic approach towards the social, most contributors stick to the conventional notion of agency that is anchored in a dualist conception of structure/agency or any mediation of this binarity. Hence, generally speaking, a large part of the literature in this field still has a poor and unsatisfactory understanding of agency, though there are promising signs, and possible points for extension can be spotted. To be able to take up new ideas on agency and reorient research, I propose taking a close look at how the conventional understanding of agency in Childhood Studies connects to wider shifts in the sciences, especially in social science.

Agency in social theory, or the structure/agency dilemma

The agency assumptions of the New Sociology of Childhood since the 1980s link conceptually to two isochronic key developments in social theory. First, they are connected to a renewed emergence and strengthening of an agency perspective, thus contesting previous and predominant structural/functional and structural/deterministic concepts of action (Ritzer & Goodman, 2004, pp. 91, 113f.). Second, as a result, this agency perspective in social science has had to dissociate its understanding of agency from older notions of "free will" and "free actors", as well as from ideas about autonomous, independent, unconditioned individuals or subjects. As King (2007) has already elaborated extensively, protagonists of the New Sociology of Childhood, in particular, painted a humanist, individualist and quasi-natural picture of children's agency, while at the same time, as sociological scholars, they paid homage to the communicative codes of the sociological zeitgeist. Thus, they connected their picture of children's agency to suitable synthetising approaches, working on what was known as structure-agency integration (Bryant & Jary, 1997, p. 3). This development in New Childhood Studies runs parallel to trends in related fields. For example, in the last two decades Anglo-American Lifecourse Research and Aging Studies have shown similar characteristics (see Raithelhuber, 2011).

The concept of agency has been a hotly debated key issue in discussion on the social within the last three decades (Carle, 2005). Roughly outlined, agency in philosophy, religious studies, social sciences and human sciences implies the idea that someone or something is endowed with a capacity or potential to do things and to make a difference. This means that he, she or it can causally impact on himself, herself or itself or on the environment in a transformative or creative manner or, alternatively, can resist such an influence from outside. Often, agency is linked to intentionality, thus representing intention or some sort of consciousness, or at least a form of practical reflexivity (Ahearn, 2010, p. 34). In many cases, agency contrasts with the concept structure. In this context, structure represents something solid and durable to explain the continuity, perpetuation, replication and distribution of relatively constant or similar human actions in time and space (Sztompka, 1994), while agency stands for the dynamic, creative moments of action. This notion is based on the idea of a continuum with two ends or poles. Thus, "free will" or "choice" is at one end, wherein agency represents the potential to bring about an uncaused cause. This notion of agency contrasts with "causation" at the other end, i.e. the notion that something or someone is caused, e.g. from outside or inside.

Since the 1970s, several theoretical approaches have been presented that have tried to describe, shed light on or criticise the interconnectedness of these antagonistic concepts. In this context, Giddens' Theory of Structuration (1984), in which agency is a core concept, has become the most prominent. This modelling of agency is reflected in many contributions in the New Childhood Studies (e.g. James & Prout, 1997, p. 5; James, Jenks, & Prout, 1998, p. 202; Mayall, 1996, p. 53), as well as offering references (e.g. Mayall, 2002, p. 33ff.) to the Realisms of Roy Bashkar and Margaret Archer (see also King, 2007). It is a well-known fact that Giddens attempts to overcome dual conceptions of the social with his key concept of a duality of structure. Hence, he defines structure as a pre-condition for action, but simultaneously claims that action reproduces structure and even has the capacity to change or modify structure. This is due to agency, as the following core quotes show:

> Agency refers not to the intentions people have in doing things but to their **capability of doing those things** in the first place (which is why agency implies power [...]). [...] Agency concerns events of which **an individual is the perpetrator**, in the sense that **the individual could**, at any phase in a given sequence of conduct, **have acted differently**. (Giddens, 1984, p. 9, author's emphasis)
>
> Action depends upon **the capability of the individual** to 'make a difference' to a pre – existing state of affairs or course of events. (Giddens, 1984, p. 14; author's emphasis)

The citations highlight a general trait of the conventional thinking on agency. According to Giddens, agency is a capacity or potential of an individual, that is a human being, to be the causal originator of action. Ultimately, this kind of individual agency rests upon a cognitive operation, independently of how much a person is conscious of this process or able to speak about it. Metaphorically speaking, agency is located relatively permanently in *one* body and thus lies hidden in *one* head until it originates action. Thus, agency is a relatively stable, essential feature or primordial quality of any individual human being, which extends and varies across the life course. Hence, it is "human agency".

Many works in social science, particularly in sociology, denounce this understanding of agency as substantialist, essentialist, humanist and individualistic (Raithelhuber, 2011, pp. 112–185). In addition, such critiques are also voiced beyond our closer intellectual environment, for example in such rising disciplines as neurology (Gazzaniga, 2011) as well as in "older" branches of science such as philosophy, in particular in moral philosophy (Honoré, 2010). A number of such contributions have roots in science and technology studies or are linked to the material turn in social and human sciences. Contributions in social and cultural sciences that intend to conceptualise agency beyond the conventional notion follow a methodological and empirical route to address the ways in which agency is produced socially and situated, i.e. in the context of everyday action, as well as the manner in which it becomes socially operative and effective. To demarcate the fundamental disparity between the ways in which agency is approached, one can distinguish between two positions. On one hand, there is the conventional notion of agency as "individual agency" or "human agency". On the other hand, we talk about "social agency" or even "collective agency" (e.g. Barnes, 2001, p. 349).

Relational/relativistic approaches towards agency

To extend our conventional notion of agency, I propose to engage deeply with relational approaches. The core argument that I want to push forward here is that a relational conception of agency can be one productive reaction towards the claim by Prout and others that we need to reflect on existing understandings of agency in the field, all the time striving for a qualitatively different approach toward agency (see Prout, 2000, p. 16; 2005, p. 65; Bühler-Niederberger & Van Krieken, 2008). A relational conception of agency reacts to the theoretically and empirically unsatisfactory determination of agency that still characterises the discussion about "childhood agency" or "children's agency" in Childhood Studies (Oswell, 2013, p. 50).

Contributions that allow a sought-after more complex perspective on agency make use of different theoretical movements. For the purpose of this chapter, I lean on contributions that can be grouped under the label "relational/relativistic" and make use, in particular, of contributions in cultural sciences (see also Bollig & Kelle, Oswell and Esser in this volume). Findings in anthropological research on agency and rituals make it clear that agency does not always have to be embodied, at least not in the sense of being restricted to solely *one* human body. It can be distributed among various participants in action. To formulate this more radically, one can say that agency can only exist in interconnectedness and be brought about in relations. According to Sax, agency should be conceived of most generally as "the ability to transform the world" (Sax, 2006, p. 474). This allows us to ask what the nature of this transformative capacity is, what it consists of and how it is made up (2013, p. 27). It seems reasonable to ask such questions in research on rituals, especially, because rituals often bring about transformations, e.g. in the context of therapies or conflict solutions (2006, p. 476). Manifestations of agency, i.e. the public instantiation and revelation of an agentic potential, play an important role in rituals. In addition, research on agency in ritual contexts also shows the significance of connectivity and collective accomplishments. Further, these accomplishments show that non-human beings, unanimated things or spiritual instances can "have" agency or be endowed with agency. To give but one example, the "agency" that a priest "possesses" when bringing together a couple is not his or her agentic potential as an individual person. Moreover, this agentic potential is distributed among various people, institutions and practices (p. 477), such as the church, the couple, the wedding contract (i.e. the sheet of paper used for it), and so on. Some of these aspects connect far back in time, for example to the authorisation that the priest received through his ordination. Only this interconnectedness of various aspects in time and space can explain the agency that becomes manifest in rituals:

> Ritual is the point at which the agency distributed among other persons, relationships, and social institutions is articulated and made manifest. (Sax, 2006, p. 478)

This is the reason why Sax concludes that ritual agency should be conceived as being distributed in networks, at best. Agency is not necessarily restricted to one single person. Indeed, this kind of limitation is actually a rare case (2013, p. 28).

Contributions such as Sax's connect with an increasing number of studies that employ a relational/relativistic perspective, most obviously when envisioning the connections between things and between human beings and things. They open up perspectives to reconceptualise and newly understand agency beyond the individualistic bias. Thus, this allows agency to be considered in the context of a fundamental sociality that embraces non-human things, both animated and unanimated (e.g. Latour, 2005). Perspectives of this kind can also be found in a number of theoretical contributions on the role of materiality in social practices (Schatzki, 2010). Others who are essentially in line with a relational approach of this kind observe how things can become mediators of agency or mediating instances. According to Gell (1998), things can become elements of a causal/relational milieu or structuring of the social in which agency is produced as well as allocated and attached to various "things". This allows us to envision the everyday practices and discourses in which humans attribute agency to other humans as well as to objects.

"[S]ocial agency" is not defined in terms of "basic" biological attributes (such as inanimate thing vs. incarnate person) but is relational – it does not matter, in ascribing "social agent" status, what a thing (or a person) "is" in itself; what matters is **where it stands in a network of social relations**. (Gell, 1998, p. 123; author's emphasis)

This form of perspectivation allows for agency to be envisioned and investigated as an essential aspect of an overall milieu, as opposed to an understanding of agency as purely an element of the human psyche (Gell, 1998, p. 20). Realistically, this approach also allows artefacts and naturefacts, i.e. "things", to be perceived as elements of a specific social identity and social agency. Hence, agents are those human beings and things that have a specific status within a network of social relations, i.e. social positions that can originate causal events in their environment. In other words, if human beings or things inherit a status of this kind, they become instances of agency. Further, Gell shows that agents are not always located solely in *one* place and that their existence is not reduced to solely *one* particular temporal segment. Thus, sometimes agents seem to have various bodies, which can appear at different places in different moments, some of them even outlasting the life of one individual (p. 21; see also Raithelhuber, 2011, pp. 162–68).

To take a third and final example, sharing this anti-individualistic understanding of agency, Holland, Lachicotte, Skinner and Cain (1998) study how human beings mediate and transform meaning. Hence, human beings bring about agency to gain control over their own behaviour, i.e. their own activities and mental processes. The authors conceive of agency as socially produced and culturally constructed activities, which are present in concrete social practices that they call "figured worlds" (p. 38). Borrowing from Vygotsky, Holland and her colleagues take on the idea of "mediating devices", i.e. gadgets or apparatuses that have a mediating, moderating and connecting quality. Human beings use these devices to control their mental processes. For example, we use a knot tied in a handkerchief to remind us that we intend to do or undo something in the future. Such devices are "external" objects that are both generalised and culturally produced. Individuals use them to entrench or embed themselves in their respective environment as well as to "bring about" change. It is essential for this approach that the assignation of meaning as well as the placement of these "things" must not be considered as an individual action, even if done fully "consciously". Moreover, such devices are part of collectively produced systems of meaning (Holland et al., 1998, p. 35). The contribution by Holland and colleagues leans heavily on the anti-essentialist work of the post-colonial Indologist Ronald Inden (1990; Holland et al., 1998, p. 42). As Inden states, agents and agencies can be conceived as being complex, changeable and in motion. They produce and reproduce each other in a dialectical process in constantly shifting situations (Inden, 1990, p. 2).

Consequences of a relational-relativistic understanding of agency

The three examples presented display a unique engagement with agency, but share a relational/relativistic perspective. Instead of asking for the quality and conditioning of "individual agency" (in the sense of capacities, features, competences, etc.), they propose investigating the socio-generative mechanisms that bring about something like "agency". Hence, if we consider "agency as an open empirical question and not as an answer given by theoretical decisions" (Passoth, Peuker, & Schillmeier, 2012, p. 5), then our attention turns towards movements and relations, i.e. towards processes, actions, situations, in which things become ligated and disconnected. Instead of asking for essences or entities, activities that can be realised come to the fore. Only then and from that position can we look at entities such as actors or subjects (Abbott, 2007, p. 9). This perspective also turns away from predominantly intentional and cognitive understandings of agency. Hence, agents are not substantialised agents, but often consist of imbricated and overlapping entities or fabrics, which are complex and in motion. Consequently, agency can be seen as a realised, situated, permuted capacity that can be accomplished through the combination of various, interconnected "persons" and "things".

What is the added value of this extended, qualitative different understanding of agency? A relational/relativistic perspective on agency suggests that, first, as researchers we do not (any longer) need to substantialise and localise agency exclusively in one individual. This is something that we human beings already accomplish well enough in our everyday practices due to our anthropocentric bias (Barnes, 2001, p. 349). Obviously, as human beings, we are inclined to take the relational characteristics of "things" within a specific context for the internal powers or the essential nature of these things in the first place (p. 349). In any case, a mere repetition of this perspective does not provide new scientific knowledge. Rather, it masks an adequate approach to agency. Second, thinking of agency merely within a dualistic perspective of agency/structure is not a viable option; however, the two concepts might be mediated. Agency is not an individual capacity that has to be asserted or analysed. To sum up, strengthening a relational/relativistic approach in Childhood Studies means staying clear of any reification of "agency", "social structures" or "individuals", as well as "networks" or "connections".

Conclusion

I started with an eclectic review of recent contributions towards agency in childhood, taking them as examples for current endeavours towards a more nuanced, differentiated understanding of agency as against tendencies that have been criticised in "early" Childhood Studies. For reasons of contrast, I differentiated between recent contributions that, on the one hand, more or less try to redesign or advance approaches to agency. My critique, which is open to question, was that they are nevertheless somehow still saturated with a binary thinking of agency/structure. At least, they do not address deeply the question of how agency is brought about socially/collectively and how it comes to be attached to certain entities, e.g. "children" or "adults", or taken away from them. Yet, on the other hand, I also took note of contributions that deploy approaches that are anchored in what I called relational/relativistic thinking. To unfold and underpin these accounts, I drew on contributions in social and cultural anthropology that allow for a dehumanised, denaturalised, de-individualised understanding of agency. To put it positively, they allow agency to be conceived as a complex, situational and collective achievement that is partly stabilised through other "humans" and "objects", or mediated by them. This extended understanding of agency is far from being an updated version of the conventional understanding of agency. The road I outlined here is not intended to support an improved or "fixed" approach towards individual or human agency, or of its shapes and functions. A fully social or collective understanding of agency that includes "objects" leads to something different. It enhances our sensitivity towards what is regarded as important and should be examined. Second, it offers a different methodological way of how to address phenomena of "agency" in childhood studies. Hence, taking the "Relation Road" is not a lazy way to level out, avoid or sideline questions of power or representation. Quite the contrary: it is a way to frustrate convenient attempts that place all these parameters in people's heads or outsource them to some factors and forces "in the background" or "in context". I think that this sensitivity and methodology also allows for a more adequate approach towards the dynamics, quick ruptures and changes in the everyday lives of children and their "others", as well as towards the fixed, durable and persistent elements across the different situations and spaces experienced by children, as for example in new programmes and practices in early childhood education and care. The argument is that we can employ relational/relativistic thinking as a heuristic method in the study of childhood or children. Theoretically and empirically, research has to start from the dynamic processes through and in which relations are brought about in time and space, and which from time to time result in the empirical production on the level of everyday life that allocates "agency", as a differentiated capacity, to human beings, e.g. as an individual capacity to children or adults. Seen in this way, "agency" can serve as a useful concept for orienting research in Childhood Studies. If we use the wider discussion on agency within this relational/relativistic perspective, then agency completely loses the essentialist, individualist and naturalist aura that still emanates from conventional approaches toward agency in the New Childhood Studies. Somehow, the seed must die in order to bear fruit.

References

Abbott, A. (2007). Mechanisms and relations. *Sociologica*, 2, 1–22.

Ahearn, L. (2010). Agency and language. In J. Jaspers, J. -O. Östman & J. Verschueren (Eds.), *Society and Language Use* (Vol. 7, pp. 28–48). Amsterdam: John Benjamins.

Alanen, L. (2010). Editorial: taking children's rights seriously. *Childhood*, *17*(1), 5–8.

Barnes, B. (1999). *Understanding Agency*. London; Thousand Oaks, CA: Sage Publications.

Barnes, B. (2001). The macro/micro problem and the problem of structure and agency. In G. Ritzer & B. Smart (Eds.), *Handbook of Social Theory* (pp. 339–352). London; Thousand Oaks, CA: Sage Publications.

Bryant, C. G. & Jary, D. (1997). Introduction. In C. G. Bryant & D. Jary (Eds.), *Anthony Giddens: Critical Assessments, Volume 2* (pp. 3–8). New York, London: Routledge.

Bühler-Niederberger, D. & Schwittek, J. (2014). Young children in Kyrgyzstan: agency in tight hierarchical structures. *Childhood*, *21*(4), 502–516.

Bühler-Niederberger, D. & Van Krieken, R. (2008). Editorial: persisting inequalities: childhood between global influences and local traditions. *Childhood*, *15*(2), 147–155.

Carle, S. D. (2005). Theorizing agency. *American University Law Review*, *55*(2), 307–387.

Corsaro, W. A. (2005). Collective action and agency in young children's peer cultures. In J. Qvortrup (Ed.), *Studies in Modern Childhood* (pp. 231–247). Basingstoke: Palgrave Macmillan.

Gazzaniga, M. S. (2011). *Who's in Charge?* New York: HarperCollins.

Gell, A. (1998). *Art and Agency: An Anthropological Theory*. Oxford: Clarendon.

Giddens, A. (1984). *The Constitution of Society*. Berkeley, Los Angeles: University of California Press.

Holland, D., Lachicotte Jr., W. & Skinner, D. (1998). *Identity and Agency in Cultural Worlds*. Cambridge, MA: Harvard University Press.

Honoré, A. (2010). Causation in the law. In E. N. Zalta (Ed.), *Stanford Encyclopedia of Philosophy* (Winter 2010 Edition). Retrieved from http://plato.stanford.edu/entries/causation-law/ (accessed 31 July 2015).

Inden, R. B. (1990). *Imagining India*. Bloomington: Indiana University Press.

Isin, E. F. (2008). Theorizing acts of citizenship. In E. F. Isin & G. M. Nielsen (Eds.), *Acts of Citizenship* (pp. 15–43). London: Zed Books.

Isin, E. F. (2009). Citizenship in flux: the figure of the activist citizen. *Subjectivity*, *29*, 367–388.

James, A. (2009). Agency. In J. Qvortrup, W. A. Corsaro & M. -S. Honig (Eds.), *The Palgrave Handbook of Childhood Studies* (pp. 34–45). Basingstoke, Hampshire: Palgrave Macmillan.

James, A. & James, A. (2012). *Key Concepts in Childhood Studies* (2nd ed.). Los Angeles: Sage Publications.

James, A., Jenks, C. & Prout, A. (1998). *Theorizing Childhood*. Oxford: Polity Press.

James, A., & Prout, A. (1990). *Constructing and Reconstructing Childhood: Contemporary Issues of Sociological Study of Childhood*. London, New York: Falmer Press.

James, A. & Prout, A. (1997). A new paradigm for the sociology of childhood. In A. James & A. Prout (Eds.), *Constructing and Reconstructing Childhood* (2nd ed., pp. 7–32). London: Routledge.

King, M. (2007). The sociology of childhood as scientific communication: observations from a social systems perspective. *Childhood*, *14*(2), 193–213.

Knappett, C. (2002). Photographs, skeuomorphs and marionettes: some thoughts on mind, agency and object. *Journal of Material Culture*, *7*(1), 97–117.

Konstantoni, K. (2012). Children's peer relationships and social identities: exploring cases of young children's agency and complex interdependencies from the minority world. *Children's Geographies*, *10*(3), 337–346.

Larkins, C. (2014). Enacting children's citizenship. *Childhood*, *21*(1), 7–21.

Latour, B. (2005). *Reassembling the Social*. Oxford: Oxford University Press.

Mayall, B. (1996). *Children, Health and the Social Order.* Buckingham: Open University Press.

Mayall, B. (2002). *Towards a Sociology for Childhood.* Buckingham: Open University Press.

Ogilvie-Whyte, S. (2003). Building a bicycle ramp: an illustrated example of the process of translation in children's everyday play activities. Paper presented to the Childhood and Youth Studies Network, 30 April 2003, University of Stirling.

Oswell, D. (2013). *The Agency of Children.* Cambridge: Cambridge University Press.

Passoth, J., Peuker, B. M. & Schillmeier, M. W. J. (2012). Introduction. In J. Passoth, B. M. Peuker & M. W. J. Schillmeier (Eds.), *Agency without Actors? New Approaches to Collective Action* (pp. 1–11). London: Routledge.

Prout, A. (2000). *The Body, Childhood and Society.* Basingstoke: Macmillan.

Prout, A. (2005). *The Future of Childhood: Towards the Interdisciplinary Study of Children.* London: Routledge Falmer.

Prout, A. (2008). Culture-nature and the construction of childhood. In K. Drotner & S. Livingstone (Eds.), *The International Handbook of Children, Media and Culture* (pp. 21–35). London; Thousand Oaks, CA: Sage Publications.

Prout, A. (2011). Taking a step away from modernity: reconsidering the new sociology of childhood. *Global Studies of Childhood, 1*(1), 4–14.

Qvortrup, J., Corsaro, W. A & Honig, M. -S. (2009). Why social studies of childhood? An introduction to the handbook. In J. Qvortrup, W. A. Corsaro & M. S. Honig (eds.), *The Palgrave Handbook of Childhood Studies* (pp. 1–18). Basingstoke, Hampshire: Palgrave Macmillan.

Raithelhuber, E. (2011). Übergänge und Agency [Transitions and Agency]. Leverkusen: Budrich UniPress Ltd.

Raithelhuber, E. (2015). Relaunching citizenship within an agency-oriented perspective: transnational lessons for social work and educational studies. In S. Köngeter & W. Smith (Eds.), *Transnational Agency and Migration – Actors, Movements and Social Support* (pp. 195–216). New York, London: Routledge.

Rammert, W. (2012). Distributed agency and advanced technology. In J. -H. Passoth, B. M. Peuker & M. W. J. Schillmeier (Eds.), *Agency without Actors?* (pp. 89–112). London: Routledge.

Ritzer, G. & Goodman, D. J. (2004). *Modern Sociological Theory* (6th ed.). New York: The McGraw-Hill Companies.

Sax, W. (2006). Agency. In J. Kreinath, J. Snoek & M. Stausberg (Eds.), *Theorizing Rituals: Issues, Topics, Approaches, Concepts* (pp. 473–481). Leiden: Brill.

Sax, W. (2013). Agency. In C. Brosius, A. Michaels & P. Schrode (Eds.), *Ritual und Ritualdynamik - Schlüsselbegriffe, Theorien, Diskussionen [Ritual and the dynamics of rituals - key word, theories, controversies]* (pp. 25–31). Göttingen: Vandenhoeck & Ruprecht.

Schatzki, T. R. (2010). Materiality and social life. *Nature and Culture, 5*(2), 123–149.

Sztompka, P. (1994). Evolving focus on human agency in contemporary social theory. In P. Sztompka (Ed.), *Agency and Structure: Reorienting Social Theory* (pp. 25–60). Langhorne: Gordon and Breach.

Taylor, C. (1985). What is human agency? In C. Taylor (Ed.), *Human Agency and Language, Volume 1: Philosophical Papers* (pp. 15–44). Cambridge: Cambridge University Press.

Thrift, N. (1996). *Spatial Formations.* London: Sage Publications.

Tisdall, E. K. M. & Punch, S. (2012). Not so "new"? Looking critically at childhood studies. *Children's Geographies, 10*(3), 249–264.

Whatmore, S. (2002). *Hybrid Geographies.* London; Thousand Oaks, CA: Sage Publications.

Woodyer, T. (2008). The body as research tool: embodied practice and children's geographies. *Children's Geographies, 6*(4), 349–362.

Children as actors in research

Chapter 7

Troubling children's voices in research

Spyros Spyrou

Contemporary Childhood Studies has celebrated the value of giving children a voice through research; children's voices have been used to establish their competence as members of society, as fully capable of reflecting and offering unique perspectives on their worlds; in short, as a means of recognising and establishing their agency. In this chapter, I draw on post-structuralist critiques of voice, which challenge its putative authenticity, treating it instead as a performative practice. I illustrate the value of troubling children's voices by looking at three features of voice – the material, the contradictory and ambiguous and the silent – which open up the possibilities for more nuanced and productive readings. From such a rethinking, children's voices escape the narrow confines of voiced utterances and enter a more fruitful conceptual space where we explore how children's voices happen.

Contemporary Childhood Studies has celebrated the value of giving children a voice through research; children's voices have been used to establish their competence as members of society, as fully capable of reflecting and offering unique perspectives on their worlds, in short, as a means of recognising and establishing their agency. This chapter builds on earlier work of mine on children's voices (Spyrou, 2011) and silences (Spyrou, 2015), which sought to critically assess and problematise the concept of voice in Childhood Studies. In the former (Spyrou, 2011), I argued for the need to critically reflect on the use of children's voices in research by attending to issues of representation as well as the need to rethink the putative claims to authenticity in child voice research by acknowledging the limits of children's voices and their complex, multi-layered and messy nature. In the latter (Spyrou, 2015), I have taken one of the difficult features of voice, namely silence, and argued that despite its putative absence, silence is neither the opposite of, nor outside of, voice but an integral part of it, hence the need to attend to it with the proper care and sensitivity. In this chapter, I extend my argument further, primarily by drawing on post-structuralist critiques of voice that challenge its putative authenticity, treating it instead as a performative practice (for instance, see Mazzei, 2010). From such a rethinking, children's voices escape the narrow confines of voiced utterances and enter a more fruitful conceptual space where we explore *how* children's voices happen. Such an exploration may allow us to push voice to its limits by looking at those aspects of children's voices that do not readily make sense (because they fail to provide a coherent narrative) or those aspects of their voices that remain unspoken but reside instead in their performative practices as silences pregnant with meaning.

It is in this sense that this chapter seeks *to trouble children's voices in research*. "To trouble" is "to unsettle", "to destabilize", "to rethink" and "to look beyond"; it is, in short, to take a critical look at the interpretive potential of children's voices in research by attending to the very social processes that give rise to them; put another way, it is to reject the all-too-easy and unproblematised desire to render children and their worlds comprehensible and transparent through a surface reading of their utterances (see Mazzei & Jackson, 2009).

Though much of what I set out in this chapter could be applied to voice research in general and not simply to child voice research, I argue that it is both necessary and productive to provide this critique of voice research to Childhood Studies for two reasons. First, because the field of Childhood Studies has not adequately engaged with such critiques so far. And second, because the power structures in childhood research – most notably, in child-adult encounters – provide a productive entry point into a critical analysis of the production of knowledge about children and childhood.

The compulsive obsession with voice in Childhood Studies

There is no doubt – and a simple search of published work in Childhood Studies will testify to this – that children's voices have long been a central preoccupation for Childhood Studies scholars. To a great extent, this is understandable. The interdisciplinary field of contemporary Childhood Studies has come about as a reaction to older disciplinary paradigms (from, among others, anthropology, sociology and psychology) that neglected, or as some would argue, totally ignored children's voices. As has been gone over many times during the last three decades, under these older schools of thought children were rendered literally speechless; it was therefore a moral, political and epistemological imperative to rectify this lack of voice in studies of childhood (Spyrou, 2011). This effort materialised as a search for "children's perspectives" and, as with other marginalised groups, voice provided the most accessible and convenient means for accumulating new research knowledge that came directly from children rather than adults (be they parents, teachers, researchers or others).

The compulsion to "capture" children's voices in research cannot be understood outside the ontological and epistemological assumptions that underpin our notions of "truth" and "authenticity" in research. As Mazzei and Jackson (2009, pp. 1–2) argue, our practices of "capturing" voice "remain attached to notions of voice inherited from metaphysics – voice as present, stable, authentic, and self-reflective". To the extent that we fail as researchers to capture our subjects' "authentic" voices, it is because of some putative limitation or inadequacy in our approach or method (MacLure, Holmes, Jones & MacRae, 2010, p. 495). Yet, voice – in all its complexity and fullness – seems to escape capture. As MacLure poignantly explains:

> But the insufficiency of voice – its abject propensity to be too much and never enough – is unavoidable. Voice will always turn out to be too frail to carry the solemn weight of political and theoretical expectation that has been laid upon it. For voice is also tied to idle, frivolous things that tarnish authenticity, weaken trust or block analysis, as least as these are usually conceived – frivolous things such as performance, appearances, inconsequentiality, vacillation and vested interest. (MacLure, 2009, p. 97)

MacLure (2009, pp. 97–98) goes on to argue that these insufficiencies of voice – be they laughter, silence, jokes, inconsistency or partiality, to name but a few – are not impediments but productive features of voice that invite us, as researchers, to explore the more nuanced meanings of what our subjects are trying to tell us. They invite us, in other words, to *trouble voice* and render it productive, starting from where our analysis would have otherwise ended. This troubling necessitates not just a rethinking of, and movement away from, claims to truth and authenticity but a reconsideration of commonly accepted methodological goals such as empathy. As Lather (2009) argues, the desire for empathy might too readily become a desire for establishing sameness between ourselves as researchers and our research subjects when distance and respect for difference should in fact guide our enquiries. The goal from this post-structuralist point of view then becomes one of rendering difference, wherever possible, productive: "the task is to produce processes and movements beyond the fixedness, or limited mobility, of presently conceptualized categories of difference" (Lather, 2009, p. 19).

In this chapter, I attempt to illustrate the value of troubling children's voices through the use of different empirical examples; in doing so, I highlight features of voice that are difficult to grasp and create a messy (though potentially productive) terrain for more nuanced readings of children's voices. The examples I provide come from research projects I have been involved with through time and are meant to facilitate reflection on and the opening up of children's voices to more critical readings; they are not meant to provide definitive and conclusive interpretations, which would, in any case, be contrary to the post-structuralist theoretical argument I make here.

Through each of the examples offered, I attempt to illustrate the possibilities for productive engagement with children's voices in research when we undertake a more "patient" and nuanced reading, which takes into account their fullness and irreducible character. Rather than providing exhaustive readings of meaning, this kind of analysis offers avenues of exploration that defy closure.

To the extent that we are offered insights into children's worlds through their words, it is because we are offered narratives of their experiences that we are able, to a greater or lesser extent, to make sense of because we situate them in their proper discursive contexts. But since this is a dialogical process – it is not just what they tell us, but also how we react to, and make sense of, what they tell us – our understandings are always partial, limited and often tenuous and revisable. It is in light of this understanding that I offer these examples of troubling as instances of productive provocation and engagement. I focus my discussion on three instances of troubling children's voices. The first one explores the possibilities for productive engagement with children's voices when they are taken to be not merely discursive but also material. The second one explores the contradictory and ambiguous in children's voices. And the third one explores children's voices through their silences. These three instances of troubling do not constitute mutually exclusive conceptual terrain but I discuss them separately to bring forth their productive potential more clearly.

Material voices

Through this first instance of troubling, I attempt to illustrate the productive terrain that opens up when children's voices are treated as both discursive *and* material constructions, which are constituted through performative practices, rather than simply as linguistic utterances imbued with meaning. Karen Barad's (see especially Barad, 2007) post-humanist perspective (termed "agential realism"), which explores the "intra-actions" and entanglements between human and non-human agents involving phenomena that are both material and discursive, provides a good entry point for rethinking voice beyond the discursive (see also Oswell and Esser in this volume).

But what does it mean to see this mutual constitution in voice? Drawing on Barad's work, Jackson and Mazzei (2012, p. 111) direct our attention to "how the material is always already discursively produced, and the discursive is always already materially produced". From this point of view, children's subjectivities and their voices are produced through the entanglement of their bodies with other human bodies and forms of matter (Jackson & Mazzei, 2012, p. 115). Children's agency is no longer seen as an individual possession but rather as the outcome of their intra-actions with other human (other children and adults) and non-human agents (e.g. material things such as books, classrooms and toys). What we are urged to account for from this perspective, then, are the performative practices of this intra-action that takes place in the discursive/material nexus (see Bollig & Kelle in this volume). As performative practices, children's voices then come to reflect both the discursive and material realities of their lives and become transformed from mere descriptions of accounts to dynamic intra-acting phenomena that produce particular understandings in research encounters (see Jackson & Mazzei, 2012, pp. 127, 132).

I illustrate this potential through an example from a study I participated in on single-parent children's experiences of poverty and social exclusion. In one of the interviews we had with a 16-year-old boy who comes from a single-parent family, he explained to us his personal sense of poverty and social exclusion using an example: "If [my friends] go to places where you need money to get in, I do not go, or, if they go somewhere to eat, I go with them, they eat and I just look at them." Though his statement is presented here somewhat out of context, it is still possible to recognise how this young person's discursive construction of the social exclusion he experiences (as a result of belonging to a single-parent family with limited economic means) is also simultaneously material; it is the material realities of his life that lead him to frame his experience discursively in the particular way he does – he is socially excluded because he is materially deprived. The discursive construction of his subjectivity is constituted through the encounters (or his *de facto* but not willing exclusion) he has with his friends. These are material encounters – encounters of human bodies with one another and encounters with non-humans (restaurants, tables, food, money) – which render his particular discursive construction meaningful. In turn, it is this discursive construction that informs the material dimension of social exclusion that he chooses to foreground through his words; that is, the material sense of exclusion acquires its meaning from being placed in the particular discursive understanding that frames it. It is in this sense that the discursive and the material are constitutive of one another and render voice as more than simply uttered speech. The fact that this young boy's words are voiced in the context of a research encounter should not, of course, be underestimated. His words are performative, not simply in the sense that they constitute a performance in the presence of the researcher, but also in the sense that they constitute a performative practice that renders his subjectivity as a member of a single-parent family experiencing poverty meaningful; he crafts his identity, in other words, by situating it within the proper discursive context where poverty and social exclusion are experienced as such because he is a member of a single-parent family.

Contradictory and ambiguous voices

In this section, I proceed to further explore what Mazzei (2009) has called the undomesticated in voice, a kind of voice that troubles (because it resists analysis) and in turn invites troubling (because it begs to be made sense of). This kind of voice is unclear, uncertain, ambiguous, multiple, undisciplined and shifting. It is a voice that cannot be made sense of readily because it defies what we, too often, consciously or unconsciously, come to assume about its putative essence – that it stands, in other words, for truth and authenticity. Our inability to see the undomesticated voice for what it is may mean that we dismiss it or that we reduce it to something other than what it is in order to make it knowable; in short, we domesticate it. Through this process of domesticating voice, we also inadvertently end up making it certain and clear, when it is anything but.

Mazzei (2009, p. 47) encourages us instead to "seek the promise of an impossibly full voice that challenges such truths and authentic meanings". Of course, this basic understanding is not new. Post-structuralists have, for quite some time now, been arguing that there is no unified subject, that meaning is unstable and indeterminate and often full of ambiguity and contradiction, and that there is a performative dimension to meaning, which challenges putative claims to truth and authenticity. Curiously enough, and despite the fascination with children's voices in Childhood Studies, post-structuralist insights have largely remained peripheral to the field. What might, then, an enquiry into the ambiguous and contradictory of children's voices provide for our understanding of children's experiences as these are narrated to us through their performative practices during our research encounters? And how might such an enquiry help produce non-essentialist accounts of children's perspectives, which are informed by the multiple and often contradictory discourses in which they are embedded?

To illustrate how the ambiguity and contradiction in children's voices may become productive through a more nuanced reading that takes into account their embeddedness in discursive fields, I turn to another study I was involved with, which explored Greek Cypriot children's knowledge, perceptions and attitudes towards foreigners who come to work in Cyprus, with a particular focus on female domestics (see Spyrou, 2009). These are women who mainly come from southeast Asia (especially from the Philippines and Sri Lanka) and provide services such as cleaning, childcare and elderly care to Greek Cypriot families. The following exchange from a focus group discussion carried out with a group of 10- to 12-year-old children reveals how contradiction and ambiguity gives rise to voices that are transgressive and undisciplined and do not, at least on the surface, make clear sense. The excerpt comes from a point in the discussion when I asked the children if they had, themselves, met any Sri Lankan women who work as domestics.

Boy A: Yes, when my grandma was alive – she has passed away now – we used to bring Sri-Lankan women [to Cyprus to help take care of her].[1] One of them lived right across from our house. She was a good person and helped us out.

Boy B: My neighbors had one [Sri-Lankan woman] as a domestic and I used to go to their house often and she was very good to me, she behaved properly, she helped out in the house and did all the chores.

Spyros: When you say she was very good, what do you mean? [question directed to Boy B]

Boy B: She behaved politely, properly, and did not complain about her job – that she had too much to do – and did what they asked her to do.

Spyros: What else?

Boy A: I know homes – I don't want to mention which ones – which exploit them very harshly. Let's say, "Go and get me that thing", because they

> do not feel like getting it themselves. She is expected to do everything. Should they be doing everything?
>
> *Spyros:* What do you think about this issue? [Directed towards Boy B]
>
> *Boy B:* Ok, he is partly right, but more so what is their job? To do those things as well. We pay them. Why should we not order them?
>
> *Spyros:* Do you consider this right, let's say? [Directed towards Boy A]
>
> *Boy A:* Not very right but sometimes yes.

A close look at the transcript and the conversation that transpires among the three of us reveals the contradictions and ambiguities inherent in the two boys' voices. To start with, in their initial statements both boys point out that the experience they each had with a Sri Lankan domestic worker left them with a positive impression: "She was a good person" (Boy A) and "she was very good with me" (Boy B). Yet their remarks are not unconditional. Both of them provide additional comments to their positive evaluations of these women. Boy A points out that she "helped us out", while Boy B states that "she behaved properly, she helped out in the house and did all the chores". Boy B further reinforces this conditional position when I ask him to justify his evaluation. When Boy A becomes critical of the relationships between Greek Cypriot employers and domestic workers and their exploitative nature, questioning essentially the right of the former to order the latter around, Boy B partly acknowledges that this is problematic but then proceeds to defend the right of employers to act in this manner: "Ok, he is partly right, but more so what is their job? To do those things as well. We pay them. Why should we not order them?" Interestingly enough, Boy A reaches a negotiated position on the issue: partly maintaining his original position and partly accepting Boy B's assertion ("Not very right but sometimes yes").

What are we to make of this exchange? A close reading of the excerpt reveals that there is no clear position by either of the boys on the issue being discussed. Despite the fact that they have opposite views on the matter at the start, as the exchange between them (through me) ensues, their statements and positions become more ambiguous and contradictory.

In fact, as I found in my conversations with other children, including children whose families employed Sri Lankan and Filipino domestic workers, their attitudes and feelings towards these women included a great deal of ambiguity and contradiction, which on the one hand, expressed a sense of intimacy and affection and on the other hand, expressed racist attitudes, which reflected difference and intolerance (Spyrou, 2009). Such understandings were not always expressed with clarity but rather occupied a fuzzy, uncertain and constantly shifting domain where children positioned themselves variously depending on the issue discussed, the context of the discussion and those present; moreover, children's understandings depended a great deal on the pertinent knowledge and experience they had and the discourses that they were able to tap into in order to make sense of the issue. Thus, to make sense of these children's voices and their ambiguous and contradictory character, one would need to consider all these parameters. These include my presence and the specific questions I ask, the presence of these particular boys who come with particular experiences and knowledge on the issue and the way they respond to me and one another at each turn of the conversation. All these parameters constitute the performative dimension of these boys' subjectivities, which take shape and form in the research encounter. Moreover, one would have to take into account the discourses that these boys access to position themselves in these ambiguous and contradictory ways (see Spyrou, 2001). Greek Cypriot children are on the one hand exposed to social discourses of equality, multiculturalism, tolerance and acceptance in school, but, at the same time, they also partake in racist social discourses – encountered in their interactions with others, in the mass media, and so on – which view these women as radically different (both physically and culturally) and inferior, an understanding which is further reinforced by the employment status of these women in people's homes and the unequal power balance that characterises relations with them. This is a complexity reflected in children's voices, which are ambiguous and contradictory.

The excerpt could of course be simply read as a clear case of children's racism: after all, they express racist opinions about these women. But another reading of the exchange – as I have indicated above – takes into account the contradictions and ambiguities that refuse to close off and finalise the meaning of the text. Such a reading defies singularity, definiteness and clarity. It also provides for a more ethical engagement with children's voices and their subjectivities as these are produced out of the complex, entangled relations they have with people, institutions and discourses. It is not just their personal experiences that matter but also the larger racist discourses in which their lives are embedded and which are enacted during the research encounter. Simply concluding that these children are racist is to attribute an identity to them when, in many ways, what we see is their struggle to make sense of the contradictions they encounter in their worlds. It is precisely the contradictions and ambiguities offered by a post-structuralist reading that make it possible to consider how children's subjectivities are crafted out of the diverse discursive and cultural resources to which they have access. The "truth" we are offered through this reading is not the only possible one and we might also expect that under a different set of circumstances these same children might reveal something quite different about their understanding of these women. The role of the interviewer-researcher, in this case, is twofold: to bring out this complexity during the research encounter by exploring instances of ambiguity and contradiction through follow-up questions and to highlight their presence when analysing the interview material.

The strength of this approach lies precisely in allowing ambiguity and contradiction to surface as legitimate positionings offering multiple and complex readings of voice as produced through research (see also Warming and Sen in this volume); there is not one dominant interpretation that emerges, but rather plausible interpretations that emerge from a close reading of the text and the research situation. Likewise, it offers productive insights into the multiple (even if limited) and complex discursive formations of children's subjectivities, children whose lives cannot be easily and conveniently reduced to a clear and single understanding.

Silent voices

In this third and last section, I illustrate the value of extending the analysis of children's voices beyond the voiced and into the realm of silence. As I have argued elsewhere (see Spyrou, 2015), silence has received scant attention by childhood scholars despite its potential for enhancing our understanding of children's voices (see also Lewis, 2010). Outside Childhood Studies, however, scholars have argued for the need to explore the fullness of voice by analysing not simply voiced utterances but also the silences that constitute our research subjects' voices (see especially Mazzei, 2003, 2007). Poland and Pederson (1998, p. 293), for example, have argued that our analyses of voice should not be exhausted with what is said but should instead explore what is left out and which can, in some cases, be equally revealing as that which is uttered. Though this is not simply a question of using the right methodologies, they argue that it is crucial to attend to the context of talk and silence, which is not limited to the interactional context of research but also extends to the institutional and cultural context where "artful agents" rearticulate social structures (Poland & Pederson, 1998, p. 303). In practical terms, and for purposes of analysis, this means highlighting and problematising silences through close and reflexive readings of research data and texts rather than dismissing them.

Of course, silences might come about as a result of diverse reasons, conditions and situations: In some cases, they might be the result of forces that silence one's voice (e.g. a teacher telling a student to keep quiet), while in other cases, they might be self-willed (e.g. keeping silent out of politeness, because one takes something for granted or because something is simply not talked about, and so on and so forth) (see Mazzei, 2003, pp. 354–366 for a more extensive discussion of types of silences; see also Baurain, 2011; Mazzei, 2004; Poland & Pederson, 1998). If silence is not an absence or omission but something that is both purposeful and meaningful (see Mazzei, 2003) then we need to extend our understanding of voice by developing ways of attending to it.

Below I provide an example of how to trouble children's silences in ways that produce more in-depth understandings of their worlds through more nuanced readings of their voices. The example comes from a focus group with four teenagers who discuss with me their experiences of living in a single-parent family. The particular exchange from which the following excerpt comes involves two of the boys in the group, Minos and Costas.

Spyros: How is life in your family?
Minos: Fine.
Spyros: Do you feel that your life is fine? Do you have any difficulties, problems that are troubling you?

Minos:	Sometimes I fight with my mom and my brother.
Spyros:	Is it because of differences you have? Are these the usual problems that every family has or is it something different?
Minos:	I don't know.
Spyros:	Is it something where your mom tells you to do something and you say "I won't do it" or she tells you "Do this" but you don't? Is it that kind of problems you have or is it other kinds of problems which are specific to your family?
Minos:	Some are like that.
Spyros:	Are you concerned about having these problems, these fights, etc.?
Minos:	Yes.
Spyros:	Do you consider this to be something serious? Or don't you take it very seriously? I do not mean that it is not serious but I am trying to understand how you see it because you mentioned it ... that is why I am asking. Is there something specific that happened and created tension in your family?
Minos:	No. Most of the times I shout, it is usually for the same reasons.
Spyros:	What do you mean?
Minos:	It is about money, let's say. My mom does not give me enough.
Spyros:	And you need more ...
Minos:	Yes.
Spyros:	And that creates extra tension and you end up arguing ... Is there anything else that is happening? Are there other reasons which might give rise to this tension?
Minos:	Nothing.
Spyros:	So, it is usually about financial issues. The rest of you? [Directed to other members of the group] We are not simply talking about problems. We are also talking about positive things that happen, things that you might like but also difficulties you might be facing.
Costas:	I do not think there is anything different from what happens in other families. Everybody fights ... money, restrictions in things we want to do.
Spyros:	Restrictions in relation to what, let's say?
Costas:	Let's say, you tell her [i.e. his mother], "I will go somewhere [to eat]" and she tells you, "No, eat at home".
Spyros:	So, it is about money again.
Costas:	Yes, sometimes.

When I start the conversation with the group and direct my attention specifically to Minos, asking about his family life, he responds with a short and simple "Fine". When I follow up with more specific questions, he proceeds to mention the fights he has with his mother and brother only to resort to another short "I don't know" response when I enquire about the reasons for these conflicts. It actually takes a few more exchanges (with mostly short responses on his part) and insistence on my part before he mentions that some of these fights are because of the financial problems that his family faces. When Costas enters the discussion, he responds with more clarity about the reasons that might give rise to such fights while he also tries to normalise these incidents by suggesting that conflicts of this type happen in all families. A close look at what the two boys say and how they respond to my questions suggests that they are not willing (especially true for Minos) to readily disclose their understandings and experiences as children growing up in single-parent families. As a researcher, I am constitutive of these children's voices not only because I guide the direction of the exchange but also because I engage in an ongoing interpretation of their voices and follow up with new questions based on these emerging understandings. Their silences are partial and negotiated with me along the way as I provide opportunities for them to make more specific responses. What I am asking them to talk about – the difficulties of living in single-parent families facing financial difficulties – is offered to me partly through their voiced utterances and partly through the silences that come attached to their words. In some cases, these silences are offered in the form of evasions (e.g. Minos' "I don't know" response); in other cases, they are offered as deflections or reworkings (e.g. Costas' attempt to produce a new interpretation of Minos' comments by reframing and normalising it: "I do not think there is anything different from what happens in other families. Everybody fights … money, restrictions in things we want to do."). My decision at some point to invite comments from children other than Minos ends up bringing Costas into the conversation, who provides a more specific understanding of Minos' earlier statements and contributes towards a more collective narrative about the effects of financial problems on children who come from single-parent families.

A close reading of the exchange reveals the nuances of these children's subjectivities as these take shape in the research encounter and through their performative practices, which span the whole range of voice – from uttered speech to silence. Along the way, and as a result of this more nuanced reading, we get an insight into these boys' understandings, which a more straightforward reading of the exchange focusing on their utterances might miss. It is their partial silences and the way they negotiate them that allows us to see how they position themselves within the research encounter – with hesitation and partial disclosure – and in relation to the specific topic we discuss. This suggests that, without its counterpart (i.e. silence), speech offers more limited opportunities for understanding children's subjectivities.

Far from being a failure on the part of the researcher to elicit speech or a failure in finding the right method to do so, silence is a constitutive element of voice. Though, in an interview/focus group discussion as exemplified above, the researcher is actively involved in the production of voice (i.e. with regards to what is said and what remains silent), it would be naïve to assume that silences would be absent from, or minimised, if the researcher limited his/her participation in the unfolding narrative (e.g. in biographic research with children where the researcher provides an initial stimulus – "Tell me about your life" – and steps back). In short, silence is not a problem to be overcome but an invitation for further reflection on voice. And though addressing the "silent" and the "absent" may not be new to qualitative research, the lack of critical reflection on this issue in Childhood Studies, which otherwise produces vast amounts of voice-based research, becomes even more vital. Reflecting on the role of language, and of voice in particular, in partially constituting children's subjectivities goes a long way in helping us understand the politics of research (see Alvesson & Skoldberg, 2009, pp. 223–224) and our own constitutive role in producing voice, both uttered and silent.

Concluding thoughts

In this chapter, I have argued for a more critical approach to child voice research, one that seeks to "trouble" children's voices by exploring their multi-dimensional character. More specifically, I have illustrated the utility of re-integrating the material in our discursive analyses of children's voices by rethinking the entanglement between the discursive and the material, which a closer look at children's voices may reveal. This kind of rethinking may allow us to bridge the gap between discourse and matter in voice research, which clearly privileges the former over the latter. Similarly, I have shown that children's voices might lack clarity and coherence and appear to be ambiguous and contradictory because of the diverse and contradictory discursive demands placed on them. This should not in any way render children's voices less real, meaningful and convincing but should instead offer an opportunity for exploring the complex and messy character of children's worlds and the processes that produce their voices. As I pointed out at the beginning of this chapter, this is not unique to child voice research. However, acknowledging the presence of contradiction and ambiguity in children's voices (rather than dismissing it as meaningless, non-consequential or a sign of ignorance) allows us to rethink our understanding of children's ontologies and the still-prevailing assumptions about children's lack of full rationality: Contradictions and ambiguities are constitutive of children's subjectivities the same way they are of adults'. Finally, I have shown in this chapter how children's silences are an integral part of their voices rather than mere omissions or absences and that paying attention to them allows for more nuanced understandings of their interpretive potential. By paying attention to them, I do not mean that, as researchers, we should try to encourage children "to speak their silences" but rather that we should recognise their silences and situate them within the local interactional contexts of the research encounter as well as the larger institutional and discursive contexts that produce them, which can potentially shed light on their meaning.

The approach put forth in this chapter also implies a rethinking of our understanding of children's agency. It suggests a turn away from substantivist notions of agency that see it as an ontological quality of the individual – the child as an autonomous and knowledgeable agent who can reflect and act on the world and, hence, potentially transform it – and towards relational ontologies that emphasise the child's relations and connections with other human and non-human agents including material realities (see Barad, 2007). Children's agency in that sense emerges out of their participation in assemblages and as a result of their interdependent relations with other agents within these assemblages (Oswell, 2013, p. 81). If we take children's voices as a modality for expressing their agency, then we inadvertently distance ourselves from claims to authenticity and truth and move towards a more fluid notion of how agency is constituted and performed through voice. Voice becomes, then, not the possession of the individual child but a co-production involving children, adults, researchers, material realities, institutions and discourses. This co-production is a coming-together – an entanglement – that surfaces under particular configurations of power and possibility in time and place and expressed through children's voices; it is a view of agency "as complex, multidimensional and ambivalent" (Valentine, 2011, p. 348) that emerges (or fails to emerge) out of the continuous rearticulation of forces.

Child researchers' desire to "capture" children's voices by making clear, certain and convincing connections between data (which are transparent and meaningful) and claims (which are supported by the evidence) short-circuits a more self-reflexive and critical analysis of voice, which looks not just at the words uttered but at the very processes that produce voice in research. My call for "troubling" children's voices does not aim to pin down and exhaust meaning by rendering it transparent through a privileged account of what children's voices mean; it is instead an invitation to produce new and different understandings that might otherwise remain hidden when we avoid engaging with the complex and messy character of children's worlds, which is offered to us through their voices.

Note

1 Brackets indicate text I have added – not children's words – to render the exchange clearer.

References

Alvesson, M. & Skoldberg, K. (2009). *Reflexive Methodology: New Vistas for Qualitative Research*. London: Sage Publications.

Barad, K. (2007). *Meeting the Universe Halfway: Quantum Physics and the Entanglement of Matter and Meaning*. Durham: Duke University Press.

Baurain, B. (2011). Teaching, listening, and generative silence. *Journal of Curriculum Theorizing*, *27*(3), 89–101.

Jackson, A. Y. & Mazzei, L. A. (2012). *Thinking with Theory in Qualitative Research: Viewing Data across Multiple Perspectives*. London, New York: Routledge.

Lather, P. (2009). Against empathy, voice and authenticity. In A. Y. Jackson & L. A. Mazzei (Eds.), *Voice in Qualitative Inquiry: Challenging Conventional, Interpretive, and Critical Conceptions in Qualitative Research* (pp. 17–26). London, New York: Routledge.

Lewis, A. (2010). Silence in the context of "child voice". *Children and Society, 24*(1), 14–23.

MacLure, M. (2009). Broken voices, dirty words: on the productive insufficiency of voice. In A. Y. Jackson & L. A. Mazzei (Eds.), *Voice in Qualitative Inquiry: Challenging Conventional, Interpretive, and Critical Conceptions in Qualitative Research* (pp. 97–113). London, New York: Routledge.

MacLure, M., Holmes, R., Jones, L. & MacRae, C. (2010). Silence as resistance to analysis: or, on not opening one's mouth properly. *Qualitative Inquiry, 16*(6), 492–500.

Mazzei, L. A. (2010). Thinking data with Deleuze. *International Journal of Qualitative Studies, 23*(5), 511–523.

Mazzei, L. A. (2009). An impossibly full voice. In A. Y. Jackson, & L. A. Mazzei (Eds.), *Voice in Qualitative Inquiry: Challenging Conventional, Interpretive, and Critical Conceptions in Qualitative Research* (pp. 45–62). London, New York: Routledge.

Mazzei, L. A. & Jackson, A. Y. (2009). Introduction: the limit of voice. In A. Y. Jackson, & L. A. Mazzei (Eds.), *Voice in Qualitative Inquiry: Challenging Conventional, Interpretive, and Critical Conceptions in Qualitative Research* (pp. 1–13). London, New York: Routledge.

Mazzei, L. A. (2007). Toward a problematic of silence in action research. *Educational Action Research, 15*(4), 631–642.

Mazzei, L. A. (2004). Silent listenings: deconstructive practices in discourse-based research. *Educational Researcher, 33*(2), 26–34.

Mazzei, L. A. (2003). Inhabited silences: in pursuit of a muffled subtext. *Qualitative Inquiry, 9*(3), 355–368.

Poland, B. & Pederson, A. (1998). Reading between the lines: interpreting silences in qualitative research. *Qualitative Inquiry, 4*(2), 293–312.

Spyrou, S. (2015). Researching children's silences: exploring the fullness of voice in childhood research. *Childhood*. DOI: 10.1177/0907568215571618.

Spyrou, S. (2011). The limits of children's voices: from authenticity to critical, reflexive representation. *Childhood, 18*(2), 151–165.

Spyrou, S. (2009). Between intimacy and intolerance: Greek Cypriot children's encounters with Asian domestic workers. *Childhood, 16*(2), 155–173.

Spyrou, S. (2001). One and more than one: Greek Cypriot children and ethnic identity in the flow of everyday life. *disClosure: A Journal of Social Theory, 10*, 73–94.

Chapter 8

Playing with socially constructed identity positions

Accessing and reconstructing children's perspectives and positions through ethnographic fieldwork and creative workshops

Hanne Warming

This chapter is based on two research projects in which the researcher played with socially constructed identity positions in different ways. It explores how children's agency in both projects influenced, and was influenced by, the research process, notably the ways in which it positioned and represented the children involved; and it documents how their agency shaped the project's results. Overall, the analysis shows that although children's (and others') agency is framed by power relations that cannot be totally suspended, playing with socially constructed identity positions opens up possibilities for new, "thicker" and more nuanced alternatives to existing representations of children's agency and their perspectives than would be possible in more naturalistic enquiries, as well as enabling them to actively influence the research process. Moreover, the analysis suggests that some of the "techniques" that were deployed to play with social identity positions may have the potential to empower children to produce a collective critique and to draw on new resources that they can use to re-negotiate their identity positions.

This chapter explores how children's agency influences the research process and product, and how children's agency is influenced by the research process, notably how it positions and represents the children involved. I approach children's agency from a post-structuralist perspective as a spatially framed process through which socially constructed identity positions and power relations are reproduced, negotiated and challenged, just as they are in adults' agency. In line with a socio-geographical approach, I understand social space not only as a place where "things happen", but as a "social action situation" where the material (including the bodily dimension) is interwoven with the discursive (Simonsen, 2001, p. 35). Though structured by webs of discursive and material relations, the social space is also changed and challenged through agents' use of the resources related to a given position (Harré, 2001) and mis-reiterations (Butler, 1993). In some cases, the spatial framing appear to be more or less identical to the institutional framing, whereas in others it goes across different institutional settings, or the opposite can be just a sub-part of the institutional setting with its own power relations and negotiations. Ontologically, the concept of spatial framing – referring to a social action situation rather than to a fixed structure – is more post-structuralist than the concept of institutional framing.

In line with Bühler-Niederberger and König (2011), I understand children's agency as framed by the intersection of the generational order and other types of power relations and socially constructed identity positions as they manifest themselves in concrete webs of relations (see also Alanen, 2013). It is these intersections that frame children's agency as they unfold in concrete social spaces. Further, children's agency is conceptualised as framed by the ontological ambiguity between dependency and independency that shapes all human agency (Cooks, 2006). Thus children's agency is seen here as a heterogeneous, spatially framed and negotiated phenomenon.

The chapter provides a critical, post-structuralist re-interpretation of research experiences from two different projects: the first involving ethnographic field work in a Danish day care institution; the second, a creative workshop with children in care.[1] Both projects aimed at empowering the involved children; the first through assessment and emphatic representation of the children's perspectives, the latter through a participatory design aimed at challenging and reconstructing the children's (unprivileged) identity positions. However, one thing is what a project aims to do, another is what actually happens. Here, I concur with others who note that while participatory research is not necessarily unequivocally good (Gallagher & Gallagher, 2008; Holland et al., 2010), it "*can* make a central contribution in providing an ethical, epistemological and political framework and in the potential for rich findings" (Holland et al., 2010, pp. 360–361). In the analysis of how children's agency influences the research process and product, and how children's agency is influenced by the research process and the way it positions and represents the children involved, I discuss whether and how the two research projects succeed in making such a contribution.

The analysis focuses on situations where the researcher plays with – or invites the children to play with – socially constructed identity positions, for instance, the researcher as an adult in a daycare setting striving for a least-adult position, or a "maladjusted child" inverting the notion of "maladjusted" so that it becomes a special value/competence instead of a stigma. The rest of the chapter is structured around the two cases. Each case consists of an introduction to the aim and research method, a presentation of the case and an analysis of the findings. The chapter concludes with a discussion that synthesises the findings from the two cases.

Ethnographic field work: playing with socially constructed positions as part of my methodology

As mentioned above, a key goal of the research in the kindergarten was to assess and emphatically represent the children's perspectives, which I approached as ambiguous and fluid rather than fixed and essential (Warming, 2011). I also acknowledge children as important gatekeepers to their own social worlds, and consequently, I decided to strive for a participant role as "least adult" (Corsaro, 1985; Mandell, 1991). In the least-adult role, the researcher makes an effort to participate in the children's everyday lives in as childlike a way as possible: playing with the children, submitting to the authority of their adult carers, abdicating from adult authority and privileges and – as suggested by Corsaro (1985) – letting the children define and shape the ethnographer's role. The rationale for doing this is that the power relations between adults and children can in some situations – due to children's mistrust or conflicting adult interests – prevent the researcher from gaining access to some part of children's social worlds (Mandell, 1991; Warming, 2011). This "least-adult role" transgresses the classic continuum of participant roles identified by Gold (1958), which runs from "complete (natural) participant" to "complete observer", as it intentionally breaks with what is regarded as a "natural" role in the field. In traditional ethnography and naturalistic enquiries, valid knowledge production depends on the researcher disturbing these natural roles as little as possible. Yet Garfinkel (1967) has clearly demonstrated that doing the unexpected and breaking the norms for role performance ("breaching experiments") can illuminate norms and expectations that are taken for granted, invisible and silent. Taking on a least-adult role can be regarded as a kind of breaching experiment that may give rise to confusion and mistrust, as Gulløv (1998) suggests. However, as the following episode from my fieldwork illustrates, it can also open up to, and invite, new role performances and position negotiations.

Case 1:[2] "You're an adult"

Gritt (a five-year-old girl) and her two friends have invited me and several children to watch their show. After some arguments about where the show is to take place, what it should be about and who should be allowed to act, the three girls arrange a makeshift stage by placing some chairs in a half circle. Gritt enters the "stage". Having instructed the audience to take their seats and her two friends to step backstage to see to the tape recorder, she introduces herself and her two friends as dancers who will perform their own choreography. "Turn it on!" she orders, pointing at the tape recorder, but her friends have trouble finding the right track, so Gritt has a go instead. It is not that easy, however, and the children struggle with the machine for a while. Meanwhile, the audience (the children) acts, at first, in an impressively disciplined manner, sitting quietly and waiting, but after some minutes, they become restless, talking louder, getting up and moving around, picking up toys and even leaving the room. Gritt turns to me and says: "Tell the audience to sit down and be quiet". "No, I'm a member of the audience myself", I protest, trying to act "least adult". However, she is not inclined to give up and continues: "You're an adult, so you have to!" "Well, then I don't want to be an adult", I say evasively. She momentarily gives up on me and turns back to the tape recorder. When she finally finds the right track, she turns to me again and says accusingly: "There, you see: they're yelling and fooling around." As I do not react to her remonstrations, she finally takes responsibility for the audience herself. First she shouts: "Shut up and sit down!" A few children obey, though most of them ignore her. Then, she puts her hands on her hips, glares sternly at the audience, and in a controlled voice, clearly articulates the following words: "We were here first, and it's our show. If you want to watch it, then sit down and be quiet. If you don't, you must leave the room". Some of the children obey and sit down, but others don't. Gritt goes up to the miscreants, putting a hand on their shoulder or pointing at them with her finger, and asks them one by one if they want to stay or leave. After a few minutes, most of the children sit down quietly in their chairs again (the others have left the room). Gritt returns to the stage, smiles brightly at the audience and says: "Ladies and gentlemen, now we can finally begin".

Analysis: playing with institutional identity positions

The institutional framing of this interaction is a kindergarten in Denmark, a daycare institution for children aged 3 to 6. The two main institutional roles (Goffman, 1959, 1961, 1974) are the inmates (the enrolled children) and the staff. The former are referred to as "children" and the latter as "adults" in every-day speech. I conceptualise institutional roles in line with Harré (2001) as *institutional identity positions* in order to emphasise that these roles are not freely chosen or deployed and cannot just be donned or discarded like masks or disguises to conceal a person's real personality. People are, in any given institutional context, positioned in roles ascribed with certain rights, duties and demands (Harré, 2001; see also Esser in this volume). Thus, a person's agency cannot totally override his/her role, but the role can be variously performed in terms of reiterations, mis-reiterations or negotiations of the institutional identity position it represents (Butler, 1993; Warming, 2011; see also Eckermann & Heinzel in this volume). It is in regard to the two main institutional roles of children and adults that I try to position myself as least adult through mis-reiterating and negotiating my institutional identity position.

In this kindergarten, it is explicitly emphasised as part of the pedagogical approach that the adult (staff) role may be performed in different ways. Yet there are still some basic scripts that define this role. For instance, the institutional identity position of being "an adult" confers privileged authority over the children and carries with it the obligation to take responsibility for keeping the peace and maintaining order, and especially to ensure that the children adhere to the institution's rules and norms.

When Gritt orders me to tell the other children to sit down and be quiet, she is acting – or rather, she is requiring me to act – in accordance with this hierar-chical child/adult position: I must take on my adult responsibility and author-ity. Her own agency is framed by this socially constructed power relationship, which at first glance might seem to assign her an unprivileged, restricted position.

However, it is exactly this construction of the child/adult relationship, which rests on my adult power and obligations, which she deploys for her own purpose. Thus, her agency is enabled in a quite surprising and powerful way by the way both our identities are institutionally framed. Or at least it would have been powerful if I had not resisted by attempting to break with an adult's role scripts. One could argue that by doing this, I also distanced myself from my self-assigned "least-adult" role, according to which I should have let the children shape my role. Gritt's insistence that I act like a real adult in accordance with conventional adult role scripts locates my behaviour somewhere in between breaching an adult institutional identity and complying with Gritt's order by letting her shape my role. Paradoxically, I react by using my power as an adult to escape the institutional position of an adult, and I distance myself from that role by taking advantage of one of the resources available to it. This episode revealed to me that I was not completely free to act "least adult", but also that I, both in worth and act (negotiation and mis-reiteration), had succeeded more clearly than before this incident in communicating my distance to the institutional adult identity position. Thus, Gritt and the incident she triggered became helpful in my future attempts to negotiate access to the children's social worlds, and I am certain that I benefited from this throughout the remainder of my fieldwork.

I will now elaborate on the analysis, paying special attention to whether and how a possible confusion caused by this playing with identity positions influenced the children's agency (or my representation of it).

Confusion: children's agency in unexpected situations

As previously mentioned, Gulløv (1998) draws attention to how violations of taken-for-granted role scripts can cause confusion and mistrust. Whether this applies to the incident involving Gritt is hard to say, but is worth examining more closely. I noticed that at first she deemed my performance unacceptable: first, she tried not once but twice to make me act in accordance with my adult role responsibility and authority, and then she blamed me for the children's unruly behaviour when she said accusingly: "There, you see: they're yelling and fooling around". However, I interpret her reaction more as angry and disappointed than as an expression of confusion, since it did not prevent her from resuming action, at least not for more than a few minutes. She quickly changed tack and assumed responsibility and authority herself, and she did this in a very forceful manner by invoking the materiality of the room: some children were allowed to stay while others were asked to leave. She also indirectly refers to the rules governing use of the room and the time slot by saying, "We were here first, and it's our show: If you want to watch it, then sit down and be quiet. If you don't, you must leave the room". The room in question was a big group room, with a door leading to the hall, and another door opening out on the playground. In the time slot for "free primary outdoor play" during which this episode took place, the children are allowed to choose whether to play in the playground, in this particular room or in one of the other rooms. There were institutionally endorsed rules for who could play where: The playground could accommodate an unlimited number of children (since all the children playing there were under adult supervision), but the rooms could only hold a limited number of children who had to agree on what game to play and were then allowed to invite other children to join them. When Gritt says, "we were here first", she means that she and her two friends had chosen the room for their game – that is, in this time slot it belonged to them and they had the right to invite other children and exclude others who disturbed them.

Besides leveraging the room's materiality and usage rules, she makes her point even more emphatic by pointedly articulating her orders to the other children, and through her body language. Thus, it is in the interplay of the physical space, the rules connected to it, Gritt's words and the way she delivers them, as well as her body language, that she succeeds in reproducing the social order of a show with a well-behaved audience and herself as director. Yet what actually happens is not a pure reproduction of the social order but rather a reframing in which Gritt has now gained a more powerful position than previously because she no longer needs adult support. She is in charge of the situation, and her actions have earned her the other children's acceptance of her authority in this particular space. This reframing was made possible because I renegotiated our identity positions through my (ambiguous) performance of a "least-adult" role. This constituted a kind of breaching experiment; however, it was not necessarily a totally unfamiliar situation for the children, as it probably resembles myriad everyday situations for them in which no adults are present in the first place. That might explain how Gritt so easily and skilfully switched to a different child role. Alternatively, one might speculate that she re-interpreted the situation and her own role performance by drawing on what I shall call secondary and periphery institutional roles, as well as roles with which she was familiar from outside the institution. In this context, secondary institutional roles include the roles of parents, siblings and child visitors from the fellow after-school institution for children aged 7–12. Other peripheral institutional roles include the role of grandparents, other relatives or caregivers, and elderly people from the village. Thus, while my performance is an intended mis-reiteration of the institutional role of an adult (e.g. a staff member), Gritt's reaction is a creative and skilful negotiation and re-positioning that draws on a vocabulary of possible ways of performing the child role enabled by the complexity and fluidity of the institutional space as well as her movement between various social spaces.

On this basis, I argue that playing with identity positions can be a way to make visible the taken-for-granted positions as well as competences and other potential ways of acting that are normally excluded and displaced by these taken-for-granted positions and related performances. Thus, playing with identity positions enables representations of children and their competences and vocabulary of actions that transcend what could be captured in a more naturalistic enquiry. I will not argue that this is necessarily a more truthful representation, but it certainly adds something to our understanding. Thus, playing with identity positions in different ways can enable a "thicker", more nuanced, multiple and ambiguous representation, which, from a post-structuralist perspective on children's identities and agency, is potentially far more interesting as it enables new ways of acting and interacting with them.

I will now turn to the issue of whether playing with identity positions creates mistrust between the researcher and the children who are the subject of the research and, if so, what the consequences there may be for access to children's social worlds and representations of their perspectives.

Lost or changed trust: consequences for, and of, children's agency

According to Luhmann (2005), trust is crucial to individuals' agency and cooperation. Thus, I found it essential to examine whether and how the trust consequences of playing with identity positions framed and reframed the children's agency and my access to their social worlds. I have elsewhere argued the impossibility of "getting under children's skin" (see Warming, 2011), and thus, here, of knowing for sure how they felt about me. However, if we follow Luhmann (2005) in defining trust as "a situated communicative act rather than as an inner feeling" (Warming, 2013, p. 13), it is possible to examine the episode outlined above from the perspective of trust building and erosion.

The moment when Gritt gives up involving me as an authority could be interpreted as an act of distrust, yet this does not paralyse her. Instead, she successfully draws on her knowledge about, and trust in, the rules for using the playroom. Her disabused trust in my adult role is replaced by another kind of trust that enables her agency. This means that although I risk losing her trust completely – or at any rate missing out on an important step in building a trusting relationship with possible negative consequences for my access to her social world – she does not appear disempowered by the situation. In fact, she soon gives me another chance by confiding what she describes as "something that the adults mustn't find out" (about how she used to cheat the adults). Her confession to me can be interpreted as a kind of test for me or as a sign that she has accepted me as "least adult"; however, it is difficult to tell which of these applies or whether something completely different is at stake. Conversely, it seems improbable that she would have given me a second chance if my reaction had led to her experiencing disempowerment. Her feelings towards me would probably have been more negative, and her inclination to engage with me in the future minimal. Rather, I believe that the potential negative consequences for my access and the research process were circumvented by Gritt's skilful agency, which enabled her to feel pride and satisfaction rather than shame and frustration during the incident in question.

Case 2: a creative workshop with children in care

I will now turn to Case 2, namely a creative workshop I held with children in care. The aim of the workshop was to develop new ideas on how to understand and support children in care, based on their own experiences and creative thinking. We wanted to develop alternatives both to "problematizing", diagnostic approaches to children (e.g. Jolivette et al., 2008; Carr, 2008) and to so-called "strength-based" approaches (e.g. Rapp & Goscha, 2011; Saleebey, 2006). While both these approaches typically rest on polar distinctions between risks/weaknesses and resilience factors/strengths (Lagoni et al., 2014), in this project we followed Rappaport (1981) in aiming towards a more dualistic view that allows for the possibility of inverting concerns about the involved children, while remaining alert to any risks and vulnerabilities (more information about the project is available at www.saerlig.ruc.dk).

Methodologically, the workshop was inspired by the so-called "future workshops" developed by Robert Jungk, Ruediger Lutz and Norbert R. Müllert back in the 1970s (see Jungk & Müllert, 1987). A future workshop is built around three phases: a critique phase, a fantasy phase and a realisation phase. The *critique* phase serves to identify real problems and frustrations rooted in people's everyday experience. This phase is also intended to release energy for creative thinking in the ensuing *fantasy* phase about how to solve these problems. In this fantasy phase, reality is suspended in order to promote creative and visionary thinking. In the third and final *implementation* phase, participants identify and plan how their visionary ideas might be partially or wholly carried out in real life (Jungk & Müllert, 1987).

Thirteen children aged 13 to 17, some living in foster families and others in residential homes for children, participated in the two-day workshop. We stayed at a luxury cottage with an indoor swimming pool and other recreational facilities in order to promote a positive and playful atmosphere, which is an important ingredient in the future workshop method. This playful atmosphere was also intended to relax the usual rules and norms to which children are subjected. By inviting children as "experts", and using the luxury vacation as a token of our recognition of their expertise and valuable contribution to our research, we also aimed to disrupt the children's everyday institutional identities. However, this time, the way that we played with socially constructed identity positions was not connected to the children's institutional identities, but rather addressed the negative labels typically used to construct their identity positions in different contexts. In analysing Case 2, therefore, I deploy a different vocabulary than that of institutional identity positions, roles and role performances used to study Case 1.

In the critique phase, we encouraged the participants to tell us whatever negative labels they had heard used to describe them personally or other children in care. We also told them that they could include labels they used to describe themselves, but that only negative ones were allowed. We wrote all these labels on posters and hung them on the walls so that the participants could see them throughout the workshop. In the fantasy phase, we asked the children to invert the meaning of each label by identifying the most positive potential way of performing the personal trait embodied in the label. Finally, in the implementation phase, we asked the participants to choose one or more labels to describe what could be done by adults in the child's environment, and by the child her/himself, to make these positive traits and their potential more visible and recognised. In this phase, they were allowed to choose whether they worked individually or in groups. Afterwards, they were asked to present their ideas to us and the other participants. They were given a range of different materials to work with, including posters, markers, scissors, glue, magazines, computers, video cameras, ordinary cameras and voice recorders, and they were free to express their ideas in different ways, e.g. through song, rap music or a theatrical performance.

The inversion that takes place during the fantasy and implementation phases is, in my view, the part of the workshop where one can experiment with identity constructions most effectively. In the following, I will give an example of how the children worked with this task, not only contributing with important input to the project, but also changing their own everyday identity positions as well as their vocabularies of action and critique.

Presentation and analysis of Case 2

Three of the participants, two girls and a boy, chose to work with the problematising label "introverted", with which they could all identify. During the fantasy phase, they inverted this label, transforming it into "being able to be alone and to immerse oneself in something". In the implementation phase, they made a poster explaining how periods of solitude and immersion can be a way to work through different kinds of trauma, with potentially positive implications for their future wellbeing and social life. In the oral presentation, they explained that adults close to the child should be aware of various aspects of these healing processes: how stressful they can be, how much potential they contain and how much the children need these periods of introversion. This awareness was deemed necessary to prevent adults from blaming the children for their introversion and/or disturbing their healing process, and instead to enable them to support it through recognition, indulgence and (extra) care. They gave examples of such healing processes from their own lives, of how adults around them normally reacted to them and how they would like them to react to support their healing processes rather than disturb them, as was usually the case – regardless of the adults' good intentions.

This, of course, was a valuable contribution to our project, which was enabled through our invitation to the children to play with identity constructions by inverting negative labels. Naturally, it depended on the children agreeing to engage with the task. Interestingly, we discovered that the impact of our experiment with identity constructions did not stop at the workshop, but continued in the children's everyday life. Thus, for instance, the foster parent of one of the girls wrote to tell us that when their daughter had returned home, she had told her foster parents what she had learned about the positive potential of periods of introversion, and had specifically asked them to accept that she needed such periods to manage her loss and grief. She also reassured them that they should not worry – she would manage and she would not isolate herself forever. She informed her foster parents that what she needed during such periods was understanding, acceptance and loving care rather than worry, questions and ill-concealed pressure to "pull herself together" and be more sociable. Invitations for social togetherness and for talking about her thoughts were welcome, she explained, as long as they were genuine and open, rather than covert orders. Her foster parents experienced this as a complete turnaround in her way of relating to them, and they concluded that the workshop had empowered the girl's – and their – agency in everyday life when it came to her introverted periods. This conclusion was supported by her foster mother's impression that her foster daughter seemed stronger and happier after the workshop.

Children's agency and the research process

The above case shows how playing with identity constructions can change children's agency in everyday life, as well as the researchers' and children's own representations of the latter's behaviour and perspectives. As researchers, we also learned how deeply it can influence the research process itself. This was evident during the summing up of the implementation phase, when we asked the children to come up with 10 recommendations for professionals working with children in care. One of these was:

> The most dangerous thing in the world is living, so if you want to protect us from the most dangerous thing, you have to protect us from life itself ... which means that we are not allowed to live our lives.

I have summed up focus groups and workshops with children in care many times, but I have never heard a response like this before. Mostly, I hear things like "they should listen more to children", "remember to ask how the child feels, and accept if she/he doesn't want to talk about it" (reported in Warming et al., 2003; Warming, 2006, 2014, 2015). We had asked for – and expected – this summary to result in similarly concrete recommendations, but instead the children delivered a far more fundamental and radical critique of adults' attitudes to children, perhaps especially children in care, indicating that adults' misplaced concern and attempts to protect them from all risks actually deprived them of an authentic life. In this way, they changed the entire agenda. Of course, much depended on our response to this "hijacking" of our research agenda. Would we take it seriously? Would we actually write their responses on the poster and incorporate them into the project as valid results? I believe that the children were aware of the risk that we would not. Thus, they delivered their first critique almost as a joke, but when we wrote it down and encouraged them to elaborate, explaining that we wanted to be able to explain their points of view to colleagues and childcare profession-als, they became very engaged and began to develop their ideas using examples.

I will argue that the children's agency and courage to criticise, as well as the nature of their critique, were partly if not entirely enabled by a research process that allowed both researchers and researched to play with socially constructed identity positions. The future-workshop-inspired format was an important facili-tating factor here. First, the playful approach made the critique less "danger-ous". Second, the inverted thinking exercise shaped the form and content of the children's critique: protection from risk, which is normally regarded as appro-priate, is here reinterpreted as the privation of life itself. The children's agency transformed the research agenda and process from a forum designed to generate concrete and constructive advice for adult use into a discussion involving radical criticism of adult behaviour and attitudes. Our encouragement to the children to elaborate further on their criticism also generated additional insights into chil-dren's perspectives on protection and care.

Concluding discussion

The two cases presented above are different in several ways. These include: (1) the research methodology: Case 1 involved ethnographic fieldwork in a natural (insti-tutional) setting and a breaching experiment where the researcher attempted to perform a "least adult" role, while Case 2 involved an experimental design inspired by the future workshop method; (2) the type of children involved: Case 1 dealt with unproblematised children aged 3–6, compared to Case 2, which involved problematised children aged 13–17 years; and (3) the identities that were exper-imented with: Case 1 involved institutional identity positions, whereas Case 2 played with identity positions related to cross-institutional, stigmatising labelling. Despite these differences, there are interesting similarities across the two cases.

First, both cases can be regarded as experiments that violate what is taken for granted by "playing with identity positions", and that thereby invite and elicit other dimensions of children's agency than would be possible in more naturalistic enquiries. Some of these forms of agency might already be familiar to the chil-dren, as I argue in the analysis of Case 1, while others might be new to them as in Case 2. While the latter might be preferable from an empowerment perspective, both ways of playing with identity positions provide us with novel insights into children's agency and perspectives that enable more nuanced, "thick" represen-tations of children than is normally possible. In Case 2, we further facilitate the representation of children's perspectives by encouraging radical criticism. In both cases, children are represented in the analysis as interdependent, competent and creative agents.

Second, in both case studies, the children's agency influenced the research process in ways that were quite surprising to the researcher, who was intention-ally open to experimentation with identity positions. In the first case, Gritt helped me to communicate my desired role as "least adult", even though the episode in question prevented me from living up to Corsaro's prescriptions for this role (Corsaro, 1985). Nevertheless, she succeeded in clearly communicating to all the children present that my role was different from that of "normal" adult staff members, which certainly expedited the children's understanding and acceptance of my position. Furthermore, the skilful and successful way she managed the situation where I failed to live up to her expectations of me counterbalanced any negative feelings she may have harboured, which might otherwise have blocked my access to her social world. In Case 2, the children transformed the research agenda from "constructive advice to adults" to "radical critique of adults". I argue that this radical critique was enabled by the special way in which we experimented with "playing with identity positions" in this project, which was inspired by the future workshop method, and which generated quite different results to partici-patory workshops and qualitative interviews that I have previously undertaken with children in care.

Overall, the analysis shows that although children's (and others') agency is framed by power relations that cannot be totally suspended (see also Sen in this vol-ume), playing with socially constructed identity positions opens up possibilities for new representations of children's agency and their perspectives as well as for them to actively influence the research process. I would not go so far as to claim that such research is unequivocally good, but I do think that it generates "thicker" and more nuanced alternatives to existing representations of children. Last, I believe that some of the methods we deployed to play with social identity positions may actually have the potential to empower children to produce collective criticism and draw on new resources that they can use to re-negotiate their identity positions.

Notes

1 The first project was my Ph.D. project, funded by Roskilde University; the second was an action research project, funded by The Obel Family Foundation.
2 This case has previously been used in an article in *Childhood*, 18(1): 39–53; see Warming, 2011.

References

Alanen, L. (2013). Childhood and Intergenerationality: toward an intergenerational perspective on child well-being. In A. Ben-Arieh, F. Casas, I. Frønes & J. E. Korbin (Eds.), *Handbook of Child Well-Being: Theories, Methods and Policies in a Global Perspective* (Vol 1, pp. 131–60). Dordecht: Springer.

Bourdieu, P., Accarde, A., Balazs, G., Beaud, S., Bonvin, F., Bourdieu, E. & Wacquant, L. (Eds.). (1999). *The Weight of the World: Social Suffering in Contemporary Society*. Stanford: Stanford University Press.

Bühler-Niederberger, D., & König, A. (2011). Childhood as a resource and labora-tory for the self-project. *Childhood*, 18(2), 180–195.

Butler, J. (1993). *Bodies That Matter: On the Discursive Limits of Sex*. New York: Routledge.

Carr, A. (2008). *The Handbook of Child and Adolescent Clinical Psychology: A Contextual Approach*. Hove: Routledge.

Cooks, A. (2006). The ethical maze: finding an inclusive path towards gaining children's agreement to research participation. *Childhood, 13*(2), 247–266.

Corsaro, W. (1985). *Friendship and Peer Culture in the Early Years.* Norwood: Ablex.

Gallagher, L. & Gallagher, M. (2008). Methodological immaturity in childhood research? Thinking through "participatory methods". *Childhood, 15*(4), 499–516.

Garfinkel, H. (1967). *Studies in Ethnomethodology.* Englewood Cliffs: Prentice Hall.

Gold, R. (1958). Roles in sociological field observation. *Social Forces, 36*(3), 217–223.

Goffman, E. (1959). *The Presentation of Self in Everyday Life.* New York: Doubleday Anchor.

Goffman, E. (1961). *Asylums: Essays on the Social Situation of Mental Patients and Other Inmates.* New York: Doubleday Anchor.

Goffman, E. (1974). *Frame Analysis: An Essay on the Organization of Experience.* London: Harper and Row.

Gulløv, E. (1998). *Børn i fokus. Et antropologisk studie af betydningsdannelse blandt børnehavebørn* [*Children in focus. An anthropological study of sensemaking among kindergarten children*]. PhD dissertation, Copenhagen University.

Harré, R. (2001). The discursive turn in social psychology. In D. Schiffrin, D. Tannen & H. E. Hamilton (Eds.), *The Handbook of Discourse Analysis* (pp. 688–706). Oxford: Blackwell.

Holland, S., Renold, E., Ross, N. J., & Hillman, A. (2010). Power, agency and participatory agendas: a critical exploration of young people's engagement in participative qualitative research. *Childhood, 17*(3), 360–375.

Jungk, R. & Müllert, N. (1987). *Future Workshops: How to Create Desirable Futures.* London: Institute for Social Inventions.

Jolivette, K., Gallagher, P. A. Morrier, M. J. & Lambert, R (2008). Preventing problem behaviors in young children with disabilities. *Exceptionality, 16*(2), 78–92.

Lagoni, K., Lavaud, M., Fjordside, S. & Warming, H. (2014). *Litteraturreview om udsatte børn og unge* [*Literature review on vulnerable children and young people*]. Retrieved from: www.saerlig.ruc.dk

Luhmann, N. (2005). *Tillid – en mekanisme til reduktion af social kompleksitet* [*Trust – a mechanism to reduction of social complexity*]. Copenhagen: Hans Reitzels Forlag.

Mandell, N. (1991). The least-adult role in studying children. In F. C. Waksler (Ed.), *Studying the Social Worlds of Children: Sociological Reading* (pp. 38-59). London, Philadelphia: RoutledgeFalmer.

Rapp, C. A. & Goscha, R. J. (2011). *The Strengths Model: A Recovery Oriented Approach to Mental Health Services.* Oxford: Oxford University Press.

Rappaport, J. (1981). In praise of paradox: a social policy of empowerment over prevention. *American Journal of Community Psychology, 9*(1), 1–25.

Saleebey, D. (Ed.). (2006). *The Strengths Perspective in Social Work Practice.* Boston: Pearson.

Simonsen, K. (2001). Rum, sted, krop og køn – dimensioner af en geografi om social praksis [Space, place, body and gender – dimensions of a geography of social praxis]. In K. Simonsen (Ed.), *Praksis, Rum Og Mobilitet* [*Praxis, space and mobility*] (pp. 17–48). Frederiksberg: Roskilde Universitetsforlag.

Warming, H. (2006). "How can you know? You're not a foster child": Dilemmas and possibilities of giving voice to children in foster care. *Children, Youth and Environments, 16*(2), 28–50.

Warming, H. (2011). Getting under their skins? Accessing young children's perspectives through ethnographic fieldwork. *Childhood, 18*(1), 39–53.

Warming, H. (2013). Theorizing trust – citizenship dynamics: conceptualisation of the relationship between trust and children's participation and citizenship in globalised societies. In H. Warming (Ed.), *Participation, Citizenship and Trust in Children's Lives* (pp. 10–31). Palgrave Macmillan.

Warming, H. (2014). The life of children in care in Denmark – a struggle over recognition? *Childhood,* online first: doi:10.1177/0907568214522838

Warming, H. (2015). Trust and power dynamics in the shaping of children's lived citizenship and participation in globalized societies, *Social Sciences Journal,* forthcoming.

Warming, H., Hansen, I. Ø., & Nielsen, M. (2003). Lærestykker fra arbejdet med og evaluering af en terapeutisk samtalegruppe for familieplejeanbragte børn [Learnings from working with, and evaluation of, a therapeutic conversation group for foster children]. *Matrix 20,* 243–285.

Section III

Agency in historical perspective

Tracing and contextualising childhood agency and generational order from historical and systematic perspectives

Meike S. Baader

The following chapter gives a historical analysis of the discursive traces of "childhood agency" in a range of educational theories. It first considers German Romanticism around 1800, then the international "progressive education" movement around the turn of the twentieth century, and finally the West German "anti-authoritarian Kinderladen movement" of the 1970s, which emerged from the protest movements of 1968. These historical periods constitute key "nodal points" in the history of childhood in Western modernity (Baader et al., 2014) – a history shaped particularly by the Romantic discourse (Cunningham, 2005). Our analysis shows that in these educational theories, children are conceived as powerful, agentive actors. This contradicts the thesis that it was only with the Childhood Studies of the 1980s that the previously dominant image of the vulnerable child was put to rest. For the schema, "strong vs. vulnerable child" is shown to have run through the modern discourse on childhood since the nineteenth century. While the various educational theories emphasise different dimensions of childhood agency, they all seek to distance themselves from a Christian conception of the "generational order".

Introduction

The concept of childhood agency has been discussed within Childhood Studies since the 1980s, primarily from a sociological perspective (see Bollig & Kelle in this volume). In focussing on "children's agency", recent work in Childhood Studies is often held to depart from earlier approaches, which are conceived as regarding children as victims: "Social studies of childhood have made available numerous studies about children's agency in circumstances and surroundings far beyond the more narrow vicinities in which children have so far been seen as victims conceptually and empirically" (Qvortrup, Corsaro & Honig, 2009, p. 5). The present chapter contradicts this view by drawing attention to conceptions of "childhood agency" within the modern educational tradition. Though Bollig and Kelle also acknowledge a tradition of reflecting on the autonomy of the child that stretches back to the Enlightenment (see Bollig & Kelle in this volume; Honig, 1999, p. 59), this tradition is not analysed in detail and has not been discussed in terms of childhood agency within particular educational theories. The present chapter, by contrast, enquires into various ways in which the child has been conceived as an actor in the history of education. It does so by considering three historical periods in which the history of childhood in the West condenses to form key "nodal points" (Baader, Esser & Schröer, 2014). This historical approach not only makes it possible to analyse the traces of "childhood agency" in educational theories, but also serves to show that what it means to attribute agency to children varies at different historical periods. What can we learn from the history of childhood, from historical Childhood Studies and from the history of academic research and knowledge in reflecting on "childhood agency"? When Prout (2000) notes that "the 'agency' in 'children's agency' remains inadequately theorised" (p. 16), a historical approach can contribute to a view of that which in various contexts has been called "agency", and can thus serve to advance its theoretical understanding. In calling for the historical contextualisation of childhood agency, the chapter is oriented around the following key theses:

1   The notion of children as actors was not introduced by the new social science-based Childhood Studies of the 1980s, but has various precursors in the history of education and of the conceptualisation of childhood, as well as in prior educational programmes and practices. These are considered here as discursive traces or prehistories, and are analysed with respect to the three historical periods noted above.

2   The comparison of these three periods in the history of education demonstrates that the notion of childhood agency, that is the appeal to the child's capacity for action, has been a part of educational theories throughout the modern age. Nevertheless, great differences can be observed in the way "childhood agency" has been conceived.

3   These differences are rooted in the way in which children are addressed, that is the manner in which they are called upon to bring forth and exercise their agency. In German Romanticism, children are urged to develop their imaginative capacities as an expression of their wilfulness and thereby to reveal the divinity that inheres within them (Schleiermacher, 1989). One hundred years later, the Swedish progressive educationalist, Ellen Key (1902; English version, 1909) addresses children as "majesty" and confers "rights" on them. In the socialist progressive education theories of the 1920s, children are encouraged to cast off their habitual subordination, which results from socialisation processes in the proletarian family (Baader, 2014a). Finally, in the post-1968, anti-authoritarian educational movement in West Germany, they are urged to express their emotions – particularly their aggressive impulses, but also their sexual drives (Seifert, 1970; Baader & Sager, 2010) – to break free from traditional conceptions of childhood and particularly the "silent childhood" (Niehuss, 2001; Seifert, 2004) of the 1930s to 1960s. Our analysis will show that childhood agency takes place in the context of particular educational programmes and visions of society.

4   In all of the above examples, the adult-child difference is a crucial element in each conception of childhood. Recent social-scientific research in Childhood Studies has repeatedly indicated the significance of generational order (Alanen, 2005). Here, at least at the theoretical level, generational order seems to be conceived as a fundamental dimension of social structures (Braches-Chyrek, Bühler-Niederberger, Heinzel, Sünker & Thole, 2011, p. 10). Yet from a historical perspective it is clear that generational order is more than simply an element of modern social structures, and that in particular historical contexts, constellations and power configurations, it is in fact called into question, negotiated, and produced and reproduced as a relational difference between adults and children. There is thus a continual process of generational ordering, in which conceptions of childhood agency and its various dimensions play a part.

5   All three of the historical constellations we shall analyse were socially critical movements that questioned the existing generational order and the supposedly predominant understanding of childhood. Our analysis shows that, in each case, the critique of the relevant generational order also constitutes a critique of Christianity. Each critique of the prevailing conceptions of the generational order is connected with different conceptions of childhood agency.

6   Since the concept of childhood agency has been thought or intoned in different ways at different points in history, it has been associated with various "forms of subjectification" (see Bröckling, 2007). For each appeal to childhood agency was bound up with a different conception of how the child – and thus the eventual adult – ought to be. To strengthen the agency of the child was – whether directly or indirectly – at the same time to strengthen that of the adult subject.

7   When childhood agency is de-historicised, de-contextualised and treated as a supposedly independent and essential capacity, then we fall into that Romantic conception of childhood, which in German Romanticism itself was based on a religious anthropology. For according to this Romantic anthropology it is precisely the child's agency that expresses its divine being. There is thus a direct link between childhood agency and a Romantic anthropology and ontology. When the notions of "childhood agency" and "children as actors" are thematised without taking into account particular historical contexts, as well as social, generational and gender relations and modes of address, then these notions are romanticised and essentialised.

Methodology and method

How historical contextualisation is to be understood depends on the position that is taken with respect to international debates on methodology and method in historical education studies (Casale, Tröhler & Oelkers, 2006). Historical contextual analysis attempts to situate its objects within the relevant historical setting and "acknowledges the overall political, social, economic, and cultural situation" (Landwehr, 2009, p. 108). In the following, historical contextualisation is understood as a form of historical discourse analysis, which enquires into discursive threads and patterns in the history of education and which sees these as part of a wider social discourse. The contextual analysis of historical discourses seeks to ensure that "a concentration on texts and other materials [...] does not let the social question become obsolete", but rather "amalgamates" (Landwehr, 2009, p. 106) these two aspects. It takes seriously, and sets out from, the "independent significance of historical material in the construction of knowledge and reality" (Landwehr, 2009, p. 106), from which it draws out connections "in order to appropriately classify the material under investigation" (Landwehr, 2009, p. 106). Since it pays particular attention to power structures, discourse analysis is well suited to an enquiry into generational differences and generational orders. Historical contextual analyses operate at a number of levels, the appropriateness of which the material and question at hand can be decided in each case. These may include a reflection on the "situational context," which asks, "who, at what time, and in what place, does something" (Landwehr, 2009, p. 107). In the following, this approach is brought to bear on our analysis of the anti-authoritarian educational movement and the West German *Kinderläden*. For the crucial question from a historico-epistemological perspective is why it should have been precisely in the 1980s that the paradigm of childhood agency became a subject of international debate, and how this might be linked to the "pedagogical constitution of the child as an actor in the wake of the '68 movement" (Baader & Sager, 2010). In this regard, the present chapter traces the way in which, in the German context, discourses on childhood agency that originated in the practical, educational field found their way into the theoretical discourse of Childhood Studies.

The following analyses focus particularly on texts and documents, that is on written historical sources. They address the question of how childhood agency is conceived there and the dimensions that are ascribed to it. In the following, "agency" is understood as an analytical category that allows the capacity for action to be described as the "effect" of various relations (Prout, 2003). When "agency" is understood as the "effect" of various relations, then this includes pedagogical calls for childhood agency, that is appeals to childhood agency. This can also be performatively produced in texts as a powerful linguistic reality (cf. Butler, 1997) (see also Eckermann & Heinzel in this volume).

It is important to make clear how a historical approach to Childhood Studies differs from an empirical, social-scientific approach. In enquiring into the notions of childhood agency or children as actors, historical research in Childhood Studies is dependent on the extant sources in this area, at least when it is not dealing with contemporary history. This is the case where two of our historical examples are concerned: German Romanticism and the progressive education movement. Becchi and Julia (1996) have noted the systematic problem faced by historical Childhood Studies in tracing "children's voices", as well as its dependence on indirect evidence. For the question of which sources come "from the child's perspective" is not independent of the manner in which agency is attributed to children in theoretical and educational conceptions of childhood. Where children's drawings and paintings were prized as forms of creative expression, as was the case among followers of Friedrich Fröbel in the mid-nineteenth century, we tend to find them – in the form of "ego-documents" or as expressions of childhood agency – in archives, since they were considered worthy of preservation. It is thus possible to establish a link between the attribution of childhood agency, the practices that children were consequently urged to engage in, and the expressions of childhood agency that are to be found in such documents. In general, historical approaches to Childhood Studies are faced with the problem that there are a larger number of sources pertaining to middle-class childhoods than to other childhoods, since practices such as letter-writing, diary keeping, and drawing were encouraged and preserved as part of a middle-class self-understanding. Finally, since we shall be concerned in the following with conceptions of childhood in different historical periods, it should be noted that childhood is understood here as the concept of a stage of life that is subject to processes of social structuring, relations of power, interactions and negotiations.

Child agents in Romanticism: imaginative, wilful and autonomous

The Romantic conception of childhood that emerged in post-Enlightenment Germany around 1800 was summed up in an exemplary manner by Friedrich Schleiermacher (1989), who stated in 1806 that in "every child the divine is revealed" (p. 18). In Germany, such Romantic notions of childhood became established in the fields of literature, painting and educational theory. In the latter domain, this development was exemplified by the work of Fröbel, whose theories were taken up internationally.

The Romantic conception of childhood was the result of complex social, cultural, and discursive historical processes (Baader, 1996; Baader, 2004a). Here it is important to see these processes as part of a critical engagement with Christianity and its narratives – a phenomenon often referred to as "secularisation". The essential precondition of the Romantic conception of childhood was the rejection of the doctrine of original sin – a gesture that of course goes back to Rousseau (Baader, 1996, pp. 35–43). It is on this basis that children came to be seen as innocent, holy or divine beings. This implies that they have a special and sacrosanct status.

Alongside its rejection of the doctrine of original sin, another key feature of the Romantic conception of childhood is the organological and holistic idea that the child already contains, in germinal form, all of the capacities that will be developed as he/she grows up. In addition, this conception critically distances itself from the *Enlightenment* view of the child. Enlightenment thinking is reproached with regarding childhood merely as a *transitorium* – as a transitional stage on the way to adulthood – and thus only as a form of "human becoming". Childhood, according to the Romantic critique, appears to Enlightenment thinking as incomplete. Furthermore, the Enlightenment regards the child as a *tabula rasa* – as a blank slate on which the ideas of its parents and the society are inscribed. The Romantic conception of the child, by contrast, sees childhood as an independent stage of life that is meaningful in itself. It is conceived as a mode of human being and emphasis is placed on the child's wilfulness, which, in contrast to the old educational tradition, is to be valued rather than broken. In his "Catechism of Reason for Noble Ladies" of 1798, Schleiermacher called upon parents to honour the "singularity and capriciousness" of their children (Schlegel, 1988, p. 143), thereby distancing himself from the fourth commandment: to honour one's parents.

In the Romantic discourse, a special role is given to the child's imaginative capacities, by means of which it repeats the divine act of creation. According to the Romantic anthropology, it is human beings' capacity for imagination – which most people lose on the way to adulthood – that testifies to their divinity – a divinity that manifests itself in the child, since most adults have fallen away from it. The innocence of the Romantic child follows in part from the critique of the doctrine of original sin, but is also due to a form of existence that has not yet been deformed by society. In sum, the specifically Romantic view of the child thus consists in: a rejection of the Christian doctrine of original sin; a departure from Enlightenment thinking and its notion of a *tabula rasa*; an anthropology according to which the child's whole developmental potential is present from the outset; and an emphasis on the wilfulness and autonomy of the child. If we add to this a quasi-religious idealisation of the child as a particularly holy or divine being, then we can speak of the Romantic *myth of childhood* (Baader, 2004a).

It was primarily Fröbel, with his concept of the kindergarten, who was responsible for translating these Romantic ideas into an educational theory. From 1848 onwards, this concept was transplanted to many other countries across the world, primarily by German emigrants. Thanks to these "travelling ideas", Fröbel himself acquired the status of a pedagogical hero, particularly in the USA, and has come to be read as a precursor of Dewey (Baader, 2004b). The main aim of Romantic educational programmes was to create a safe and nurturing space in which children could develop their capacities with as little hindrance as possible. This was also the reasoning that lay behind the concept of the kindergarten. A key element of Fröbel's educational theory – particularly of his account of children's play – was the idea of autonomous activity (*Selbsttätigkeit*), in which children were urged to engage. There was then a religious justification for the high estimation of children's play as a genuinely child-specific form of expression (Baader, 1996).

These Romantic conceptions of childhood and of the mother-child relationship (Baader, 2014; 2015b) were extremely influential. "Romanticism", as Cunningham (2005) puts it, "was much more influential as a body of ideas than as an active force in day-to-day child-rearing within the middle-class home" (p. 72). Nevertheless, in the German context, the kindergarten programme, along with Fröbel's so-called "play gifts" (*Spielgaben*), allowed these Romantic ideas to become a genuine part of day-to-day child-rearing and educational practices. In Cunningham's (2005) view, "Romanticism embedded in the European and American mind a sense of the importance of childhood, a belief that childhood should be happy and a hope that the qualities of childhood, if they could be preserved in adulthood, might help redeem the adult world. In becoming more child-oriented in this way, society has radically changed its ideas on the relationship between childhood and religion" (p. 72).

Romanticism developed a conception of childhood subjectivity, rooted in an essentially childlike form of "autonomy" (in the sense of a divine drive to create), on which the Romantic anthropology was based. But it was also Romanticism that conceived children as "strangers" in the modern world (Richter, 1987). Within the field of New Childhood Studies, children are at times described in such Romantic terms, such as when Chris Jenks describes the child as a "stranger", "he inhabits our world and yet seems to answer to another" (Jenks, 1982, p. 9; for a critical view, see Baader, 2004a). A number of educational practices were derived from this Romantic conception of childhood. These included gardening work, active play and "guided" play using the Fröbel play gifts. All of these activities were supposed to stimulate children's capacity for autonomous activity.

Child agents in the progressive education movement: lively, eugenically fit and emotionally sensitive

The accounts of childhood given by progressive educationalists around 1900 followed those of the Romantics in many respects, yet were as diverse as the progressive education movement itself. The idea of autonomous activity played an important part in the movement's reworking of Romantic educational theory. For the progressive education movement, as for the Romantics, the child's defining features are its "innocence, naturalness, and individuality" (Esser, 2013, pp. 231–234). The child is thus essentially strong and autonomous. Following the Romantics, the Swedish progressive educationalist, Key (1902), refers to the "holy child" and emphasises its wilfulness and strength of will (p. 76). She also speaks of the majesty of the child, who is to be served by adults (p. 35, p. 120). In this way, Key, like Schleiermacher, explicitly distances herself from the biblical fourth commandment. In doing so, she draws both on Fröbel and on the classical and Romantic myth of childhood, which lays weight on the child's wilfulness.

For Key, the source of the child's energy lies in its healthy body, at least when its parents conform to the right eugenic picture – that is when they are neither alcoholics nor mentally disabled. In itself, the child is not fragile but lively and healthy – provided it is raised and taught by its mother in natural surroundings. The threat or danger to the child comes rather from the school institution and from the Christian doctrines of sinfulness. In this regard, Key (1902) writes of "soul murder[s] in the schools" (p. 143). At this point the child takes on the figure of a victim – a victim created by the restrictive character of educational institutions. This trope can also be found in the work of Maria Montessori, who also saw potential in eugenics and who herself referred to Key (Baader, 2005, p. 268). It is characteristic of both educationalists that they associate the image of the child suffering within a false educational institution with that of the suffering Christ (Baader, 2005, pp. 123–274). In Key, the strong and active child is thus contrasted with the vulnerable child who has been robbed of her vitality by the combined forces of religious education and the school (Baader, 2015a). The child is a victim of the school institution and of religious education. She is urged to develop her agency through physical training, exercise in the open air and through artistic and creative activity. Above all, she should display strong emotions (Baader, 2012). Key's conception of childhood agency goes hand in hand with a Nietzschean, social-Darwinian essentialism, in which it is a question of giving expression to nature and life themselves. In Key, the Romantic conception of childhood is determined in an evolutionary, social-Darwinian, Nietzschean and vitalistic manner. By living out its vital nature and feelings, the child can contribute to the "higher development of humankind". But even these vital forces, which, in true *Lebensreform* style, the child is to express, are themselves understood as deriving from a divine energy, and thus appear as essences.

In its practical application, Key's version of the progressive education movement's conception of childhood agency involves physical training – a central element in the youthful cult of the body and the country boarding schools (*Landerziehungsheime*) – and forms of physical conditioning, which recent scholarship on the progressive education movement has discussed (Baader, 2014a; Hagener, 2010; Oelkers, 2011).

Child agents in the 1968 movement: self-assertive, able to say no, resistant, liberated and political

In the West German *Kinderläden* movement, children were trained to continually exercise their agency. The movement emerged from parental initiatives in West Berlin, Frankfurt am Main and other West German university cities. These parents and activists were driven by a desire not to bring their children up to be obedient, quiescent and silent citizens; they did not want well-behaved, conformist children. They therefore distanced themselves from the child-rearing methods of their parents' generation and attacked its conception of the generational order, which they perceived as being based on subordination and a hierarchically determined generational difference (see Hungerland in this volume).

In the wake of the historical experience of National Socialism and the studies on *The Authoritarian Personality* (1950) by Theodor Adorno and other members of the Frankfurt Institute for Social Research, the founders of the *Kinderläden* asked themselves how they could raise their children to be self-assertive, capable of saying no and resistant. Critical skills and anti-authoritarianism were important concepts for the movement, even if the latter term was often strongly contested. Rather than raising children to be obedient, it was now a question of training them in forms of disobedience. The members of this highly diverse movement distanced themselves both from the "silent childhood" of the 1950s, to which recent historical research has attended (Niehuss, 2001; Seifert, 2004), and from the educational norm of a "familial pedagogy of good behaviour" (Mollenhauer, 1968, p. 136), which dominated the educational programmes of the West German kindergartens of the day (Aden-Grossmann, 1987, p. 130). These were criticised as much as the prevailing intra-familial child-rearing practices. The object of their critique was a "familialised childhood" restricted primarily to the interior space of the family and subject to a gender-based division of labour, where the mother was accorded sole responsibility for child-rearing (Baader, 2014b). Opposing itself to this familial approach, the *Kinderläden* movement was based around the group of children or the children's collective. Its critique of the middle-class nuclear family was informed by a political reading of psychoanalytic theory (Kauders, 2011). The contact that parents would have with other adults and with the children's collective in the *Kinderläden* would, as the reasoning went, "blast open" the restrictive Oedipal structure of the middle-class nuclear family.

The *Kinderläden* educational programme was based on Wilhelm Reich's concept of child self-regulation. Children were to be jointly responsible for deciding when they would play, eat or sleep, and were to be actively involved in decorating the *Kinderläden* space (Breiteneicher, 1971; Baader & Sager, 2010). They were also supposed to become better acquainted with their emotions and needs, and to develop a "cultivated" sense of their bodies (Seifert, 1970). The aim was to raise a liberated, happy child and, on this basis, an adult subject "capable of pleasure and love" (Seifert, 1970; Baader & Sager, 2010, p. 264; Baader, 2012). This also involved the "liberation of child sexuality", which played a significant role in some conceptions of the *Kinderläden*. These perspectives on child sexuality drew on Reich's sexual theories (Sager, 2015) and ranged from the necessary lifting of taboos to a problematic blurring of boundaries. In general, the *Kinderläden* were characterised by the de-hierarchisation of the generational difference; children were addressed as actors, and adults renounced their authority while also reflecting on their educational practice, for the "teacher must herself be taught" (Breiteneicher, 1971, p. 7). The concept of self-regulation (which children were to be made capable of by the age of three) and the call for children to exercise their agency were closely connected and occupied a central place in the *Kinderläden* educational programme (Seifert, 1970).

Childhood agency was not only ascribed to individual children, but also to the group of children or the collective. According to the rather heterogeneous *Kinderläden* programmes, childhood agency is also the agency of the children's collective. This point was illustrated by a photograph of three children walking over a piano keyboard (Breiteneicher, 1971, cover image), which became an icon of the *Kinderläden* movement. Children were allowed to engage in such activities, just as they were allowed to hit adults – as is illustrated in a television documentary on the *Kinderläden* from 1969 (Bott, 1970). For the adults, such manifestations of childhood agency constituted signs that the project of "teaching disobedience" was succeeding. In the context of the *Kinderläden* programme, childhood agency amounted to a politicised form of agency. The drive-based conception of the subject that lay behind the notion of "self-regulation" was grounded in essentialist claims. Yet these no longer had a religious underpinning, but were based on Reich's version of the psychoanalytic theory of drives.

This conception of childhood agency led to the involvement of children in the process of designing the *Kinderläden* space and planning the timetable and rhythm of the day (Baader & Sager, 2010). It was in this context that the "situational approach" evolved. This approach, which was initially developed by Jürgen Zimmer (2007) and which is still widely employed in German child day-care centres today, sets out from the questions which children themselves pose. Children are thus addressed as agents, for it is ultimately their questions that serve to structure the day-to-day educational activities of the kindergarten (Fthenakis & Textor, 2000). The approach was closely associated with an attention to "child cultures" – a concept that came to prominence in German debates in the 1970s and later entered the discourse of Childhood Studies (Baader, 2011).

The child's right to say "no" was considered an important aspect of its agency. This was thematised in an exemplary manner in the *Nein-Buch für Kinder (No-book for Children)*: "Mother and father be honoured, but children have a right to complain" (Stiller & Kilian, 1973, p. 35). Like Schleiermacher's "Catechism" of 1798 and Key's *The Century of the Child* of 1900, the *Nein-Buch für Kinder* also seeks to have done with the fourth commandment. This is likewise true of the controversial "bible" of the *Kinderläden* movement: a collection of texts by the English progressive educationalist Alexander S. Neill published in German in 1969 under the title *Theorie und Praxis der antiautoritären Erziehung* (*The Theory and Practice of Anti-Authoritarian Education*).

In sum, we can say that from the Romantic movement around 1800 through the progressive education movement around 1900 and up to the pedagogical theories of the West German *Kinderläden* movement around 1970, the appeal to childhood agency and the child's capacity for action – whether conceived as wilful, majestic or resistant – went hand in hand with a critique of a religiously legitimated generational order. This critique was levelled against the subordination of children to their parents and thus against a hierarchised, strongly power-based and religiously grounded conception of the generational difference.

Since the *Kinderläden* movement emerged from the 1968 protest movement, its critique of a hierarchical generational structure and its associated appeal to childhood agency and the child's right to say "no" and resist were rooted in a politicised context. In regard to the problem of the "complicity of children" (Bühler-Niederberger, 2011), the question arises here of whether, in an educational context in which children are encouraged to develop resistant behaviour, their saying "no" represents a form of complicity. There were, however, limits to the domains in which the child was encouraged to say "no": In the context of sexuality, the right to a "no" did not feature (Baader, 2012, 2015c; Sager, 2015).

On the basis of a consideration of the West German *Kinderläden* movement, certain paths can be reconstructed that led to the emergence of West German childhood sociology and an associated conception of childhood agency, and that brought forms of knowledge and practices – in the sense of "situated knowledges" (Haraway, 1988) – from the *Kinderläden* movement to the social sciences. In order to examine the connection between the West German *Kinderläden* movement and the emergence of New Childhood Studies from the sociological sciences in the German Federal Republic, these "traces" could be pursued through further studies.

Conclusion and further perspectives

As our historical analysis indicates, conceptions of childhood are closely intertwined with the historical, political and social contexts. This is not trivial, because there is "a tendency of children's culture to give the appearance of existing outside a political context" (Renner, 2015, p. 304). In the historical periods analysed above, we encountered discourses on childhood and children that conceive the latter as strong and endowed with agency and a capacity for action. They are not seen as being vulnerable. If they are under threat, it is from the prevailing social structures, but they are not in themselves defined by any special vulnerability.

It was also shown that those educational programmes that called for the nurturing of children's agency defined themselves in contradistinction to the dominant educational programmes of the day, which were reproached with turning children into "victims". This was the charge that we saw Key level against the traditional school system and religious education. Our analysis thus shows that the binary opposition between actor status on the one hand and victim status or vulnerability on the other has been deeply embedded in the Western discourse on childhood since the nineteenth century. In addition, we saw that what was conceived in earlier educational theories as the child's (essential) autonomous activity came to be reconceived as "agency" by new, social-scientific approaches. This can be seen as an expression of the "scientification of the social" that took hold in the 1970s and 1980s (see Raphael, 1996).

In sum, four elements are particularly important in theorising and systematically reflecting on childhood agency from a historical perspective. First, the prevailing political, educational, institutional and organisational contexts must be taken into account. The consideration of these contexts also needs to take into account the prevailing conceptions of childhood as ways of "framing" childhood agency. Second, it is important to enquire into the forms of agency that are attributed to children in such conceptions. Third, the attribution of childhood agency is often bound up with a negotiation of generational orders in the relevant contexts. Fourth, it is necessary to analyse the relevant dimensions of childhood agency. These include physical forms of childhood agency, which are also part of processes of subjectification. In Key's view, children should strengthen their bodies through exercise, fresh air, and sojourns in nature; according to the *Kinderläden*, they should physically express their aggressive impulses and become acquainted with their body as a sexual body. Distinguishing between these different dimensions is not only necessary where childhood agency is concerned, but also – and likewise from a relational perspective – in regard to childhood vulnerability (Baader, 2015a).

In all of the historical examples discussed above, children are urged to develop their agency and to make their voices heard precisely because they represent the promise of an alternative modernity or society. In the accounts we have analysed, the agency attributed to them is that which might save or redeem the world, whether this is their imagination and wilfulness in the Romantic era; their contribution to the higher development of humanity through a Nietzschean vitalism or a social Darwinism (which does not apply to all children equally) in Key; or, in the 1968 movement, their self-production as subjects who have liberated themselves from social constraints and who are able to push through social transformations. The corresponding forms of subjectification – first, imaginative and creative; second, physically energetic and eugenically healthy; and third, fully liberated and politically critical – differ greatly from one another. Nevertheless, in some respects, the essentialism in these theories of the subject is carried over from the one to the others.

All of these theories challenge the prevailing generational order at a fundamental level, yet all do so from different perspectives. This shows how closely the question of childhood agency is tied to that of generational order and generational ordering. All of the theories, from 1800 to the 1970s, attempt to throw off a Christian religious conception of the generational order – one that is legitimated by the Ten Commandments. This conception lies, as it were, underneath the historical stage and forms a – partly hidden – discursive thread within the negotiation of the Western "model of modern childhood" (see Mierendorff, 2014) up to the 1970s.

References

Aden-Grossmann, W. (1987). *KinderGarten: Eine historisch-systematische Einführung in seine Entwicklung und Pädagogik* [*Kindergarten. A historic and systematic introduction into its development and pedagogical concepts*]. Weinheim: Beltz.

Adorno, T. W., Frenkel-Brunswik, E., Levinson, D. J. & Stanford, R. N. (1950). *The Authoritarian Personality*. New York: Harper and Row.

Alanen, L. (2005). Kindheit als generationales Konzept [Childhood as generational concept]. In H. Hengst & H. Zeiher (Eds.), *Kindheit soziologisch* [*Childhood Sociologically*] (pp. 65–82). Wiesbaden: VS.

Baader, M. S. (1996). *Die romantische Idee des Kindes und der Kindheit: Auf der Suche nach der verlorenen Unschuld* [*The Romantic Idea of Children and Childhood: Researching the Lost Innocence*]. Neuwied: Luchterhand.

Baader, M. S. (2004a). Der romantische Kindheitsmythos und seine Kontinuität in der Pädagogik und in der Kindheitsforschung [The Romantic Myth of Childhood and its Continuity in Education and Childhood Studies]. *Zeitschrift für Erziehungswissenschaft, 7*(3), 416–430.

Baader, M. S. (2004b). Froebel and the rise of educational theory in the United States. *Studies in Philosophy and Education, 23*, 427–444.

Baader, M. S. (2005). *Erziehung als Erlösung: Transformationen des Religiösen in der Reformpädagogik* [*Education as Release: Transformations of the Religious in Progressive Education*]. Weinheim: Juventa.

Baader, M. S. (2011). An den großen Schaufensterscheiben sollen sich die Kinder von innen und die Passanten von außen die Nase platt drücken. Kinderläden, Kinderkulturen und Kinder als Akteure im öffentlich-städtischen Raum seit 1968 [Kinderläden, Children's Culture and Agency in Urban Spaces since 1968]. In M. S. Baader & U. Herrmann (Eds.), *68 – Engagierte Jugend und Kritische Pädagogik: Impulse und Folgen eines kulturellen Umbruchs in der Geschichte der Bundesrepublik* [*Progressive Youth and Critical Education. Impulses and Consequences of a Cultural Change in Western Germany*] (pp. 232–251). Weinheim: Juventa.

Baader, M. S. (2012). Childhood and happiness in German Romanticism: progressive education and the West German anti-authoritarian Kinderläden movement of the 1968. *Paedagogica Historica, 48*(3), 485–500.

Baader, M. S. (2014a). Die Kindheit der sozialen Bewegungen [The Childhood of Social Movements]. In M. S. Baader, F. Esser & W. Schröer (Eds.), *Kindheiten in der Moderne: Eine Geschichte der Sorge* [*Childhood in the Modern Era. A History of Care*] (pp. 154–189). Frankfurt/M.: Campus.

Baader, M. S. (2014b). Die reflexive Kindheit [The Reflexive Childhood]. In M. S. Baader, F. Esser & W. Schröer (Eds.), *Kindheiten in der Moderne: Eine Geschichte der Sorge* [*Childhood in the Modern Era. A History of Care*] (pp. 414–455). Frankfurt/M.: Campus.

Baader, M. S. (2015a). Vulnerable Kinder in der Moderne in erziehungs- und emotionsgeschichtlicher Perspektive [Vulnerable Children in the Modern Era from the Perspective of a History of Education and Emotion]. In S. Andresen, C. Koch & J. König (Eds.), *Vulnerable Kinder: Interdisziplinäre Annäherungen* [*Vulnerable Children: Interdisciplinary Approaches*] (pp. 99–101). Wiesbaden: Springer VS.

Baader, M. S. (2015b). Modernizing early childhood education: the role of the German women's movement after 1848 and 1968. In H. Willekens, K. Scheiwe & K. Nawrotzki (Eds.), *The Development of Early Childhood Education in Europe and North America: Historical and Comparative Perspectives* (pp. 217–234). Houndmills: Palgrave Macmillan.

Baader, M. S. (2015c). Pedo-sexuality: an especially German history. *Child*, special issue of *WSQ, 43*(1/2), 315–322.

Baader, M. S., Esser, F. & Schröer, W. (Eds.). (2014). *Kindheiten in der Moderne: Eine Geschichte der Sorge* [*Childhood in the Modern Era. A History of Care*]. Frankfurt/M.: Campus.

Baader, M. S. & Sager, C. (2010). Die pädagogische Konstitution des Kindes als Akteur im Zuge der 68er-Bewegung [The Pedagogical Constitution of Children as Actors in the Movement of the 1968]. *Diskurs Kindheits- und Jugendforschung* [*Discourse Childhood and Youth Studies*], 3, 255–269.

Becchi, E. (2004). Le XXe siècle. In E. Becchi & D. Julia (Eds.), *Histore de l'enfance en occident*. Tome 2: Du XVIIIe siècle à nos jours [*History of Western Childhood*. Vol. II: from 18th Century to our days] (pp. 358–433). Paris: Seuil.

Bernstein, R. (2011). *Racial Innocence: Performing American Childhood from Slavery to Civil Rights.* New York: University Press.

Bott, G. (Ed.). (1970). *Erziehung zum Ungehorsam: Antiautoritäre Kinderläden [Education to Disobediance: Anti-authoritarian Kinderladen Movement].* Frankfurt/M.: März.

Braches-Chyrek, R., Bühler-Niederberger, D., Heinzel, F., Sünker, H. & Thole, W. (Eds.). (2011). Deutungen und Bilder von Kindern und Kindheit [Interpretations and Images of Children and Childhood]. In Promotionskolleg Kinder und Kindheiten im Spannungsfeld gesellschaftlicher Modernisierung, *Kindheitsbilder und die Akteure generationaler Arrangements* [Graduate School: Children and Childhood in Modernization and Society, *Images of Childhood and the Actors of Generational Arrangements*] (pp. 9–18). Wiesbaden: VS.

Bröckling, U. (2007). *Das unternehmerische Selbst: Soziologie einer Subjektivierungsform [The Entrepreneurial Self: Sociology of Forms of Subjectivation].* Frankfurt/M.: Suhrkamp.

Breiteneicher, H. (1971). *Kinderläden: Revolution der Erziehung oder Erziehung zur Revolution? [Kinderläden: Revolution of Education or Education for Revolution?]* Reinbek: Rowohlt.

Bühler-Niederberger, D. (2011). *Lebensphase Kindheit: Theoretische Ansätze, Akteure und Handlungsräume [Childhood as a Phase of Life: Theoretical Approaches, Actors and Arenas of Actions].* Weinheim: Juventa.

Butler, J. (1997). *Excitable Speech. A Politics of the Performative.* New York: Routledge.

Casale, R., Tröhler, D. & Oelkers, J. (2006). *Methoden und Kontexte: Historiographische Probleme der Bildungsforschung [Methods and Contexts: Historiographical Problems of Educational Research].* Göttingen: Wallstein.

Cunningham, H. (2005). *Children and Childhood in Western Society since 1500.* Harlow: Pearson Longman.

Esser, F. (2013). *Das Kind als Hybrid. Empirische Kinderforschung (1896–1914) [The Child as a Hybrid. Empirical Child Study (1896–1914)].* Weinheim, München: Beltz Juventa.

Fthenakis, W. & Textor, M. R. (Eds.). (2000). *Pädagogische Ansätze im Kindergarten [Pedagogical Approaches in the Kindergarten].* Weinheim: Beltz.

Hagener, M. (2010). *Der Hauslehrer: Die Geschichte eines Kriminalfalls [The Private Tutor: History of a Criminal Case].* Berlin: Suhrkamp.

Haraway, D. (1988). Situated knowledges: the science question in feminism and the privilege of partial perspectives. *Feminist Studies, 14*(3), 575–595.

Honig, M. -S. (1999). *Entwurf einer Theorie der Kindheit [Sketch of a Theory of Childhood].* Frankfurt/M.: Suhrkamp.

Honig, M. -S. (2009). How is the child constituted in childhood studies? In J. Qvortrup, W. A. Corsaro & M. -S. Honig (Eds.), *The Palgrave Handbook of Childhood Studies* (pp. 62–77). Houndmills: Palgrave Macmillan.

Jenks, C. (Ed.). (1982). *The Sociology of Childhood: Essential Readings.* Aldershot: Avbury.

Kauders, A. (2011). Drives in dispute: the West German student movement, psychoanalysis, and the search for a new emotional order, 1967–1971. *Central European History, 44,* 1–21.

Key, E. (1902/1992). *Das Jahrhundert des Kindes [The Century of the Child].* Neu herausgegeben und mit einem Nachwort von Ulrich Herrmann. Weinheim: Beltz.

Key, E. (1909). *The Century of the Child.* New York: G. P. Putnam.

Landwehr. A. (2009). *Historische Diskursanalyse [Historical Discourse Analyses].* Frankfurt/M., New York: Beck.

Mierendorff, J. (2014). Die wohlfahrtsstaatliche Kindheit (1914–1945) [The Childhood of the Welfare State (1914–1945)]. In M. S. Baader, F. Esser & W. Schröer (Eds.), *Kindheiten in der Moderne: Eine Geschichte der Sorge* [*Childhood in the Modern Era. A History of Care*] (pp. 20–30). Frankfurt/M.: Campus.

Mollenhauer, K. (1968). *Erziehung und Emanzipation: Polemische Skizzen* [*Education and Emancipation: Polemic Sketches*]. Munich: Juventa.

Neill, A. S. (1969). *Theorie und Praxis der antiautoritären Erziehung* [*Theory and Practice of Anti-authoritarian Education*]. Reinbek: Rowohlt.

Niehuss, M. (2001). *Familie, Frau und Gesellschaft: Studien zur Strukturgeschichte der Familie in Westdeutschland 1945–1960* [*Family, Woman and Society: Studies of the History of Family in Western Germany 1945–1960*]. Göttingen: Vandenhoeck & Ruprecht.

Oelkers, J. (2011). *Eros und Herrschaft: Die dunklen Seiten der Reformpädagogik* [*Eros and Power. The Dark Side of Progressive Education*]. Weinheim: Beltz.

Prout, A. (2000). Childhood bodies: construction, agency and hybridity. In A. Prout (Ed.), *The body, childhood and society* (pp. 1–18). Houndmills: Palgrave Macmillan.

Prout, A. (2003). Kinder-Körper: Konstruktion, Agency und Hybridität [Children's bodies: Construction, agency and hybridity]. In H. Hengst & H. Kelle (Eds.), *Kinder-Körper-Identitäten* [*Children, Bodies and Identities*] (pp. 33–50). Weinheim: Juventa.

Qvortrup, J., Corsaro, A. W. & Honig, M. -S. (Eds.). (2009). *The Palgrave Handbook of Childhood Studies.* Houndmills: Palgrave Macmillan.

Raphael, L. (1996). Die Verwissenschaftlichung des Sozialen als methodische und konzeptionelle Herausforderung für eine Sozialgeschichte des 20. Jahrhunderts [The scientification of the social as methodological and conceptual challenge of a social history of the 20th century]. *Geschichte und Gesellschaft, 22*(2), 165–193.

Renner, K. J. (2015). The ambiguous role of agency in childhood studies. *Child,* special issue of *WSQ,* 43(1/2), 304–307.

Richter, D. (1987). *Das fremde Kind: Zur Entstehung der Kindheitsbilder des bürgerlichen Zeitalters* [*The Strange Child: The Making of Images of Childhood in the Bourgeois Era*]. Frankfurt/M.: Fischer.

Sager, C. (2015). *Das aufgeklärte Kind: Zur Geschichte der bundesrepublikanischen Sexualaufklärung (1950–2010)* [*The Sexual Educated Child. A History of the Sexual Education in Western Germany (1950–2010)*]. Bielefeld: transcript.

Schlegel, F. (1988). *Kritische Schriften und Fragmente in sechs Vol. (Vol. 2: Athenäums-Fragmente)* [*Critical Scriptures and Fragments in Six Volumes. (Volume 2: Athenäums Fragments)*]. E. Behler & H. Eichner (Eds.). Paderborn: Schöningh.

Schleiermacher, F. (1989). *Die Weihnachtsfeier* [*The Festival of Christmas*]. Zürich: Manesse.

Seifert, C. (2004). *Wenn du lächelst, bist du schöner! Kindheit in den 50er und 60er Jahren* [*When you are laughing, you are more beautiful*]. Munich: dtv.

Seifert, M. (1970). *Kinderschule Frankfurt, Eschersheimer Landstraße. Vorgänge: Eine kulturpolitische Korrespondenz* [*Children's School Francfort, Eschersheimer Landstrasse (Landstreet). Events: Cultural Political Correspondences*], 5, 158–162.

Stiller, G. & Kilian, S. (1973). *Nein-Buch für Kinder: Hinterher ist man schlauer* [*The No-book for Children. Afterwards You Are More Intelligent*]. Weinheim: Beltz & Gelberg.

Zimmer, J. (2007). *Das kleine Handbuch zum Situationsansatz* [*The little handbook for the situational approach*]. Berlin: Cornelsen.

Chapter 10

Martha Muchow's research on children's life space

A classic study on childhood in the light of the present

Günter Mey

In the scope of Childhood Studies, the methodological claim will be made here that childhood research is not research about children so much as research from the point of view of children. This contribution connects these considerations to certain issues of developmental research by discussing the study "The Life Space of the Urban Child" conducted by Martha Muchow in the 1920s to 1930s. Muchow's innovative design of combining various methods (e.g. cartography, interviews, essay writing and various observations) is an outstanding example of how studies can be conducted in such a way as to obtain a complete picture of a complex psychological phenomenon, to the extent that these various methods provide different perspectives of the topic at hand. Going beyond the question of how we collect data, Muchow also stressed that research into children must involve a specific adult (researcher) and a specific child and that a simplistic view of children needs to be overcome. Taking this into account, this contribution discusses the premise that it is easy to make statements about seeing the world through their eyes, but that we have to recognise the differences between how adults and children perceive things. In particular, the point is stressed regarding how far statements made by adults about children can be seen as statements of a child's point of view. In contrast to widely used models, which either reconstruct childhood from the adults' points of view or against the background of the individual's own childhood memory, this contribution argues for consequently considering childhood as a construction created by different generational constellations.

Introduction

In recent years, it has become almost self-evident to research explicitly into the child's perspective rather than researching about children. This shift in research direction has established itself particularly in the context that emerged in Great Britain and Scandinavia in the mid-1980s with the involvement of Sociology and Education Studies under the label of "Childhood Studies", which then, in the 1990s, extended to many other countries (James et al., 1998; Corsaro, 2005; Qvortrup et al., 2011; Woodhead & Montgomery, 2003).

Developmental Psychology was not immediately involved in the formation of Childhood Studies, and indeed there were initially strong critiques of (mainstream) Developmental Psychology (e.g. Mayall, 1996; Burman, 2005) from within Childhood Studies. Nevertheless, conceptualisations from within Developmental Psychology did provide a productive series of points of contact to the research direction of Childhood Studies. This is particularly true since the traditional conceptualisation of *development* and its grounding in an exclusively biological idea of maturity has become less popular within mainstream Developmental Psychology itself. This has been the case for a long time in critical Developmental Psychology or discursive Developmental Psychology, or more generally in cultural Developmental Psychology – even in this area of the discipline the focus is now placed on the idea that children are (self-)effective and capable of agency.

In the course of this review, older studies from the early phase of Developmental Psychology were rediscovered, and it became clear that the "grandfathers" (and in this context in particular, the "grandmothers") of the discipline had at their disposal a separate repertoire of methods through which they investigated the child and its life-world *more closely* (Mey, 2000, 2010).

As diary studies defined the developmental research on childhood, it was particularly those early works that experienced a renaissance, not only because they permitted the representation of complex developmental processes, but also because they did more justice to the child's experience and perspective. The works of Clara and William Stern and their rigorous, long-term observation of the development of their three children (1965 [1907]; see Lamiell, 2010) can be highlighted in this context. In addition, there was much regard for Kurt Lewin and his filmic studies of *Das Kind und seine Welt* (*The Child and Its World*) directed by Eberhard Frowein (1931). Lewin's film – only rediscovered at the end of the 1970s – made the child's specific life-worlds vividly accessible (van Elteren, 1992). Lev Vygotsky needs to be included amongst these figures, as he stands for the development of a culture-oriented (developmental) psychology (Valsiner, 2000), as does the most well-known developmental psychologist, Jean Piaget (1929), who has been re-read and reinterpreted in terms of ethnography (Duveen, 2000).

The following contribution examines Martha Muchow's study, "The life space of the urban child" (Muchow & Muchow, 1935), which was carried out in the 1920s and 1930s at the Hamburg Institute for Psychology. The Institute was directed by William Stern and was one of the most significant centres for research into pedagogical and developmental psychology at the time (Kreppner, 2005). Muchow's study is typical of research into psychological/pedagogical approaches to children and young people that were shaped in the Weimar era (Billmann-Mahecha, 2015; Krepper, 2015).

This chapter begins by briefly introducing Muchow's work, as well as demonstrating its unique qualities, namely its view of the child as agent, and the incorporation of that perspective into her analytical method. Furthermore, this contribution reflects on the construction of children within childhood research, the way in which this is shaped in specific historical contexts, and how children, either explicitly or implicitly, are ascribed a particular subject position.

A classic and its (non-)reception

Muchow's work on the city as the life-world of children began in the Hamburg district of Barmbek in the late 1920s. In collaboration with her students, Muchow dedicated herself for many years to the observation of children in this working-class area. She sought to make visible not only the experience of how children use the places at their disposal, but also how children of differing ages (from kindergarten age to the onset of puberty) generally perceive and adapt public space (streets and squares), and how children seek out adult-regulated places and orient themselves in this *adult* world.

Since Martha Muchow committed suicide in 1933, in the face of the drastically changing political climate of the National Socialist regime and the fierce denunciations made against her, the results of this research were only published posthumously by her brother, Hans Heinrich, in 1935 (Muchow & Muchow, 1935). For a long time the publication was forgotten, which also says much about how work and researchers denigrated by National Socialism were dealt with in the post-war era in Germany (Geuter, 1993 [1988]). This was the fate not only of Muchow, but also of Lewin, Stern, and many other researchers. Muchow's "Life Space" study was only rediscovered and reprinted by Jürgen Zinnecker in the 1970s (Muchow & Muchow, 1978 [1935]). Since then it has been republished in 1998 and 2012, and is considered a milestone in studies of children's life-worlds. In terms of Muchow's work in non-German speaking countries, the "Life Space" study has only recently appeared in English for the first time – with a scholarly apparatus providing a commentary and extrapolations from the perspectives of psychology, pedagogy and sociology (Mey & Günther, 2015).

Muchow's study is now receiving greater attention, since her work was innovative not only in the first third of the twentieth century, due to its research object and method, but also because, at the time of its first reprint more than 40 years later, it stimulated research into socialisation processes (Zinnecker, 1978), which investigated the everyday life of children in urban environments (Zinnecker, 1998). Within psychology, the study was – alongside its reception in the field of the "history of psychology" (e.g. Bringmann, Lück, Miller & Early, 1997; Miller, 1997) – highly valued in the field of Environment and Development, which was becoming established in the 1980s (Görlitz, Harloff, Mey & Valsiner, 1998; Wohlwill, 1985; Mey, 2001). Following on from this reception, the work was taken up within a variety of disciplinary contexts, thanks to its understanding of children as *individual agents*, of peer groups or children's culture and the processes of (self-)formation and the appropriation of life-worlds (which Muchow describes as "creative transformation" ["*Umschaffen*"]). (For a contemporary overview of the impact of the study, see Faulstich-Wieland & Faulstich, 2012; Behnken & Zinnecker, 2015; Mey, 2012.)[1]

Muchow's view that the conventional research question of showing "how the city – as a particular world – is able to influence and shape the young people who live in it" (Muchow & Muchow, 2015 [1935], p. 63) was "insufficient, and possibly even wrong in the long term" (p. 63), led to her formulating the following shift in perspective:

> Hence the objective was no longer to investigate how a described life in a city influences children who live there, but to show how children transform their "city" into their environment, and how thereupon the "world lived by the child" represents the city. (pp. 63–64)

Muchow's "re-discoverer", Zinnecker (1978), saw that she called for the overcoming of the reductive assumptions underpinning research into environments, social groups and milieus. Of particular importance was the way she broadened the partial, narrow view of familial and pedagogical socialising bodies, precisely because the study revealed the importance of "street socialization" and highlighted the relevance of developmental spaces that were created and occupied by the children themselves. Muchow's early work already contains issues of theoretical frameworks that were programmatically formulated in the 1980s: These "new" positions emphasise the individual as a "productive processor of internal and external reality" – as outlined by Hurrelmann (1983) – or understand children "as producers of their own development", as introduced by Lerner (1982).

Alongside this new understanding of the subject, Muchow also proposed an altered methodological approach in which observation, interviews and essays were triangulated in order to do justice to different modes of urban perception. Following on from a series of theoretical considerations dealing with Stern's critical personalism, his concept of "personal world" (Stern, 1930), and J. J. von Uexküll's (1921) concept of *Umwelt* (environment), as well as Muchow's engagement with phenomenology, Muchow's investigation into the "Life space of the urban child" was conducted in three specific steps: First, the life space "in which someone lives"; second, the life space "that someone experiences"; and third, the life space "that someone lives". Specific but related methods were used to access each of these life spaces: All three life spaces were formulated to assist in communicating a complex image of the places where children gather, of their activities at these different places and, above all, of the manner in which they *adapt* and transform ("*umschaffen*") these places. Using pre-prepared city maps, children were asked to draw the places they *knew* well, such as where they played and met with friends, as well as the places they *did not know as well*, for example, places where they did not spend much time. The children were asked to use different colours to indicate the relevance of these different places. The researchers explored the life space that the children experienced by interviewing the children about the location and characteristics of their play spaces and other play areas, as well as about the nature of the games they played there. These questions were supplemented with written materials, such as essays on the theme "What did you do last Sunday?" The life space in which the children *lived* formed the main part of Muchow's study. In order to explore this space, the behaviour of the children was observed during a variety of times of the day, days of the week and weather conditions, recording how they dealt with that part of the urban environment. Muchow selected different, contrasting places – playgrounds, a wharf/harbour area, a quiet street, a thoroughfare, a department store, and so on – to gain a comprehensive insight into the variety that comprised "The life space of the urban child".

In all the descriptions of how children appropriate their city environments/life-worlds, what becomes apparent is Muchow's determination to show "that there is no 'space independent of the subject'" (Muchow & Muchow, 2015 [1935], p. 141), as well as the fact that the world of children and the world of adults is clearly different, because they relate to the world in different ways. According to Muchow, we recognise the "true 'life space' of the urban child":

> [o]nly when we see how children deal with particular and substantially characterized pieces of adult environment, and how this results in a totally different observational structure of how they 're-live' a certain urban section into their world. (p. 143)

This life space – and Muchow wishes to emphasise this – "is not constructed alongside that of urban adults (since much of the adult world is also lived in by the children!), but is superimposed, or better, interspersed" (p. 144). The reform pedagogue Muchow, who remains attentive to how the social relationship between children and adults (and pedagogues) is formed, calls at the same time for a *different* way of seeing children's autonomy, and to take children seriously in their unique individuality.

In particular, her method expresses the attempt to turn towards everyday experiences, and to orient itself around the subject's perspective and the reconstruction of that perspective. This attitude is evident in the comments of Annelise Westermann, who participated in the study as a research assistant:

> Thus I learned to always describe things very precisely, to always speak of the individual child. Its world and its experiences had to be respected. All in all, our motto was to start out with experiences – to ferret them out, which was a matter of course at the time, or at least an aim that was seriously pursued, and to accompany life's turns throughout our research, without smoothing things out too much. (1979, p. 58)

Taken as a whole, the research programme of that time can be characterised as a form of qualitative research (Mey, 2015) shaped from the perspective of the subject. It also organises its applied and combined methods through the use of contrasting sites of investigation and presents an analysis that reveals moments of a "thick description" (Geertz, 1973) – which "even between the lines do not betray any sense of prescription" (Billmann-Mahecha, 1994, p. 214).

Michael-Sebastian Honig explicitly recognises the value of the "Life Space" study when he observes that Muchow succeeded "in perceiving the world 'with the eyes of the children' and representing this 'child's perspective'" (1999, p. 37). Of particular significance for Honig is the "ambiguity, seldom acknowledged, but important for the methodology of childhood research, of the reform-pedagogical focus for children, that the recognition of the individuality of children includes an emphasis on the difference between adults and children" (p. 37).

Reflections on the structuring of research situations

Since researchers are always also adults who live daily lives as researchers in their field of research and act as non-researchers in everyday situations, the following reflections are made in order to explain why Muchow's direction is absolutely necessary. We need to understand why childhood research (meaning both the choice and application of methods) should be shaped in terms of a self-reflexive approach. We also need to grasp why the difference between adults and children must be insisted upon and, correspondingly, why one's own assumptions, including unexamined preconceptions about the "other", must be interrogated.

An instructive example is provided by Franz Breuer (2001) with regard to his analysis of child sport cultures. In his preliminary considerations, he assumed that children tended to "feel 'intimidated' when coming into contact with adults who were not known to them" (p. 21), and he suggested methodological arrangements to remedy this. These included avoiding the use of the term "interview" in front of the children; instead, they were more circumspectly told that the situation was about "talking with them about their sporting activities" (p. 21). In addition, a technical arrangement was facilitated through which small, inconspicuous recording devices were used, so that the child's "willingness to converse" was not diminished. The fact that this *child-appropriate* process failed to have the desired result became clear to Breuer through some of the children's reactions,

> with which we hadn't reckoned [...]. After word had got around in the location where we were investigating children's sports activities that people/ adults were running round carrying out interviews, there was frequently a "scramble" amongst the children wanting to take part in the process. It was the children themselves who introduced the term "interview": "I would also like to be interviewed", and the like. Some of the children expressed their disappointment that during the conversations a proper or large-scale

microphone wasn't being used. Many children asked when and whether the recording would be "broadcast". (p. 21)

This example illustrates that the *child adequacy* of any method can hardly be answered unambiguously once and for all. Each evaluation of a method as *child adequate* necessarily contains preconceptions about children and childhood arising from the evaluation's particular historical context. Through a comparison of German childhood research at the beginning and the end of the twentieth century, Jürgen Zinnecker (1999) has shown that, for example, the relationship between political and psychological/pedagogical motives has become reversed. Today – also under the influence of legislative regulation (e.g. the UN Convention on the Rights of the Child) – the principle is foregrounded that children have a right "to be heard and to express their view of the world" (p. 75). Zinnecker correspondingly predicts that:

> The design of research projects will as a result in future be interrogated as to whether they respect the human rights of children. Is the voice of the child being heard? Is the research conducted with the "informed consent" of the children? Are the children able to participate in the evaluation according to their ability to do so? (p. 75; cf. Alderson, 1995; Alderson & Morrow, 2011).

Following Zinnecker's point of view, the difference between earlier research positions and those of today is visible in the work of Clara and William Stern (1965 [1907]), the latter having been Martha Muchow's mentor, as mentioned above. Stern and Stern emphasised at the beginning of the previous century that children should not be informed of the purpose of the research. (The idea that they could be actively involved in shaping or partly conducting the study was not one that occurred to the researchers at that time.) The authors explained their precautionary measures as follows:

> This ignorance seems to us to be an absolute requirement of the research projects, on the one hand, in order not to damage the character of the children, and on the other, to ensure that the children's expressions have the genuineness that derives from naivety. (Stern & Stern, 1965 [1907], p. iv)

To this extent, the construction of children and childhood plays a role not only at the stage of data interpretation (regardless of whether the data is qualitative or quantitative), but also already at the data collection stage, and presumably even beforehand, at the point of refining the research question and focusing on questions that appear interesting or are indeed answerable at all. These constructions are an expression of prevalent images of children/childhood as empirically comprehensible conceptions and historically determined constructions.

From such a point of view, particular perspectives clearly emerge in the study of the "The life space of the urban child". For example, Imbke Behnken and Michael-Sebastian Honig ask whether one can assume in Muchow's work that there is a "naturalising" of the notion of the actor (2012, p. 12) in the way that she sees children as individuals, even when she is dealing with groups of children or a theoretical and empirical understanding of children and/or their culture as "social places". In this context, Behnken and Honig point out that, as Muchow's work is embedded in a "heritage of reform pedagogy", she "personalises social relationships and somehow sets children in opposition to the social world as a kind of ideal collective operating from an Archimedean point of view, so to speak" (p. 12).

On the question of conducting research "from the children's perspective"

From this point of view, we must come to a second question that Martha Muchow addresses even if only implicitly, but which is central to contemporary childhood research. The question regards how far adult statements about children and childhood are – or can be – statements made from a child's perspective, as opposed to simply statements *about* children made by adult researchers (see also Spyrou and Warming in this volume). In order to obtain an adequate answer to this question, there must be full disclosure on the researcher's part about the presumptions that influence the conceptualisation of the research (situation), as in the case of Breuer's work. Since childhood research is research that is mediated, structured (sometimes in advance), and produced by adults, understanding the relationship between adult researchers and children as research subjects, as well as the role of the researchers, becomes as important as understanding the researched child itself. Childhood can only be understood as something that is constructed through generational relations.

Without an explicit regard for how generational relations construct notions of childhood, children's perspectives will ultimately be judged by comparative frameworks that can only lead to statements *about* children. Two fundamental points to consider here are: (a) childhood is perceived through one's own adult perspective; and (b) childhood is frequently related to one's own memories of the experience of having been a child. Both comparative frameworks may fall back on empirical knowledge about children, e.g. from other studies. In the same way, the observations may be shaped by a partially implicit understanding of an *ideal* childhood.

With regard to (a) (the evaluation from an adult perspective), the difficulty is that differences, or the differentiated nature of the child (also in comparison with adult standards), is viewed and described as deficient, because these

> are [exclusively] measured against the restrictive conditions of formalised adult communication (the dominance of ground-rules, formal value

systems, a rationalised view of the world [...]). A large part of the adult misunderstanding of children is to be understood as the result of an all too rigid insistence on adult-centred conventions of communication and of what is considered normal behaviour. (Hülst, 2012, p. 65)

This mode of observation was characteristic, above all, of traditional approaches within Developmental Psychology (and is of course prevalent today in everyday discourse, as well as being reproduced in pedagogical institutions, either implicitly or, indeed, sometimes quite overtly). It expresses itself in descriptions such as "children cannot yet do a particular task" or "children make mistakes" or "children are limited in what they can do", and so on.

In this respect, conceptions of children are problematic when children are understood too strongly in terms of the development of a more or less scientific and rational adult conception of the world. This fact explains why, within Childhood Studies, children are described, following Jens Qvortrup (1994), as "beings" rather than "becomings" (even if this is a distinction that tends towards not-infrequent exaggeration, which is in itself problematic), because within a rational adult perspective or comparative framework, no one asks whether the child's view of the world and itself possesses its own logic, or whether children's forms of representations should act as a starting point – and one that is quite differently configured to that of adults.

In relation to (b) (the recollections of one's own childhood), one first of all has to bid farewell to the illusion of "faithfully preserved memories of one's own youth and childhood", as Muchow's contemporary, Siegfried Bernfeld, stated (2010 [1922]) in the context of analysing introspection. In contrast to an earlier episte-mological and anamnestic optimism, today, cognitive and autobiographical models in Developmental Psychology assume that experiences and all forms of thought (the construction of meaning) made in earlier life cannot be recalled exactly by adults (Oswald & Krappmann, 1995). Yet, even if we were to assume that ideal introspective memories of childhood experiences were accessible, then this would mean disregarding the fact that childhood and children's experiences vary according to historical conditions, and that the adults' childhood is different from "child-hood as experienced today". Such problematic confusions are common, as, for example, Anton Bucher (2001) shows through his interviews with pedagogues, which demonstrate that the majority of children today are viewed as less careful, less robust and less attentive. In contrast, these pedagogues describe their own childhood in considerably more positive terms. In various research and everyday contexts, one can see such conceptions and presumptions according to which pre-vious generations view their own childhood and youth more positively than that of those who came after them, and analyse the members of that later generation more negatively (and in part as deficient, since they are uninterested and apolitical).

Both comparative frameworks allow us to see that research *from the child's perspective* has its own limits if it does not put the encounter between adult researchers and researched children at the centre of methodological reflection. The shared production of a generational hierarchy has to be made the starting point for the reconstruction of childhood and the description of children. Instead of a naive attitude that presumes that we, as adult researchers, can "really" adopt the perspectives of children, can see the children's worlds "through their eyes", and can speak with the "voices of the children", we need instead to make it clear *who is speaking*. Only under this precondition can we make sure that researchers *give* children a voice – nothing more, but also nothing less.

Taking this into account, all and any (well-intentioned) approaches to the participation of children must rethink their objective of "giving the children a voice" and aim for research *with* children instead. The idea of allowing children to participate directly (or more directly) in the research activity, for example, or to design the research questions together with the researchers, or to shape the research process in conjunction with them – as research collaborators (Porter et al., 2010; Hart, 1997) – needs further investigation. No matter how necessary it is to integrate the interests and views of children (potentially also to share some of the "power", and thus go beyond Muchow's conception of research), one still has to be aware of differences within social categorisation. Children, whether they collaborate or not, are, when all is said and done, children, and adult researchers remain adults, with their own specific perspectives, subjectivities and social and cultural definitions.

Concluding remarks

The observation that children are agents was new for its time in Muchow's work; however, contemporary childhood research may take this assumption for granted. How far and in what way the child is considered to be an agent, or indeed the general conception of agency, differs greatly between then and now. The terminology, however, remains very much the same. Originally it denoted an emphasis on thinking *from the child's perspective* (and acting upon this pedagogically, by placing the child at the centre of the research). This was then addressed in Developmental Psychology approaches underpinned by theories of socialisation taking into account child–environment interaction (or transaction). This was also acknowledged in the recognition that children are agents in their own development, and we now see this in the differential understanding of children as beings (instead of becomings). This growing differentiation is due in part to the position to which children are ascribed – and is also dependent on the disciplinary perspective in question. The discipline not only establishes the framework within which childhood is understood as an independent life-situation and as a "social space", but also frames studies on childhood, and the perspective taken regarding children and childhood.

In conceiving of childhood research as something that requires an understanding of the differences between children and adults, and of childhood as part of the generational hierarchy, it is important to conceptualise research from the children's perspective in relational terms. This understanding of the interactive relationship between researchers and their subject has been formulated program-matically for a long time in qualitative social research (Mruck & Mey, 2010) and finds expressions in its fundamentals (in particular, the principles of openness, foreignness/otherness and communication; Mey, 2010). At the same time, one needs to keep in mind that, depending on the theoretical standpoint, the concep-tion of the research subject may be formulated in quite different ways.

This kind of reflection on perspective is by no means novel: it can be found in many places. Alongside sociological research dealing with childhood, as well as that conducted with qualitative methodology, this can also be seen in the realm of phenomenology (e.g. Graumann & Kruse, 1998), which was also relevant for Muchow; she completed her doctoral studies in this field. Merleau-Ponty (2010), in a critical reply to Piaget, his predecessor as the Chair of Psychology in Geneva, argued that science from an adult perspective can *only* ever speak *about* children and what that science considers children to be. In pedagogical phenomenology, Meyer-Drawe (1984/2001) emphasises individuality, foreignness/otherness and difference, even in children's sense of their own bodies, as something that marks children and adults as distinct.

In other words, we need to keep the difference between adults and children perpetually in view, in line with works such as Martha Muchow's. Doing so, as Behnken and Honig (2012, p. 13) observe, maintains the opportunity "for perceiving children *as children,* and it also generates practical distinctions that are rendered objective within the concept of knowledge termed 'child'". But beyond this, we can also focus on those differences, as Beatrice Hungerland (2015) concludes in her contribution on "Children as actors – Muchow's life space study and its implications for 'new' childhood studies":

> Different from many researchers, Muchow did not match the children in her study with prevalent ideas of what defined good and proper childhood. The children she met in the streets were working-class children who lived under tough social conditions. Although these underprivileged children lived in ways that did not meet the ideals of middle-class childhood, she focused on their potentials and competences and was curious to learn about how they got along. (p. 264)

As Hungerland puts it, future studies following Muchow's approach and taking into consideration the perspectives of children may not only help to answer questions about disparities between living conditions of adults and children and about diversities among children, but moreover at the same time may serve to enhance their social position.

Note

1 See also the documentary film *Auf den Spuren von Martha Muchow* (*In search of Martha Muchow*) (Mey & Wallbrecht, 2016; incl. English subtitles).

References

Alderson, P. (1995). *Listening to Children: Children, Ethics and Social Research.* Ilford: Barnardo's.

Alderson, P. & Morrow, V. (2011). *The Ethics of Research with Children and Young People: A Practical Handbook.* London: Sage Publications.

Behnken, I. & Honig, M.-S. (2012). "Der Lebensraum des Großstadtkindes": Eine Pionierleistung der Kindheitsforschung [The Life Space of the Urban Child. Pioneer Work in Childhood Research]. In M. Muchow & H. H. Muchow (new expanded edition, I. Behnken & M.-S. Honig, eds.), *Der Lebensraum des Großstadtkindes* [*The Life Space of the Urban Child*] (pp. 9–16). Weinheim: Juventa.

Behnken, I. & Zinnecker, J. (2015). Martha Muchow and Hans Heinrich Muchow: the life space of the urban child – the loss and discovery, connections and requisites. In G. Mey & H. Günther (Eds.), *The Life Space of the Urban Child: Perspectives on Martha Muchow's Classic Study* (pp. 3–27). New Brunswick, London: Transaction Publisher.

Bernfeld, S. (2010 [1922]). *Vom Gemeinschaftsleben der Jugend: Beiträge zur Jugendforschung* [*Community Life of the Youth. Contributions to Youth Research*] (new edition). Charleston, South Carolina (BiblioLabs LLC): BiblioBazaar.

Billmann-Mahecha, E. (1994). Qualitative Sozialforschung in der Psychologie der Weimarer Republik: Beispiele aus der Kinder- und Jugendpsychologie [Qualitative social research in psychology in the Weimar Republic. Examples taken from child and adolescent psychology]. *Psychologie und Geschichte, 5*(3/4), 208–217.

Billmann-Mahecha, E. (2015). Martha Muchow's life space study in the context of contemporary childhood and adolescent research. In G. Mey & H. Günther (Eds.), *The Life Space of the Urban Child: Perspectives on Martha Muchow's Classic Study* (pp. 47–59). New Brunswick, London: Transaction Publisher.

Breuer, F. (2001). Qualitativ-methodische Untersuchung von Kinderwelten [Qualitative Inquiry of Children's Life Worlds]. In G. Mey (Ed.), *Qualitative Forschung in der Entwicklungspsychologie. Potentiale, Probleme, Perspektiven* [*Research report of the Department of Psychologie of the School of Social Sciences, University of Technology, Berlin*]. Forschungsbericht aus der Abteilung Psychologie im Institut für Sozialwissenschaften der Technischen Universität Berlin, 1, 19–23. Retrieved from http://psydok.sulb.uni-saarland.de/volltexte/2004/336/ (accessed 21 October 2015).

Bringmann, W. G., Lück, H. E., Miller, R. & Early, C. E. (Eds.). (1997). *Pictorial History of Psychology.* Chicago: Quintessenz.

Bucher, A. (2001). "Die Kinder sind nicht mehr so glücklich wie wir". Kindheitsglück in der Sicht von ErzieherInnen ["Today Children Are Not As Happy As We Were." Childhood Happiness from the Educators' Perspective]. In I. Behnken & J. Zinnecker (Eds.), *Kinder, Kindheit, Lebensgeschichte: Ein Handbuch* [*Children, Childhood, Life Story*] (pp. 33–46). Seelze-Velber: Kallmeyer.

Burman, E. (2005). Engendering development: some methodological perspectives on child labour. *Forum Qualitative Sozialforschung/Forum: Qualitative Social* Research, 7(1), Art 1. Retrieved from http://nbn-resolving.de/urn:nbn:de:0114-fqs060120 (accessed 21 October 2015).

Corsaro, W. A. (2005). *The Sociology of Childhood.* Thousand Oaks: Pine Forge Press.

Duveen, G. (2000). Piaget ethnographer. *Social Science Information, 39*(1), 79–98.

Faulstich-Wieland, H. &. Faulstich, P. (2012). *Lebenswege und Lernräume: Martha Muchow: Leben, Werk und Weiterwirken* [*Life Paths and Learning Spaces: Martha Muchow: Life, Work, Outreach*]. Weinheim: Beltz Juventa.

Geertz, C. (1973). Thick description: toward an interpretative theory of culture. In C. Geertz (Ed.), *The Interpretation of Cultures: Selected Essays* (pp. 3–20). New York: Basic Books.

Geuter, U. (1993 [1988]). *The Professionalization of Psychology in Nazi Germany* (translated by Richard Holmes). Cambridge: Cambridge University Press.

Görlitz, D., Harloff, H. J., Mey, G. & Valsiner, J. (Eds.). (1998). *Children, Cities, and Psychological Theories: Developing Relationships.* Berlin: de Gruyter.

Graumann, C. F. & Kruse, L. (1998). Children's environments. The phenomenological approach. In D. Görlitz, H. J. Harloff, G. Mey & J. Valsiner (Eds.), *Children, Cities, and Psychological Theories: Developing Relationships* (pp. 357–369). Berlin: de Gruyter.

Hart, R. A. (1997). *Children's Participation: The Theory and Practice of Involving Young Citizens in Community Development and Environmental Care.* London: Earthscon/UNICEF.

Honig, M.-S. (1999). Forschung "vom Kinde aus"? Perspektivität in der Kindheitsforschung [Research "Taken From Child's Perspective"? Perspectivity in the Childhood Research]. In M.-S. Honig, A. Lange & H. R. Leu (Eds.), *Aus der Perspektive von Kindern? Zur Methodologie der Kindheitsforschung [From the Children's Point of View? The Methodology of Childhood Studies]* (pp. 33–50). Weinheim: Juventa.

Hülst, D. (2012). Das wissenschaftliche Verstehen von Kindern [Understanding Children Scientifically]. In F. Heinzel (Ed.), *Methoden der Kindheitsforschung: Ein Überblick über Forschungszugänge zur kindlichen Perspektive [Methods of Childhood Studies: An Overview of Research Approaches to Children's Perspective]* (2nd ed., pp. 52–77). Weinheim: Beltz Juventa.

Hungerland, B. (2015). Children as actors – Muchow's life space study and its implications for "new" childhood studies. In G. Mey & H. Günther (Eds.), *The Life Space of the Urban Child: Perspectives on Martha Muchow's Classic Study* (pp. 251–266). New Brunswick, London: Transaction Publisher.

Hurrelmann, K. (1983). Das Modell des produktiv realitätsverarbeitenden Subjekts in der Sozialisationsforschung [The individual as a productive processor of internal and external reality. A model in socialisation research]. *Zeitschrift für Sozialisationsforschung und Erziehungssoziologie, 3,* 91–103.

James, A., Jenks, C. & Prout, A. (1998). *Theorizing Childhood.* Cambridge: Polity Press.

Kreppner, K. (2005). Heinz Werner and the psychological institute in Hamburg. In J. Valsiner (Ed.), *Heinz Werner and Developmental Science* (pp. 55–74). New York: Kluwer Academic/Plenum Publishers.

Kreppner, K. (2015). Martha Muchow – a life devoted to educational enlightenment and to the scientific foundation of understanding children's worlds. In G. Mey & H. Günther (Eds.), *The Life Space of the Urban Child: Perspectives on Martha Muchow's Classic Study* (pp. 29–46). New Brunswick, London: Transaction Publisher.

Lerner, R. M. (1982). Children and adolescents as producers of their own development. *Developmental Review, 2,* 342–370.

Lewin, K. (1931). *Das Kind und die Welt [The Child and the World]* (Director: E. Frowein). Hagen: FernUniversität Hagen.

Lamiell, J. T. (2010). *William Stern (1871–1938): A Brief Introduction to His Life and Works.* Lengerich: Pabst Science Publishers.

Mayall, B. (1996). *Children, Health and Social Order.* Buckingham: Open University Press.

Merleau-Ponty, M. (2010). *Child Psychology and Pedagogy: The Sorbonne Lectures 1949–1952* (translated by Talia Welsh). Evanston, IL: Northwestern University Press.

Mey, G. (2000). Qualitative research and the analysis of processes. Considerations towards a "qualitative developmental psychology", *Forum Qualitative Sozialforschung/Forum: Qualitative Social Research, 1*(1), Art. 10. Retrieved from http://nbn-resolving.de/urn:nbn:de:0114-fqs0001107 (accessed 21 October 2015).

Mey, G. (2001). Auf den Spuren von Martha Muchow [In Search of Martha Muchow]. *Psychologie und Geschichte*, *9*(1–2), 107–122.

Mey, G. (2010). Qualitative developmental psychology. In A. Toomela & J. Valsiner (Eds.), *Methodological Thinking in Psychology: 60 Years Gone Astray?* (pp. 209–230). Charlotte: Information Age Publishers.

Mey, G. (2012). Auf den Pfaden von Martha Muchow [In Search of Martha Muchow]. In M. Muchow & H. H. Muchow (new edition, I. Behnken & M.-S. Honig, eds.), *Der Lebensraum des Großstadtkindes* [*The Life Space of the Urban Child*], (pp. 179–192). Weinheim: Beltz Juventa.

Mey, G. (2013). "Der Lebensraum des Großstadtkindes": Eine Pionierarbeit zu Forschung von kindlichen Lebenswelten ["The life space of the urban child" - A pioneer work for researching children's life worlds]. In K. Westphal & B. Jörissen (Eds.), *Vom Straßenkind zum Medienkind: Raum- und Medienforschung im 21. Jahrhundert* [*From Street Child to Media Child. Space and Media Studies in the 21st Century*] (pp. 22–38). Weinheim: Beltz Juventa.

Mey, G. (2015). Muchows methodological heritage – pioneering qualitative research. In G. Mey & H. Günther (Eds.), *The Life Space of the Urban Child: Perspectives on Martha Muchow's Classic Study* (pp. 235–249). New Brunswick, London: Transaction Publisher.

Mey, G. & Günther, H. (Eds.) (2015). *The Life Space of the Urban Child: Perspectives on Martha Muchow's Classic Study*. New Brunswick. London: Transaction Publisher.

Mey, G. & Wallbrecht, G. (2016). *Auf den Spuren von Martha Muchow* [*In Search of Martha Muchow*] (DVD, 45 min; incl. English subtitles and bonus material). Lengerich: Pabst Science Publishers.

Meyer-Drawe, K. (2001 [1984]). *Leiblichkeit und Sozialität: Phänomenologische Beiträge zu einer pädagogischen Theorie der Inter-Subjektivität* [*Corporeality and sociality: Phenomenological Contributions to an educational theory of inter-subjectivity*] (3rd ed.). Munich: Fink.

Miller, R. (1997). Martha Muchow and concept of life space. In W. G. Bringmann, H. E. Lück, R. Miller & C. E. Early (Eds.), *Pictorial History of Psychology* (pp. 337–341). Chicago: Quintessenz.

Mruck, K. & Mey, G. (2010). Grounded theory and reflexivity. In A. Bryant & K. Charmaz (Eds.), *The Sage Handbook of Grounded Theory: Paperback Version* (pp. 487–510). London: Sage Publications.

Muchow, M. & Muchow, H. H. (1935). *Der Lebensraum des Großstadtkindes* [*The Life Space of the Urban Child*]. Hamburg: Riegel.

Muchow, M. & Muchow, H. H. (1978 [1935]). *Der Lebensraum des Großstadtkindes* [*The Life Space of the Urban Child*] (reprinted version, edited & introduced by J. Zinnecker). Bensheim: päd-extra.

Muchow, M. & Muchow, H. H. (1998 [1935]). *Der Lebensraum des Großstadtkindes* [*The Life Space of the Urban Child*] (reprinted version, edited & introduced by J. Zinnecker). Weinheim: Beltz.

Muchow, M. & Muchow, H. H. (2012 [1935]). *Der Lebensraum des Großstadtkindes* [*The Life Space of the Urban Child*] (new expanded edition, ed. by I. Behnken & M.-S. Honig). Weinheim: Beltz Juventa.

Muchow, M. & Muchow, H. H. (2015 [1935]). The life space of the urban child. In G. Mey & H. Günther (Eds.), *The Life Space of the Urban Child: Perspectives on Martha Muchow's Classic Study* (pp. 61–146). Brunswick: Transaction Publisher.

Oswald, H. & Krappmann, L. (1995). Kinder [Children]. In U. Flick, E.v. Kardorff, H. Keupp, L.v. Rosenstiel & S. Wolff (Eds.), *Handbuch qualitative Sozialforschung* [*Handbook of Qualitative Social Research*] (2nd ed., pp. 355–358). Munich: Beltz/PVU.

Piaget, J. (1929 [1926]). *The Child's Conception of the World*. London: Routledge & Kegan Paul.

Porter, G., Hampshire, K., Bourdillon, M., Robson, E., Munthali, A., Abane, A. & Mashiri, M. (2010). Children as research collaborators: issues and reflections from a mobility study in sub-Saharan Africa. *American Journal for Community Psychology*, 46(1–2), 215–227.

Qvortrup, J. (1994). Introduction. In J. Qvortrup, M. Bardy, G. Sgritta & H. Wintersberger (Eds.), *Childhood Matters: Social Theory, Practice and Politics* (pp. 1–24). Aldershot: Avebury.

Qvortrup, J., Corsaro, W. A., Honig, M.-S. & Valentine, G. (Eds.). (2011). *The Palgrave Handbook of Childhood Studies*. London: Palgrave Macmillan.

Scholz, G. (1994). *Die Konstruktion des Kindes: Über Kinder und Kindheit* [*The Construction of the Child. About Children and Childhood*]. Opladen: Westdeutscher Verlag.

Stern, W. (1930). *Studien zur Personwissenschaft: Erster Teil: Personalistik als Wissenschaft* [*Studies of Personhood: First Part: Personality as Science*]. Leipzig: Barth.

Stern, C. & Stern, W. (1965 [1907]). *Die Kindersprache* [*Children's Speech*]. Darmstadt: Wissenschaftliche Buchgesellschaft.

Uexküll, J. J. v. (1921). *Umwelt und Innenwelt der Tiere* [*Environment and Inner World of Animals*] (2nd rev. ed.). Berlin: J. Springer.

Valsiner, J. (2000). *Culture and Human Development*. London: Sage Publications.

Van Elteren, M. (1992). Kurt Lewin as filmmaker and methodologist. *Canadian Psychology/Psychologie canadienne*, 33(3), 599–608.

Westermann, A. (1979). Auf die Welt eines jeden einzelnen zu achten, war ihr wichtig [Pay attention to the world of each single child—that was important for her] (interviewed by G. Koch). *päd. extra*, 6, 56–58.

Wohlwill, J. F. (Ed.). (1985). Martha Muchow, 1892–1933: her life, work, and contribution to developmental and ecological psychology. *Human Development*, 28, 198–224.

Woodhead, M. & Montgomery, H. (2003). *Understanding Childhood: An Interdisciplinary Approach* (Childhood, Vol. 1). Chichester: Wiley.

Zinnecker, J. (1978). Recherchen zum Lebensraum des Großstadtkindes. Eine Reise in verschüttete Landschaften und Wissenschaftstraditionen [Investigation on the life space of the urban child. A journey into buried life worlds and scientific traditions]. In M. Muchow & H. H. Muchow (reprinted version, edited & introduced by J. Zinnecker), *Der Lebensraum des Großstadtkindes* [*The Life Space of the Urban Child*] (pp. 10–41). Bensheim: päd extra.

Zinnecker, J. (1998). Nachwort am Ende des Jahrhunderts [Epilogue at the end of the century]. In M. Muchow & H. H. Muchow (reprinted version, edited & introduced by J. Zinnecker), *Der Lebensraum des Großstadtkindes* [*The Life Space of the Urban Child*] (pp. 55–66). Weinheim: Juventa.

Zinnecker, J. (1999). Forschen für Kinder – Forschen mit Kindern – Kindheitsforschung: Über die Verbindung von Kindheits- und Methodendiskurs in der neuen Kindheitsforschung zu Beginn und am Ende des 20. Jahrhunderts [Research about children – researching with children – childhood research: Links of the discourses about childhood and methods at the beginning and the end of 20th century]. In M.- S. Honig, A. Lange & H. R. Leu (Eds.), *Aus der Perspektive von Kindern? Zur Methodologie der Kindheitsforschung* [*From the Children's Point of View? The Methodology of Childhood Studies*] (pp. 69–80). Weinheim: Juventa.

Chapter 11

"Children need boundaries"

Concepts of children's agency in German parents' guidebooks since 1950

Beatrice Hungerland

The following chapter starts out from the assumption that children's agency manifests itself in relation to processes of generational ordering. These processes are closely connected to the social order in general, and as key elements of the social hierarchy reveal themselves to be a consistent, if variable, factor. The analysis of parent guidebooks published in Germany from 1950 onwards illustrates the malleability of the concept of children's agency and how this concept corresponds to differing forms of generational order, forms that themselves are influenced by historical events and wide-ranging social discourses. For the period under discussion, we can identify four distinct forms of socially desirable child agency. Into the 1960s, there is the continuation of authoritarian structures of subordination that are only undone in the 1970s through the emergence of democratic family structures informed by a higher degree of pedagogical expertise. A new, more broadly conceived child agency can be seen in the "Kinderladen" and anti-authoritarian education movement, something that, however, has become increasingly constrained since 1990.

The institutionalised generational order determines how far children can operate as actors who play an active role in shaping the social worlds of which they are part – and vice versa. The social categories at stake – children and adults, who possess their own different spheres of action – are perpetually being constructed in the discourses and practices of generational production. "The generational structure depends upon the children's capability for action (as well as upon the others involved); appropriate forms of generational capability for action are determined by the actors' positions within social structures; the historically formed social practices of 'generationing' ensure that structures and capacity for action are (internally) interconnected" (Alanen, 2005, p. 79)[1].

This chapter demonstrates how specific patterns of generational order, as components of an overarching social structure, can either enable or restrict children's capacity for action. Generational order is understood here as a structural element in society, a "core component in social hierarchies" (Bühler-Niederberger, 2011, p. 214) that is characterised as a space of protection and training through the historical, cultural and social institutionalisation of childhood. The basis for this institutionalisation is the social construction of the "otherness" of "the child" (see also Wihstutz in this volume), which can manifest itself in different ways but always serves to justify the particular treatment of children and frames the unique interaction between adults and children as a relationship of care and tutelage.

The analysis here relates to discourses in parent guidebooks, addressed to mothers and fathers, which discuss questions of child pedagogy and childcare (Höffer-Mehlmer, 2003, p. 7). These kinds of books are storehouses of knowledge that bear witness to the norms and values of a particular society, epoch or culture. They can often be used to reconstruct explicit and implicit historical knowledge about pedagogy (e.g. for Germany: Oelkers, 1995; Schmid, 2008; international: Hardyment, 2007; Hulbert, 2003).

In the present study, parent guidebooks serve as data for analysing understandings of childcare and pedagogy, and identifying what these understandings tell us about the legitimation of changing intergenerational power relationships and constructions of children's agency. It takes a discourse analysis approach underpinned by the sociology of knowledge, following Foucault's assumption that in discursive practices, language constructs as forms of knowledge the objects that it describes (Foucault, 1972; Keller, 2007, 2011). The authors of the guidebooks are viewed as purveyors of knowledge, speaking as social actors, experts and representatives of specific discourses and implementing these discourses across institutional and other areas of social practice. "Such actors [...] orient themselves in their (discursive) practice around the rules of the specific field of discourse, for example, the publishing demands of media reporting or of scientific discourse. [...] They are spokespersons and representatives of large social groups" (Keller, 2007, p. 43).

This study does not set out to discover whether the forms of "generationing" recommended in the guidebooks were actually carried out by parents in practice, nor whether children do indeed operate within the spaces of possibility open to them or try to transgress them and thereby use their "agency" to help establish or transform generational structures. The study focuses on identifiable concepts of childhood agency that are situated within broader social structures. Social, political and economic developments leave their mark in emerging conceptions of the generational order and the agency of children. Insights gained into the construction of childhood agency and generational hierarchy will therefore be set alongside broader historical developments (see also Baader in this volume).

The study analyses guidebooks that were published from 1950 onwards in West Germany, taking into account publications that appeared in the unified Federal Republic after 1990. The (West) German discourse corresponds to a supranational development that can be traced in most Western countries (in Europe, the USA), i.e. the transition from authoritarian hierarchical relationships between children and parents to more negotiated generational relationships. This supranational development is evident in the large majority of international guidebooks that were translated into German and published in Germany. At the same time, a national specificity is evident in discussions about generational patterns and childhood agency, one that can be explained by historical developments in Germany from the post-war period onwards through to the unification of the nation in 1990. This discourse is characterised by, amongst other things, a family-focused socialisation of the young child and a fear of child tyrants (Gebhardt, 2009) – which is probably responsible for the emergence of an explicit counter-model in the anti-authoritarian "Kinderladen" movement (Baader, 2014).

The method adopted is based in grounded theory (Strauss & Corbin, 1996). Following the consideration of relevant academic research, the data were framed into an open-ended research question (Hungerland, 2002). Data selection was grounded in theoretical sampling and principles of minimum and maximum variation. Following the detailed analysis of one hypothetically significant document, a further guidebook was chosen for analysis. As a result, it was possible to identify key-related characteristics, to establish a typology and thus classify a specific discourse. Different sources that present new or divergent ideas and concepts were taken into account as a way of capturing the full spectrum of generational relationships. In the period under examination, numerous variations were identified in how children's agency was conceptualised, both in terms of the children's potential as well as the advice that was presented either to enable or restrict this potential.

The analysis here is mainly focused on assertions and proposals regarding the upbringing of babies, infants and pre-school children. Parental care and education are accorded a particularly important role in this first stage of life, as they "lay the foundation stones" on which later socialising institutions can and should build. In addition, the family hierarchy is naturalised more strongly in early childhood by contrast with later years. The child is also unquestioningly seen as a "product" of its parents' care and pedagogical attention.

In what follows, four versions of socially desirable childhood agency in post-war Germany are presented within the context of each specific generational order. These are typologies of discourse patterns that exist alongside others but can be read, thanks to their fundamental characteristics, as new patterns emerging in a particular period. Evidence for this is provided by one German-language source in each case.

The post-war era and the continuity of authoritarian hierarchical structures

Parent guidebooks published in (West) Germany into the 1960s are marked by the situation of the post-war era and the phase of reconstruction. There are references to material shortages, limited living space, low-technology households and large families. No mention is made of the previous support of large parts of the population for the ideology of the National Socialists. Indeed, the most widely disseminated parent guidebook of the Nazi era, Johanna Haarer's

Die deutsche Mutter und ihr erstes Kind (*The German Mother and Her First Child*, first published in 1934) was edited more for language rather than content when it was republished in post-war Germany (Berger, 2000), right up to 1987, the year of the author's death. It recorded more than 1.2 million sales in that time (Benz, 1988). Haarer's pedagogical ideas, very much in line with NS ideology, can be found – in milder form – in numerous works by other authors of parent guide-books at the time. One can recognise an effort to re-establish normality as quickly as possible after the insecurities of the war years, something that is particularly striking in the focus on the certainties of traditional bourgeois conceptions of the family. It is much less common to come across guidebooks published at this time in Germany that explicitly advocate new conceptions of the family, as was the case in the USA with books that promoted the democratisation of family life or com-municated to parents the insights of developmental psychology (Hulbert, 2003).

In the following detailed analysis of the 480-page guidebook *Mother and Child* (*Mutter und Kind*) by Hannah Uflacker – a standard reference book in West Germany at the time – we see that the guidebook presents clear prescriptions for the organisation of life according to a traditional pattern of generational and gender hierarchy. The child's room for manoeuvre is restricted here in terms of active co-determination within the family.

> If something is forbidden by the parents, then this must be non-negotiable. Any revocation, however well-intentioned, undermines the principles of education. (Uflacker, 1963, p. 444)

The mother is principally responsible for providing for and educating the chil-dren, the father merely a marginal figure. Both help construct the generational hierarchy, even if the full-time mother and the full-time working father have dif-fering levels of contact with the child. As adults, they are equally empowered to assert their authority over the child. The basic assumption is that becoming a member of a community is not a voluntary process, and that parents must estab-lish a hierarchy at an early stage.

> We all have to learn, however, to fit into our community, and nothing creates more problems than a delay in teaching this. (Uflacker, 1963, p. 439)

Punishment, monitoring, regulation and subordination – the subjugation of the child within the generational hierarchy – is the self-evident, unquestioned expres-sion of the social order. Obligatory obedience and adaptation to the hierarchy are the structural limitations of children's agency. The parents are encouraged to establish the unconditional subordination of the child. Otherwise, they are in danger of producing an anti-social egoist.

> The child must never be allowed to assert its will through any form of defi-ance. Most bright children will recognize the effectiveness of this strategy straight away, and quickly become household tyrants. (Uflacker, 1963, p. 432)

Not only will the child tyrannise its parents, but it will have problems in later life. The "natural" fact that parents need to intervene, and monitor and limit the child's room for manoeuvre, is framed in terms of natural metaphors:

> It's up to the parents to decide whether this young child's ground will be fertile or whether the good seeds will be suffocated by weeds. (Uflacker, 1963, p. 436)

The children's independent room for manoeuvre is restricted and directed at this stage in order to enable agency in the future; in other words their ability to act when adults. The prescriptions for adults relate to almost all everyday activities, setting narrow limits for the child within clear and non-negotiable structures that manifest themselves in a strict time regime that gives the parents a high degree of control over the life of the child.

Together with the time that (in particular) the mother spends with the child, "being left to its own devices" is also considered important for the child's development. This time opens up potential space for manoeuvre outside the adults' control; how the children use that time remains a subject of speculation – the guidebook has nothing more to say.

Children's playtime is subject to clear prescriptions, both in terms of its timespan as well as in its purpose and orientation. Play is less about having fun and more about teaching the children about rules and hierarchy. The guidebook demonstrates, moreover, how parents can develop the competence of their children so they can contribute to the family upkeep and harmony. Children should make a contribution to the community and participate by learning to fulfil obligations:

> Obedience has been regarded as one of the most important ways of educating a strong-willed person, but there are other training methods. The first is the performance of duties. In teaching her child to be independent, the mother can see how happy and proud her child feels when it is allowed to help. (Uflacker, 1963, p. 451)

In conclusion, we see that this guidebook – like most of its time – seeks to reproduce a restrictive and hierarchically structured generational order that sets extremely narrow boundaries for children's agency.

Economic miracle and the expansion of education – children become democrats

The Western world's assumption that it was technologically pre-eminent was undermined by the Sputnik crisis in the USA and Western Europe in reaction to the launch of the first Soviet artificial satellite in 1957. The resulting public discussion reflected the conflict between the political systems of capitalism and communism. Demand rose for fundamental reforms to the education system to ensure the supply of qualified human capital (Seiverth, 2007) and the maintenance of the supposed supremacy of capitalism. Education experts in West Germany also called for the expansion and democratisation of the education system.

After the initial years of post-war reconstruction, demand had grown for highly qualified workers, and education was increasingly viewed as an opportunity for personal growth. In the course of this discussion about education policy, the education system expanded in West Germany and there was a considerable rise in the number of individuals participating in education (Drewek, 2001). The increasing importance placed on education also affected the understanding of children's room for manoeuvre in parent guidebooks for pre-school children. Emphasis was placed on the rich potential at the child's disposal, a potential that was to be developed in a goal-oriented fashion. In the new guidebooks, we can see a loosening, or liberalisation, of the generational order; an education in democratic thinking is viewed as a new, important aspiration that was to be promoted in the family from an early age. This right to a voice changed the position of children and expanded their room for manoeuvre within the family, even if there was no questioning of the adults' responsibility to control the rules of engagement.

From the 1960s, German-language parent guidebooks increasingly included translations from English-speaking, predominantly American, authors, who made the results of developmental psychology popularly accessible. A range of authors also wrote about democratic education within the family, making up for what the US occupying army had tried, but barely managed to do, in its attempts at denazification in West Germany.

The call for better education, the promotion of children's competencies and the construction of a more democratic society, all of which find expression in the guidebooks, can be directly contextualised: education and knowledge were said to enable mature citizens to make rational decisions. Childcare and education became a project that demanded particular knowledge and skills from parents, who were addressed by the new guidebooks through titles such as *Parent School* (*Elternschule*)[2], *Parenting Driving Licence* (*Elternführerschein*)[3] or *Baby-School* (*Baby Schule*, orig. *Teach Your Baby*)[4]. These titles suggest that parents were being trained to become specialised experts in their field, something that was also evident in the 1972 guidebook by the child and adolescent psychotherapist Thomas Zottmann. He provides, for each stage of child development, between 10 and 12 "pedagogical lessons" intended to provoke reflection about children and education. These lessons are directed at both parents; as part of this professionalisation of parenting, fathers were more explicitly involved in their offspring's education.

The principles of strictness and obedience are replaced by a focus on children's own competencies and potential. The generational hierarchy is no longer viewed as something "natural", and parents have to legitimise their position through their ongoing acquisition of pedagogical expertise:

> Intelligent parents know that the status quo is never fixed, neither in children's development or anywhere else in nature. This is why they must be prepared, and should not allow themselves to be surprised by steps forward in their child's development. (Zottmann, 1972, p. 53)

When parents are learners themselves, the hierarchy begins to level out. This new arrangement leads to a new form of childhood agency, in which children have more time and space at their disposal. Independence and self-confidence are identified as important characteristics that parents should encourage, as they are a valuable investment in their children's future. Parents are encouraged to help their child reach new horizons in later life, no longer through learning to obey, but through the development of their child's active personality.

> Overcoming obstacles will mean that later in life, the adult will be less afraid of the boss's office. Every higher branch reached on a tree increases the likelihood that tomorrow s/he will reach a more elevated position in her chosen profession. (Zottmann, 1972, p. 109)

Such pedagogical goals indicate a more individualised vision of personality that is linked to a complex society, which makes multifarious demands on the individual. That individual's survival depends on the early experience in taking on responsibility, and on learning how to be a competent social actor.

In line with an emphasis on the development of pre-school capabilities in childhood, play takes on more of a pedagogical function than before. Parents are responsible for carefully preparing this, as well as ensuring that it proceeds in a regulated and responsible fashion.

> Everything the adult does in later life is present in embryonic form in the child's play activities. Parents can have a profound influence on the future fate of the one-year-old. (Zottmann, 1972, p. 46)

Precision and punctuality remain important learning outcomes in the new social context, but the advice regarding discipline and training becomes less rigid. Therefore, both parents and children gain greater room for manoeuvre. Such a fundamental readiness to disband positions of power ultimately implies the transformation in generational arrangements necessary for the emergence of democratic structures in the family. In the "democratic family", every member, even the youngest, has the fundamental right to have his/her needs recognised. In spite of this relative openness, it must still be acknowledged that the child does not take up a special position within the family and is granted no special privileges.

The revolution: "back to nature" – children as actors in a new world

From the 1970s onwards, and principally in the 1980s, parent guidebooks contain genuinely new conceptions of generational order and alternative ideas about childhood agency. After 1968, driven on by the student movement, discontent with traditional social norms and goals had led to calls for the reorganisation of the education system. In the 1970s, alternative methods of pedagogy and collective forms of education in the anti-authoritarian West German "Kinderladen" movement sought to enact the "revolution of the bourgeois individual". This movement sought to develop emancipatory models that ran counter to traditional education practices. These models were intended for application in other areas of society in due course (Roth, 1976, p. 10). The radical implementation of idealistic pedagogical concepts, which aimed to create a new society through the schooling of "new" citizens, led to an intensive, enduring theoretical engagement with the roles of parents and educators. Guidebook authors turned to writers such as A. S. Neill, who, over several volumes, had written about his experiences in the free school at Summerhill that he had founded in 1921. According to Neill, compulsion-based society was to be revolutionised through a pedagogical method in which the child was afforded as much freedom as possible in its development. Parental authority should be reduced to a minimum, and mutual trust should become the basis of human interaction (Neill, 1969). The reception of psychoanalytical writings, in particular by Wilhelm Reich (1971), but also by Erich Fromm and representatives of the Frankfurt School, drew parents' attention to the role of the family in the suppression of drives. In this analysis, family structures encouraged the formation of the authoritarian personality that was the basis for the power relations dominant in a capitalist society. The new guidebooks were shaped by a desire to allow children to develop as freely as possible. These books propose a generational order that not only understands children as equal to adults, but at times views children's agency as even more valuable. Since they possess the potential, children are viewed as embryonic social innovators. The adults have to recognise and protect this potential, allow it to unfold smoothly and, if necessary, subordinate their own needs to those of their offspring.

The following quotations come from Barbara Sichtermann's 1981 guidebook, *Life with a Newborn Child* (*Leben mit einem Neugeborenen*). Sichtermann, an important voice of the 1968 generation, presented her book as a critical "counter-model" to conventional guidebooks. She ascribes a high level of agency to the newborn child within all areas of family life. She does not question the child's capacity for action, and demands support and respect for the child's needs. In order to understand these in the correct fashion, the book demands close proximity and an intimate coexistence between child and parent.

"Specialist knowledge" – which, in earlier guidebooks, formed the basis of a good and proper education – is now rejected. In its place, the main drivers are child emotion, sensuality, corporeality and instinct.

> I believe there is only one qualified specialist who can educate the educators: the child, and through this "counter-model" I would like to help you to learn from your child. (Sichtermann, 1981, p. 27)

Such intensive support of child agency is not a restriction placed on parents but a necessary condition for the transformation of a way of life.

The presence of a newborn child can bring about a transformation in the social atmosphere, producing more helpfulness, patience and consideration for others. (Sichtermann, 1981, p. 245)

Parents can and indeed should learn from the "unformed" child, and gain more awareness of their own needs. Ultimately, the whole of society could and should be fundamentally changed by this (renewed) orientation towards the child. Parents should therefore protect the child's natural needs from a potentially hostile environment. Children should be able to rely on adults' support to achieve an untroubled interaction with the world. Paying attention to the child is not only the responsibility of the mother or father, but a task for every adult.

Each child develops as a social actor in its own individual way, and this individuality has to be discovered and carefully developed by the adults:

The most important thing in the life of a newborn child is the adults' willingness to experiment, to try things out spontaneously. Don't allow rules to determine the course of your day, but make imagination and spontaneity your guiding principles. This is possible since you are dealing with the utter novelty of a newborn child: nothing like it has existed before – how can you know what it wants, what it will reject, and how it will react? (Sichtermann, 1981, p. 11)

In principle, the child as social actor should be confronted with neither spatial nor temporal limits. For Sichtermann, a routinised life not only impedes the child's healthy development but also limits the lives of the adults, and their ability to surrender themselves to life with their child.

If life with a newborn child is going to take on a fresh breath of life, then we have to undo the tangled knots of ritual that have wound themselves around our lives and threaten to suffocate them. We have to consciously strive to undo the formal structuring of our behaviour. (Sichtermann, 1981, p. 179)

The child's world should not be a restricted space; rather, the whole material world should be at its disposal:

Children want "objects to work with"; even at six months, they want to do everything that adults do, and they are only interested in toys if adults also play with them. There would be serious consequences for the child's development if you were to refuse to give your child access to the objects you use in everyday life. (Sichtermann, 1981, p. 165)

Conventional spatial divisions between adults and children should be undone wherever possible – starting with sleeping environments, then proceeding to the borders of the world of work, undoing the separation between the public and private spheres that might limit the potential of children's agency:

> Take the sleeping newborn child to places where you are not expected: to a cafe, to a public event, to an outdoor swimming pool, on board the train. If your fellow citizens tell you this is not the proper place to bring a sleepy infant, you can respond by informing them that this also partially depends on them as fellow citizens. (Sichtermann, 1981, p. 151)

Ultimately, the abolition of the dominant generational order should proceed from the parent-child relationship to affect all aspects of social life, and definitively undo the ghettos that are created by "a rigid separation of the generations in terms of place, time and activity within everyday life" (Sichtermann, 1981, p. 242).

"Competent children" within the boundaries of negotiated agency

Socio-political developments exert an influence on the shaping of intergenerational relationships, something that is very noticeable in the case of German unification. Unification led not only to a great sense of insecurity but also to increased opportunities in the east. In addition, long-term unemployment transformed education into an indispensable investment, but also led to increased competition, as well as to fears that emerged with increasing globalisation and internationalisation.

Since the 1990s, there has been a general uncertainty about how to manage children, and parental incompetence has become a popular theme in the German media. While general awareness of pedagogical questions is increasing, this itself is leading to uncertainty about the correct way to proceed. Public discourse in Germany is marked by hazard scenarios nourished from a variety of sources. Alongside questions raised by ever more heterogeneous family structures and new familial models, there was also the need to negotiate with very different models of education and pedagogical concepts in the wake of unification with East Germany in 1989. Early years' childcare outside the family had been expanded in the GDR, because the state was interested in developing children as "socialist personalities"[5]. The majority of mothers had been integrated into the labour market, which, however, took a serious downturn in the post-unification years. The number of children's day-care centres also expanded in the West; since 1996 in unified Germany a nursery place has been guaranteed by law for every child over 3 years of age.

In 2001, the "Pisa shock" had major repercussion for Federal education policy. German schoolchildren performed below average in the PISA (Programme for International Student Assessment) comparative international study of

43 countries. In addition, the study made clear that in Germany the education system reproduced a social inequality that disadvantaged children from poorer families and immigrant backgrounds in a way seen in no other country. The ensuing debates led to education reforms that were, however, marked by great disagreement. Amongst the consequences of these reforms were the raising of the profile of day-care centres as educational institutions, and an increase in pedagogical assistance, also in online form. Within the federal initiative "Early Years Help", there has been, since 2009, an expansion of local forms of support for "parents and children from the onset of pregnancy and the early years of life"[6].

Children Need Boundaries (*Kinder brauchen Grenzen*): the title of the guidebook discussed below programmatically marks the direction taken by advice books for parents. This book, first published by Jan-Uwe Rogge in 1993, was highly successful and was republished in 2008 in a new edition, cited below. In truth, the book is not primarily directed towards the restriction of children's agency – in fact, limits are understood as a precondition for becoming a successful social actor. The child, according to Rogge's ideas, needs limits in order to gain a sense of self and to experience him/herself as an autonomous and unique individual.

> Children want clarity and orientation; they want to know where they stand. (Rogge, 2008, p. 149)

Since the image of the child as a competent social actor has become accepted as the norm, the role of the parents in this model is different from earlier patterns. The setting of limits for children is not simply down to the power of the adults; instead, children's agency is intended to emerge through individually negotiated, clearly identifiable and feasible limits.

> The older the children become, the more important it becomes that they look for their own solutions, and learn to act independently. (Rogge, 2008, p. 149)

Children are perceived as partners in negotiation – albeit within a framework that is not arbitrary but continues to be set by adults.

> It is the child's prerogative to test limits, even in younger years. It is the parents' duty to fulfil their responsibility as educators, and deal with any excessive and transgressive child behaviour in a clear fashion. (Rogge, 2008, p. 14)

Within the family, every member has equal rights to assert their own interests, but also equal responsibility towards the community. On the one hand, the child is viewed as an equal partner, while on the other, as an initiate, it has the right to special treatment and care. Parents have to establish and maintain binding structures within which the child can develop. Respect for the individuality of the child is the starting point for pedagogical activity – and for the facilitation of children's agency:

> Children come into the world as unique personalities, and should not be continually measured against other children. This, then, is the pedagogical approach: education is a form of relationship, and one can only teach if one enters into a relationship. (Rogge, 2008, p. 28)

The guidebooks' new concern is with the maintenance of the child's independent personality. The pedagogical goal is the development of a high degree of self-accountability that enables the child to recognise not only its own rights and potential, but also its limits and responsibilities:

> As a father or mother I am not solely responsible for the actions of you, my child. You are responsible for yourself. I give you freedom in so far as I can, given my responsibilities as a teacher, but you also have to learn to take responsibility for what you do. (Rogge, 2008, p. 18)

The goal is individual agency, which is not only maintained but also shaped, negotiated and directed by a self-aware social actor. Such an actor is conscious of its strengths and weaknesses, of what it can do, but also of its (inner and outer) limits. Through self-discipline and self-reflection, the child should be in a position to formulate its own demands and translate these in a socially responsible way.

> There are good reasons to involve children in the decision-making progress, as this also requires them to be willing to develop the courage of their own convictions and to take responsibility for them. (Rogge, 2008, p. 65)

An actor of this kind not only understands the need for self-determination in him/herself, but also accepts the individuality and demands of others. Every other individual is viewed as a potential partner with whom the requirements of a common situation are negotiated. Limits are seen as challenges that require reflection on whether they can be overcome without creating tensions. It is the role of the parents to create the space for such child agency:

> The consequences of transgression have to be clear. The child has freedom. If it can respect limits and keep to agreements, then the consequences will not arise. If the child transgresses or fails to keep to agreements, then it has to experience the consequences. (Rogge, 2008, p. 49)

The balancing act between individualisation and social adjustment should be maintained with a light touch; joy and fun, not an obstinate clinging to principles, should be the determining characteristics of family life and learning. Part of each individualised negotiation should be the rejection of universal formulae and perfectionism:

> Children want parents who master the art of 'making do' as well as the art of giving support and guidance; in certain situations, parents won't always have the answer or the perfect solution. (Rogge, 2008, p. 169)

In this concept of child agency, the child's competence as a social actor forms the basis of generational interaction, and the capacity for action results from communication between parents and children – insofar as the children agree with the parents' goals. For, ultimately, the adults are the ones who set the framework within which child agency emerges. More than before, the key to parenting is the production of cooperative situations and a common set of arrangements that in the end promote children's participation.

Conclusion

If we trace the development of normative parenting expectations in German guidebooks from the post-war era to the present, we see more than just a willingness to give children more opportunities to participate. Expectations also become ever more complex and ambiguous, and make ever greater demands of both parents and children – something possibly connected with increasing uncertainty on both sides. While in the 1970s it was enough to acquire knowledge of developmental psychology in order to define what was possible for children, pedagogical demands have become significantly more complex. The ideas of "anti-authoritarian education", which sought to reduce the limits imposed on the child's time and space, have continued to influence the discourse, with the result that children are increasingly perceived as competent social actors. At the same time, however, there have been growing calls to police the boundaries of child agency, leading to wide-ranging investigations into how this might be done in an appropriate way. The development of a self-confident personality able to deal with contemporary demands requires, on the one hand, giving children the space to participate in debate – which allows them to gain experience as social actors at an early age. On the other hand, the regulated and planned setting of limits is viewed as indispensable for this development. The concrete setting of limits ought to be done in response to the individual personality of the child, its stage of development and the needs of the parents as well as the specific (temporally changing) family arrangement. The material and institutional conditions that shape the lives of parent and child must also be taken into account. The limits set must be constantly adapted and yet remain intelligible. Such demands ultimately turn the parents back upon themselves: continuous self-improvement is required – although the same also applies for the children. Children have to learn to be partners in negotiation at an early age in order to influence the shaping of generational relationships.

These, however, remain as strongly hierarchical as before, dominated by the fact that the adults remain the arbiters of the (variable) rules of the game.

The above analysis has shown how adaptable and yet persistent the idea of child agency has been and how this has changed in relation to different conceptions of generational order, which are themselves influenced by historical events and far-reaching social discourses. This is visible in the development of the German discourse in parent guidebooks – something that is equally well documented for other countries, in particular the USA. The analysis of the mutual influence (or rejection or disregard) of international discourses about child agency within generational hierarchies is a fascinating potential area of future research.

Notes

1 Unless otherwise indicated, all translations were commissioned by the author.
2 Bönninghausen (1972).
3 Spahn (1976).
4 Painter (1974/orig. 1971).
5 Up to 1989, the GDR had the densest network of child nurseries in Europe, attended by 80 per cent of all 0- to 3-year-olds in the country.
6 Available online at www.fruehehilfen.de/fruehe-hilfen/was-sind-fruehe-hilfen (accessed 21 October 2015).

References

Alanen, L. (2005). Kindheit als generationales Konzept [Childhood as a generational concept]. In H. Hengst & H. Zeiher (Eds.), *Kindheit soziologisch* [*Childhood sociologically*] (pp. 65–82). Wiesbaden: VS.

Baader, M. S. (2014). Die reflexive Kindheit [The reflexive childhood]. In M. S. Baader, F. Esser, & W. Schröer (Eds.), *Kindheiten in der Moderne. Eine Geschichte der Sorge* [*Childhoods in the Modern Era: A History of Care*] (pp. 414–455). Frankfurt/M., New York: Campus.

Benz, U. (1988). Brutstätten der Nation. 'Die deutsche Mutter und ihr erstes Kind' oder der anhaltende Erfolg eines Erziehungsbuches [The nation's breeding grounds. 'The German mother and her first child' or the persistent success of a educational book]. *Dachauer Hefte*, 4(4), 144–163.

Berger, M. (2000). Frauen in der Geschichte des Kindergartens: Johanna Haarer [Women in the history of the Kindergarten: Johanna Haarer]. In M.T. Textor (Ed.), *Kindergartenpädagogik Online-Handbuch* [*Online Handbook Paedagogy of the Kindergarten*]. Retrieved from www.kindergartenpaedagogik.de/1268.html.

Bönninghausen, I. v. (1972). *Spiel mit mir - lern mit mir. ZDF Elternschule* [*Play with me - learn with me. ZDF Parent's school*]. Cologne: Verlagsgesellschaft Rudolf Müller.

Bühler-Niederberger, D. (2011). *Lebensphase Kindheit. Theoretische Ansätze, Akteure und Handlungsräume* [*Childhood as a phase of life: Theoretical approaches, actors and arenas of actions*]. Weinheim, Munich: Juventa.

Büchner, P., Fuhs, B., & Krüger, H.-H. (1997). Transformation der Eltern-Kind-Beziehungen? Facetten der Kindbezogenheit des elterlichen Erziehungsverhaltens in Ost- und Westdeutschland [Transformation of parent-child relationships? Facets of child-relatedness in east and west German parenting]. In H.-E. Tenorth (Ed.), *Kindheit, Jugend und Bildungsarbeit im Wandel: Ergebnisse der Transformationsforschung* [*Changes in Childhood, Youth and Educational Work: Results of Transition Research*] (pp. 35–52). Weinheim: Beltz.

Dessai, E. (1981). *Erziehung ohne Elternstress: Wie Eltern und Kinder besser miteinander auskommen* [*Education without stress: how parents and children get along better*]. Munich: Kindler.

Dewey, J. (1964). *Demokratie und Erziehung: Eine Einleitung in die philosophische Pädagogik* [*Democracy and Education. An Introduction to the Philosophy of Education*]. Braunschweig: Westermann.

Dodson, F. (1975). *How to Father. The Extraordinary Guide That Helps the Father Perform His Vital Role.* New York: Signet.

Drewek, P. (2001). Bildungssysteme und Bildungsexpansion in Deutschland. Zur Entwicklung ihres Verhältnisses im historischen Vergleich [Educational systems and educational expansion in Germany. A historical comparison of the development of their relation]. *Zeitschrift für Pädagogik, 47*(6), 811–818.

Epting-Kullmann, A. (1955). *Vom Handwerk des Erziehens* [*The Craft of Education*]. Gelnhausen, Berlin-Dahlem: Burckhardhaus-Verlag.

Foucault, M. (1972). *The Archaeology of Knowledge.* New York: Pantheon.

Gebhardt, M. (2009). *Die Angst vor dem kindlichen Tyrannen: Eine Geschichte der Erziehung im 20. Jahrhundert* [*Fearing the Child Tyrant: A History of Education in the 20th Century*]. Munich: DVA.

Haarer, J. (1949/1961). *Die Mutter und ihr erstes Kind* [*The mother and her first child*]. Munich: Carl Gerber.

Hardyment, C. (2007). *Dream Babies: Childcare Advice from John Locke to Gina Ford.* London: Francis Lincoln.

Höffer-Mehlmer, M. (2003). *Elternratgeber: zur Geschichte eines Genres* [*Parents Guidebooks. The History of a Genre*]. Baltmannsweiler: Schneider Hohengehren.

Hörl, R. (Ed.). (1971). *Kinder in ihrer Welt - Kinder in unserer Welt: Kleines Praktikum für Eltern und Erzieher* [*Children in their world - children in our world: a short traineeship for parents and educators*]. Frankfurt/M., Hamburg: Fischer Bücherei.

Hulbert, A. (2003). *Raising America: Experts, Parents, and a Century of Advice about Children.* New York: Knopf.

Hungerland, B. (2002). *"Wie viel Zeit für's Kind?" Zur gesellschaftlichen Produktion generationaler Ordnung durch elterliche Zeitinvestition* [*"Time for your child?" Parental time investment for producing the generational order*]. Retrieved from http://elpub.bib.uni-wuppertal.de/edocs/dokumente/fbg/paedagogik/diss2002/hungerland.

Jugendwerk der Deutschen Shell (Ed.). (1985). *Jugendliche & Erwachsene '85: Generationen im Vergleich* [*Adolescents and Adults: Comparing Generations*]. 5 Vols. Opladen: Leske & Budrich.

Keller, R. (2011). The Sociology of Knowledge Approach to Discourse (SKAD). *Human Studies 34*(1), 43–65.

Keller, R. (2007). Diskurse und Dispositive analysieren: Die Wissenssoziologische Diskursanalyse als Beitrag zu einer wissensanalytischen Profilierung der Diskursforschung [Analyzing discourses and dispositifs: The input of a sociological discourse-analysis to profiling the discourse analysis]. *FQS, vol. 8 no.2 art. 19.*

Neill, A. S. (1969). *Theorie und Praxis der antiautoritären Erziehung: Das Beispiel Summerhill* [*Summerhill: A Radical Approach to Child-rearing*]. Reinbek bei Hamburg: Rowohlt.

Oelkers, J. (1995). *Pädagogische Ratgeber: Erziehungswissen in populären Medien* [*Educational guidebooks: paedagogical knowledge in popular media*]. Frankfurt/M.: Diesterweg.

Painter, G. (1974): *Baby-Schule: Programmiertes Intelligenztraining für Kleinkinder* [*Teach Your Baby*]. München, Gütersloh: Bertelsmann Ratgeberverlag.

Reich, W. (1971). *Massenpsychologie des Faschismus* [*The Mass Psychology of Fascism*]. Cologne: Kiepenheuer & Witsch.

Rinken, B. (2012). *Gender- und Familienbilder in Elternratgebern - Heterogene Sichtweisen* [*Images of gender and family in parents' guidebooks - heterogeneous perceptions*]. Munich: DJI. Retrieved from http://d-nb.info/1033246034/34.

Ritter, P. & Ritter, J. (1972). *Freie Kindererziehung in der Familie* [*The Free Family*]. Reinbek: Rowohlt.

Rogge, J.-U. (2008). *Das neue Kinder brauchen Grenzen* [*Children Need Boundaries*]. Reinbek: Rowohlt.

Roth, J. (1976). *Eltern erziehen Kinder - Kinder erziehen Eltern: Elterninitiativen nach der Kinderladenbewegung* [*Parents educate children - children educate parents: parent initiatives after the Kinderladen movement*]. Cologne: Kiepenheuer & Witsch.

Schlißke, O.(1956). *Evangelisches Elternbuch* [*A Protestant parent's guide*]. Gütersloh: Rufer.

Schmid, M. (2008). *Erziehungsratgeber in der ersten Hälfte des 20. Jahrhunderts – eine vergleichende Analyse* [*Educational guides in the first half of the 20th century: A comparative analysis*]. Berlin: Weissensee- Verlag.

Seiverth, A. (2007). *Traumatisierung und Notstandssemantik. Bildungspolitische Kontinuitäten vom Sputnik- zum PISA-Schock* [*Traumatization and semantics of crisis: continuities in educational policies from Sputnik- to PISA-Shock*]. *DIE* 50(1), 32–35.

Sichtermann, B. (1981). *Leben mit einem Neugeborenen: Ein Buch über das erste halbe Jahr* [*Life with a Newborn Child. A Book on the First 6 Months*]. Frankfurt/M.: Fischer Taschenbuch.

Spahn, C. (Ed.). (1976). *Der Elternführerschein: Ein Kurs zur Erziehung des Kleinkindes* [*The parent's license: a course for toddler's education*]. Munich: Goldmann.

Spivak, G. C. (1988). Can the Subaltern Speak? In C. Nelson & L. Grossberg (Eds.). *Marxism and the Interpretation of Culture* (pp. 271–313). Chicago: University of Illinois Press.

Strauss, A. L. & Corbin, J. (1996). *Grounded Theory: Grundlagen Qualitativer Sozialforschung*. Weinheim: Beltz Psychologie Verlags Union.

Uflacker, H. (1963). *Mutter und Kind* [*Mother and Child*]. Gütersloh: Bertelsmann Verlag.

Winiewicz, L. & Spiel, W. (1973). *Elternschule* [*Parents' school*]. Vienne, Darmstadt: Koch's Verlag.

Zottmann, T. M. (1972). *Die ersten 5 Jahre: 73 pädagogische Lektionen für junge Eltern* [*The first 5 years: 73 educational lessons for young parents*]. Stuttgart: Ernst Klett.

Transnational and majority world perspectives of agency

Chapter 12

Exploring children's agency across majority and minority world contexts

Samantha Punch

This chapter reflects on recent debates concerning children's agency in a variety of contexts across both the majority and minority worlds. It draws on examples from a range of settings, including families, schools, residential care and rural communities within Asia, Latin America and Europe. In particular, it explores current critiques of the concept of children as social actors, considering the limitations and nuances of children's agency within the generational order. The chapter questions why there continues to be a gap between the academic discourse of childhood agency and arenas of policy and practice. It suggests that by engaging in a cross-cultural dialogue between the majority and minority worlds, our understanding of children's agency could be enhanced.

Introduction

Within Childhood Studies, and in line with the new paradigm of the sociology of childhood as set out by Prout and James in 1990, there has been a wealth of empirical studies over the last 25 years that demonstrate children's agency. However, the theoretical developments for moving this paradigm forward have been limited in contrast to the abundance of empirical evidence, which illustrates the diverse ways that children are social actors. Hence, this edited collection contributes to recent literature that critiques a taken-for-granted understanding of children's agency (for example, Hoang & Yeoh, 2014; Oswell, 2013; Tisdall & Punch, 2012). In particular, this chapter has three key aims. It begins with an exploration of current critiques of the concept of children as social actors, outlining the limitations and nuances of children's agency within the generational order. The chapter then examines why there continues to be a gap between the academic discourse of childhood agency and arenas of policy and practice. It ends by suggesting that an engagement in cross-cultural dialogue between the majority and minority worlds[1] could enhance our understanding of children's agency.

Recently, there have been critiques emerging of children's agency that question or problematise what agency really means for different groups of children and young people (Bordonaro & Payne, 2012; Mizen & Ofusu-Kusi, 2013). This chapter builds on this literature as it suggests that a more nuanced definition of children's agency is required, which locates it within the structural constraints of the generational order. Within Childhood Studies, the pervasiveness of children's agency has been a strong focus for empirical work, becoming almost a taken-for-granted mantra (Tisdall & Punch, 2012). This emphasis was necessary to counteract past models of child development and socialisation, by showing that children are not passive beings (Mayall, 2006). There has been a tendency to see it everywhere (Oswell, 2013), even when it may surprise us, in order to document that children are not necessarily helpless, nor passive, when faced with very difficult situations. For example, researchers have explored agency in relation to child soldiers (Rosen, 2007), child prostitutes (Montgomery, 2009) and street children (Hecht, 1998), as these examples counteract a more traditional, stereotypical view of such children as passive victims.

However, as Mizen and Ofusu-Kusi point out, children's agency is "a much used but largely unexamined concept" (2013, p. 363). There are not many explicit definitions or conceptualisations of children's agency. The term tends to be a little vague and lacks clarity:

- ability "to choose to do things" (Mizen & Ofusu-Kusi, 2013, p. 363).
- children's capacity to do (Oswell, 2013, p. 3).
- ability to act creatively and make things happen (James, 2009, p. 42).

It is not necessarily clear what the difference is between exercising one's agency or power. Robson et al. describe children's agency as the "capacities, competencies and activities through which they navigate the contexts and positions of their lifeworlds" (2007, p. 135), but they are not explicit as to how agency relates to other concepts such as power or participation. The limitations of children and young people's agency in specific contexts may often be acknowledged but not sufficiently problematised, as Bluebond-Langner and Korbin (2007) indicate:

> What is less clear is the degree of agency, the impact of that agency, let alone the nature of that agency – points that could also be made about the agency of adults – singly or in groups. Children, like adults, do not escape structural constraints. (p. 242)

It is now recognised that it is not enough to say that children have agency; a more nuanced exploration of their agency needs to be considered. By scrutinising children's situated agency in context, it is possible to disentangle the type and nature of their agency as well as the outcomes and consequences attached to asserting agency or not.

Critiquing children's agency

Agency can be accepted uncritically as being a positive action that can mask the complexities of the process:

> Children and young people's agency should certainly be a contested and scrutinised concept rather than one which is taken-for-granted, unproblematised or assumed inherently to be positive and desired by all children and young people. (Tisdall & Punch, 2012, p. 256)

It is also important to consider from whose perspective children's agency is considered to be positive or negative. Benwell's (2013) research on children's use of outdoor space in South Africa indicates that, as adults, we should not always assume that children want to resist adult authority. He warns about reinforcing the "adults versus children" narrative, as he suggests that adults' behaviour does not always impact on children's lives in negative ways. There is often an assumption that adult-imposed structure or adult power over children is negative and something that children should assert their agency to resist or counteract. What happens when children do not assert their agency and are passive or dependent? Is that necessarily negative or does it depend on whether they choose to be passive or active? Hoang and Yeoh's work with children "left behind" by migrant parents in Vietnam suggests that "agency is as much about inactivity as activity" (2014, p. 14).

This discussion links to the concept of vulnerability, which is often perceived as an inhibitor to children's ability to assert their agency. Bluebond-Langner and Korbin (2007) question the place of vulnerability when so much emphasis is on children's agency. As Rosen (2007) asks: Are child soldiers innocent victims of war who should be protected or are they moral agents who should be held responsible for their violence? These and other authors point out the tensions between attributing children's agency as opposed to acknowledging their structural position of vulnerability in extremely constrained contexts (Tisdall & Punch, 2012). For example, in African case studies there is a tendency for adults only to see vulnerability and there is not enough focus on children's agency (Payne, 2012; Pells, 2012).

In contrast, others suggest that there is sometimes too much focus on agency, which underplays children's position of vulnerability (Bluebond-Langner & Korbin, 2007). For example, street children are sometimes only perceived by adults as threats, whereby adults tend to assume that street children's agency is inappropriate rather than recognising their vulnerability. Mizen and Ofusu-Kusi (2013) argue that vulnerability in such contexts should be seen as driving agency rather than as denying children's capacity to act. Hoang and Yeoh remind us that emphasising agency over structure can lead to "uncritical celebrations of migrant children's agency [which] mislead us when we turn our attention to those immobile children whom the migrant parents have left behind" (2014, p. 4).

Thus, when the type of agency is linked to the outcomes and consequences of children's agency, this is often connected to moral judgements about what is perceived to be a positive or negative type of agency. A key problem arises when children see their actions as positive but adults impose a negative judgement on what they are doing or do not take the time to understand it from the children's point of view. Bordonaro and Payne (2012) refer to this as ambiguous agency: when children's agency threatens the existing moral and social order or contrasts with idealised notions of minority world childhood.

Ambiguous agency raises questions about the extent to which children's agency is perceived by adults as appropriate, moral or responsible. If children's agency is considered to be negative, challenging or problematic (at least from the adults' perspective), then it is more likely to be questioned or attempts to be made to curtail it. As Hoang and Yeoh state, "children's agency is contingent on a social construction of childhood that is neither static nor universally uniform" (2014, p. 3), but it is also important to recognise that "adult perceptions of children's agency and needs, in turn structures these processes" (2014, p. 1). Hence, in order to understand the nature and outcome of children's agency, it must be located within the generational order that shapes it.

Furthermore, Holt (2011) argues that, whilst children and young people's agency has been key to the development of Childhood Studies and to the inclusion of children and young people's perspectives in academic discourses, it is also

> paradoxically integral to the marginalization within contemporary societies of children and young people (and others, such as disabled people) who cannot achieve this ideal of independence and autonomy. (Holt, 2011, p. 3)

It is important to consider aspects of children's lives where they have limited agency or exclude children or situations when they cannot assert agency. Ansell (2013) has suggested that instead of the concepts of "agency" and "rights", perhaps "power" and "justice" would be more appropriate terms to use. However, switching terms does not seem to solve the issue as there is a similar lack of clarity, and they also have their limitations conceptually. Developing a clearer definition of agency is a way forward. However, in order to do this, it is necessary to problematise children's agency to reveal the complexities and ambiguities of applying theoretical ideas in practice, particularly when social realities are complex and contradictory.

There have been some recent moves to problematise children's agency, and it would now be helpful to bring together some of these critiques in order to develop a more nuanced picture where children's agency is not polarised as either active or passive. As Oswell argues, it should not be about "a simple binary, having or not having agency, capacity and power" (2013, p. 269). A continuum of agency seems a more appropriate conceptualisation that "varies depending on opportunistic and constrained contexts, created and expected identities, positions of power/lessness, lifecourse stage, and state of emotions and wellbeing" (Robson et al., 2007).

A couple of key studies in majority world contexts have taken forward this idea of a continuum of agency by developing notions of "thicker and thinner" agency (Klocker, 2007) or "tactical" agency (Honwana, 2005) (critically: see Esser in this volume). Klocker's research with child domestic workers in Tanzania describes how they work extremely long hours with low pay and face a range of potential abuse. She suggests that a notion of thick and thin agency can be helpful in understanding the continuum of children and young people's constrained agency in different contexts:

> "thin" agency refers to decisions and everyday actions that are carried out within highly restrictive contexts, characterized by few viable alternatives. "Thick" agency is having the latitude to act within a broad range of options. (Klocker, 2007, p. 85)

It is possible for a person's agency to get "thicker" or "thinner" over time and space, and across their different relationships. Honwana's research with child soldiers in Mozambique uses the term "tactical agency" to show how they "cope with the concrete and immediate conditions of their lives.... Their actions, however, come from a position of weakness" (2005, p. 49). Thus, tactical agency includes vulnerability and it is about an ability to cope whilst at the same time being an "agency of the weak". Her analysis leads her to conclude that child soldiers have an in-between status where they are both child and adult, victim and perpetrator, guilty and innocent.

These examples indicate the importance of understanding the relational nature of children's agency. White and Choudhury's (2010) work exploring children's rights in communities in Bangladesh stresses that children's agency is not autonomous, and needs to be supported by adults. Thus, it is collective agency rather than individualised. My own work in rural Bolivia also points to the role of negotiated interdependencies (Punch, 2001a, 2015b) in understanding children's position as social actors. It is interesting that much of the research that highlights the relationality and nuances of children's agency has emerged from majority world contexts. By opening up a greater dialogue and developing a more global approach to Childhood Studies, there are opportunities for learning from the majority world (Punch, 2015a). Certainly, a focus on relationships can shed light on the complexities and interconnections of childhoods across both majority and minority world contexts (Cannella & Diaz Soto, 2010; Hopkins & Pain, 2007; Jeffrey & Dyson, 2008; Tisdall & Punch, 2012).

Exploring the gap between discourses of Childhood Studies and arenas of policy and practice

As we have seen, in academic research there is widespread recognition that children are competent social actors. Yet despite many positive moves forward, why does there continue to be a gap between the academic theory of children's agency and the arenas of policy and practice? Why does it seem that practitioners are sometimes reluctant to embrace the new paradigm of the sociology of childhood, working within child development models where children are not readily perceived as competent social actors, and adults need to act in their best interests (James, 2005)?

An empirical example that illustrates this comes from research on food practices in residential child care in Scotland. When both inter- and intra-generational perspectives were sought, it emerged that some of the residential staff's intentions of providing stability and security when delivering food for children in care could be interpreted by children as control and surveillance rather than as a caring gesture (McIntosh et al., 2010). This mismatch of perceptions regarding children's agency was linked to tensions between children's rights to participation and their rights to protection (Punch et al., 2012). When participation was enforced in inflexible ways, it was not experienced in terms of learning or caring by the children but in terms of excessive control by staff or an example of the imbalance of power between adults and children more generally.

Similar gaps between academia and practice have been highlighted in parts of the majority world. For example, Pells' (2012) research with children in Rwanda shows how discourses of vulnerability and victimhood are more dominant than those of children's agency and participation. Payne (2012) also found that adults tended to impose moral judgements on child-headed households in Zambia, leading to questions about who is at risk and from whose point of view. Both of these studies in African contexts argue that children's agency can be treated in a tokenistic manner in practice by adults, who continue to work within child development models where children are more likely to be perceived as passive and vulnerable rather than as potentially competent social actors.

Some may argue that this is why a continued focus on children's agency is required, as it still has not trickled down enough into practice (Mayall, 2006). Is there a resistance to the new paradigm of childhood because adults' assumptions are ingrained with the development models of childhood as a period of dependency on adults? However, perhaps the notion of children's agency is not being embraced because it does not resonate enough with adults' views of children. Is that partly because the language of the academic discourse of Childhood Studies is not accessible enough to practitioners and parents? Is children's agency not seen as appropriate or relevant to apply to everyday practice, or is it because agency has not been sufficiently located within the generational order?

It is clear that children's agency needs to be understood from both adults' and children's perspectives (Hoang & Yeoh, 2014). Prior to the new 1990s paradigm of the sociology of childhood, research on children tended to be conducted from the adults' viewpoint. The empirical studies of the 1990s and 2000s strove to counteract this bias by focusing on children's views. It is now recognised that in order to fully understand children's lives, both adults' and children's voices should be considered. Hence, it is timely to unpack children's agency rather than take it for granted, and it should be positioned within the generational order. If the limitations of children's agency are acknowledged, and if vulnerability is accounted for, then perhaps the discourses of agency would be more likely to reflect the complexities of children's social status.

Children's agency and the generational order

In their book *Conceptualising Child-Adult Relations*, Alanen and Mayall (2001) made a strong case for the use of the term "generationing" as a structural feature of child-adult interactions. It is surprising that their theoretical ideas have not been explored empirically in an explicit way. The generational order tends to be implied but not really engaged with, and consequently, the generational order is less developed theoretically than the gender order. It could be that Childhood Studies has been so busy with the business of trying to get children's voices heard and children's issues on the policy agenda that there has been a tendency to over-emphasise children's agency, resulting in an under-selling of the generational order. Perhaps in order to offer an alternative to developmental models of children as passive dependents (see also Holt, 2011), we have been a little too keen to stress the notion of children as competent social actors?

For example, if we consider the process of gender becoming mainstreamed within the field of development studies, we can see a parallel neglect of the generational order. In the past, approaches to development were criticised for being male-dominated and gender-blind (Boserup, 1970). These critiques began in the 1970s and, about 20 years later in the 1990s, gender issues were more regularly recognised as relevant to development; now, gender has been integrated into most development thinking. In contrast, issues relating to age and generation continue to be marginalised in most development programmes. There are some development projects that focus specifically on children and young people, but broader community projects tend to integrate gender whilst overlooking age. As we have seen, the new paradigm of the sociology of childhood emerged in the early 1990s, yet 25 years later, children and young people's perspectives regarding development issues are not regularly sought, despite evidence that this can lead to negative consequences for their lives (see, for example, Ansell, 2005).

Therefore, in order to reach a more nuanced conceptualisation of children's agency, it has to be considered in relation to the generational order. Oswell's recent book, which gives an overview of much research on children's agency, says that as sociologists of childhood we have to be careful not

> to see children's agency everywhere or to see it as a universal, unitary phenomenon. It is the task of a sociology of children to document that capacity when observed, but also to recognise incapacity, abuse, power relationality, torture and exploitation. But the task also relies on a recognition of children's dependency. (Oswell, 2013, p. 280)

By drawing on my empirical work in rural Bolivia from the mid-1990s through to 2014, I shall extend this thinking on children's agency further by focusing on the relationality of the generational order, considering the relations between children and adults, and between children and other children in terms of inter-dependencies, rather than children's dependency. The chapter will argue that children's agency can be understood in relation to negotiated and constrained interdependencies within and across generations. The remainder of this section will map how this conceptual framework has developed from a majority world context and has been applied to research in Scotland, a minority world setting (see also Plows, 2012).

During the mid-1990s, I explored rural Bolivian children's agency in relation to their work. The structural constraints that children faced included poverty, a cash-limited, subsistence economy and cultural views of child-adult relations where adult discipline tended to be harsh. Nevertheless, children had a range of strategies for asserting their agency and combining work, school and play (Punch, 2001a). They negotiated their position within the generational order, both in their child-adult relationships and in their sibling relations. It was clear that household interdependencies enhanced children's bargaining power despite the range of structural constraints that limited their opportunities (Punch, 2007). The rural Bolivian Childhood Studies also revealed that children's opportunities for work, education and migration depended to some extent on their birth order position. For example, sometimes older siblings could enable younger siblings to pursue education by helping out financially with migrant remittances, but there was most pressure on the youngest sibling of the household, regardless of gender, not to migrate but to stay behind and care for older parents (Punch, 2014).

In rural Bolivia, like some other parts of the majority world, relations of inter-dependence between parents and children, and between siblings, are important over the life course, as family networks help to protect individuals against eco-nomic instability and social risks (Bühler-Niederberger & Schwittek, 2014). In a majority world society with no welfare benefits, young people often have a strong sense of family responsibilities, including caring for their parents when they are old (Mills & Blossfeld, 2005). In rural Bolivia, such obligations and duties of care are negotiable in practice, particularly as they tend to be worked out with siblings, often influenced by birth order position. Hence, the concept of "negoti-ated interdependencies" emerged (Punch, 2001a). On returning to Bolivia ten years later, and alongside personal communication with Penny Vera-Sanso[2], it became clear that it was also important to emphasise the constraints attached to these negotiated interdependencies:

> a term which reflects how young people in the majority world are con-strained by various structures and cultural expectations of family responsibili-ties yet also assert their agency within such limitations as they balance both household and individual needs. (Punch, 2014)

Vera-Sanso had pointed out the risk of overemphasising children's agency and choice, which would mask the limitations. Thus, by situating children's agency within the structural context, it was possible to explore children's vulnerabilities and the thinness of their agency in precarious situations.

My follow-up study in rural Bolivia ten years later illustrates shifting interdependencies between generations and over the life course, as household relations and obligations are negotiated and worked out, rather than fixed. For example, Marianela is one of seven siblings who had always contributed to her household, looking after animals and performing agricultural and domestic work. When her older brothers migrated to work in Argentina, she had to take over their responsibilities, so the household divisions of labour during childhood often depended more on birth order position rather than gender (Punch, 2001b). Later, in return, her brothers offered to pay for her secondary school education, which involved migrating to a nearby town. After much thought, she declined, as evidence suggested that a secondary education was unlikely to lead to an alternative livelihood: She had seen several of her peers fail and waste scarce resources (Punch, 2015b).

Marianela became a domestic worker in the nearby town, and she and her siblings would take turns to go back to the rural community during holidays to help their parents harvest the land. During the economic crisis in Argentina, her brothers who had migrated to work on agricultural plantations were unable to return and she had to give up her job for several months to go and help her parents (Punch, 2014). Meanwhile, her brothers continued to send back remittances to the household. Finally, at 20 years old, Marianela migrated to the south of Argentina to join one of her brothers who found her a job. All of the siblings put pressure on their youngest brother not to migrate but to stay and care for their older parents. This example shows how negotiated and constrained household interdependencies exist both within and across the generations. It illustrates the importance of explicitly bringing in the generational order as part of the structural context (Punch, 2007) in order to understand children's agency at the level of both adult-child relations and relations between children.

As Vanderbeck (2007) has argued, it is necessary to explore patterns of intergenerational change in order to understand how the actions of one generation can impact on those of another. Recently there has been a global trend that indicates that there is a growing emphasis on the education of young people (Jeffrey & Dyson, 2008; Punch, 2015a). Yet young people's increased education status is not necessarily resulting in better-paid urban employment characterised by low wages and long hours (Jeffrey et al., 2008). A study of young people in rural Vietnam, China and India found that the changing livelihood transitions of youth add to the burden of the older generations in rural areas, particularly older women, who are losing the traditional labour contributions of young people whilst not being compensated with remittances from well-paid urban jobs (Punch & Sugden, 2013). A consideration of children's agency and generational issues reveals the importance of exploring age relations across the life course as well as relationally between the generations, considering the role of siblings, birth order position, peers, friends and boyfriends/girlfriends (Punch, 2015b).

Cross-cultural learning and children's agency

Through a critical discussion of the use and limits of the concept of childhood agency, this chapter has moved forward academic debates on children's agency by contributing thoughts from research in the majority world. The link between the concept of agency and the structural constraints of the generational order has not been sufficiently established so far. This chapter has emphasised the need to take into account the ways in which agency relates to other concepts such as power or participation, and to be aware of the impact of processes of generationing (see also Alanen & Mayall, 2001). An overemphasis on children's agency, rather than a focus on its location within the generational order, risks overlooking the limits of children's agency or emerging with a binary view of it. The lack of a clear and suitable definition of children's agency as a relational concept that also encompasses children's potential dependency is not just an academic question, but also relates to the challenge of using the term appropriately in practical and political contexts.

As this chapter has pointed out, many theories and concepts of Childhood Studies have been developed in the minority world and used in majority world contexts, but rarely is the learning process reversed. This chapter has shown that by drawing on examples of children's agency in majority world countries, an understanding of children's potential as social actors is located within the generational order. This more nuanced approach to children's agency is also useful for understanding children's agency and generational positioning in the minority world. This chapter also points to another area that has tended to be neglected within the generational order, and that is intra-generational relations, particularly birth order and sibling composition. When considering concepts such as agency and power, greater focus tends to be centred on adult-child relations rather than relations between children. This chapter has illustrated the importance of age, birth order and sibling composition as intra-generational factors that shape the generational order and should also be considered in minority world household divisions of labour.

As a result of my research in rural Bolivia, it was clear that a sociology of sibling relations was under-developed. With the exception of recent work, such as Edwards et al. (2006) and Bacon (2012), most research had been carried out by psychologists, not sociologists. When intra-generational relations during childhood are considered, we tend to examine issues of gender, age, ethnicity and class, but birth order is still overlooked as a social variable. In a subsequent project on sibling relationships in Scotland with families with three children,

I explored the ways in which agency and power between siblings is different from that between parents and children (Punch, 2005). This research showed how different locations in the birth order are socially constructed and each position has relative advantages and disadvantages attached to it. However, in practice, the ways in which these emerge are fluid and have to be negotiated on a regular basis (McIntosh & Punch, 2009). There is a recognised birth-order hierarchy with particular expectations and roles linked to different birth-order positions, but they are not fixed. Thus, birth order can also shape the opportunities and constraints regarding children's ability to assert their agency, but birth order is often neglected as a key part of the generational order.

This chapter has highlighted the importance of exploring children's agency in the context of both inter-generational and intra-generational relations. Not only should both kinds of generational relationships be considered, but they also need to be understood from both adults' and children's perspective to reach a more nuanced picture of processes of generationing. This chapter has shown that in order to grasp the intricacies and complexities of the generational order, children's agency should be explored in relation to the negotiated and constrained inter-dependencies within and across generations. This conceptual framework focuses on relational processes within the generational order, indicating the dynamic and contingent nature of children's agency, which is situated in a social and cultural context. It encourages consideration of enabling and constraining processes that reveal both positive and negative aspects of agency and interdependencies from generational perspectives.

This chapter has illustrated the potential for greater dialogue across majority and minority worlds (Cannella & Diaz Soto, 2010; Jeffrey & Dyson, 2008; Punch & Tisdall, 2012). In particular, it contributes to the growing literature that demonstrates how the minority world can also learn from concepts developed in relation to majority world childhoods (Panelli et al., 2007; Punch, 2015a; also Wihstutz in this volume). Focusing only on children and young people's perspectives regarding agency and participation is no longer sufficient; greater emphasis is needed on the intricacies, complexities, tensions, ambiguities and ambivalences of processes of generationing across both majority and minority world contexts.

By drawing on majority world examples, this chapter has suggested that the development of the concept of children's agency should also include a consideration of their vulnerability as well as the interdependencies between children and adults. The notions of shifting interdependencies between generations and over the life course, or taking into account other intra-generational relations (such as birth-order position) are also of relevance for minority world contexts. Thus, this chapter has indicated the potential usefulness of a greater integration of the empirical findings and theoretical insights from research in majority world contexts, which can be applied to a discussion of minority world childhoods.

Notes

1 The majority world refers to the economically poorer continents of Asia, Africa and Latin America. The terms majority and minority worlds are preferred as they shift the positive emphasis towards the poorer countries, reminding us that the more common global experience of childhood is that of the majority world, where they combine work, school and play, rather than having a privileged minority world childhood dedicated to play and school (Punch & Tisdall, 2012).

2 This discussion took place at a Conference on "Social Reproduction across the Lifecourse" on 18 March 2011 at Birkbeck College with Penny Vera-Sanso from the Department of Geography, Environment and Development Studies (GEDS), Birkbeck College, University of London.

References

Alanen, L. (2012). Disciplinarity, interdisciplinarity and childhood studies. *Childhood, 19*(4), 419–422.

Alanen, L. & Mayall, B. (2001) (Eds.). *Conceptualising Child-Adult Relations.* London: Routledge Falmer.

Ansell, N. (2005). *Children, Youth and Development.* London: Routledge.

Ansell, N. (2013). *The Case for a Conceptual Reframing of Childhood Studies: Rights and Agency or Justice and Power?* RGS-IBG Conference, London, 30 August 2013.

Bacon, K. (2012). Beings in their own right? Exploring children and young people's sibling and twin relationships in the minority world. *Children's Geographies, 10*(3), 307–320.

Benwell, M. (2013). Rethinking conceptualisations of adult-imposed restriction and children's experiences of autonomy in outdoor space. *Children's Geographies, 11*(1), 28–43.

Bluebond-Langner, M. & Korbin, J. (2007). Challenges and opportunities in the anthropology of childhoods: an introduction to "Children, Childhoods, and Childhood Studies". *American Anthropologist, 109*(2), 241–246.

Bordonaro, L. & Payne, R. (2012). Ambiguous agency: critical perspectives on social interventions with children and youth in Africa. *Children's Geographies, 10*(4), 365–372.

Boserup, E. (1970). *Women's Role in Economic Development.* London: George Allen & Unwin.

Bühler-Niederberger, D. & Schwittek, J. (2014). Young children in Kygyzstan: agency in tight hierarchical structures. *Childhood 21*(4), 502–51.

Cannella, G. S., & Diaz Soto, L. (2010). *Childhoods: A Handbook.* Oxford: Peter Lang.

Edwards, R., Hadfield, L., Lucey, H. & Mauthner, M. (2006). *Sibling Identity and Relationships: Sisters and Brothers.* London: Routledge.

Hecht, T. (1998). *At Home in the Street: Street Children of Northeast Brazil.* Cambridge: Cambridge University Press.

Holt, L. (2011). Introduction: geographies of children, youth and families, disentangling the socio-spatial contexts of young people across the globalising world. In L. Holt (Ed.), *Geographies of Children, Youth and Families* (pp. 1–8). London: Routledge.

Hoang, L. & Yeoh, B. (2014). Children's agency and its contradictions in the context of transnational labour migration from Vietnam. *Global Networks,* online first: doi:10.1111/glob.12057.

Honwana, A. (2005). Innocent and guilty: child soldiers as interstitial and tactical agents. In A. Honwana & F. de Boeck (Eds.), *Makers and Breakers: Children and Youth in Postcolonial Africa* (pp. 31–52). Oxford: James Currey.

Hopkins, P. & Pain, R. (2007). Geographies of age: thinking relationally. *Area, 39*(3), 287–294.

James, A. (2009) Agency. In J. Qvortrup, W. Corsaro & M.-S. Honig (Eds.), *Palgrave Handbook of Childhood Studies* (pp. 34–45). London: Palgrave Macmillan.

James, A. (2005). Life times: children's perspectives on age, agency and memory across the life course. In J. Qvortrup (Ed.), *Studies in Modern Childhood: Society, Agency and Culture* (pp. 248–265). Basingstoke: Palgrave Macmillan.

Jeffrey, C. & Dyson, J. (2008). *Telling Young Lives: Portraits of Global Youth.* Philadelphia: Temple University Press.

Jeffrey, C., Jeffery, P., & Jeffrey, R. (2008). *Degrees without Freedom? Education Masculinities and Unemployment in North India.* Palo Alto: Stanford University Press.

Klocker, N. (2007). An example of thin agency: child domestic workers in Tanzania. In R. Panelli, S. Punch & E. Robson (Eds.), *Global Perspectives on Rural Childhood and Youth: Young Rural Lives* (pp. 81–148). London: Routledge.

Mayall, B. (2006). Values and assumptions underpinning policy for children and young people in England. *Children's Geographies, 4*(1), 9–18.

McIntosh, I., Punch, S., Dorrer, N. & Emond, R. (2010). You don't have to be watched to make your toast: surveillance and food practices within residential care for young people. *Surveillance and Society, 7*(3), 287–300.

McIntosh, I. & Punch, S. (2009). 'Barter', 'deals', 'bribes' and 'threats': exploring sibling interactions, *Childhood, 16*(1), 49–65.

Mills, M. & Blossfeld, H. (2005). Globalization, uncertainty and the early life course: a theoretical framework. In H. Blossfeld, E. Klijzing, M. Mills & K. Kurz (Eds.), *Globalization, Uncertainty and Youth in Society* (pp. 1–24). London: Routledge.

Mizen, P. & Ofosu-Kusi, Y. (2013). Agency as vulnerability: accounting for children's movement to the streets of Accra. *The Sociological Review, 61*, 363–382.

Montgomery, H. (2009). *An Introduction to Childhood: Anthropological Perspectives on Children's Lives.* Chichester: Wiley-Blackwell.

Oswell, D. (2013). *The Agency of Children: From Family to Global Human Rights.* Cambridge: Cambridge University Press.

Panelli, R., Punch, S. & Robson, E. (Eds.). (2007). *Global Perspectives on Rural Childhood and Youth: Young Rural Lives.* London: Routledge.

Payne, R. (2012). 'Extraordinary survivors' or 'ordinary lives'? Embracing 'every-day agency' in social interventions with child-headed households in Zambia. *Children's Geographies, 10*(4), 399–412.

Pells, K. (2012). "Rights are everything we don't have": clashing conceptions of vulnerability and agency in the daily lives of Rwandan children and youth. *Children's Geographies, 10*(4), 427–440.

Plows, V. (2012). Conflict and coexistence: challenging interactions, expressions of agency and ways of relating to work with young people in the minority world. *Children's Geographies, 10*(3), 279–292.

Prout, A. & James, A. (1990). A new paradigm for the sociology of childhood? Provenance, promise and problems. In A. James & A. Prout (Eds.), *Constructing and Reconstructing Childhood: Contemporary Issues in the Sociological Study of Childhood* (pp. 7–33). London: The Falmer Press.

Punch, S. (2015a). Possibilities for learning between childhoods and youth in the minority and majority worlds: youth transitions as an example of cross-world dialogue. In J. Wyn & H. Cahill (Eds.), *Handbook of Children and Youth Studies* (pp. 689–701). Singapore: Springer.

Punch, S. (2015b). Youth transitions and migration: negotiated and constrained interdependencies within and across generations. *Journal of Youth Studies, 18*(2), 262–276.

Punch, S. (2014). Young migrant trajectories from Bolivia to Argentina: changes and continuities in an era of globalisation. In A. Veale & G. Dona (Eds.), *Child and Youth Migration: Mobility-in-Migration in an Era of Globalisation* (pp. 21–43). Basingstoke: Palgrave Macmillan.

Punch, S. (2007). Generational power relations in rural Bolivia. In R. Panelli, S. Punch & E. Robson (Eds.), *Global Perspectives on Rural Childhood and Youth: Young Rural Lives* (pp. 151–164). London: Routledge.

Punch, S. (2005). The generationing of power: a comparison of child-parent and sibling relations in Scotland. *Sociological Studies of Children and Youth, 10,* 169–188.

Punch, S. (2001a) Negotiating autonomy: childhoods in rural Bolivia. In L. Alanen & B. Mayall (Eds.), *Conceptualising Child-Adult Relations* (pp. 23–36). London: Routledge Falmer.

Punch, S. (2001b). Household division of labour: generation, gender, age, birth order and sibling composition. *Work, Employment & Society, 15*(4), 803–823.

Punch, S. & Sugden, F. (2012). Work, education and out-migration among children and youth in upland Asia: changing patterns of labour and ecological knowledge in an era of globalisation. *Local Environment, 18*(3), 255–270.

Punch, S. & Tisdall, K. (2012). Exploring children and young people's relationships across majority and minority worlds. *Children's Geographies, 10*(3), 241–248.

Punch, S., McIntosh, I. & Emond, R. (2012). "You have a right to be nourished and fed, but do I have a right to make sure you eat your food?" Children's rights and food practices in residential care. *International Journal of Human Rights, 16*(8), 1250–1262.

Robson, E., Bell, S. & Klocker, N. (2007). Conceptualizing agency in the lives and actions of rural young people. In R. Panelli, S. Punch & E. Robson (Eds.), *Global Perspectives on Rural Childhood and Youth: Young Rural Lives* (pp. 135–148). London: Routledge.

Rosen, D. (2007). Child soldiers, international humanitarian law, and the globalization of childhood. *American Anthropologist, 109*(2), 296–306.

Tisdall, K. & Punch, S. (2012). Not so 'new'? Looking critically at childhood studies. *Children's Geographies, 10*(3), 249–264.

Vanderbeck, R. M. (2007) Intergenerational geographies: age relations, segregation and re-engagements. *Geography Compass, 1*(2), 200–221.

White, S. & Choudhury, S. (2010). Children's participation in Bangladesh: issues of agency and structures of violence. In B. Percy-Smith & N. Thomas (Eds.), *A Handbook of Children and Young People's Participation* (pp. 39–50). London: Routledge.

Chapter 13

Do the "mollycoddled" act?

Children, agency and disciplinary entanglements in India

Hia Sen

The concept of agency, which has enjoyed considerable significance in Childhood Research since the 1980s, is not as celebrated in the South Asian context. The debate surrounding childhood in these countries was for a long time primarily centred on issues of policymaking or human rights. Research addressing these concerns did not use an agentive approach for child labourers or children from various marginalised communities as their very situations of disempowerment made them researchable children. This chapter is based on the experience of fieldwork conducted with 10- to 12-year-old children from middle-class families in Kolkata. The discomfort with the concept of agency in the context of protected children from well-off Bengali families has been explored to understand how concepts travel across transcultural academic contexts and, in the process, become entangled with different academic legacies. Central to the chapter is the concern that middle-class Indian children can be a source of awkwardness to scholars trained in India, who are caught between the allure of an approach that favours "agentive children" and the longstanding legacy in South Asian historiography of seeking "protest" only among certain groups that conform to a notion of classical subalternity.

Until about a decade ago, the overwhelming majority of social science literature on childhood in India was on those children who were captive in the dismal situations that at that time typified many of the developing countries to the world at large. The concept of children's agency was at that point well in circulation in the social sciences in the Anglo-Saxon academia, owing in great part possibly to the appearance of James and Prout's work in 2002. When I began my doctoral research in 2009, it was hard to come by works on childhoods in India that did not draw attention to themes of persecution or shortsighted policymaking for which whole communities suffered acutely. That there was little engagement with the concept of agency in these works appeared unproblematic at that point, given that the children they spoke of and often the communities they were from were by definition disempowered. The research of that period was also characterised by a near absence of childhood outside the contexts of labour, poverty, trafficking and poor educational policies. Their very disempowerment made certain groups of children worthy of notice in research. In hindsight, of course, all of this seems much less unproblematic than it was at that time. I have attempted to use hindsight as analytical stilts in order to locate my awkwardness that was the byproduct of particular disciplinary trainings within the contexts of disciplinary histories and changing political-academic climes.

This chapter is an offshoot of my fieldwork experiences from the years 2009–2011 in the city of Kolkata with children who were primarily from Bengali, middle class backgrounds. I did my fieldwork in two rounds, staying in Kolkata for a total of seven months over this period. As I moved back and forth from one academic context to another, it became increasingly apparent that theories, concepts and the ways of identifying these in the field could not remain the same when they travel to different academic contexts. In this chapter, through a reflection of my own awkwardness with the concept of agency when confronted with children from middle-class Indian families, I have argued the need to chart the travels of the concept of agency, its entanglements with other disciplines and the *theoretical flotsam* it washes up along the way. Particularly in an academic context where engagement with the notion of agentive children is undeniably favoured in contemporary Sociology and Anthropology, examining the possible implications of these travels of the concept of "agency" is crucial as more scholars join the ranks of childhood ethnographers, framing their research agendas according to their location in transcultural academia.

In 1988, the publication of Spivak's essay about a regional project that addressed the lacunae in colonial historiography generated a chain of articles in the next one and a half decades musing over the politics of representation in South Asian historiography. The titles of several of these articles imitate Spivak's original title, *Can the Subaltern Speak?*[1] (Spivak, 1988). Most, though not all of these, are related to the Subaltern Studies project that was founded by the historian Ranajit Guha in collaboration with fellow historians. The title of this chapter too fashions itself after this style, in order to gesture towards a certain disciplinary history that has sculpted the academic landscape in India, beyond the discipline of History.

A decade ago, the scholars as well as the principles that were behind the 'new Childhood Studies' were particularly attractive to a generation of researchers interested in sociological and anthropological research on childhood, an area that prior to the 1990s was dominated by writings on socialisation. This corpus of childhood research that existed before appeared archaic and problematic for its adultism when compared to the newer work. The notion of "agentive children" appeared to be the code that would open the door to the vibrant scene of contemporary Childhood Studies. Almost a decade ago, as a student in Delhi, I read James and Prout (2002) at the Teen Murti Library in New Delhi and found the agentive approach to childhood greatly appealing when around me the abounding literature on childhood was primarily of the other kind (Sekar, 1993; Weiner, Burra & Bajpai, 2006). It made sense that children had to be seen as actors in their own right. The engagement with liberal notions of agency or action theories or practice theories was relatively unproblematic when reading them (see also Wihstutz in this volume for a critique of liberal concepts of agency). It was another matter altogether when one began fieldwork armed with a notion that children were capable of autonomous action and resisted or bargained with the domination of adults. At one level, agency appeared to consist of making children's voices be heard, though at other times it appeared to mean that children were constantly challenging, subverting and foiling the impositions made on them by adults. It put me in a predicament, given the kind of research I wanted to do, the kind of middle-class children I interviewed and the kinds of concerns about resistance and dominance that existed in Indian academia.

It is this predicament that this chapter probes, locating the discomfort with agency within the context of disciplinary history and institutional practices through which theories and their political, methodological implications travel across academic contexts and acquire different meanings for researchers in different contexts. Researchers do often find themselves caught between the representational politics, idioms, and so on of academia in which they are trained and those that generate theories with which one works. I have explored the influence of the Subaltern Studies project in post-colonial academia, particularly in shaping the notion of "agency" and the incongruity of seeing protected middle-class Bengali children as "agentive" against this established tradition of seeking the "right kind of marginalized".

The field and the predicament

In 2009 when I started outlining my research area, I knew that I wanted to work on childhood and how predominant notions translate into lived experiences of children. I also knew that I wanted to contextualise it within the Bengali-speaking middle classes. It was a self-conscious move away from any themes of pathos of South Asian childhood that I was at that time loath to explore. The German academic scene, to which I arrived, offered a varied array of work on childhood and held out possible directions for research. A work that I found compelling was Zinnecker's writing on West German youth (Zinnecker, 1990; Watts, Fischer, Fuchs & Zinnecker, 1989) and on childhood as a *Bildungsmoratorium* in which Zinnecker (2001) did not adhere to a teleological model to understand the privileging of a childhood invested in leisure careers, but wrote about the possibility of analysing this cultural moratorium as a "counterworld" to adult production (Zinnecker, 2001, p. 43). The framework appeared all the more appropriate in the context of West Bengal where the notion of a protected childhood invested in education was central to the middle class as early as the late nineteenth century.

Although there have been shifts in the middle classes in the region of Bengal over the years, particularly owing to the economic liberalisation of India in the 1990s, the middle class's preoccupation with education has, if anything, been accentuated. Moral outrage from sections of the middle class about the eroticisation of children in reality television is a reminder of the "sacralisation" (Zelizer, 1994) of a childhood dedicated to the pursuit of "good culture".

Zinnecker's argument about childhood as a cultural moratorium was built against the backdrop of a rapidly industrial society. My own interests were in charting the contours of a cultural moratorium of childhood that emerged in part as a legacy of the colonial past (Sen, 2014). The Bengali *bhadralok* or the gentry that emerged in colonial Bengal harboured contempt for manual work and businesses to a certain degree, associating them with people from lower castes or those from other ethnic groups (Chatterjee, 1985). This legacy, to an extent, shaped the contemporary middle classes in West Bengal, and the cultural moratoria of childhoods became all the more central to the Bengali middle class, which privileged the pursuit of leisure careers to distinguish itself from other classes and ethnic-linguistic groups.

Once the broader area was worked out, I had to consider how I would go about my fieldwork. I chose to look at narratives of three cohorts. Of these, the cohort which comprised of 10- to 12-year-old children who narrated their everyday activities was central to my work. The interviews with children emerged more from a pragmatic than an ideological concern. The centrality of children's accounts was not owing to a "commandment to listen to the voices of children" (Bluebond-Langner & Korbin, 2007, p. 243) but to have a firsthand account of how their childhood was lived (Sen, 2014, p. 79).

After a few days, the very reasons that made Kolkata a prudent "field" made accessing children and interviewing them that much more difficult. Adults hovered about everywhere. I had, true to my interest, pursued children where the cultural moratorium placed them – I went to various afterschool tuitions, swimming classes, homes, and on one occasion met 11-year-old girls in the piano room of a school. It appeared challenging to find the children alone at any point. Much of this was not deliberate. Adults sometimes happened to be within earshot because even in swimming classes for children, the enclosure was the space available for both children who practiced and their parents who talked, drinking tea, exchanging information about schools and tests, and checking the time before they would accompany their children to another tuition or singing class. Whenever I talked to the children in their houses or apartments, at almost every interview there were one or more adults present.

One of the challenges of fieldwork was striking a balance between what the children would say and eliciting that which was not said owing to the presence of adults. It was one of the most disconcerting aspects of the interviews, though it wasn't that parents were against the interviews. Rather, their enthusiasm at times to have their children interviewed ensured their presence or involvement in case the child faltered.

I had not reckoned with the presence of adults in almost every aspect of the children's everyday lives. Children ages 9 to 12, particularly single children, slept with their parents, stepped out of the house with their parents and the adults were around even in their leisure hours, making up for playmates children had little access to outside of school. At first it didn't pose much of an issue. It was only after I returned to Germany that, in the course of conversation with a Professor who had extensively worked with children, I mentioned the involvement of adults at the interviews. My anecdotes were met with horrified incredulity that I was keeping the interviews. I was told to start afresh as the interviews were not valid.

Of course, it was exasperating to have adults cut into conversations with the children. The contexts were not always desirable, but I had little choice. My discomfort with what I was doing grew upon hearing that the interviews weren't "proper". In the second phase of my fieldwork, I was determined to do something about the issue and keep the interviews "unspoilt". But the presence of adults, even in the conversation with the children, was daunting.

In a context where there are sometimes as many as four adults in the family living in a two-bedroom apartment, the presence of adults in the house during the interviews was usual. I was chary of asking them, however politely, to be in another room while I talked to their child. Again, being left alone in a room did not ensure ironclad privacy. There was one instance when I asked Rwiti, an 11-year-old girl, what she watched on the television. She hesitated and a voice from the adjoining room prompted, first *National Geographic* and then *Taare Zameen Par* (a film in Hindi released a few years before about a dyslexic boy. The film ironically upheld the assertion that parents can lose their children if they push them too hard).

There were times when I'd ask girls and boys if they had friends of the other gender, particularly after hearing the names of their friends. The children almost always emphatically said they didn't. A 12-year-old girl, Mridula, who asserted that there were no boys who were friends, said after a few seconds of reflection, "but I talk to some boys in tuition". Boys, too, had similar responses. It could have been owing to a number of reasons; the fact that parents and teachers frowned upon romantic inclinations could have had a bearing on their response. Though parents did not overtly criticise girl-boy friendships – and, in fact, in the swimming classes, girls would talk to boys – romantic interests were considered threatening as they distracted children from their studies. On these few occasions, I despaired and I wondered how "agency friendliness" could be achieved in my work. If an adult in the same room as the child "thinned" the agency of the child (Klocker, 2007), an adult prompting the child's replies was worse (see also Esser in this volume for a critique on an understanding of agency as being either thick or thin).

At the same time, the child-adult relationships in the family were anything but fixed in a format. In one interview session, the mother and grandmother of the 11-year-old girl I was interviewing were present in the room. As I was interviewing her mother, Rwiti came and placed herself on the sofa beside her mother. The mother protested, at which she indignantly said, "Ah great! When I was talking you were sitting there throughout"[2]. These were occasions when the prospects of my research felt less formidable. It was much more comforting when the children *talked back*, for this was the closest to the notion of agency to which I felt I had to be loyal.

It was not so much that I was not convinced that children were actors in their everyday lives. The point was *where to look* for this action, which I felt would have to be akin to a rebellion or a conniving manipulation of adults who dominate. With these protected children, who spent almost all day moving from one supervised context to another learning singing, watching television with parents, being accompanied by parents to tuitions, I couldn't discern mutinous tendencies of the kind I thought counted as "agency". These were the mollycoddled children who were not only protected from paid work and sexual experiences, but were also kept away from domestic chores in many families. If there was a hidden transcript of children's agency, I wondered if I would know how not to miss it.

The Subaltern Studies project

The notion of hidden transcripts already had some currency in Indian academia, though not in relation to childhood research. It perhaps had more to do with the works of Guha (1982) than that of Scott (1990) and the Subaltern Studies project, which emerged in the 1980s and became one of the most influential schools of work in Indian academia, sculpting particular interests and forming discursive moulds of domination and resistance.

The emergence of this school has been traced to political circumstances when there was a growing disillusionment with orthodox Marxist theory and practice, particularly in the aftermath of an armed Maoist struggle, which was abortive (Sarkar, 1999). The term "subaltern" avoided the economic reductionism of the term "class", yet implied the relation of dominance-exploitation. A central concern of the school was the critique of the Western colonial power-knowledge. The colonial historiography was countered in these writings, for its elitism, as also the nationalist historiography, which primarily saw the nationalist movement as spearheaded by a western educated Indian intelligentsia, and which therefore was also elitist (Guha, 1982).

It is within this project that the most potent notion of agency in Indian academia emerged. The agency referred to is primarily the agency of the indigenous persons who were mute and peripheral in the earlier form of history writing. The subalterns are primarily peasants, women and persons from the former untouchable or Dalit castes in these writings. A dominant premise was that the subordinate people of South Asia have no consciousness as subject agents in the elitist historiography in the three forms – nationalist, colonialist and Marxist. There was no consideration of them creating their own history (O'Hanlon, 1988). The restoration of these histories was a central concern.

The implications of romanticising the "authentic" indigenous voice that emerges from a position of this kind are comparable with the questions of authenticity of the child's voice that James (2007) cautions against (see also Spyrou in this volume). In order to assert the subaltern as an actor, a particular idiom of protest by the subaltern was given centrality. As the prime concern of the subaltern historians was the subaltern as an actor, the reading of different sources also had to consider action on the part of the peasant, tribal or the lower castes. This action was central. The idiom of the subordinate in effect traced out the kind of action, which would be interpreted. As the subordinate's voice was previously not heard owing to its marginalisation by the power-knowledge, its "recovery" would therefore be in acts of insubordination. In doing so, "the original presence" (O'Hanlon, 1988, p. 196) would be "restored". This meant that a particular kind of action would be of interest to a subaltern historian, the act of defiance or protest.

O'Hanlon (1988) says that "the very notion of restoration of an original presence suggests – and particularly so where the presence is an 'insubordinate' or resistant one – the means by which it is to be done" (p. 196). Some implications of this idiom of the active subaltern are of interest in the context of seeing children as agents. I shall discuss them as two distinctive points, though in effect they make up the idiom as a whole.

What counts as action?

The affinity between the agenda of "recovering voices" as it emerged in European microhistory (Dayton, 2004) as well as the Subaltern Studies project and the notion of agency as it emerged in Childhood Research is of significance to ethnographers from adjacent disciplinary contexts who grapple with the concept of "agency" in the field. The capability of the child as a subject-agent and the agency of the slave emerge from the same set of liberal humanist values. Johnson (2003) says:

> To put this another way: the term "agency" smuggles a notion of the universality of a liberal notion of selfhood, with its emphasis on independence and choice, right into the middle of conversation about slavery against which that supposedly natural (at least for white men) condition was originally defined. (p. 115)

This is perhaps not as apparent in Childhood Research as in the historical writings, but there is a certain triumph in hearing the voices, which oppose that of adults, of the structures and the discourses, which had kept them in subordination. In this context, my conviction about hearing children's voices became tenuous in Kolkata for the children's worlds were peopled with adults. At some points, it felt as if there were more adults than children in the children's accounts of their everyday lives. I mention two different contexts from the field.

In the months of my fieldwork in Kolkata, I interviewed more than 30 children between ages 9 and 12. At one point I had toyed with the idea of asking them to produce maps of the regions of the city that they were familiar with in their everyday lives, and then I abandoned the idea. However, during interviews with some of the children, names of certain localities would come up and I'd pursue the theme. A few of the children used generic names of spaces, like "*para*" (neighbourhood), to refer to their unsupervised ventures to the grocer's, or to adjoining neighbourhood playgrounds. Some of them knew the names of neighbourhoods their tuitions or other classes were in, but the majority of children would be accompanied by adults. They would be accompanied to the bus stop by their parents, and in the interviews they mentioned that their parents would stand at the bus stop until they left. Outside of the school, parents – particularly mothers – would be present at the swimming club or sports classes, sitting on the doorsteps of houses when the children were at tuition, and would accompany the children home.

This was the extent of the involvement of adults in the lives of children from the Bengali middle class. When I asked them if they played outside of the house or went out by themselves, most children made it clear that this was out of the question. If they resented it, it wasn't something encountered during my fieldwork. Some of them negotiated with the available resources of space and playmate and played with parents within the house. In the winter of 2010, some of the children talked about playing badminton. "Corridor badminton" was mentioned (Sen, 2014, p. 157), played with parents. One boy said he played with his grandfather on the terrace. The constant accompaniment was in effect the kind of practice that Alanen (2001) terms *"generationing"* (p. 135), though this was also true of adolescents as well to a great extent.

I wondered what the children thought about their context. The limited number of places that children could go to and be in unsupervised was certainly not unquestioned by the children. For instance, walking along the pathway adjacent to a swimming pool on a December evening, I asked a 10-year-old boy if he heard stories about his parents' childhood. Some distance away, the mothers and fathers of the children, including his own, were sitting, drinking tea and talking. The roar of traffic and honking of cars and buses could be heard beyond the gates of the swimming club. Shouryajit nodded, telling me what he knew of his parents' childhood. I asked him if he thought they were any different from his. He said yes, then was quiet as we walked, and then launched into a narrative about a day his mother was lost as a child, and couldn't find her mother. I was quiet, wondering if he would relate it to the question asked, when he concluded his narrative with: "But now ... it's ... we can't even get lost". The statement made sense in the context of our earlier conversation about the one time he was "almost" lost when he was allowed to go the barber's with an older boy.

Children were particularly wary of talking about conflicts with parents. If the parents were out of earshot, the question would be greeted with hesitation but also a smile and they wouldn't always elaborate their answers. The word *"porashuna"* or studies would be mentioned as a reason and sometimes they explained that there would be a "fight" if they "played too much". The choice of the word *fight* was an interesting one. It suggested a conflict between equals and could be contrasted with the term "scolding" used by some of the children and by respondents of the older cohorts when speaking about conflicts with parents. A few children spoke of corporal punishment. But noticeably, references to being slapped were often talked about humorously by children, using terms that trivialised the incident; for example, Ishan, an 11-year-old boy, said his parents were annoyed if he played "too much" and didn't study. "Ma gives me one whack" (laughs). The effect of saying "one whack" is different than "I was beaten" and also connotes a different image of the adult-children balance of power. The strategy of joking was applied by children to refer to conflict with parents, instead of simply talking about being beaten.

A few children laughed at themselves and the tactics of dodging studies or circumventing parental rules. Rwiti, a 10-year-old girl, talked about annoying her parents, saying, "Like ... when I don't study, then my mother says I must study, and I say 'In a bit Ma' ... and then like that no studying is done"[3]. These anecdotes were almost always given humorously with a laugh, subverting the power of the adult by making the incident funny in their script and referring to ways of getting round the rules.

These were undoubtedly conversations that made me feel that I was in the "right". I would applaud myself for reading subversion in speech in which some form of defiance was performed, irrespective of its "actuality". At this point, I would revert to the Subaltern Studies project. I would like to refer to the model of this project, which O'Hanlon considers the product of the unguarded pursuit of subjectivity and agency, and "its tendency to suppress strategies and efforts at resistance which do not take the masculine form of a full-blooded rebellion by a subject-agent such as it tends to have enshrined within it" (O'Hanlon, 1988, p. 213). The protest sought by this model is conventional.

The reference to my field is to bring out the imperative felt to seek children's agency in a particular form. It is as James (2007) says that the anthropological concern for giving voice to children is "somewhat of a new research orthodoxy". If Anthropology and History in South Asia have learnt to hear voices that were once peripheral, then they have learnt to hear them when they speak in one kind of a language: that of rebellion. The dissident child is therefore the child as subject-agent.

Whose voice must be listened to?

In the last few years, there has been noticeable critical reflection on the liberal theories of action (O'Hanlon, 1988; Ahearn, 2001; Mahmood, 2001; Johnson, 2007). Scholars have also explored the differing connotations of agency when different theoretical models from action theory to practice theory are embraced (Ahearn, 2001). In recent times, the clarity of the concept of children's agency has also been questioned (Bordonaro & Payne, 2012), and the pitfalls of "giving voice" to children have been discussed (James, 2007; Bluebond-Langner & Korbin, 2007; Honig, Lange & Leu, 1999; see also Spyrou in this volume).

In many postcolonial contexts, this reviewing of agency has meant the abandonment of an approach that equates agency with the "free will" exercised by "completely autonomous individuals" (Ahearn, 2001, p. 115). The implication of an approach like this in Childhood Research in the developing countries is the growing visibility of children from particular contexts. The recognition of the agency of children in these circumstances is not without its difficulties. Bordonaro and Payne (2012) draw attention to an "ethical conundrum" that is posed in acknowledging the agency of children involved in "morally ambiguous actions" (p. 369).

A central concern in this chapter is a representational conundrum that is posed by the appetite of Childhood Research for children's agency and is complicated by the disciplinary histories in postcolonial academia. In a reversal of earlier historiographical practices, certain groups of people are singled out in the Indian academia, in History and the other social sciences and analysed through the lenses of action and practice theories. Owing to this academic legacy in which the dispossessed have symbolic preeminence, the agency of persons from certain groups or communities is of greater interest in research than others. Those who have borne the brunt of epistemic violence twice, in the colonialist and the nationalist elite historiography, are of particular interest in post-colonial academia.

It does not raise eyebrows, therefore, that much of the research on children in South Asia centres on certain contexts – the child labourers who are predominantly from a lower caste, child prostitutes, children from religious minorities, Dalit children, tribal children. Agency is not the predominant concern in these works, but there are some exceptions like Dyson's research (2007) on child workers in the Himalayan forests. Das (1989), in a nuanced writing on agency, privileged the voices of children. But the children whose voices interested her had lost their families in the anti-Sikh riots of 1984 and were put up in two community camps in Delhi. These were children who, in the literal sense, were dispossessed.

In other developing countries, the attempt at researching children's worlds from an agentive approach is perhaps more evident. Klocker's research (Klocker, 2007) on Tanzanian girls involved in domestic work, devised a quantification of agency by employing terms like "thin agency" (p. 85) taking into account the actions in restrictive contexts. Though this approach is not unproblematic, it offers a possibility of diluting the sharpness of the idiom of protest that is attributed to certain groups in the Subaltern Studies tradition. The assumption that poverty stricken Tanzanian girls can "assert" agency (p. 83) implies that even the weakest of the lot is capable of action, however feeble. It is nevertheless disconcerting that "agency" is written in conjunction with the verb "assert" (p. 83).

That the worlds of middle-class children are largely absent in the research on developing countries and from scholars trained in these countries is not arbitrary. I have drawn attention to this question of invisibility in this chapter. When analytical devices quantifying agency are being devised for children in developing countries, these would be incongruous to research on protected, middle-class children whose contexts are restrictive in a different sense than that of the Tanzanian girls. This is the representational conundrum for children whose "comfortable" situation coupled with their docility renders them invisible in certain academic contexts.

Conclusion

The term "mollycoddled" has been employed as a rhetorical gesture. It intends to draw attention to the ideology that underlies the interest of childhood researchers in India. That everyone, regardless of generation or degrees of protection enjoyed by them, is capable of action is not of concern in this context. But the privilege or the misfortune of being greatly protected, being mollycoddled, makes children from a certain background incongruent to a conceptual framework that recognises protest as action.

Childhood Studies in South Asia are, if at all, in an embryonic form. However, interest in questions of agency, childhood and children is emerging from different quarters of academia and also certain non-governmental organisations[4]. This makes it all the more important to locate the concept of agency in its travels and in institutional practices and histories. The need to look at not just disciplinary pasts but also transdiciplinary histories is central in this context.

The Subaltern Studies project has without doubt been a powerful influence on scholars of South Asia in the disciplines of history, sociology and anthropology. In the Preface to the first volume of Subaltern Studies, Guha (1982) states that the word "subaltern" should be understood as the name "for the general attribute of subordination in South Asian society whether this is expressed in terms of class, caste, age, gender and office or in any other way" (p. vii). But an interest in the subordination of children though generationing practices has been peripheral to this strand of writing. It, however, played a crucial role in epitomising subalternity in India by selecting certain groups – peasants, tribals, women from certain backgrounds. The concept of agency in India radiates from an understanding of action generated from Subaltern Studies. I have argued that this tradition inflects the notion of agency in research on children and singles out children in particular contexts.

The extent of protection, regimentation and adults in the children's everyday lives was at times a cause of despair during my fieldwork in Kolkata. The tension underlying my fieldwork as I moved between the academic contexts was sometimes dispelled. But where child soldiers were in armed conflict, the children I was talking to moved between home, school, tuitions and singing lessons. Even their primary playmates at times were adults who supervised them in varying degrees. I wondered how one would read agency when children, on being asked to switch off the television, do just that. Mahmood's work (2001) on the dilemma of employing a feminist lens to analyse Egyptian women's involvement in a religious movement inimical to their "emancipation" is closest to the concerns of this chapter. The training of the women in piety, their docility, is an annoyance to the emancipatory politics of feminist theory. The awkwardness of working with coddled, "docile" children, when the general mood in Childhood Research favoured actions that go against the grain, similarly revealed the hegemonic status ascribed to action-centred research on children.

The central contention of this paper is that concepts travel. They travel even within a cultural context. The ideological imperatives and idioms of the concept of agency are overlooked outside the context of South Asian historical writings. Therefore, when the concept of the child as an agent is addressed in South Asia, researchers would be more willing to listen to some voices, or to voices when they obey a specific script. The idiom of subordination is predominant in colonial history. This could be the reason there are Women Studies in India than Gender Studies, Dalit Studies than Caste Studies. The imperatives to valorise a subject who previously had no voice, and to listen for a kind of rebellion inscribed in that voice emerges from this academic context and could have an effect on the direction of childhood research in India. This relation between subalternity and agency can be found even in recent writings. Vallgårda (2014), for example, argues how colonial understandings distort the agency of subalterns. Although in her analysis of the encounter between Danish missionaries and natives in South India she argues that there are no autonomous subalterns, the agency of a native woman is identified in her symbolic act of running away from the Danish missionaries.

This exploration of the entanglements of agency with other disciplinary soils made visible the fine cracks between my field and that of other researchers working on children in other contexts. Even if every one of them worked with a steadfast conviction of children's agency, the notion of a community in a sense was misleading. The travels ensure that there are cracks. As Said says, "There seem to be too many interruptions, too many distractions, too many irregularities interfering with the homogenous space supposedly holding scholars together" (Said, 1983, p. 159).

There is a paradox involved. The middle classes of Bengal have been perceived as agents of change, rebellious, having been foremost in the protest against the colonial administration. In contemporary India, the middle classes have been seen as spearheading social movements, political changes and legislative changes. But the mollycoddled middle-class children are something of a conundrum. They do not upend the dominant construction of childhood as other groups of children in India do, nor do they run from the enclosures of protection. Where, as children, they have the potential to claim visibility as representationally marginalised and generationally subordinated to adults, this potential is reduced by their middle-class location. The script of "protest" is not their lot. Though it doesn't have a voice in the colonial historiography, the protected middle-class child, therefore, is not a subaltern.

Notes

1 Though a number of articles have titles parodying Spivak's title, some of the most notable in terms of their academic engagement with the questions raised by Spivak are Maggio, J. (2007). Can the subaltern be heard? *Alternatives*, 32, 419–443; Prakash, G. (1994). Can the "subaltern" ride? A reply to O'Hanlon and Washbrook. *Comparative Studies Society and History*, 34(1), 168–184. A recent article is Vallgårda, K. (2014). Can the subaltern woman run? Gender, race and agency in the colonial missionary texts. *Scandinavian Journal of History*, 39(4), 472–486.

2 I have also recorded the conversation elsewhere (Sen, 2014, p. 96) with a slight variation in the translation from the original lines in Bengali.

3 The conversation has also been discussed elsewhere (Sen, 2014, p. 100) with a variation in translation.

4 A few indicators are found. There is a sociologist from India on the editorial board of the journal *Childhood*. In 2013, a conference called "Childhoods in South Asia: Comparative and Historical Perspectives" was organised by the Australian National University. Four years ago a research institute of women studies in Hyderabad commissioned a project to children's writers that would assume the perspectives of children from marginalised groups. The interest in childhood and children's agency can thus be identified in the Indian academic context.

References

Ahearn, L. M. (2001). Language and agency. *Annual Review of Anthropology, 30*, 109–137.

Alanen, L. (2001). Childhood as a generational condition: children's daily lives in a central Finland town. In L. Alanen & B. Mayall (Eds.), *Conceptualizing Child-Adult Relations* (pp. 129–143). London: RoutledgeFalmer.

Bluebond-Langner, M. & Korbin, J. E. (2007). Challenges and opportunities in the anthropology of childhoods. An introduction to "children, childhoods and childhood studies". *American Anthropologist, 109*(2), 241–246.

Bordonaro, L. I. & Payne, R. (2012). Ambiguous agency. Critical perspectives on social interventions with children and youth in Africa. *Children's Geographies, 10*(4), 365–372.

Chatterjee, P. (1985). The fruits of Macaulay's Poison Tree. In A. Mitra & S. Sen (Eds.), *The Truth Unites. Essays in Tribute to Samar Sen* (pp. 70–89). Calcutta: Subarnarekha.

Das, V. (1989). Voices of children. *Daedalus, 118*(4, Another India, Fall), 262–294.

Dayton, C. H. (2004). Rethinking agency, recovering voices. *The American Historical Review, 109*(3), 827–843.

Dyson, J. (2007). Respite and rupees: the impact of a new market opportunity on the everyday lives of children and young people in the Indian Himalayas. In D. K. Behera (Ed.), *Childhoods in South Asia* (pp. 29–42). Oxford: Pearson Education Limited.

Guha, R. (Ed.) (1982). *Subaltern Studies I. Writings on South Asian History and Society*. Delhi: Oxford University Press.

Honig, M., Lange, A. & H. R. Leu (Eds.) (1999). *Aus der Perspektive von Kindern? Zur Methodologie der Kindheitsforschung [From the Children's Point of View? The Methodology of Childhood Studies]*. Weinheim: Juventa.

James, A. (2007). Giving voice to children's voices. Practices and problems, pitfalls and potentials. *American Anthropologist, 109*(2), 261–272.

Johnson, W. (2003). On agency. *Journal of Social History, 37*(Fall 1), 113–124.

James, A. & Prout, A. (2002). *Constructing and Reconstructing Childhood: Contemporary Issues in the Sociological Study of Childhood* (repr). London: RoutledgeFalmer.

Klocker, N. (2007). An example of "thin" agency: child domestic workers in Tanzania. In R. Panelli, S. Punch & E. Robson (Eds.), *Global Perspectives on Rural Childhood and Youth: Young Rural Lives* (pp. 83–94). London: Routledge.

Mahmood, S. (2001). Feminist theory, embodiment, and the docile agent: some reflections on the Egyptian Islamic revival. *Cultural Anthropology, 16*(2), 202–236.

O' Hanlon, R. (1988). Recovering the subject subaltern studies and histories of resistance in colonial South Asia. *Modern Asian Studies*, 22(1), 189–224.

Said, E. W. (1983). Traveling theory. In E. W. Said (Ed.), *The World, the Text, and the Critic* (pp. 157–181). Cambridge, MA: Harvard University Press.

Sarkar, S. (Ed.). (1999). *Writing Social History* (4th ed.). New Delhi: Oxford University Press.

Scott, J. C. (1990). *Domination and the Arts of Resistance: Hidden Transcripts.* New Haven: Yale University Press.

Sen, H. (2014). *"Time-out" in the Land of Apu: Childhoods, Bildungsmoratorium and the Middle Classes of Urban West Bengal.* Wiesbaden: Springer VS.

Sekar, H. (1993). *No Light in Their Lives: Girl Child Labour in the Match Industry of Sivakasi.* Noida: National Labour Institute.

Spivak, G. C. (1988). Can the subaltern speak? In C. Nelson & L. Grossberg (Eds.), *Marxism and The Interpretation of Culture* (pp. 271–313). London: Macmillan.

Vallgårda, K. (2014). Can the subaltern woman run? Gender, race and agency in the colonial missionary texts. *Scandinavian Journal of History*, 39(4), 472–486.

Watts, M., Fischer, A., Fuchs, W. & Zinnecker, J. (1989). *Contemporary German Youth and Their Elders: A Generational Comparison.* New York, Westport: Greenwood Press.

Weiner, M., Burra, N. & Bajpai, A. (2006). *Born Unfree: Child Labour, Education and the State in* India. New Delhi: Oxford University Press.

Zelizer, V. A. (1994). *Pricing the Priceless Child: The Changing Social Value of Children.* Princeton: Princeton Univ. Press.

Zinnecker, J. (1990). What does the future hold? Youth and the sociocultural change in the FRG. In L. Chisholm, P. Büchner, H. Krüger & P. Brown (Eds.), *Childhood, Youth and Social Change: A Comparative Perspective* (pp. 17–32). London: Falmer Press.

Zinnecker, J. (2001). Children in young and aging societies: the order of generations and models of childhood in comparative perspective. In T. J. Owens & S. L. Hofferth (Eds.), *Children at the Millennium: Where Have We Come From? Where Are We Going? Advances in Life Course Research, Volume 6* (pp. 11–52). Amsterdam: Elsevier Science & Technology.

Context matters!

On non-working children's citizenship in South Indian children's rights initiatives as a practice

Laura B. Kayser

In recent years, children's agency in enforcing and formulating their rights has been discussed with reference to the concept of citizenship. While children's active role within working children's movements is generally considered a paragon of this kind of agency, their far more widespread participation in activities against child labour has so far received scant recognition. Using findings from field research with non-working children and young people on their activities against child labour in two children's rights initiatives in South India, this chapter explores the meaning of lived citizenship from these children's perspectives in their institutional and everyday contexts. Drawing on the concept of citizenship as a practice referring to rights (Lister, 2007), an alternative conceptualisation of children's citizenship is developed based on children's practices in children's rights movements from children's own perspectives. The analysis highlights the importance of matters of context for their citizenship practices. It reveals the relevance of the generational order for the children's citizenship, which is characterised primarily by their own and their target group's status as children. The exploration of these children's practices provides new insights into the characteristics and challenges of realising citizenship as a child in the Majority World (among other places). Furthermore, the results question the widespread notion of non-working children's activities against child labour as non-agentic and emphasise the need to rethink normative assumptions about what constitutes "real" agency.

Children's rights-related agency and the matter of context

Since the adoption of the United Nations Convention on the Rights of the Child (UNCRC), participation has become the "new norm in children's rights practice and policy" (Reynaert *et al.*, 2009, p. 529). In both the Minority and Majority Worlds, there are large numbers of initiatives working on the implementation of this principle by promoting and fostering children's voices and their active role in their lives (Reynaert *et al.*, 2009; Bourdillon, 2004). Many of these efforts are directed at children's participation in enforcing and formulating their own rights.

Recently, this has been discussed with reference to the concept of citizenship. In line with the "New" Sociology of Childhood (James & Prout, 1990; James, 2009), these accounts highlight children's active role in society, as well as their current social and political contributions. This involves a critique of children's (marginalised) position in society. Conceptualising children's citizenship as an actual practice referring to rights (Lister, 2007) has been highlighted as a particularly promising way to look at and recognise children's respective activities as an expression of their agency in this regard (James, 2011; Invernizzi & Williams, 2008a; Milne, 2013).

Against a perceived tendency for both childhood and children's rights studies "to nurture normative and political positions that deal with improving respect for children's agency" (Hanson 2014, p. 442), the recent years have seen an increasing demand for critical views on the claims of children's rights in general (Reynolds *et al.*, 2006, p. 443; Reynaert *et al.*, 2009), and on the concept of agency in relation to the worldwide implementation of children's rights and children's active role in this endeavour (Tisdall & Punch, 2012). This approach proposes a new focus for the study of children's rights and children's related agency that goes beyond mere recognition and is concerned with children's actual practices and their contexts. Regarding children's rights, this implies an examination of the meaning of these rights in practice and of children's own perspectives on their rights in their various real-life contexts (Tisdall & Punch, 2012; Reynolds *et al.*, 2006; Hanson, 2014). As Tisdall and Punch (2012) point out, it is still an open question what it actually means for children to exercise agency within children's rights initiatives. In line with this critical and context-sensitive approach to children's agency, the need to conceptualise childhood not only from Minority World childhoods (as a specific context) has been voiced. Where minority childhood ideals – such as scholarisation (see Boyden, 1997) – are applied to a Majority World framework (Tisdall & Punch, 2012), this becomes particularly relevant.

This new perspective corresponds well with a concept of lived citizenship that is concerned with the ways children themselves experience this kind of agency in their different real-life contexts (Lister, 2007; James, 2011; Invernizzi & Williams, 2008b). While children's active role in working children's movements and their claims (right to work and education) are generally considered a paragon for children's lived citizenship (Liebel, 2008; Invernizzi, 2008), the corresponding and more widespread practices of non-working children against child labour are perceived differently. These are not considered authentic expressions of children's agency, because they agree with international policies (Invernizzi & Milne, 2002, p. 404; critically: Stasiulis, 2002).

The chapter uses empirical findings from a qualitative study on non-working children's activities against child labour in two children's rights initiatives in South India to question this common notion. It explores the meaning of lived citizenship from these children's perspectives in their institutional and everyday contexts and draws on the concept of citizenship as a practice referring to rights

(Lister, 2007) to further develop an alternative concept of children's citizenship in relation to children's rights. The results highlight the relevance of matters of context for the children's citizenship practices. By looking at citizenship as an actual practice, the chapter thus conceptualises agency empirically, starting from children's own lived experiences in children's rights initiatives. In this regard, it points to the need to rethink normative assumptions about what constitutes "real" agency.

The chapter begins by outlining the concept of children's lived citizenship as a practice referring to children's rights and presents two empirical accounts from children's rights movements ("Conceptualising children's citizenship as a practice referring to children's rights"). It goes on to introduce the framework of the study at hand ("The study: non-working children's practices against child labour in two South Indian children's rights initiatives") and presents findings on the meaning of contextual factors for children's citizenship practices ("Children's citizenship practices from children's perspectives: matters of context") in relation to, first, institutional versus everyday contexts ("Citizenship practices *within* and *without*: institutional and everyday contexts") and, second, the fundamental context of the generational order ("Citizenship as a practice *by* children *for* children: context of the generational order"). In the final section, these findings are used to outline the defining characteristics of an alternative concept of children's citizenship as a practice, which is discussed in relation to the debate on children's (rights-related) agency ("On the matter of context for an alternative concept of children's lived citizenship in relation to children's rights").

Conceptualising children's citizenship as a practice referring to children's rights

"Children are almost everything that the non-citizen is" (Cockburn, 1998, p. 107) and have mostly been conceptualised with regard to their future citizenship status, based on an adult norm (p. 107). However, with reference to the New Sociology of Childhood and its aim to highlight children's active role (James, 2009), several attempts have been made to revise the theoretical concept of citizenship to include children and promote the recognition of children's agency. Along this line, several authors have developed difference-centred citizenship concepts to accommodate children's practices as expressions of citizenship (including theirs) as one that is (necessarily) different but of equal "value" (Moosa-Mitha, 2005; Cockburn, 1998; Lister, 2007; Invernizzi & Williams, 2008a). Despite their differences, these accounts highlight the need for a different and broader understanding of citizenship because of children's social position within the generational order (Moosa-Mitha, 2005; Cockburn, 1998; Lister, 2007; Invernizzi & Williams, 2008a). Their inherent aim to promote children's potential as citizens now is still evident in recent contributions on children's citizenship (e.g. Larkins, 2014; Cheney, 2012; Tisdall et al., 2014).

Against this background, a concept of *lived* citizenship has been highlighted as especially promising for looking at and understanding children's practices as expressions of citizenship (James, 2011; Invernizzi & Williams, 2008b). Drawing on feminist models that conceptualise citizenship from positions of social marginalisation (Kabeer, 2005), Lister (2007) proposes an understanding of children's citizenship as a socio-political, active and participative kind of lived practice, which is directed at enforcing rights. Looking at children's actual practices makes it possible to recognise children as *doing* citizenship, despite their lack of a formal citizen status (Lister, 2007; Smith et al., 2005). This conceptualisation involves the demand to develop it from the perspectives of the marginalised themselves, as something that is characterised by its realisation "from below" (Smith et al., 2005, p. 2; see also Liebel, 2008). In this regard, everyday and informal forms of citizenship become particularly relevant, so that one needs to look at children's present citizenship practices in actual, everyday contexts (Lister, 2007). As James (2011) points out on this matter of context, this must include an examination of children's experiences in relation to the given contexts and their ways of acting within these contexts in their everyday life.

Despite the call to engage with children's perspectives on this lived citizenship (for example Liebel, 2008; Jans, 2004; James, 2011), studies on the issue are rare. This is especially true for children's citizenship in relation to children's rights. However, there are two accounts that refer to children's citizenship as a lived practice referring to (children's) rights that use empirical examples, which are very similar to the one presented here. The first account describes a citizenship "from below" in reference to children's rights-related practices in working children's movements in the Majority World (Liebel, 2008), whereas the second study outlines a more "global" kind of citizenship in relation to children's practices in a Canadian children's movement (Stasiulis, 2002). Both offer important insights into the defining characteristics of children's citizenship as a practice in relation to children's rights and will be used to further develop an alternative concept of children's citizenship.

In Liebel's (2008) example from the working children's movement, he describes children's citizenship as a self-organised kind of practice that children realise in their everyday lived realities, distancing it from institutional contexts. It takes place in a specific Majority World context and addresses instances of (children's) rights violations in children's own real-life contexts. The citizenship he describes evolves from a situation of powerlessness, and includes children's claim to determine and enact their own rights – a critique of existing anti-labour laws for children in particular – as well as the idea of entitlement to an equal status in relation to adults. It is also characterised by children's awareness of a shared concern (as children) and is a highly collective phenomenon, as Liebel notes (Liebel, 2008).

Stasiulis (2002), on the other hand, refers to a kind of lived citizenship that aims to advocate children's rights globally (no child labour/poverty, pro-education) in line with the UNCRC. It is a media-prone form of citizenship, which, in contrast to Liebel's account, is mostly directed at more disadvantaged children in (poor) Majority World contexts. Despite these differences, the children's practices on behalf of (other) children reveal a similar understanding of existing commonalities between all children globally. Because they share the position as children, they feel best placed to understand and advocate on behalf of (other) children's situations and concerns. Their practices, too, question children's experiences of powerlessness and include the claim to actively participate in the realisation of children's rights (Stasiulis, 2002). Looking at children's citizenship as an actual *practice* draws attention to the contexts in which children have to realise their citizenship and the significance those contexts have for their practices (James, 2011; Tisdall & Punch, 2012). In the current debate, the matter of context is mostly referred to in order to differentiate between "less agentic" forms of children's participation in formal initiatives set up for them by adults on the one hand, and their "real" agency in child-initiated informal activities in children's everyday lives on the other (Liebel, 2008, p. 42; Invernizzi, 2008). While these are not the only relevant contextual factors for children's lived citizenship, the clear distinction between institutional and everyday contexts for children's citizenship is difficult to maintain when considering children's actual practices, as the analysis will show.

As mentioned with regard to the concepts of children's citizenship, the generational order and children's marginalised and powerless position constitute another, particularly relevant contextual factor for the characteristics of children's citizenship (Lister, 2007; Liebel, 2008; Roche, 1999). However, not much is known about *how* the generational order becomes meaningful for children's citizenship practices. Adding another aspect to the lack of insight into the particularities of this relation, James (2011, p. 169) emphasises the need to consider the specific "cultural politics of childhood" of children's respective real-life contexts in order to understand the meaning and characteristics of their citizenship from a childhood studies perspective. This also applies to the relation between children and adults within participatory spaces (e.g. children's rights initiatives), as Taft (2014) points out. With regard to the Indian context of the study at hand, this generational order seems to consist of a relatively dominant and strongly asymmetrical age hierarchy that does not support the notion of children's active role (Saeed, 2014; Nieuwenhuys, 2009).

The study: non-working children's practices against child labour in two South Indian children's rights initiatives

The research (a diploma thesis project) took place over a period of six weeks in spring 2009 in two children's rights initiatives (urban/rural) in Tamil Nadu,

South India, where non-working children played an active role in activities against child labour. Both initiatives attach great importance to children's participation and run programmes to promote and facilitate it, especially regarding children's rights. While the urban initiative operates in a medium-sized city and runs a child-led children's rights group, the rural initiative has established children's parliaments as participatory spaces for children. Both work with children from marginalised groups, mostly Dalit communities.

The study set out to explore these non-working children's perspectives on their practices against child labour, their subsequent meaning-making and experiences within the initiative and in their everyday lives. To this end, several group discussions and individual interviews were conducted with children and young people (aged 12 to 21) engaged in the initiative's activities, as well as with staff and volunteers, with the help of gatekeepers from a local Christian college. The children were asked about their past and present activities against child labour as well as their reasons for this active role. The analysis drew on the reconstructive approach of the documentary method, with its focus on implicit and collective knowledge (Bohnsack, 2008) to gain access to the children's meaning-making and experiences regarding their citizenship practices (for a more detailed description and another example of how to use the documentary method in children's agency research, also see Dreke in this volume). It focused on two group discussions with children from the urban children's rights initiative (group 1: age 12–14; group 2: age 14–17), as group discussions are considered particularly suitable to illustrate children's collective perspective and corresponding experiences based on their shared spaces of experience *as children* in a specific context (Mayall, 2008; see also Heinzel, 2000; Bohnsack, 2008). The methodology's focus on a meaning beyond the literal also addresses the particularities arising from the "translation dilemmas" (Temple & Young, 2004) of the research setting. The interviews were carried out in Tamil – the children's native language – with the help of a local interpreter and later translated into English (Temple & Young, 2004). Starting from the group discussions, patterns of children's orientations structuring their anti-child labour practices were reconstructed in relation to their shared spaces of experience. In a second step, the reconstructed characteristics of children's citizenship practices were further differentiated and developed using the remaining interviews as well as the two above-mentioned empirical examples of children's lived citizenship in relation to children's rights. The reference to distinct empirical cases served as an approximation to the methodology's reliance on a systematic comparison (Bohnsack, 2008), considering the exploratory approach of the study.

Children's citizenship practices from children's perspectives: matters of context

Looking at children's lived citizenship from children's own perspectives, the study found the matter of context to be highly relevant. The following section reports findings that offer important insights into the meaning of different contextual factors for their citizenship practices. First, it presents findings on the meaning of institutional vs. everyday (real-life) contexts for children's citizenship practices (4.1) and, second, it elaborates on the context of the generational order and its fundamental relation to children's citizenship practices (4.2) from the non-working children's perspectives.

Before turning to the main findings, it is necessary to make some general remarks on the children's activities against child labour. First of all, it became apparent that children's lived citizenship took on different forms. In addition to participation in demonstrations set up by the initiatives, their strategies involved talking to children and their parents as well as organising support for bringing children back to school. Overall, their accounts reveal a strong commitment to become active in support of children's rights and concerns. This goes along with a specific notion of child labour. Their emotionally upset reaction to the topic of child labour and their references to horrific stories of long working hours, violence and death that they know or have heard of in their immediate environment clearly show that they associate it with serious maltreatment of children by adults. Their aim is therefore to help children out of unbearable work situations and enable them to go to school – a good, violence-free school – which they see as the proper place for all children.

Citizenship practices within and without: institutional and everyday contexts

Both the group discussions and the interviews revealed that children's active role against child labour was not limited to their participation in activities set up for them by the initiatives, such as the protest march outlined below. Instead, children also aimed to realise their citizenship individually in their everyday lives outside the initiative. The strong contrast between children's ways of relating to those efforts in an everyday context on the one hand, and their participation in the institutional context on the other, indicates that these spaces are fundamentally different in regard to the experience for children's citizenship practices and their attached meaning.

When asked about their activities against child labour, children in both discussion groups immediately brought up the initiative's annual protest march with great enthusiasm and highlighted their practices relating to the event. Overall, the march emerges as the crucial (and positive) framework for the children's understanding of their citizenship practices against child labour. This focus is not surprising as all the children were taking part in the preparations for the protest march at the time of the interviews. Nevertheless, several characteristics of the children's perspective on their citizenship become visible. One of these is that it marks the (institutional) context of the march and the children's corresponding citizenship practices as inherently collective in nature. They speak consistently as members of a group ("we") when referring to the protest march and their related practices. Second, when those accounts are compared with children's statements on individual efforts in everyday contexts, the protest march emerges even more clearly as the relevant and positive space of experience for the children's citizenship practices. Third, their way of relating to their activities against child labour primarily with reference to the initiative and its programmes suggests that, from their perspectives, their citizenship is closely linked to their experiences within the children's rights initiative. On the whole, the initiative emerges as the main context in which the children locate their more successful activities against child labour.

Outside the initiative's enabling and supportive environment, the children's citizenship practices clearly face a very different response, as illustrated by the children's accounts. While many children have a personal history of individual endeavours against child labour in their everyday life, those are voiced only on request – quite unlike the protest march. This second, everyday context for their citizenship practices constitutes a very different space of experience. Compared to the preceding enthusiasm with which they referred to the march, the children showed much less excitement when contributing with regard to this other issue, and were even reserved. Their parallel accounts of attempts to bring children back to school reveal a mostly individualised space of experience. Here, children's efforts are not met with success; instead, the children are confronted with their limited possibilities and lack of power. Accordingly, they frame their practices in terms of the confrontations with limits, for example, by referring to the reasons for child labour, which they locate in areas beyond their immediate control and power. This results in them giving a very different meaning to their citizenship practices in this everyday context, which they do not conceive as an essential part of "what they do against child labour", despite their apparent attempts. The fact that this difference is based on a perception of limited success suggests that a tangible impact is important for the meaning that children attach to their citizenship practices.

The differences between these two contexts thus point to the relevance of the responses they receive to their claim to citizenship in the area of children's rights. There is a sharp contrast in this regard: while children's active role seems to meet a negative response outside the initiative's immediate environment, it is precisely this strong commitment to children's rights that earns them recognition within the initiative.

The relevance of institutional vs. everyday contexts and their characteristics can be further differentiated by drawing on accounts from the rural children's rights initiative. This comparison underlines the differences in children's citizenship practices in relation to the *specific* characteristics of this everyday context. With their knowledge of children's rights and their active role in their implementation, the children in the two initiatives face very different environments for the realisation of their citizenship. The rural children's citizenship practices take place in an area with a long history of anti-child labour/pro-education campaigning, as well as children's participation in children's parliaments. The local forms of children's work are mainly within limited, and mostly formal, sectors. These children's accounts present a more positive everyday context for their citizenship practices, along with broader support from adults, even outside the initiative. The environment of the urban children's rights initiative, in contrast, poses a much less transparent and manageable context for targeting child labour in general. In the city, children work in many different and mostly informal sectors, and there are no existing structures on which children's participation can build.

Citizenship as a practice by children for children: the context of the generational order

As the previous section suggested, my study found a strong relationship between the forms and characteristics of children's citizenship practices, their corresponding meaning-making and children's position within the generational order. This section presents important new insights into that relationship that goes beyond the more general statements referred to above. In both of the focussed group discussions, the highest interactive density was in the sequences dealing with children's position and the role in activities against child labour *in relation to adults*. As such, they give access to the most relevant orientations regarding the children's citizenship practices (Bohnsack, 2008). Using findings from the study, the following section will show that and *how* their position within the generational order is crucial for the children's perspectives on their citizenship. It shows that children's position constitutes a fundamental contextual factor alongside the institutional and everyday contexts presented above.

The group discussions show that the overall framework for children's citizenship practices against child labour is a confrontation between the children's strong commitment to act *as* children *for* children and their powerless position within the generational order of their real-life contexts. References to their limits stand out as a prominent feature in all their accounts. One example would be indicating reasons behind child labour that are beyond children's immediate control; i.e. in adult-controlled contexts, such as the school or family. Surprisingly, this reference to their limited possibilities as children and their reliance on adult support can also be found in relation to the protest march, which otherwise constitutes a markedly positive context for their citizenship practices, as shown above. The group discussions and individual interviews revealed an experiential space in which children are constantly confronted with their powerless position. This issue appears to be of particular importance for the younger children.

Faced with these limitations and their lack of power, the children develop strategies to exert influence by drawing on adults or collective action as a resource.

While this common reference to the use of specific strategies hints at a context in which their (perceived) potential impact as children is rather limited, even more important is that it portrays a kind of citizenship that has to be achieved in the face of resistance and opposition. This notion of opposition to their citizenship practices leads to another important aspect of children's citizenship in relation to the generational order. The children differentiate pointedly between their own concerns as children and those of adults when talking about their contributions to the protest march. This differentiation was illustrated by a heated discussion on the role of the adults in this march. While the relation between children and adults is therefore a relevant, if contested, issue in relation to children's rights, it is the idea that children's voices and concerns are inherently different from and opposed to those of adults that is essential for their perspectives on their citizenship. Even within the initiative, where adults encourage children's active role, a clear distinction is drawn between children and adults. The study found that the children are very conscious about their position in relation to adults, a consciousness further emphasised by their use of the pronoun "we" whenever that relation is concerned. It highlights their collective identity and sense of belonging to the social group of "children" for their citizenship practices.

Though adults are seen as vital to achieve children's citizenship because of their access to essential resources and protection, they are commonly framed as a possible threat to children's aims. The references made by the children reveal a shared belief that adults cannot be trusted to stand for children's concerns and well-being. Children's intentions, however, are generally presented in a very positive light. In one group discussion in the rural initiative, the children even attributed children with specific qualities for enforcing children's rights, generally: their moral superiority and great potential for attracting public attention. It is their misgiving about adults and their perception that adults are responsible for children's misery, for example in labour situations, which frame their idea that they themselves, *as children*, have to step in and be advocates for (other) children. This is closely related to a feeling of responsibility towards children worse off than they are. In this regard, their knowledge and privileged position as non-working members of children's rights initiatives distinguish them from other children.

As a result of these findings, a two-fold meaning of the generational order for children's citizenship practices can be defined. On the one hand, the generational order poses a barrier and limits the chances these children have to affect and thus positively achieve their citizenship in relation to their mostly adult-dominated life worlds. On the other hand, it is exactly this powerlessness of children that motivates their commitment to *living* citizenship as children for (other) children. The results thus provide further information on the relevance of the generational order as an important contextual factor for children's citizenship, citizenship that can only be understood in relation to their position as children within this order.

On the matter of context for an alternative concept of children's lived citizenship in relation to children's rights

Looking at children's citizenship practices from children's own perspectives highlights the importance of contextual factors. It is important to note that some caution should be used in generalising these findings, due to the exploratory approach of the study as well as the small size and specific character of its sample. However, the results can be used to expand the current understanding of those matters of context (institutional vs. everyday ones; generational order) in relation to children's lived citizenship and the meaning they attach to it. They clearly point out the need to take different dimensions of context into account when thinking about (or promoting) children's participation in relation to children's rights.

It becomes apparent that the non-working children carry out their citizenship practices in two fundamentally different contexts, one institutional and one everyday. Whereas the children's rights initiative and its associated programmes have emerged as a particularly promising and positive context, children's individual experiences with their citizenship outside this supportive environment are framed by accounts of limited possibilities and impact. This contradicts the clear distinction that has been drawn between children's participation in formal initiatives set up for them by adults, and children's active role in child-initiated informal activities that take place in their everyday lives (Liebel, 2008; Invernizzi, 2008). Rather, the findings suggest that children's participation in children's rights initiatives generates "spill-over effects" for their everyday lives outside these initiatives. In this regard, the results also emphasised differences in children's citizenship practices that relate to the *specific* characteristics of this everyday context.

The strong relationship between the generational order of children's real-life contexts and the forms and meaning of their citizenship practices is another important, and interconnected, finding of the study. Similarly to recent observations (particularly Liebel, 2008; Stasiulis, 2002), the non-working children's citizenship is characterised by an understanding of a shared concern as children, thus re-affirming the significance of this contextual factor for the lived citizenship of children in general. My study complements these accounts by pointing out that this kind of citizenship in relation to children's rights is one specifically *by* children *for* (other) children. Going beyond previous statements on the importance of the generational order for children's citizenship, the current study reveals a two-fold relationship between the generational order and children's citizenship practices. As demonstrated above, it is exactly the same powerless position *as children* which, on the one hand, poses barriers to the children's citizenship practices and, on the other hand, serves as the essential motivation to act on behalf of (other) children. Moreover, the findings indicate that this characteristic is based on children's notion of an inherent difference and even opposition between their interests as children and those of adults. Adults are generally seen in a (very) negative light. The children's strong collective identity as children can thus only be understood in relation to the respective generational order of their real-life contexts.

A further comparison with the accounts by Stasiulis (2002) and Liebel (2008) can be used to refine the concept of children's citizenship practices in relation to children's rights from the children's perspective, as well as to highlight the specific characteristics of the non-working children's citizenship. Unlike the pro-work claims of the working children's movements (Liebel, 2008), the aims of the non-working children do not oppose an existing international policy. Their citizenship is, instead, motivated by the perceived lack of endorsement of children's rights in their everyday life. There, their conformity with international policies does not make it considerably easier for them to realise their citizenship, as their accounts show. Consistent with Liebel's description of the working children's citizenship, they claim children's rights as *their* rights and actively refer to those rights or point at their violations in their own life worlds (Liebel, 2008). The comparison with Stasiulis' account of the Canadian children's "global citizenship" (p. 530) points at yet other characteristics of the non-working children's citizenship. Both the Canadian and the South Indian children share the aim to help *other* children whose life situations are perceived as unbearable. Nonetheless, their different life worlds account for an important difference in this regard. Whereas the Canadian children do not share the real-life contexts of the children for whom they advocate, the children from the South Indian initiative personally know children in labour situations, or are "at risk" of being child labourers themselves. Furthermore, the contrast with the media-prone kind of citizenship Stasiulis describes calls attention to the differing options and resources for citizenship practices in Minority vs. (poor) Majority World contexts. In this regard, the Canadian children's access to mass media clearly differs from the more local forms open to the South Indian children from marginalised communities.

With reference to the call to examine the meaning of children's rights and children's participation in children's rights initiatives in their real-life contexts (Tisdall & Punch, 2012; Hanson, 2014), the present study suggests that children's active role might pose considerable challenges for children, particularly in relation to their position in the specific generational order. However, it seems that children themselves are content to play a leading role in this endeavour. Furthermore, the study demonstrates that non-working children's activities "against child labour" have a lot more in common with the working children's citizenship "from below" (Liebel, 2008) than usually acknowledged. It also constitutes an active and participative practice that includes a strong commitment to children's rights. As such, it has to be read as an expression of children's agency (Lister, 2007). This conclusion challenges the common notion of not equating these children's practices with "real" agency because of the apparent conformity of their goals with international policies. It instead paints a more nuanced picture that draws on children's own perspectives. Moreover, it points to the need to reconsider the normative assumptions underlying the attribution and acknowledgement of agency to children's activities in general.

References

Bohnsack, R. (2008). *Rekonstruktive Sozialforschung. Einführung in qualitative Methoden* [*Reconstructive social research. Introduction to qualitative methods*] (7th rev. ed.). Stuttgart: Barbara Budrich. [In German]

Bohnsack, R. (2010). Documentary method and group discussion. In R. Bohnsack, N. Pfaff & W. Weller (Eds.), *Qualitative Analysis and Documentary Method in International Educational Research* (pp. 99–124). Opladen, Farmington Hills: Barbara Budrich.

Bourdillon, M. (2004). Children in development. *Progress in Development Studies,* *4*(2), 99–113.

Boyden, J. (1997). Childhood and the policy makers: a perspective on the globalization of childhood. In A. James & A. Prout (Eds.), *Constructing and Reconstructing Childhood: Contemporary Issues in the Sociological Study of Childhood* (pp. 190–229). London, New York: Routledge Falmer.

Cheney, K. E. (2012). Killing them softly? Using children's rights to empower Africa's orphans and vulnerable children. *International Social Work, 56*, 92–102.

Cockburn, T. (1998). Children and citizenship in Britain. A case for a socially interdependent model of citizenship. *Childhood, 5*(1), 99–117.

Hanson, K. (2014). "Killed by charity?" Towards interdisciplinary children's rights studies. *Childhood, 21*(4), 441–446.

Heinzel, F. (2000). Kinder in Gruppendiskussionen und Kreisgesprächen [Children in group discussions and circle time]. In F. Heinzel (Ed.), *Methoden der Kindheitsforschung. Ein Überblick über Forschungszugänge zur kindlichen Perspektive* [*Methods in childhood studies. An overview on research approaches to children's perspective*] (pp. 117–130). Weinhein/Munich: Juventa. [In German]

Invernizzi, J. (2008). Everyday notions of working children and notions of citizenship. In J. Invernizzi & J. Williams (Eds.), *Children and Citizenship* (pp. 131–141). London: Sage Publications.

Invernizzi, A. & Milne, B. (2002). Are children entitled to contribute to international policy making? A critical view of children's participation in the international campaign for the elimination of child labour. *The International Journal of Children's Rights, 10*(4), 403–431.

Invernizzi, A. & Williams, J. (Eds.). (2008a). *Children and Citizenship.* London: Sage Publications.

Invernizzi, A. & Williams, J. (2008b). Notions of children's citizenship. In A. Invernizzi & J. Williams (Eds.), *Children and Citizenship* (pp. 1–7). London: Sage Publications.

James, A. (2011). To be (come) or not to be (come): understanding children's citizenship. *The ANNALS of the American Academy of Political and Social Science, 633*(1), 167–179.

James, A. (2009). Agency. In J. Qvortrup, G. Valentine, W. Corsaro & M.-S. Honig, M. (Eds.), *The Palgrave Handbook of Childhood Studies* (pp. 34–45). Basingstoke: Palgrave.

James, A. & Prout, A. (1990). *Constructing and Re-Constructing Childhood.* Basingstoke: Falmer.

Jans, M. (2004). Children as citizens: towards a contemporary notion of child participation. *Childhood, 11*(27), 27–44.

Kabeer, N. (2005). The search for inclusive citizenship. Meanings and expressions in an interconnected world. Introduction. In N. Kabeer (Ed.), *Inclusive Citizenship: Meanings and Expressions* (pp. 1–27). London, New York: Zed Books.

Larkins, C. (2014). Enacting children's citizenship: developing understandings of how children enact themselves as citizens through actions and acts of citizenship. *Childhood, 21*(1), 7–21.

Liebel, M. (2008). Citizenship "from Below": children's rights and social movements. In A. Invernizzi & J. Williams (Eds.), *Children and Citizenship* (pp. 32–43). London: Sage Publications.

Lister, R. (2007). Why citizenship. Where, when and how children? *Theoretical Inquiries in Law, 8*(2), 693–718.

Mayall, B. (2008). Conversations with children. Working with generational issues. In P. Christensen & A. James (Eds.), *Research with Children: Perspectives and Practices* (2nd ed., pp. 109–124). London: Routledge Falmer.

Milne, B. (2013). *The History and Theory of Children's Citizenship in Contemporary Societies*. Dordrecht, New York: Springer.

Milne, B. (2005). Is "participation" as it is described by the United Nations on the Rights of the Child (UNCRC) the key to children's citizenship? In A. Invernizzi & B. Milne (Eds.), *Children's Citizenship: An Emergent Discourse on the Rights of the Child, Journal of Social Sciences*, Special Edition 9 (pp. 31–42). Delhi: Kamla-Raj Entreprises.

Moosa-Mitha, M. (2005). A difference-centred alternative to theorization of children's citizenship rights. *Citizenship Studies, 9*(4), 369–388.

Nieuwenhuys, O. (2009). Is there an Indian childhood? Editorial. *Childhood, 16*(2), 147–153.

Reynaert D., Bouverne-de-Bie, M. & Vandevelde, S. (2009). A review of children's rights literature since the adoption of the United Nations Convention on the Rights of the Child. *Childhood, 16*(4), 518–534.

Reynolds, P., Nieuwenhuys, O., & Hanson, K. (2006). Refractions of children's rights in development practice. A view from anthropology – introduction. *Childhood, 13*(3), 291–302.

Roche, J. (1999). Children: rights, participation and citizenship. *Childhood, 6*(4), 475–493.

Saeed, S. (2014). Children and young people's participation in India: framing law, policy and the media. In Tisdall, E. K. M., A. M. Gadda & U. M. Butler (Eds.), *Children and Young People's Participation and Its Transformative Potential: Learning from Across Countries* (pp. 91–112). Basingstoke: Palgrave Macmillan.

Smith, N., Lister, R., Middleton, S. & Cox, L. (2005). Young people as real citizens: towards an inclusionary understanding of citizenship. *Journal of Youth Studies, 8*(4), 425–443.

Stasiulis, D. (2002). The active child-citizen: lessons from Canadian policy and the children's movement. *Citizenship Studies, 6*(4), 507–538.

Taft, J. K. (2014). 'Adults talk too much': intergenerational dialogue and power in the Peruvian movement of working children. *Childhood*, online first: doi: 10.1177/0907568214555148.

Temple, B. & Young, A. (2004). Qualitative research and translation dilemmas. *Qualitative Research, 4*(2), 161–178.

Tisdall, E. K. M., Gadda, A. M. & Butler, U. M. (Eds.). (2014). *Children and Young People's Participation and Its Transformative Potential: Learning from across Countries*. Basingstoke: Palgrave Macmillan.

Tisdall, E. K. M. & Punch, S. (2012). Not so "new"? Looking critically at Childhood Studies. *Children's Geographies, 10*(3), 249–264.

Section V

Agency in institutions of childhood

Chapter 15

Agency

Educators' imaginations as triggered by photographs of pre-school children

Claudia Dreke

"Agency" is not only a (childhood)-sociological concept, but, in connection with the concept of "children as competent actors", has also become a normative idea shaping the professional work of educators. The educators are meant to recognise the children's learning activities and document their specific capabilities. In this chapter, this process is illustrated through the example of two photographs from a German kindergarten. From an institutionalist perspective, photographs serve as the symbolic visualisation of the kindergarten as institution. Both photographs can, however, be read as illustrating forms of agency that actually contradict the intentions of the educators expressed in the accompanying captions. In actual fact, the photographs make visible desirable forms of agency. This contradiction and its institutional context are discussed under the concept of "generational order".

Since the 1980s, one of the topics much debated in child sociology has been the idea that children are "social actors" and the use of the concept of "agency" to emphasise their active participation in society. At the same time, the concept of "socialisation" has come under attack more and more in arguments bolstering the idea of children as autonomous actors and, on ethical grounds, criticizing research whose methods did not support that idea (James, 2008; Bühler-Niederberger, 2011, p. 166; Punch & Tisdall, 2012; Hungerland & Kelle, 2014). These arguments have also begun to strongly influence pedagogical institutions. National curricula in, for example, Brazil and New Zealand, integrated the concept of children as "agents" and sought to establish appropriate pedagogical methods (Kaga et al., 2010, pp. 95, 48). In this way, "children's agency" has not only become a key concept in educational policy and academic discourse, but it is now setting normative standards for the academic discipline of pedagogy. It is also seen as answering to the need for "autonomous, independent and entrepreneurial individuals" in late modern society (Vandenbroeck & Bouverne-de Bie, 2006, p. 139).

Even in debates on the professionalisation of educating small children, the concept of the "child as an actor in its own educative processes" (Ruppin, 2015, p. 8) has become dominant since the 1990s. The "new image of the child" is conceived as a practical ideal that has to guide pedagogical methods, as can be seen in most regional curricula developed since 2004.

But this conception of childhood is not as new as many of its proponents seem to believe, and has not been inspired solely by recent sociological innovations. The Romantic movement of the late eighteenth century, in fact, inspired the debates on educational reform at the end of the nineteenth century; this, in turn, fuelled the reform movement of the late 1960s and the 1970s in Germany with its "Kinderladen" movement. This inspired and encouraged children to autonomously unfold their particular abilities. After 1990, this conception was reinforced in the transformation of the educational institutions of the former GDR. It sometimes created the impression that the lack of historical perspective is often accompanied by a romantic overestimation of children's abilities (Baader, 2005 and in this volume).

Seen from an institutionalist perspective (Rehberg, 2002, 2014), the "child as an actor" can be understood as a way to conceptualise the kindergarten. It will be used to show how typologies of actors and of forms of agency can be meaningful in an institutional context. The empirical data consist of photographs, which were intended to demonstrate the specific abilities of children in pedagogical documentation. Photographs of this kind are increasingly being used to show children as autonomous actors. How they are intended and how inner contradictions cannot be avoided will be shown in the final part of this chapter.

"Agency" as a way of thinking about childhood in kindergarten

According to Rehberg (2002, 2014), institutions are social regulators that give expression to the principles and claims to validity of a particular social order. They can reify into guiding principles, which stabilise this order and shape long-term power relations. In this way, they suggest a meaningful reality offering humans a "cultural mould" (Rehberg, 2014, p. 53). They mediate between a meaning that has become a structure and actors who relate to this meaning.

Kindergarten can be considered one such institution. After its creation in the nineteenth century, it became the target of continuous demands for reform: Children were expected to be educated there, and not simply supervised and raised by adult females[1] (Reyer, 2006). The Kinderladen movement of the 1970s was not the first to raise the issue of the "generational order" (Alanen, 2005) as a form of "relational inequality" (Betz, 2010), but it forcefully proposed a "de-hierarchization" of this order (Baader & Sager, 2010, p. 255). Grell (2010, p. 154) tied this idea to the concept of "self-education", which has become prominent in contemporary educational theory. The child as a "self-educating actor" can be seen as a reversal of the traditional institutional idea of the kindergarten in which the child was an "object of education". Now, generational relationships inside the institution have to change and with them role expectations regarding educators and children.[2]

According to Rehberg (2014, p. 53), symbolic forms suggest the legitimacy of institutions and make them visible. Thus, they are essential for validating institutions' guiding principles (Rehberg, 2002, p. 47). These forms become visible in material symbols, ritual actions and gestures, as well as in forms of language and habitus. They are seen as "embodiments" of the institutions and strengthen them by their very visibility (pp. 48f). By contrast, organisations are understood here as formal, purpose-oriented associations. Any existing kindergarten is a rationally conceived organisation; at the same time, it relates to the institutional form of the "kindergarten" in general by its symbolic forms and its general claim to legitimacy (Rehberg, 2002, p. 49).

Accordingly, guiding principles define the aims of childhood education and the kindergarten in a symbolic form. Yet related claims to or assertions of validity do not exclude the possibility of creative responses or of competing meanings of guiding principles being offered by all "stakeholders" such as children, educators, parents, policymakers, and so on. Their meanings can be analysed in order to shed light on the complex connections between structures and actors and to understand how institutional demands can be translated into plans for action and human self-identification (Rehberg, 2014, p. 54). This analysis gives an insight into forms of institutional meaning in which "agency" plays a prominent role.

Institutional stakeholders such as children and educators can be understood in principle as actors in social interaction (e. g. Mead, 1975; Denzin, 1977). They interpret one another's behaviour and react to the intentions they detect in it. Nevertheless, social interactions are always both facilitated or limited by institutions and their hierarchies. In this sense, the following section concentrates on institutionally defined typologies of actors (e.g. "independent children") and on corresponding forms of agency as they are symbolically realised in kindergartens. Here, Raithelhuber's questions (2012) as to the social production of agency become important – who is granted which agency, and who is allowed to do what? For this reason, the perspective adopted in this chapter derives from approaches in childhood sociology, which critically reflect on the ascription of substantial agency to children and seek to understand structure and agency in relational terms (Bühler-Niederberger, 2011; Esser, 2014; Bollig & Kelle, 2014).

The following analysis of two photographs taken in a kindergarten is guided by the assumption that it might be illuminating to question the ideas of "agency" and "children as actors" in kindergartens, where these concepts are normative. The photographs were intended to be used as tools of internal "documentation".

Visualisation in the kindergarten

Visual data, such as photographs, are increasingly being used to examine and analyse child education. Kindergarten educators are expected to observe the development of each child, and to use these observations in shaping educational strategies (Cloos & Schulz, 2011; Sparrman & Lindgren, 2010; Pettersson, 2013). Photographs are not only integrated into the children's portfolios but are also part of the internal auditing process for pedagogical work.

Visual data in kindergartens that have been produced for pedagogical purposes have, in contrast to textual data (Cloos & Schulz, 2011), seldom been investigated. Research has been conducted on self-produced video data (Pettersson,

2013) or TV programmes. Methods of discourse analysis have been used to question "visual documentation" and their new "normalizing practice" (Sparrman & Lindgren, 2010). The production, selection and interpretation of photographs in pedagogical documentation have so far not stood at the centre of analysis.

In an institutional perspective, it might be assumed that those photographs will be chosen for public presentation, which can legitimise the work done in the kindergarten. Rehberg (2014, p. 89) describes the public sphere in this context as a "legitimizing space of resonance"; i.e. the photos are presented to have an effect on other stakeholders. It can be assumed that, in this respect, they are somehow successful because they are intended to "document" what is going on in the kindergarten. In our context, however, they are understood as visualisations in which institutional hierarchies are symbolically represented. In this respect, they need not be consonant with the intentions of those presenting the "documentation".

For our analysis, the question of who selects and presents which photographs according to which criteria is of paramount importance. It is they who present the symbolic expression of the institution. Thus, we can ask *how* the institution is symbolically represented. For this purpose, we can use methods for the sociological analysis of pictures (Pilarczyk & Mietzner, 2005; Bohnsack, 2008, 2009). These involve photographs being understood as including the constructive inputs of all those involved in the interactive production of the photographs.

Photographs as a collective product

It is assumed here that photographs never directly reproduce reality, but instead include political, social and moral assumptions. Therefore, they are themselves seen as a way of constructing reality (Pilarczyk & Mietzner, 2005, p. 106). They can be analysed from the different perspectives of the different roles taking part in the production of these pictures: the photographer, the person represented, the initiator, the user, the addressee and the recipient, or, in this particular context, the educators, the children, the management of the kindergarten and the parents. In consequence, photographs can be helpful in investigating the perspectives and attitudes of all persons involved.

It is the photographer and the subject, in particular, who are implicated in the act of creating a new social setting by means of photographs (Bohnsack, 2009, p. 31). Bohnsack emphasises that interpretations of the world are not simply made visible in photographs, but that they become part of the social world they claim to represent. In reference to Karl Mannheim, Bohnsack presupposed the existence of guiding pre-reflexive, a theoretical knowledge about social scenes, gestures and mimicry as well as "incorporated knowledge" as defined by Bourdieu. This is relevant for our approach of analysing institutions, as such "incorporated knowledge" can also indicate the symbolised guiding principles of the institution.

Since photographs of children (and adults), in contrast to texts, can show bodies, they are particularly helpful in analysing the relations between children, their body and society. It is obvious that representing the body is important in order to understand children as social actors (Prout, 2000).

Method: the selection of the data and the approach

The photographs presented here are part of a series of eight pictures that were exhibited in a kindergarten near Berlin. They are part of a larger collection owned by this kindergarten. I shall discuss the first picture in detail, and then refer to the second one for a brief comparison. They came to my attention in 2012 during one of numerous internship visits undertaken as part of my role as a teacher. Both photographs had captions that explained the scenes represented. The manager of the kindergarten told me that they were intended to inform parents about their children's learning activities, showing them as "actors". Here and in later conversations she constantly referred to the discourse of "available meaning", which dominates child pedagogy. To avoid any misleading impressions, she insisted on her right to have the final say in choosing the photographs displayed and their accompanying "expert commentaries". This very insistence emphasises the role ascribed to photographs in the professional work of the kindergarten. My particular interest being the selection criteria, I asked the manager to show me photographs that, from her point of view, were suitable to different extents for public display. She designated the first photograph shown here as "just about presentable", a choice of words to which I will return.

The following interpretation uses the "documentary method" devised by Ralf Bohnsack (2008, 2009). It distinguishes between four levels of interpretation: "pre-iconographic level of meaning", "iconographic interpretation", "formal composition" and "iconological/iconic interpretation" (Bohnsack, 2008, p. 14). Here, I am skipping the pre-iconographic interpretation, in which all details in the photograph would be considered. After a brief summary of the iconographic interpretation, I will proceed to the formal composition of the photograph – of its surface composition and the perspective it uses. In this, I shall try to avoid any reference to prior textual knowledge; the picture should be seen as it is. This can be helpful in moving from "recognizing" to "seeing" the contents of the picture (Bohnsack, 2008, parts 23–27). This will be followed by a description of body postures, facial expressions, gestures and the relationship between represented and representing bodies. The interpretation of the social meaning of the photograph intends to find out HOW the cultural or social phenomenon (understood here as the kindergarten in its broad sense) is produced. Then, the captions that had been added by those who organised the exhibition will be confronted with our previous interpretation. In this way, possible previous suggestive ascriptions will become discernible and with them, the intentions of organisers of the exhibition.

Interpretation of the first photograph

The first photograph is a rectangular landscape format, 15.8 cm × 11.4 cm (Figure 15.1). At first glance, it seems to show the German version of Ludo (Mensch ärgere dich nicht) in which four smaller bodies and one larger body are taking part. All of them are seated at a table and only partially visible. The surroundings contain a range of functional fixtures and equipment.

Figure 15.1 First photograph.

A striking presence in the picture, due to their colour and form, are the rectangular surfaces of the table and the Ludo game boxes. Their surfaces run like a track from the foreground to the upper right and draw attention to the empty chair and the edge of the cupboard. If one further extends the vertical boundaries of the game items, both the forehead of the semi-visible figure and the front part of the largest body's right hand become visible – especially the index finger. As this hand covers the right hand of the person sitting in front of the semi-visible figure, it emphasises what remains hidden. The figure in the background is the only one that can be seen from the front and whose head is neither cut off nor partially concealed. In addition, the black board around which the figures are sitting is located in the centre. Both the large figure and the small figure at the front of the table appear to be particularly important elements of the composition (Figure 15.2: planimetric composition).

The perspective from which the picture is taken elevates the photographer above the scene and established his or her distance to it. Apparently, he/she is standing, and is both close to and removed from the ongoing social activity. If one extends the vertical lines of the shelf and the cupboard in order to establish the vanishing point, it becomes clear that these lines point back to the photographer. As a result, the photographer draws attention not only to the board, the index finger and the small body at the front, but also to her- or himself; and this, as a result, draws the photographer into the action (Figure 15.3: perspective).

Figure 15.2 Planimetric composition.

Figure 15.3 Perspective.

Particularly striking is the right hand with the extended index finger, which belongs to the largest figure and points to the right edge of the picture. Since the lower half of the right arm with the extended index finger crosses the left arm, the gesture is difficult to understand. While the left hand, by touching the board, suggests that it is related to the game, the other hand gestures beyond the board itself. At the same time, due to this and also thanks to the bending of the arms, the same gesture appears to be uncertain. This effect is heightened by the chosen section, the perspective and the rectangular form, which makes her appear compact in relation to the small figures. Another important point in this respect is the figure's location in the upper left-hand corner of the photograph. The figure's posture indicates that the table is too small for her. Thus, this figure appears to be out of place because of both the ambiguous gesture and her size in contrast to the table and the smaller figures. While the two figures in the foreground seem to be looking at the gesture, the third figure sitting at the front and apparently emphasised by the composition is looking ahead at the (black) board. The contrast to the two figures beside it is even sharper. This figure is not looking at the gesture made by the larger figure.

Preparedness for play and emotional control

The posture of the three figures, turned towards the Ludo board, can be read as indicating their being prepared to participate in the game. This would presuppose that they are actually able to play the game or at least learn how to play it. However, since the large figure is showing something instead of being designated as a potential co-player, and preparedness to play rather than the activity of playing is being shown, some doubts about their abilities are not out of place. In addition, attention is drawn to the attitude of the small figures. They seem to be prepared for a game, which in translation is called "Come on, don't get angry", an allusion to the imperative to control one's emotions. The picture focusses on the small bodies, indicating that they are in need of emotional mastery rather than the large figure. The photograph thus shows, beyond the difference in body sizes and forms, a common-sense understanding of the hierarchical roles of children and adults and hierarchies of their specific capabilities.

The pointing gesture as the symbol of the generational order

This role difference is even more salient if we analyse the space in which the children are playing. The game board is at the far end of the upper right edge of the table, so the dice can only be thrown on the board, which will disturb the game itself. By contrast, this position is suitable for the smaller bodies to pick up and move figures. Moves appear to be both limited and enabled by the adult. Considering the fact that she has placed her hand on the board but is not touching any figures, she appears to be more powerful than the children, controlling the game and the space where the game is taking place.

This differentiation is given greater weight by the large figure's pointing gesture, which belongs to the gesticular vocabulary of pedagogues (Pilarczyk & Mietzner, 2005, p. 171). Prange (2005) proposes "pointing" as the fundamental structure of pedagogy in education, a thesis that Ricken (2006) has modified, suggesting that it is *one* fundamental form of educational practice. According to Ricken, pointing is a gesture that simultaneously indicates something to oneself and to others, at the same time directing others' attention. Thus, pointing elicits a response and posits mutual understanding. Still, Ricken argues, it simultaneously attempts to guide or dominate mutual understanding. Pointing is a gesture that makes a claim to authority.

The large figure in the photograph is thus the one who claims to be authoritatively pointing something out to others. Within the kindergarten, this gesture indicates that the adult is the teacher, who dominates social relationships with children: It suggests that they are people who are expected to respond to the gesture. The children are thus defined as children in a social or pedagogical sense and the situation itself as a pedagogical one. Put in Goffman's terms (1977), through her bodily presence she provides the primary social framework for the scene in which she positions herself as a teacher. To this extent, the gesture of pointing and the gesture of her left hand make manifest the claim to a hierarchical generational relationship. Both gestures can be understood as the symbolic representation of this relationship. They are part of training that establishes a social difference and imposes a claim to authority (Wulf, 2014, p. 182).

However, this symbolic representation does not get a straightforward response by the prominent child at the front: it is not looking at the gesture, but is concerned with something beyond it. In relation to the adult it appears small. This is emphasised by its central position – from the perspective of the photographer – which makes the relationship between the two people all the more significant. The child is shown in relation to the (institutionally mediated) gesture as indifferent to its symbolic content. This causes the gesture to appear less dominant. With regard to the other figures, it is at least unclear whether they relate to the gesture.

The bodies may themselves adopt positions and orientations, but it is the photographer who frames them and causes the educator to appear marginalised. Her institutionally ascribed power position is weakened in this way, while the (handicapped) position of the child at the focus of the photograph is strengthened. As a result, a fracture emerges in the hierarchical relationship in which the adult is seen as superior and powerful, and the child as subordinate. The position of the educator appears to be as lacking in routine and sovereignty as that of the photographer. Since the photographer alludes to her own presence by means of the perspective she had chosen, she reinforces the impression of disarray, which is reflected in her own ambivalent position.

Thus, the picture reveals a moment of crisis: the generational order is not secure. Ambivalence is reflected in another element in the picture: the empty chair at the end of the "track". Even a minor shift in perspective would have rendered it less present. The educator would have appeared more prominently. Yet, because of the framing of the picture, the ambivalence is stressed. This leads to the following questions: Where do the educators belong? As co-players on the children's side; as referees of children's activity; as observers from a distance? This uncertainty can be understood in terms of new institutional expectations concerning educators and the generational relationship. According to these expectations, educators should step back from the hitherto unambiguous role of directing and educating adults and allow more autonomous space for the children and their activities.

This analysis is not meant as a criticism of allegedly unprofessional photographic practice by kindergarten workers. Rather, it looks at their uncertainty in this new situation. The photograph may have been taken under spatial and temporal constraints, but the fact that it was chosen for the public display, and that this choice was confirmed by the manager, establishes it as a symbol of the changing institution of the kindergarten. This is underlined by the fact that it was accompanied by an (anonymised) "expert commentary".

The caption

> Linus T., Linus M. and Phil-Jonas play Ludo together with Tina. The children enjoy counting the dots on the dice and then move the figures the correct number of steps.
>
> Documented by Christine Meier and Teresa Schmitz[3]

This caption is surprising. There is no visual evidence of collective play, nor any indication of children playing or the joy they might be experiencing. The discrepancy between picture and text instead makes it possible to see that we are dealing with the educators' anticipatory ascription of activity and emotion to children. The form of agency that is ascribed to them is of a joyful game that leads to correct calculations. One of the tenets of the romantic view of children is that they enjoy playing, and learn in the process. This can be seen as corresponding to Fröbel's theory of play (Baader, 1996, p. 232). Since the caption emphasises the correct calculations conducted by the supposedly playing children, the game is pedagogically instrumentalised. In contrast to Huizinga's definition of playing (Huizinga, 1996, p. 22), here it appears to be a didactical tool. Thus, the caption "corrects" the ambivalence in the relationship between the educator and the children, converting the latter into self-educating actors who fulfil adults' expectations. The caption also points to the educators' intention to represent and power to define items. In this way their authority is restored.

Why did the manager think that this picture was not quite presentable? Apparently, the educator and her gesturing finger were too dominant, and the photograph was less convincing as a document of children's autonomous agency. Still, the photograph was apparently displayed because the gesture was demonstrative and not admonishing, and thus not quite an expression of judgemental pedagogy.

In contrast, the following photograph and its commentary, shown on the same poster, were praised by her.

The second photograph

This photograph (Figure 15.4) is different in several respects to the previous one. In the foreground, it shows the figure of a single 3- to 4-year-old child, dressed in winter clothing, with a rucksack attached to a long stick resting on his left shoulder and looking at the photographer. It was taken outdoors in cold weather. One might think of a "hiking day". The child, with the rucksack, dominates the composition, along with the long stick stretching diagonally across more than two thirds of the picture. Large areas beside him restrictively frame his body, while two other children are only partially visible. This photograph has also been taken by the supervisor and the vanishing point is located beyond the door of the building to which the cobbled path leads.

Figure 15.4 Second photograph.

Because of his posture, rucksack and stick, the child appears to be in contrast to the children behind him. Due to the position of his upper left arm in the middle of the picture, his carrying the rucksack is a salient feature. In addition, he is smiling at the photographer, to whom he is closer than the other children. His smile conveys trust and a willingness to cooperate. His cooperation appears all the more important since the child is on the path, and the slight twist in his lower body shows that he is about to move forward. Nevertheless, he is standing still, as if pausing and presenting his upper body with a slight turn towards the photographer and the beholder.

By means of the perspective and the landscape format, the photographer changes the child into a "cute dwarf" and in this way stresses the difference between childishness and adulthood. By using the picture composition and perspective to emphasise the characteristics of rambling – the wooden stick, the rucksack, the general hiking atmosphere – the picture refers to the motif of Romantic wayfaring. Yet the child himself is not moving forward but stands halfway between the indoors and the outside. While the perspective directs the viewer's gaze towards the building and thus towards the interior, the child's lower body points in the opposite direction. This intended moving-away from the protective building appears to be arranged by the photographer. The child is standing still and smiling, and in this way demonstrates "competent compliance" (Bühler-Niederberger, 2011, p. 202).

The motif of the wanderer, the twee perspective and the singling out of the child refer to a romantic idealisation of the child. The hierarchy between adults and children seems to be particularly evident in this context, but it is also a hierarchy that is recognised by the child.

The contrast to the (anonymised) expert commentary is striking:

> It's hiking day and Jonas has come up with a good idea to carry his rucksack. He hangs it on a stick, because the straps of his rucksack keep slipping off his shoulders.
>
> Documented by Christine Meier and Teresa Schmitz

Again, the caption is used to emphasise the child's autonomous initiative. By praising the invisible "good idea", the documenting educators posit themselves as authoritative actors. Their praise can be seen as a claim to power and as an instrument of dominance (Paris, 1995), which reproduces and re-affirms the generational order.

The allusions to the Romantic (ideal) image of the child are continued on the textual level in describing the boy as inventive and almost genius-like. The manager's praise was prompted by seeing that such small children can have such good ideas, as the caption suggests. The documentation is nevertheless ambivalent, in that the agency that is ascribed to the child apparently increases in relation to the smallness of the child – the smaller, the more inventive. In this way, the picture becomes ideological: It constructs the child in his status as a (romanticised) child in a figurative sense – in the interests of the educators.

Conclusion

Using photographs as symbolic means to visualise social relations in kindergarten, we asked two questions. How can social regulations be demonstrated? What significance do concepts and expectations in child pedagogy, such as agency, have for attempts to show the expected effects of agency? Both the statements of the manager and the commentaries to the photographs show that educators are expected to view and treat children as actors with specific abilities. In this way, photographs are thought to affirm the orienting concepts of pedagogical institutions. Yet a closer look at the pictures enables us to detect contradictions. What is visible in the pictures is different from what is ascribed to them by educators.

In the first photograph, the children are imagined as happily playing and counting, although neither aspect is visible in either their expressions or gestures. From an institutional perspective and close analysis of the photograph, the gestures of the educator and the reactions of the children show an ambiguous generational relationship. It is contradicted in the caption in favour of the educators' authority. The difference to the second photograph consists of the fact that the commentary ascribes the child a creativity that the picture does not show, and also a different form of agency, namely "competent compliance" as a child (Bühler-Niederberger, 2011, p. 202). At the same time, the relationship between the educator and the child appears to be particularly asymmetrical.

It is precisely the claim the captions make – that they offer a correct interpretation of the photograph – that allows us to see how educators in the kindergarten see themselves and their children and what is expected of them. Beneath the surface, the hope for autonomous agency is changed into a *desirable* agency. This is particularly visible in the second photograph, which is intended to prove the expressly praised inventive spirit of the child on the basis of a romantic idealisation. However, the commentary to the first picture also allows one to recognise a form of romanticisation in that the children are imagined in the caption as playing joyfully, whereas this appears doubtful on the visual level.

What also emerges is the authority of the educators, which contradicts their explicit intentions. On the one hand, this photo only just escaped censorship. As formulated by the caption, the manager saw it presenting a negative connotation of institutional authority and pointing to a tradition of alternative liberal and liberalising education. Ironically, the picture could be seen as unintentionally stressing authority. Indeed, the visible authority of educating adults in the second picture underlines, in terms of both the picture and the text, the hierarchical difference between children and adults.

To this extent, the guiding principle of the socially regulated education of children in an asymmetrical generational relationship is not represented in this kindergarten as a straightforward act of adult authority. Instead, the social regulation of the generational relationship finds expression in forms of documentation that disavow pedagogical authority, while nonetheless revealing it in a veiled form that can even serve to enhance that authority. This is particularly true when only the child is shown and the educator is invisible.

The idealisation of competent children who are active without any recognisable prompting from adults leads one to examine the flip side of this equation: Which are the "active" children and which are not? Certainly, there are some empirical indications that the ascription of activity and independence is a criterion for the production of social inequality in kindergarten (Beyer, 2013, p. 230).

In the final analysis, we see the subtle power of the guiding principle of a kindergarten pedagogy, regulated by the generational order, which cannot be undone through mere good intentions nor through a belief in children's "agency". This seems to confirm the assumption made by Bühler-Niederberger (2011, p. 185) that children can only be "actors *as children*" [emphasis of the author]. Which forms of agency are preferred and legitimised in which particular social contexts must remain the subject of further research.

Notes

1 On the debate about education in connection with a specific understanding of family and gender, see Baader (2008).
2 The empirical connections between the conceptions of children, normative expectations and pedagogical measures have been evidenced in primary schools, for example see Dreke (2012, 2014) in relation to conceptions of social hierarchy held by teachers in Italy and Germany, and see Alexi (2014) with reference to forms of interaction between teachers.
3 Names of the educators who have taken the photographs and have given the photo this title.

References

Alanen, L. (2005). Kindheit als generationelles Konzept [Childhood as a generational concept]. In H. Hengst & H. Zeiher (Eds.), *Kindheit soziologisch* [*Childhood sociologically*] (pp. 65–82). Wiesbaden: VS.
Alexi, S. (2014). *Kindheitsvorstellungen und generationale Ordnung* [*Concepts of childhood and generational order*]. Opladen: Budrich.
Baader, M. S. (1996). *Die romantische Idee des Kindes und der Kindheit. Auf der Suche nach der verlorenen Unschuld* [*The romantic concept of the child and of childhood. In search of the lost innocence*]. Neuwied: Luchterhand.
Baader, M. S. (2005). *Erziehung als Erlösung* [*Education as salvation*]. Weinheim, Munich: Juventa.
Baader, M. S. (2008). Öffentliche Kleinkinderziehung in Deutschland im Fokus des Politischen. Von den Kindergärten 1848 bis zu den Kinderläden in der 68er Bewegung [Public early education in Germany in the political focus: From the Kindergartens 1848 to the Kinderläden of the 68-movement]. In J. Ecarius & H. Malmede (Eds.), *Familie und öffentliche Erziehung. Theoretische Konzeptionen, historische und aktuelle Analysen* [*Family and public education. Theoretical conceptions, historical and current analyses*] (pp. 267–290). Wiesbaden: VS.
Baader, M. S. & Sager, K. (2010). Die pädagogische Konstitution des Kindes als Akteur im Zuge der 68er-Bewegung [The pedagogical constitution of the child as an actor in the course of the 68-movement]. *Diskurs Kindheits- und Jugendforschung, 3*, 255–267.
Betz, T. (2010). Die Kindergesellschaft. Wie Kindheit und Ungleichheit zusammenhängen [Childhood society. The relation of childhood and inequality]. *Sozial Extra* 11/12, 37–40.

Beyer, B. (2013). *Soziale Ungleichheit im Kindergarten. Orientierungs- und Handlungsmuster pädagogischer Fachkräfte* [*Social inequality in the Kindergarten. Orientation and action patterns of educational staff*]. Wiesbaden: VS.

Bohnsack, R. (2008). The interpretation of pictures and the documentary method (64 paragraphs). *Forum: Qualitative Research, 9*(3), Art. 26, http://nbn-rsolving.de/urn:nbn:de:0114-fqs0803267 (last accessed 10 October 2014).

Bohnsack, R. (2009). *Qualitative Bild- und Videointerpretation. Die dokumentarische Methode* [*Qualitative Interpretation of Pictures and Videos. The Documentary Method*]. Barbara Budrich: Opladen & Farmington Hills.

Bollig, S. & Kelle, H. (2014). Kinder als Akteure oder Partizipanden von Praktiken? Zu den Herausforderungen für eine akteurszentrierte Kindheitssoziologie durch Praxistheorien [Children as Actors or as Participants of Practices? The challenges of practice theories to an actor-centered sociology of childhood]. *Zeitschrift für Soziologie der Erziehung und Sozialisation, 34*(3), 265–281.

Bühler-Niederberger, D. (2011). *Lebensphase Kindheit. Theoretische Ansätze, Akteure und Handlungsräume* [*Childhood as a phase of life: Theoretical approaches, actors and arenas of actions*]. Juventa: Weinheim.

Cloos, P. & Schulz, M. (2011). Die Beobachtung und Dokumentation kindlicher Tätigkeiten. Eine Einleitung [Observation and documentation of children's activities. Introduction]. In P. Cloos & M. Schulz (Eds.), *Kindliches Tun beobachten und dokumentieren. Perspektiven auf die Bildungsbegleitung in Kindertageseinrichtungen* [*Observing and documenting children's activities. Perspectives on educational support in day care centres*] (pp. 7–18). Weinheim, Basel: Juventa.

Denzin, N. (1977). *Childhood Socialization. Studies in the Development of Language, Social Behavior and Identity*. San Francisco: Jossey-Bass Publishers.

Dreke, C. (2012). *Künftige Lebenswege von Schulkindern. Deutungsmuster sozialer Ungleichheit von Lehrkräften in Italien und Deutschland* [*Children's roadmaps into the future. How Italian and German teachers construct social inequalities*]. Wiesbaden: VS.

Dreke, C. (2014). Bewegung im sozialen Raum? Schulische Sozialisation und künftige soziale Platzierungen von Kindern aus der Sicht von Lehrkräften in Italien und Deutschland [Movements in the social space? School socialization and future social positioning of children in the perspective of teachers in Italy and Germany]. *sozialer sinn, 1*, 29–54.

Esser, F. (2014). Agency revisited. Relationale Perspektiven auf Kindheit und die Handlungsfähigkeit von Kindern [Agency revisited. Relational perspectives on childhood and the capacities of children]. *Zeitschrift für Soziologie der Erziehung und Sozialisation, 34*(3), 233–245.

Goffman, E. (1977). *Rahmen-Analyse. Ein Versuch über die Organisation von Alltagserfahrungen* [*Frame Analysis: An Essay on the Organization of Experience*]. Frankfurt/Main: Suhrkamp.

Grell, F. (2010). Über die (Un-)Möglichkeit, Früherziehung durch Selbstbildung zu ersetzen [On the (Im-) Possibility to replace early education by self-education]. *Zeitschrift für Pädagogik, 56*, 154–167.

James, A. & Prout, A. (1997/2004). *Constructing and Reconstructing Childhood: Contemporary Issues in the Sociological Study of Childhood*. London: Routledge.

Huizinga, J. (1996). *Homo ludens. Vom Ursprung der Kultur im Spiel* [*Homo Ludens: A Study of the Play-Element in Culture*]. Reinbek bei Hamburg: Rowohlt.

Kaga, Y., Bennett, J. & Moss, P. (2010). *Caring and Learning Together. A Cross-national Study of Integration of Early Childhood Care and Education within Education*. Paris: UNESCO.

Mead, G. H. (1975). *Geist, Identität und Gesellschaft aus der Sicht des Sozialbehaviorismus* [*Mind, Self, and Society: From the Standpoint of a Social Behaviorist*]. Frankfurt am Main: Suhrkamp.

Paris, R. (1995). Die Politik des Lobes [Policy of Praise]. *KZfSS: Sonderheft, 35,* 83–107.

Pettersson, K. E. (2013). *Playing a Part in Preschool Documentation. A Study of How Participation Is Enacted in Preschool Documentation Practices and How It Is Affected by Material Agents.* Lindköping University.

Pilarczyk, U. & Mietzner, U. (2005). *Das reflektierte Bild. Die seriell-ikonografische Fotoanalyse in den Erziehungs- und Sozialwissenschaften* [*The reflected picture. Serial-iconographic photo analysis in educational and social sciences*]. Bad Heilbrunn: Klinkhardt.

Prange, E. (2005). *Die Zeigestruktur der Erziehung. Grundriss der Operativen Pädagogik* [*The structure of indicating in education. Outlines of the operational pedagogy*]. Paderborn: Ferdinand Schöningh.

Prout, A. (2000). Childhood bodies: construction, agency and hybridity. In A. Prout (Ed.), *The Body, Childhood and Society* (pp. 1–18). Houndmills: Macmillan.

Raithelhuber, E. (2012). Ein relationales Verständnis von Agency. Sozialtheoretische Überlegungen und Konsequenzen für empirische Analysen [A relational understanding of agency. Social theoretical reflections and consequences for empirical analyses]. In S. Bethmann, C. Helfferich, H. Hoffmann & D. Niermann (Eds.), *Agency. Qualitative Rekonstruktionen und gesellschaftstheoretische Bezüge von Handlungsmächtigkeit* [*Agency. Qualitative reconstructions and theoretical concepts of the power to act*] (pp. 122–153). Weinheim, Basel: Beltz Juventa.

Rehberg, K. -S. (2002). Institutionen, Kognitionen und Symbole – Institutionen als symbolische Verkörperungen. Kultursoziologische Anmerkungen zu einem handlungstheoretischen Programm [Institutions, cognitions and symbols – institutions as symbolic embodiments. Cultural sociology comments on an action theory research program]. In A. Maurer & M. Schmid (Eds.), *Neuer Institutionalismus* [*New institutionalism*] (pp. 39–56). Frankfurt am Main: Campus.

Rehberg, K. -S. (2014). Die "Öffentlichkeit" der Institutionen [The "Public" of institutions]. In H. Vorlaender (Ed.), *Institutionen als symbolische Ordnungen* [*Institutions as symbolic orders*] (pp. 85–118). Baden-Baden: Nomos.

Reyer, J. (2006). Einführung in die Geschichte des Kindergartens und der Grundschule [Introduction into the history of kindergarten and elementary school]. Bad Heilbrunn: Klinkhardt.

Ricken, N. (2006). Klaus Prange. *Die Zeigestruktur der Erziehung. Grundriss der Operativen Pädagogik* [*Klaus Prange. The structure of indicating in education. Outlines of the operational pedagogy*]. Paderborn: Ferdinand Schöningh.

Ruppin, I. (2015). Einleitung [Introduction]. In I. Ruppin (Ed.), *Professionalisierung in Kindertagesstätten* [*Professionalization in day care centres*] (pp. 7–24), Weinheim, Basel: Beltz Juventa.

Sparrman, A. & Lindgren A. -L. (2010). Visual documentation as a normalizing practice: a new discourse of visibility in preschool. *Surveillance & Society, 7*(3/4), 248–261.

Tisdall, E. K. M. & Punch, S. (2014). Not so "new"? Looking critically at childhood studies. In S. Punch & E. K. M. Tisdall (Eds.), *Children and Young People's Relationships. Learning across Majority and Minority Worlds* (pp. 249–264). London, New York: Routledge.

Vandenbroeck, M. & Bouverne-de Bie, M. (2006). Children's agency and educational norms. A tensed negotiation. *Childhood, 13*(1), 127–143.

Wulf, C. (2014). *Die Bilder des Menschen. Imaginäre und performative Grundlagen der Kultur* [*The images of men. Imaginary and performative basics of culture*]. Bielefeld: transcript.

Chapter 16

Agency and the conceptualisation of minors in child protection case files

Timo Ackermann and Pierrine Robin

Political and scientific discourse increasingly stresses that children are actors with their own rights. However, the limits of agency are particularly clear when children become victims of violence. This is especially the case with abuse and maltreatment. In this chapter, we aim to provide insight into the production of agency in this particular institutional setting. We analyse how children and children's agency are represented and conceptualised in ten child protection case files produced by the child protection services. We analyse the form in which agency or the deprivation of agency is produced through assessments undertaken by the child protection services. In this sense, agency is not treated as a human property but as an effect of the interaction between social workers and children through assessments and the preparation of cases in documentation work.

In child protection policy, children are regarded more as objects in need of protection rather than as subjects with rights (Wolff et al., 2013b; Robin, 2013). Moreover, more often than not they are treated as vulnerable human beings in need of protection rather than potential autonomous actors (Wolff et al., 2013b). These views are tied to the emergence of child protection policy in nineteenth-century Europe, and are linked to the view that the state should intervene in private family life to protect weaker members of the family unit. However, as Youf (2002) has stressed, child protection policy was also an attempt to conserve the social order that existed at the time and pursued demographic objectives. Child protection legislation was not put in place to promote human and children's rights; rather, it was aimed at integrating children who found themselves on the fringes of society.

Several difficulties immediately arise in designing a system for children's participation in care. First, care relationships are unequal; they create dependency. Moreover, children in care cannot choose whether professionals should deal with their "case". Such relationships of care are established by the professionals themselves; they work with children who clearly possess less power (Robin, 2013). This situation is confounded by the fact that the field of child protection is constituted of multiple actors with potentially diverging interests.

Nevertheless, the status of children in care has evolved considerably since the adoption of the United Nations Convention on the Rights of the Child (UNCRC, 1989). States that have signed the Convention recognise children as rights holders, and this includes recognising their socio-economic and civil rights. Therefore, these states must grant children protection, provide them with services and secure effective possibilities for child participation in decisions that affect their lives. The UN Convention also enhances the rights of children in care; for instance, children in care must be provided with the opportunity to be heard in any judicial and administrative proceedings that directly affect them. Similarly, children in care have the right to be heard during assessments of their situation. Nevertheless, the Convention has been widely criticised for its historical and cultural abstraction of childhood and for ignoring the diversity of childhood in various contexts (Morrow & Pells, 2012). This criticism has led some organisations to focus on certain child-specific problems. For example, in this context, the Council of Europe focusses on the rights of marginalised children in Europe. In 2005, the Council published recommendations on the rights of children living in care. These recommendations set out a number of specific rights, including the right to take part in the decision-making process and individual care plans (Council of Europe, 2005). However, unlike the UNCRC, these guidelines are not legally binding. In 2009, the European Committee for Social Cohesion evaluated the application of the Council of Europe's recommendations and highlighted numerous obstacles to their implementation (Council of Europe, 2009). Morrow and Pells (2012) warn of viewing children as passive victims rather than social agents with capacities. Moreover, they demonstrate that legalist strategies "often start with conceptions of vulnerability, which do not necessarily reflect the priorities of children's everyday lives" (p. 915).

The German situation provides a useful case with which to discuss children's agency in the field of European social protection. Germany has namely implemented a familialist social model of care that treats individuals as members of a family. Accordingly, the provision of individual rights to family members is viewed as a move towards the destruction of the social fabric (Robin, 2013). Germany also has a long tradition of participatory legal frameworks. Since 1989, when the regulatory framework underwent an important change, particularly regarding the assessment process, Germany's child welfare system has increasingly offered possibilities for children and their parents to participate in care. These reforms moved the primary responsibility for conducting assessments to administrative services. This was in accordance with the principle of double subsidiarity: State intervention is to be supplementary to the role of parents in raising their children, and courts can only intervene after the local authority has done so. This process is viewed as bolstering voluntary help, and ensuring this is done prior to imposing compulsory care. The assessment process is conducted by social workers from the *Jugendamt*, the central agency in charge of child protection. The *Jugendamt* treats the process as an attempt "to systematically determine the extent to which the well-being of the child is threatened by any element connected to his/her environment, in order to propose appropriate action" (Boutin & Durning, 2008, p. 77). The assessment process can be conducted in the form of a diagnosis before assistance has been provided, as part of a further process aimed at assessing the child's situation and developing an individual care plan. Decisions on childcare must consider the best interests of the child, who also has the right to participate in the process. This takes place in the wider context of the changing field of social work, and follows a contractual approach that provides more freedom than other methods but also gives more responsibility to children and their families (Astier, 2007).

Our research was conducted in the context of a larger research- and practice-based project (Wolff et al., 2013). Our work is based on the assumption that although the German legal framework foresees the broad opportunities for participation, it sometimes seems to be more geared towards the perspectives of adults. Furthermore, previous research has demonstrated some of the difficulties associated with participation in German child protection services (Pluto, 2007). Our research seeks to provide a better understanding of how children are seen in child protection services and the extent to which their voices are considered. Based on the assumption that agency is relational and produced by diverse actors, we assume that agency is not a human property but the effect of social interaction between social workers and children in the assessment process. We studied written reports that were produced as part of the working process in the child protection services offices and as part of this interaction. In doing so, we sought to study how minors are conceptualised in child protection records. The aim was to provide an understanding of agency in child protection processes. Studying assessment processes in Germany, where the culture of participation is high and has been implemented for many years, could provide useful insights into the production of agency in this particularly complex and ambivalent institutional setting. Children are seen as vulnerable, but they are also recognised as rights holders. Consequently, the German setting provides a good example with which to rethink agency in the field of vulnerability. At the same time, we also aim to question notions of children as naturally passive individuals when confronted by vulnerable situations.

Theoretical framework

To understand the participation of children in the assessment process, children's evolving agency within interaction needs to be studied empirically. In line with relational social theory, which was presented in the first part of this book, we approach agency as an effect of social relations in a specific context. Thus, we view children's agency as tied to and influenced by the generational order and as interacting with other power relations and socially constructed identity positions (see Bühler-Niederberger, 2011). Agency is therefore not a human property, but an assemblage (Oswell, 2013), an arrangement that is negotiated between various actors, which in our case means between social workers and parents within the organisational setting provided by the *Jugendamt*. Thus, we study children's agency – in analysing one part of the institutional setting – as a heterogeneous, contextually shaped and negotiated phenomenon.

Children's agency has been widely studied in the field of Childhood Studies, principally through the analysis of participatory processes in the context of interdependence and reciprocity (Lansdown, 2010). For Smith (2002), participation is not a linear process, nor does it flow from adult to child; it is a reciprocal activity in which children and adults build common understandings and knowledge. Emotion and effective communication are essential if common understandings are to form. Children's participation is linked to adults' representations of children. However, it is also related to children's vulnerabilities and capacities, and their perceptions of the services available to them. Moreover, Stoecklin (2013) argues that the extent to which children develop their agency and participation depends on their interaction with adults, and the dynamic contexts in which children live; furthermore, Stoecklin argues that this is a non-linear, lifelong process (p. 454). At the same time, participation takes place within a framework of power dynamics.

For a long time, there was very little empirical research analysing children's participation in child protection processes (Cashmore, 2002). However, the issue of children's place in decision-making processes in child protection has recently been subjected to extensive research; most of this research has been conducted in Britain and Germany in the field of Childhood Studies. In her article "Participation and Emotions: Troubling Encounters between Children and Social Welfare Professionals", which was based on interviews with social workers, Pinkney (2011) noticed a huge disjuncture between policy texts on participation and the everyday experiences of social workers. In formal policy texts, participation is generally presented as uncomplicated. However, interviews with social workers are littered with references to the emotional complexity of their work with children. Pinkney highlights the sense of ambivalence among social workers about their abilities and willingness to listen to children. She argues that organisations, such as social services, develop socially structured defences aimed at distancing professionals from the people with whom they work. Pinkney demonstrated "how professionals either consciously or unconsciously develop ways of working and talking with and about children which seek to minimize their own anxieties and defend them psychically from stress" (p. 39). Furthermore, she points out that this should alerts us "to the complexities involved in listening and the different ways that adults and children listen as well as the different way they assess whether they have been listened to" (p. 40). Studies conducted in Australia have underlined the difficulty of conceiving of children as subjects during the assessment process (Mason & Michaux, 2005).

Professionals demonstrate a greater ability to communicate with parents than with children during the assessment process; they fear that asking children direct questions about their situation will make them more vulnerable. Children's views rarely appear in assessments and are never a key factor in decisions (Mason & Michaux, 2005). Pluto (2007) in Germany and Leeson (2007) in the UK have come to similar conclusions. In interviews, professionals argue that they are convinced of the need for participation; however, studies show that children are barely seen or heard during the assessment process (Pluto, 2007; Leeson, 2007). In analysing conversations between social workers and children, van Nijnatten and Jongen (2011) show that "professionals are often unclear about the status of the information the children are supposed to provide. They scarcely explain the goal of the encounter, what they expect from the children and whether they have free choice to tell or keep silent. As a result, the children showed confusion, and remained silent, even when they had a strong view, or did not enter into an exchange of information by getting and remaining involved in play" (p. 549). This is why Holland (2001) refers to a process of the "ongoing silencing of the voices of children". In dangerous situations, professionals are especially unlikely to engage in a process of meaningful child participation. Participation by children is encouraged primarily to get them to accept assistance rather than to give them the possibility of shaping assistance. Children's words are used to justify the point of view of the professionals (Katz, 1995). Iversen (2014) came to the same result after analysing 35 child assessment interviews in Sweden. She concludes that although social workers sometimes invoke the category of the competent, participating child, they also construct them as troublesome if children try to make decisions about how counselling should proceed. She notices that social workers "describe willing children as competent, unwilling children as developing, and children attempting to rule in counseling as problematic" (p. 274). Participation is predetermined and only considered valid when children follow the proposed model of intervention. This represents a limited form of participation that only respects children's wishes if they agree with the intervention proposed by social workers. In this sense, participation is not used to question existing power relations; on the contrary, it strengthens them.

Most of these studies were based on interviews or conversations; few drew on case studies or written assessments. In contrast, this chapter provides an alternative view of agency in the context of child protection by analysing ten case files compiled by the child protection services. We seek to understand how children and their agency are represented in case files and analyse the form of agency or deprivation of agency that is produced through documentary work; *how children and their status as actors are produced in practices of documenting child protection processes*[1]. After presenting our methodological framework and research methods, we describe some of the results of our study.

Methodological framework and research methods

This study is based on ten case files from the German child protection services that were collected as part of a research project led by Reinhart Wolff and Uwe Flick (2013)[2] between 2009 and 2011 from 40 child protection services throughout Germany. The ten cases involved 18 minors (ten girls and 8 boys) ranging from one month to 20 years of age (Ackermann & Robin, 2014).

The case files usually contain a wide spectrum of documents. The first pages typically document the personal details of the child and his or her parents, such as date of birth, address and, in the case of the parents, occupation. As social workers are obliged to document all of their actions, the files usually consist of written notes from meetings with parents, home visits or team meetings held between the social workers themselves. The case files also usually contain reports on the child's development written by other professionals. These reports were written by people such as teachers, doctors and psychologists, and were assembled by the social workers for use in the child's assessment. In our analysis, however, we focussed on the reports written by social workers, using other professionals' accounts as contrasting material only.

These case files constitute a specific type of document; they are "standardized artefacts" or even "fictions" (Wolff, 2004) produced for an organisation (Garfinkel, 2008). Records merely provide an "appearance of legitimacy, rationality and efficiency" (Wolff, 2004, p. 505). In this sense, the files provide legitimacy to the actions that were carried out (Luhmann, 2005). Social workers leave "institutionalized traces" in their case files that lead to "conclusions about activities, motives, and the reasoning of its author" (Wolff, 2004, p. 503, our translation). Documents such as case files now serve as an increasingly important source of data for the social sciences. Although these documents should not be taken as proving what "really" went on in specific cases, they do provide insight into the established conceptualisations. Furthermore, they are sources of information about relevant organisational and institutional contexts and illustrate how these professionals responded to and acted within them (Hall et al., 2003).

Our analysis revolved around a "process of breaking down, examining, comparing, conceptualizing, and categorizing data" (Strauss & Corbin, 1998, p. 61). In examining the case records, we treated them as communicative (Wolff, 2004), active documents (Prior, 2003) that were directed at potential readers. Notes and documentation practices are addressed to colleagues, supervisors and other professionals such as judges, or even service users, parents or the children themselves. This led us to attempt to reconstruct communicative meanings, the documents' messages and the conceptualisations of children they expressed.

We followed a process that could be described in terms of grounded theory methodology. We started with open or initial coding, and went through the material line by line (Charmaz, 2014, p. 47). Concepts from childhood and child maltreatment theory, such as agency and participation, guided our analysis as "sensitizing concepts" (Strauss & Corbin, 1998, p. 41). We developed our understandings using constant comparison, following our theoretical interest based on sampling sequences (Strauss & Corbin, 1998, p. 176). We treated each case as a whole, with a story, but also used cross-case comparisons (Patton, 1990). Focussed coding was then undertaken by using "the most significant and/or earlier codes to sift through lager amounts of data" (Charmaz, 2014, p. 57). We then developed our main, more abstract categories through the continual process of axial coding (Charmaz, 2014, pp. 60–63) by comparing our codes and their relation to each other.

Research results

We found three main ways of conceptualising children and their agency: the invisible child, the child as an object and the child as a disturbing and discomforting actor. These three depictions are traces of the social interaction that takes place in the assessment process. Some case files tended to follow one of these particular conceptualisations. However, *different* constructions of the children were evident in most of the case files. Moreover, the ways in which the children were described also changed during the course of a case; for example, a child may have first appeared as an object of care, but later become invisible for much of the time.

The invisible child

It soon became clear to us that the case files lacked basic information on subjects such as the numbers of children in danger, their gender or their age. Sometimes it was not even clear whether a child had been involved in a case until we had finished reading the entire case file. The voice of the child seemed to be almost non-existent. Only one file documented a meeting held alone, face-to-face with a minor. However, most of the other meetings were solely undertaken between adults, or with children who were obviously being excluded from the talking; at least, their positions were sketched out briefly or not reported at all. Thus, during our early work, we realised that information about children was not considered as crucial as we had expected. This observation is sort of similar to that made by Garfinkel (2008) in his work "Good reasons for bad records". Garfinkel showed that medical practitioners were not including the information *he* had expected them to include in their records. He argued that they do so for good reasons; their practices reflected the situational and organisational rationality. In our case, social workers mainly focused on adults' worlds, perspectives and interests. Social workers act as if they are merely collecting information and sampling "objective" data. Their interest in adults' discourse, including that of the parents and of adults from related institutions, resulted in a focus on statements made by adults. Although a focus on adults' perspectives (which made children invisible) occurred repeatedly in the case files, it was particularly pronounced in two of them. These cases completely lacked a depiction of childhood and, as such, made its analysis impossible. This led us to create our first category: the invisible child.

The child as an object

When children were mentioned in the records, they generally appeared as objects in need of help (in nine of our records). We differentiated between three subcategories in which children were constructed in this manner: *the child as a victim of an accident, the child as a victim of neglect and maltreatment and the child with needs*. These subcategories mostly concerned cases of negligence or physical violence and involved small children. The first of these depictions referred to a history of child maltreatment. The long-term violence that these children had undergone was ignored and the children were viewed *as victims of accidents* (Sellenet, 2006). The records contained a case in which a child had suffered numerous fractures, but social workers maintained that the child had not been maltreated. The mother was described as a "loving" mother, and it seemed to be difficult for them to imagine that a "loving" mother could maltreat her child. Children who are constructed as *victims of accidents* are not only seen as passive, but they are also not even viewed as victims of violence. In contrast, in the cases in which minors were described as *victims of maltreatment*, social workers aimed to protect children from potential risks. Instances of suspicion often led to a further search for information. However, numerous rapid interventions were also conducted, especially when disastrous living conditions were reported. In these cases, the social workers reacted quickly: They ensured that other social workers got involved with the family, conducted home visits or even removed the child from the family. Children in these cases were regularly described as passive actors who had already suffered or who were in need of protection from further harm. Children often had very little agency in these situations, as social workers were focussed on the "objective" statements made by adults. This was also the case with the *child with needs* category. In these cases, social workers expressed concern about a child's basic needs and invoked the image of an age-based, continuous form of child development. In one case, a social worker searched for and identified "age-based development, but with difficulties using language" (Case 10, p. 31). A three-year-old girl was said to be "dressed decently and able to articulate herself in an age-appropriate way" (Case 9, p. 3). However, the author of the file argued that "the girl had hardly changed" (Case 5). This demonstrates that social workers used their casework to compare "ideal" stages of child development (regarding weight, language, etc.) with the child's "real" stage. In fact, social workers often treated the children as passive actors, but they documented their own efforts to change parents' attitudes. Still, social workers often expressed doubts as to whether they could really help children fulfil their needs (Cases 6 and 2). In these three conceptualisations, children are treated as objects of adult care and are viewed as in need of adult care in all three of these subcategories.

The child as a disturbing and discomforting actor

In five cases, children were conceptualised mainly as disturbing actors. These cases mostly concerned older children and were focussed on issues of psychological or sexual violence. Although these children were interpreted as actively shaping their (family) lives, they were also described in terms of different subcategories: They were *deviant actors, active actors in need of normalisation, and averted protagonists.*

Deviant actors were often described as having problems at school and displaying abnormal behaviour. Teachers had reported "aggressive" and "sexualized" behaviour in school and this had been documented in the case files. These children made "uncontrolled sounds", did not complete their homework; they "hit" and, in some cases, "attacked" other students. Such reports clearly implied that the child's behaviour needed to change because it otherwise made "normal" school attendance impossible: "if children are to carry out their tasks at school, they need individually tailored structures that also involve consequences; and children need a firm day-to-day routine" (Case 7). Such forms of normalising work (Foucault, 1993) were also evident in our other subcategories.

In one of the cases, a child who had been described as *an active actor in need of normalisation* also appeared to have been "normalised" through professional casework, as the child was now supporting her siblings and family. In the view of the social worker, this had led the child to assume a role that did not follow the linear pathway of a child's development:

> When she looks after her sister, she looks like a small pedagogue supporting her sister; more like an adult. She takes on responsibility for her little sister and her mother. Steps must be taken so that she can return to her role as a child. (Case 9, p. 43)

The girl in this case was viewed as having entered the adults' sphere; as such, she had to "return to her role as a child". Although recent research (Liebel, 2011) suggests that our lives develop continually from birth to death, the social worker drew a clear boundary between the adult world and the world of children. This resulted from the complex scenario with which the social workers were confronted. On the one hand, they aimed to strengthen the girl's ability to support her family, but they also wanted to protect her from situations they perceived as harmful, such as from taking on "too much" responsibility.

When children's active roles were accepted, their influence was typically limited to the family sphere. In these cases, children's activities therefore had no impact on the public sphere or on the professional decision-making process. Nevertheless, we did find one child – who had actively sought professional support – described as a protagonist (Liebel, 2010). The girl had spoken to her teacher about situations in which she felt that her father's behaviour had been strange or awkward. Her father's actions could certainly be categorised as sexual abuse, and the girl was clear that she wanted the abuse to stop. However, she also wanted her father to stay with her family and asked her teacher to treat the matter confidentially. Despite this, management of the process was taken out of the girl's hands and the worried teacher informed her colleague as well as the local child protection team without the girl's consent. The social workers were worried too: Numerous meetings were held with teachers and social workers from a specialised sexual abuse service, yet the girl was not involved. Finally, the social worker in charge decided to "confront" the father, and did so without the girl's consent. The father denied the accusation and the confrontation failed to solve the situation. Moreover, after the girl had spoken with a friend, a rumour spread through the school that she had been raped by her father. The social workers were alarmed and asked a judge to remove the girl from her home. However, the girl denied that rape had occurred and stated that her friend had misunderstood her. A gynaecological examination proved that she had not been raped. The doctor's diagnosis was used by the judge to clear her father. But the girl was harassed in school because of the rumours and had to change schools. Moreover, she stayed with her family and broke off all contact with the social workers. In this case, a minor asked adults for support and even told them how she wished the assessment process to be undertaken (confidentially, among other things). Nevertheless, the decision-making process was taken out of her hands.

Conclusion

Our analysis of ten case files from child protection services demonstrates that children are mostly made invisible or viewed as objects of care. This led social workers to apply an adult-centred perspective and focus on parents' problems. The case files mainly describe how the parents acted, what they thought and how they reacted to the social workers. Consequently, they ignored children's perspectives. This of course makes it very difficult for minors to ensure that their interests are considered in decision-making processes that concern their own lives. Even when children were conceptualised as actors, they were typically treated as actors whose actions have to be restricted. Our results are similar to those of Iversen (2014), who concluded that although social workers sometimes invoke the category of the competent, participating child, they also construct children as troublesome when children try to make decisions. This is particularly the case when children attempt to influence the manner in which counselling should be undertaken as part of a predetermined process. Opportunities for participation are bound to the organisational context reflected in the case files: In our study, this meant a top-down participatory form of social interaction focussed mainly on adults as clients, and far less on children. In this sense, children's agency is tied to adults' representations and understandings of children, and to children's vulnerabilities and capacities.

This understanding of children's agency is linked to the asymmetric relationship between professionals and children. Indeed, during the assessment process, parents are heard more than their children; this implies that children's voices are of less value than those of adults. It was not until the 1980s that children's voices began to be heard, but their voices remain fragile when faced with dominant adult speech. To make their voices and rationales heard, children, as "minors", have to amplify their efforts in the face of professionals who, caught up in the parents' narrative, can ignore children's interpretations. Indeed, social workers are highly focussed on the "plausibility" of their casework (Ackermann, 2014) and this means using all of the available information to construct a case. However, children's speech is often considered untrustworthy. Leeson (2007) argued "this fits with the nature of current social work practice being risk-averse" (p. 274).

This research provides an opportunity to rethink agency in the field of vulnerability in a particular institutional setting characterised by its complexity and ambivalence. Our conclusions question both notions of children being naturally passive in vulnerable situations and as naturally active. Agency is not a human property but an effect of chains of transaction between various and independent social actors (in this case at least, parents, social workers and children). It is expressed in relational networks between adults and children, themselves characterised by power imbalances, and emerges through ambivalent interpersonal relations. As Burkitt (2015, p. 15) shows, "in interrelation, interdependence and interactions with others, interactants are always active and passive, powerful and yet vulnerable to various degrees, acting on others and being acted on by those others". Moreover, we need to remember "that relations and interdependencies have an emotional dimension to them, which usually involves feelings of compulsion, attachment, loyalty, affiliation, identification, trust, love, need, friendship, or their opposites and, most crucially, ambivalences" (p. 14).

How, in this context, can we strengthen children's involvement in assessments of their own situation? Jaffé (2001) has shown that the quality of children's participation in the assessment process depends on adult representations of the children's world and, vice versa, on children's representations of the adult world. This requires recognising the plurality of a child's verbal and non-verbal means of expression, supporting the emergence of their point of view, encouraging participation, not at an imposed time, but at a time chosen by the children, offering them real choices between different means of assistance and accepting their views. Instead of simply imposing an external view of their situation onto the children, it is time for assessments to acknowledge children's own understandings of their situations and to take their views into consideration.

Notes

1 Our main interest was to understand how children were conceptualized. Moreover, we sought to analyse the effects on agency which result from practices of record keeping. We focused on the conceptions of childhood, child maltreatment and agency that were mobilized by social workers.
2 The project's main subject was improving organizational structures and standards. It aimed to learn from the failures in child protection processes in 42 departments in Germany (Wolff & Flick, 2013). The project was completed in 2011. See also the report on children in care in Wolff (2013). For the German situation, and for background information about our research project, see Wolff, Biesel & Heinitz (2011).

References

Ackermann, T. & Robin, P. (2014). Kinder im Kinderschutz. Zur Konstruktion von Agency in amtlichen Entscheidungsprozessen [Children in child protection. Construction of agency in decision making processes]. In D. Bühler-Niederberger, L. Alberth & S. Eisentraut (Eds.), *Kinderschutz: Wie kindzentriert sind Programme, Praktiken, Perspektiven* [*Child protection. How child-centered are programs, practices, perspectives*] (pp. 64–81). Weinheim, Basel: Juventa.

Ackermann, T. (2014). Entscheiden über Fremdunterbringungen: Praktiken der Fallerzeugung [Decision making about out-of-home-placement. Practices of constructing cases]. In B. Bütow, M. Pomney, M. Rutschmann, C. Schär & T. Studer, (Eds.), *Sozialpädagogik zwischen Staat und Familie* [*Social pedagogy between state and family*] (pp. 153–173). Wiesbaden: Springer.

Astier, I. (2007). *Les nouvelles règles du social* [*The new rules of social order*]. Paris: PUF.

Boutin, G & Durning, P. (2008). *Enfants maltraités ou en danger: L'apport des pratiques socio-éducatives* [*Maltreated children: report about socio-educatives practices*]. Paris: L'Harmattan.

Bühler-Niederberger, D. (2011). *Lebensphase Kindheit: Theoretische Ansätze, Akteure und Handlungsräume* [*Childhood as stage of life. Theoretical approaches, actors and scopes for action*]. Weinheim, Munich: Juventa.

Burkitt, I. (2015). Relational agency, relational sociology, agency and interaction. *European Journal of Social Theory*, online first, doi: 10.1177/1368431015591426

Cashmore, J. (2002). Promoting the participation of children and young people in care. *Child Abuse and Neglect*, 26(8), 837–847.

Charmaz, K. (2014). *Constructing grounded theory*. Thousand Oaks: Sage Publications.

Council of Europe (2005). *Recommendation Rec (2005) 5 of the Committee of Ministers to member states on the rights of children living in residential institutions.*

Council of Europe (2009). *Rights of Children in Institutions. Report on the implementation of the Council of Europe Recommendation* Rec (2005) 5 on the rights of children living in residential institutions.

Foucault, M. (1993). *Discipline & Punish: The Birth of the Prison.* New York: Vintage.

Garfinkel, H. (2008). *Studies in Ethnomethodology.* Bodmin Cornwall: MPG Books.

Hall, C., Juhila, K., Parton, N. & Poso, D. (Eds.) (2003). *Constructing Clienthood in Social Work and Human Services. Interaction, Identities and Practices.* London, New York: Jessica Kingsley.

Holland, S. (2001). Representing Children in Child Protection Assessments, *Childhood, 8*(3), 322–339.

Iversen, C. (2014). Predetermined participation Social workers evaluating children's agency in domestic violence interventions, *Childhood, 21*, 274–289.

Jaffé, P. D. (2001). L'expertise judiciaire des capacités parentales: subjectivité de l'évaluation, utilité du rapport [Judicial expertise of parental skills: subjectivity of assessment]. In Viaux, J. L. (Ed.), *Ecrire au juge* [*Letter to the judge*] (pp. 119–132). Paris: Dunod.

Katz, L. G. (1995). *Talks with Children of Young Children.* Norwood: Ablex.

Lansdown, G. (2010). The realisation of children's participation rights. Critical reflections. In B. Percy-Smith & N. Thomas (Eds.), *A Handbook of Children and Young People's Participation: Perspectives from Theory and Practice* (pp. 11–23). London, New York: Routledge.

Leeson, C. (2007). My life in care: experiences of non-participation in decision-making processes. *Child and Family Social Work, 12*, 228–277.

Liebel, M., in collaboration with Robin, P. & Saadi, I. (2010). *Children, droits et citoyenneté, Faire émerger la perspective des children sur leur droit* [*Children, rights and citizenship, children's point of view of their rights*]. Paris: L'Harmattan.

Luhmann, N. (2005). *Legitimation durch Verfahren* [*Procedural legitimation*]. Frankfurt/M.: Suhrkamp.

Mason, J. & Michaux, A. (2005). *The Starting out with Scarba Project: Facilitating Children's Participation in Child Protection Process*. Paddington: The Benevolent Society.

Morrow, V., & Pells, K. (2012). Integrating children's human rights and child poverty debates: examples from young lives in Ethiopia and India, *Sociology, 46*(5), 906–920.

Oswell, D. (2013). *The Agency of Children: From Family to Global Human Rights*. New York: Cambridge University Press.

Patton, M. Q. (1990). *Qualitative Evaluation and Research Methods*. Newbury Park: Sage Publications.

Pells, K. (2012). Rights are everything we don't have: clashing conceptions of vulnerability and agency in the daily lives of Rwandan children and youth. *Children's Geographies, 10*(4), 427–440.

Pinkney, S. (2011). Participation and emotions: troubling encounters between children and social welfare professionals. *Children & Society, 25*(1), 37–46.

Prior, L. (2003). *Using Documents in Social Research*. New Dehli: Sage Publications.

Pluto, L. (2007). *Partizipation in den Hilfen zur Erziehung, eine empirische Studie* [*Participation in child welfare services. An empirical study*]. Munich: Verlag Deutsches Jugendinstitut.

Robin, P. (2013). *L'évaluation de la maltraitance, Comment prendre en compte le point de vue de l'enfant?* [*Assessment of child maltreatment, how can we take into account the point of view of the child?*] Rennes: Presses Universitaires de Rennes.

Sellenet, C. (2006). *L'enfance en danger. Ils n'ont rien vu?* [*Maltreated child. They didn't see anything?*] Paris: Belin.

Smith, A. B. (2002). Interpreting and supporting participation rights: contributions from sociocultural theory. *The International Journal of Children's Rights, 10*(1), 73–88.

Stoecklin, D. (2013). Theories of action in the field of child participation. In search of explicit frameworks, *Childhood, 20*(4), 443–457.

Strauss, A. & Corbin, J. (1998). *Basics of Qualitative Research: Techniques and Procedures for Developing Grounded Theory*. Thousand Oaks, CA: Sage.

United Nations General Assembly (1989). *Convention on the Rights of the Child*. Retrieved from UN Office of the High Commissioner for Human Rights website: www.ohchr.org/en/professionalinterest/pages/crc.aspx.

van Nijnatten, C. & Jongen, E. (2011). Professional conversations with children in divorce-related child welfare inquiries. *Childhood, 18*(4), 540–555.

Wolff, R., Flick, U., Ackermann, T., Biesel, K., Brandhorst, F., Heinitz, S & Rönsch, G. (2013a). *Aus Fehlern lernen: Qualitätsmanagement im Kinderschutz* [*Learning from failure. Quality management in child protection systems*]. Leverkusen: Barbara Budrich.

Wolff, R., Flick, U., Ackermann, T., Biesel, K., Brandhorst, F., Heinitz, S., Patschke, M. & Robin, P. (2013b). *Kinder im Kinderschutz: Zur Partizipation von Kindern und Jugendlichen im Hilfeprozess: Eine explorative Studie* [*Children in Child Protection. Participation of children and young people. An explorative study*]. Cologne: NZFH.

Wolff, R., Biesel, K. & Heinitz, S. (2011). Child protection in an age of uncertainty: Germany's response. In N. Gilbert, N. Parton & M. Skivenes (Eds.), *Child Protection Systems: International Trends and Orientations* (pp. 183–203). New York: Oxford University Press.

Wolff, S. (2004). Dokumenten- und Aktenanalyse [Analysis of documents and records]. In U. Flick, E. V. Kardorff, H. Keupp, L. V. Rosenstiel & S. Wolff (Eds.), *Handbuch qualitative Sozialforschung: Grundlagen, Konzepte, Methoden und Anwendungen* [*Handbook of qualitative research. Basics, concepts, methods and usages*] (pp. 502–514). Weinheim: Beltz, PVU.

Youf, D. (2002). *Penser les droits de l'enfant* [*Thoughts about children's rights*]. Paris: PUF.

Chapter 17

Children as social actors and addressees?

Reflections on the constitution of actors and (student) subjects in elementary school peer cultures

Torsten Eckermann and Friederike Heinzel

In this chapter, the concept of "children as addressees" is introduced. In this process, the paper outlines a conceptual framework to overcome a one-sided research perspective in which actors are either seen as creative and autonomous individuals in their own right or as passive recipients "simply internalizing society and culture" (Corsaro, 2014, p. 18). This attempt can be understood as a praxeological rehabilitation of childhood(s) within the school as an institution. The main question is: How do children as actors and addressees generate addressing practices under school conditions, and to what extent in this process do they fall back on previously shown addressing practices in order to "institute" themselves as (student) subjects? Drawing on the work of Judith Butler, we represent a non-subjectivist subject theory and a non-actor-centred actor theory, respectively.

With the emergence of the "new" Childhood Studies in the 1980s, the concept of "children as social actors" was established. In contrast to an adult-centred perspective that ascribes children a status as future members of society and focusses on children merely as "adults-in-the-making", the concept of "children as social actors" emphasises the full and active membership of children in and for society (Bühler-Niederberger, 2011). Thus, childhood is not only seen as a stage of preparing for adulthood – "that is, children exist with reference to what they will become – competent, rational adults" (Whyness, 1999, p. 354). Moreover, children cannot be conceptualised as passive recipients of socialisation; instead, "children as social actors" actively take part in the production of childhood(s) (see also Esser, 2009). From this point of view, the concept of "children as social actors" seems to be fruitful for Childhood Studies both in regard to aspects concerning research ethics (e.g. turning away from children as objects of research) as well as to methodological considerations (e.g. "from the children's perspective") (Heinzel, 2012; Honig, 1999).

Although the concept of "children as social actors" was ground-breaking for Childhood Studies and greatly influenced the (re-)thinking of childhood, it has also provoked severe criticism. Bühler-Niederberger (2011), for example, argued that it is necessary to take into account the fact that the two key concepts of "children as social actors" and the "generational order" are bound together. The one-sided view fails to understand that children's acts are always embedded in a generational order. Similarly, Winterhager-Schmidt (2002) points out that the concept tends to overemphasise the autonomy of the child and underestimate the impact of the social (e.g. the peer group) and institutional (e.g. school) contexts. Another criticism arises from the term "actor", which refers to the tradition of methodological individualism (Schmidt, 2012). Methodological individualism conceives the actor as the central element of social life, neglecting the complex interplay between the actor's acting and social structure.

Closely linked to the concept of "children as social actors" is the idea of children's agency. In line with the concept of agency (James, 2009), "children as social actors" are attested a capacity to act; however, this capacity remains opaque as to its concrete theoretical underpinning. Agency is rarely theorised in Childhood Studies (Valentine, 2011). Therefore, there is a reason for further discussion on the following questions: How is the term "agency" to be understood? And how can "agency" be empirically investigated? This is the starting point for our contribution. Based on the practice theory approach (Schatzki et al., 2001), we focus on how children and their peers engage in constituting actors and (student) subjects via practices of addressing one another, and look at how these processes can be theoretically and empirically investigated. In the everyday processes of negotiation within the context of peer culture at elementary school, especially, children and their peers address each other as "someone", whereby they become socially constituted. We argue that children's agency cannot be taken for granted as a more or less "natural" ability, but that it is embedded in a dynamic social practice including bodies, school artefacts and things.

Following these assumptions, this chapter aims to shed light on the possibilities and limitations of the practice theory perspective for Childhood Studies regarding the concept of 'children as social actors' as well as the concept of agency. The argument will be developed in four steps: First, the main aspects of the theoretical framework will be outlined ("Theoretical framework: actors and agency"), followed by a brief description of the concept of "addressing" ("Concept of 'addressing'"). In a second step, we focus on the praxeological approach as well as practices of addressing in everyday teaching ("Practice theory perspectives: addressing practices of the actor's and subject's constitution within everyday teaching"), followed by a short description of the applied research methods ("Methodological notes concerning the empirical reconstruction of the actors' and subjects' constitution within addressing acts"). In the third step, we will illustrate – based on videotaped classroom observations – in how far "agency at work" can be empirically investigated ("Case study"). Finally, the results and implications for Childhood Studies will be discussed ("Conclusion").

Theoretical framework: actors and agency

The pioneering work *Constructing and Reconstructing Childhood* by James and Prout (1990) marks a break to the relative absence of children from sociological research and contributed significantly to today's self-image of Childhood Studies.

James and Prout (1990) developed a new perspective on the "child as a social actor" as follows: "children are seen and must be seen as active in the construction of their own lives, the lives of those around them and of the societies in which they live. Children are not just the passive subjects of social structures and processes" (James & Prout, 1990, p. 8). The perspective presented here in a programmatic manner attempts to conceptualise children not as passive reality-processing actors, but as active actors producing meaning and constructing social reality. According to this view, social reality cannot be reductively limited to a pre-structured social world by the adult generation. Rather, social reality is located within the daily social practice, which is interactively shaped by both adults *and* children.

James and Prout's (1990) concept of "children as social actors" is clearly linked to the tradition of interpretative social research such as symbolic interactionism. The primary interest of the "traditional paradigm of socialization" was mainly limited to the question of which past biographic class-specific influences determine the current actions of the child. However, "new" Childhood Studies conceptualises the social actor as a "meaning-producing being" whose actions are given a meaning only within face-to-face interaction. Thus, the focus is placed on the everyday social practices in the here and now (Kelle & Breidenstein, 1996). However, in the initial concept, the question of how exactly the "child as a social actor" develops its agency was neglected; it is only later that it was specified (James et al., 1998).

In order to close this gap, the authors refer to Giddens' (1984) practice theory approach. Giddens' starting point is the duality of agency and structure, which needs to be overcome. He rejects the idea that actions and structures are independent entities, believing that, instead, they relate to each other in a recursive manner. Social structures not only limit the actors' agency, but also enable action at the same time. In this process, social practices play a crucial role because the actors reproduce the conditions that enable their actions both *in* and *through* social practices. By using Giddens' theory (1984), James and Prout (1990/2003) refer to an approach that emphasises the relevance of the actor. With recourse to Giddens' theory, Elliott (2014, p. 58) points out that in "contrast to approaches that downgrade agency, Giddens argues that people are knowledgeable about the social structures they produce". For Giddens, actors are reflexive and have a "discursive consciousness", which is discursive available knowledge regarding one's own actions, which, however, is only used in practice. Thus, Giddens grants actors an ability to take action with the capacity to reflect on their actions and thus "do agency" by using their reflexive knowledge. However, at the same time Giddens does not intend to solve the "agency structure problem" in an actor-centred manner and fails to pay attention to the mutual dependence of the actors' action and social structure.

According to Esser (2009) and despite the broad reception of Giddens' practice theory, there is a risk within the academic field of Childhood Studies that the duality between "agency" and structure is not given up, but instead fixated upon. The "agency" of the child is opposed to structure such as pedagogic institutions (e.g. school) or to adults as representatives of these structures who restrict their actions, ignoring the fact that social structures are themselves products of social interaction.

Concept of "addressing"

With the concept of "addressing", we take a step back concerning the remarks on Childhood Studies because, according to representatives of the post-structuralist strands of theories, actors are not fixed entities and may not be presupposed to analysis. Instead, they are always understood in a processual and relational manner. The work by Butler (1997/2001) is essential for this process-based understanding of the constitution of the subject (for a feministic, post-structuralist and queer theory perspective on childhood, see also Castañeda, 2001; De Graeve, 2015; Robinson, 2013). She conceptualises the subject as being "attached" *in* as well as *through* language. The subject emerges "as a consequence of language" (Butler, 2001, p. 101) and necessarily remains within its terms. Furthermore, subjects are always involved in power relations and discourses. In addition there are those titles such as "mother, researcher, human being, disabled person, child[1], worker, foreigner, topmodel, manager, Islamist, Turk" (Villa, 2013, p. 66)[2] which provide potential subject forms and positions for the individuals. These subject forms are then occupied by the different individuals and thus allocate them a place in the social order. During this process, however, subjects are not interchangeable with individuals; instead, they can be understood "as (re-) presentations of individuals who are worthy of recognition or are rather intelligible" (p. 66).

In order to develop her theoretical approach, Butler (1997/2001) used Althusser's (1971) "theory of interpellation". Althusser assumed that subjects are transformed into subjects by the process of an invocation, thus, by a call or an addressing. Through these addressing practices subjects are, then, being requested to speak, to act and to be recognised *as someone*. This recognition *as a specific subject* excludes other forms of subjects, such as the ability to act or speak like a "child", "mother" or "researcher". Thus, the subject constitution is a matter of selection.

Within the theory developed by Butler and similar to the position of Childhood Studies, the process of subject constitution cannot be seen as a "developmental event" (in the sense of the children *becoming* and adults *being* subjects). As Butler (1997, p. 11ff.) insists, the "subject reiterates its subjection" and therefore reinvokes the "conditions of its own subordination" through current practices of addressing. Thus the "subject emerges both as the *effect* of a prior power and as the *condition of possibility* for a radically conditioned form of agency". This understanding of the subject's constitution offers the possibility to understand subjects neither as being deterministically shaped by structures nor as being entirely autonomous. Instead, a paradoxical simultaneity is assumed: The subject constitutes him- or herself and acquires agency through subordination to subject forms and subject positions that are offered to the subject by addressing. Practices of subordination and empowerment likewise exist within the constitution of the subjects. Thus, Butler (1997/2001) breaks with the assumption that subordination and empowerment are thought of separately. Instead, subordination presents a form of empowerment.

Although the act of addressing is conducted by concrete individuals, it does have an "institutional structure" to which the individuals submit. As Althusser (1977) underlines, subjects are addressed by ideological state institutions such as churches, educational institutions, families and political parties. Addressing is thus always accompanied by antecedent meanings: If an individual is addressed as a "girl", then this addressing is accompanied by antecedent images, meanings and norms (from the media, everyday actions, research discourses, etc.).

In summary, it can be noted that Butler's concept of addressing offers a promising theoretical framework that has been proven to be compatible with the practice theory and profitable for Childhood Studies. One point of particular importance is that Butler does not apply an actor model in which the actors are provided with characteristics (cf. Giddens' "reflexive actor"), which are then seen as causative for their actions. Rather, subjects and actors constitute themselves in iteratively performed acts of addressing, which produces the subject by addressing it (Ricken, 2013). Butler's approach clearly emphasises that the subject is not simply produced by an abstract power, "but comes to be in and through her concrete relations to others" (Magnus, 2006, p. 95).

However, it must be pointed out that it is not always entirely clear to what extent Butler's theory takes into account non-discursive addressing, which would then – with regard to the agency concept – assume a child to be linguistically competent. However, in this context we argue for a practice theory understanding whereby speech acts themselves represent social practices that take place "as addresses" *via* (e.g. gaze, voice) and *through* (e.g. words, which are incorporated into the limbs, strengthening the backbone) the addressee's *body*.

In order to formulate and develop Butler's concept of addressing using practice theory to an even greater extent, we will focus on the practice theory perspectives in the following section.

Practice theory perspectives: addressing practices of the actor's and subject's constitution within everyday teaching

The above remarks indicate that Butler's theory primarily considers discursively constituted addresses. Praxeological theoretical approaches (see also Bollig and Kelle in this volume), however, focus on "silent" addressing practices. They focus on the performance of practices concerning production and reproduction of forms of subjects that have always been used (Reckwitz, 2010, p. 35). Here, practices are "the place where subjects exist, form and are formed" (Reckwitz, 2010, p. 39).

At the same time, practices presuppose subjects as their medium, with practices and subjects constituting each other. Subjects acquire practices through their actions, which in turn make the subjects recognisable, visible and acknowledgeable by others (Alkemeyer, 2013). In this light, the subject is determined "neither antecedently nor subordinately to the social but in fact as running simultaneously analytically" (Reh & Rabenstein, 2012, p. 226). This practice theory perspective does not presuppose the actors' agency; instead, it assumes that it is only during the performed actions that it is decided "what agency is and who receives it" (Alkemeyer, 2013, p. 48). In this context, agency is both a necessary *condition* in order to be capable of acting in social practice and a *result* since agency only derives from social practice.

In relation to learning and teaching practice, this means that actors in school are already familiar with field-specific logics and action requirements and "perform" subject forms day after day, which have been allocated to them through addressing practices. Thus, they are regarded as subjects who have a defined place in school: pupils and teachers.

McHoul (1978) demonstrated that addressing practices play a key role in everyday teaching concerning the organisation of communication in class. However, addresses cannot be reduced to a mere response of a collective or an individual pupil. In fact, addresses implicate a stimulative nature that underlies the norm to answer and to act *as* a pupil. In line with these findings, Wenzel (2010, p. 35) pointed out that school lessons are trying to "socialize pupils to show a public behavior". Thereby children "train" themselves during class in school, addressing practices whereby they receive an "official" status as a pupil in front of the school public. Through these acts of addressing, they relate themselves to school norms of acceptability.

Methodological notes concerning the empirical reconstruction of the actors' and subjects' constitution within addressing acts

Based on the previously described theoretical background, we attempt to show in the following section how it is possible with the help of videotaped observations to empirically approximate microprocesses of the actors' and subjects' constitution during addressing acts carried out by primary school pupils in a learning setting at school.

Here, our analysis focusses on the sequential reconstruction of the acts of addressing (Reh & Ricken, 2012). Through these acts children position themselves with regard to each other and address each other as something or someone. Furthermore, it is decided during the performance of these actions who or what – as a result of the conducted addressing – the addressee becomes socially. In line with practice theory, it is assumed that acts of addressing also appear in the children's physical and bodily practices.

In order to analyse the following case study, results were used from the research project "KoText" ("Cooperative peer feedback during text revision in primary German classes"). The project data collection started in 2010 and was funded by the German Research Foundation (DFG). The project combines quantitative methods (e.g. questionnaire, standardised tests) and qualitative methods (e.g. micro-ethnography). Here in this chapter, however, we focus solely on the qualitative part of the study. This part of the study aims to investigate the interaction processes and negotiation among primary school children (3rd grade) during the cooperative revision of their own texts in German language classes. The final sample consists of 132 students (between the ages of 8.5 and 10 years) who work in 44 learning groups (cf. Heinzel et al., 2013). These learning groups were videotaped for later analysis. Solely gender-homogenous groups were put together, corresponding to the children's choice (students filled out a questionnaire that included the measurements of the sociometric peer status). Referring to "*micro-ethnography*" (also known as the ethnographic microanalysis of interaction), we use the video-recorded "data"[3] for a fine-grained, sequential analysis of face-to-face-interaction, or more precisely of *body-to-body interaction* among the students (including bodily movements, gazes, gestures), and examine how the elementary school students organise or manage the group work process (Erickson, 1992/2006; Streeck & Mehus, 2005). Our previous analyses show that the children are confronted with specific requirements (e.g. "clarifying who should begin") while they work together cooperatively. Below we will describe a group that is dealing with requirements concerning "waiting" and "reading out loud".

Case study

The chosen group consists of three girls: Anna, Elaysa and Shania. Before the start of the group work, the girls go to their desk with the text in their hands. There is already a table microphone on the desk, which serves to record the group work. This is when the first scene begins, which we provided with the heading "protecting the text".

Waiting: "protecting the text"

Anna, Elaysa and Shania have just taken a seat at the desk. Anna sits across the desk from Elaysa and Shania. She bends over the desk with her upper body and asks Elaysa: "What did you get, Elaysa?" Elaysa then quickly pulls the text which she is holding in both hands towards her body in order to read it and looks at Anna without speaking. Then Anna turns her attention again to her own text. Shania then points out that the group work is being recorded: "Look, it is being recorded". Shortly afterwards Anna touches the table microphone. She gets directly admonished by Shania: "No, no". Anna replies: "That was by mistake"; she now pushes the microphone aside. When Shania points with her pen to Elaysa's text and says something to her (which the observer cannot understand), Elaysa again quickly pulls her text towards her body and continues to read.

We are now going through the description step by step ("linebyline") to understand the practical logic of the actions: Anna turns towards Elaysa and offers her to engage in interaction. She expresses interest and relates to the content of Elaysa's story by asking, "What did you get, Elaysa?" Here, the "double" addressing is striking: "you..., Elaysa?": She is trying to identify the addressee within the group precisely. Because of the co-presence of a third person, the "*you*" on its own seems undifferentiated. However, Anna does not only use "*you*", a form of addressing that tends to be used in an intimate peer context: She additionally addresses the "public of the group" by using an additional "official" addressing by name. Due to the addressing by name, Elaysa becomes visible as actor and accordingly as a (student) subject within the group. At the same time, she is involuntarily exposed because she did not speak on her own initiative.

Elaysa indicates through her physical re-addressing that she refuses the offer to interact by not answering the question. Instead, she tries to "protect her text" and thereby herself from this "public" evaluation. Afterwards, Shania intensifies the public character of the situation by pointing out again that the group work is being recorded. When Shania refers to Elaysa's text once more at the end of the scene, it is significant that Elaysa again shows the same reaction as already described. Elaysa is trying to avoid the "public" examination and tries to protect her text. We now continue with the next scene, which takes place in the group immediately afterwards.

Waiting: "monitoring the text"

> Anna gets up from her seat. Shania and Elaysa both look at their own texts. Anna returns to her seat, places her pencil case on the desk, gets out a pen and sits down. She moves her pen towards the text. Shania says to Anna, "You are not supposed to write anything in your own text". Elaysa directly comments: "No, you are not allowed to write in your own text". Shania puts up her hand. Elaysa now reaches across the table to Anna's text, folds the sheet of paper and repeats: "We are not allowed to write in the text; we are supposed to keep it covered". Anna replies that she did not write in it. Shania's hand is still up.

In this scene the text still remains the focus of attention. The description magnifies the interaction process like a magnifying glass. From this micro-level perspective, the description shows that Anna's action to move her pen towards the text leads to Elaysa's and Shania's reaction: They both directly admonish Anna for her behaviour. At first glance, these admonishments are very irritating, particularly taking into account that the action of moving a pen to a text is quite a normal action in a school context. Furthermore, this action is not only seen as needing to be justified (e.g. "Anna, what are you doing there?"): Anna's action is also directly admonished by using – or, as Butler (1997/2001) would say, by directly (re-)citing – the classroom norm. Elaysa and Shania's addresses assume the role of "*calls to order*" and achieve an impact not only through underpinning physical actions ("folding the sheet of paper") but also by being repeated. In this process, Elaysa repeats the school norm that has already been "proclaimed" by Shania. This obviously implies an agreement between the two concerning the relevance and the actualisation of the classroom norm, whereby the latter is necessary for the establishment of a pedagogic interaction.

Both address themselves in a mutualising way as "controllers of the text" and "guardians of the school norm". At the same time, Anna is addressed as the only one in the group who is not aware of the school norm and therefore must be explicitly reminded of it. Thus Anna is addressed as a school student subject who relies on "monitoring" and "controlling". The addressing "You ... in your own" clearly shows that Anna cannot freely do what she wants with her own text. Making changes in her own text makes her behaviour look self-determined, which obviously disturbs the norm of heteronomy. Compliance with these norms is then demanded by Shania and Elaysa through their *"calls to order"*.

We now take a leap in time (about 2 minutes) – as if fast-forwarding the videotape slightly – to the "official" beginning of the group work. During the fast-forwarded intermediate phase, the teacher has explained the task to the children. They are now supposed to read out their stories to the group.

Reading: "quieting others"

> Elaysa begins to read out "The story of the mermaid"; in the meantime Shania turns towards another group and requests silence with a "Shhh". For a moment Anna has her text still lying open in front of her, but Shania then closes it and puts it aside. Thereupon Elaysa suddenly stops reading and says to Anna: "Hey, it's my turn". While Elaysa continues reading, Anna slowly pulls the closed text from the end of the desk towards herself. Elaysa continues to read out the story and when she finishes reading, Shania asks, "Is that it?" Elaysa affirms this. Anna asks, "Haven't you written any more?" Elaysa answers in the negative. Shania then explains, "Now it's my turn". Anna then smiles and says, "Yes, my one is the longest".

The group work has now officially started: Elaysa begins to read out her text. The description shows that the observer focusses less on the reading, but more on the "subplots" that take place in the meantime. First, the description shows that through her "Shhh", Shania indicates that she exerts a controlling influence not only within her own group but also in regard to "disturbing factors" from outside her group. She carries out practices of claiming silence, which within the pedagogic context represents constitute practices, and which are here called "quieting". Furthermore, it becomes obvious that within this scene, the "monitoring" of Anna's text is continued, albeit in a slightly varied form: The text is not only simply closed, but is also taken away without anything being said. Elaysa reinforces Shania's order-producing behaviour by stopping her reading and saying, "Hey, it's my turn". Thus, she claims an active audience. At the end of the reading, Shania finally takes over marking the ending ("Was that it?") for Elaysa and thus shows that she feels responsible for the course of action within the group. Elaysa's affirmation is followed by Anna's question ("Haven't you written any more?") through which Anna obviously wants to show that she expected a greater amount of text and is making a social comparison. Her final comment, at least, ("Yes, my one is the longest") confirms the impression that Anna wants to outdo Elaysa and Shania in terms of the amount of text. The reading out in the group continues; it is Shania's turn.

Reading out: "measuring the text"

> Shania reads out her text until the word "hoarse" comes up. She asks, "Do you know what 'hoarse' means?" Elaysa and Anna reply in the negative, shaking

their heads, so Shania explains: "'Hoarse' means that you can't talk and can't say a word properly". She then continues to read out her text but interrupts again several times in order to give further explanations. Thereby she is stalling now and then. In the meanwhile Anna occupies herself with "measuring" her text with the help of the span between her thumb and her index finger. Then Shania leaves the desk. When she returns, she says to Anna, "Now you can read". Anna replies with an 'OK', then asks: "Shall I also read out the heading?" Shania and Elaysa almost simultaneously answer with a drawn-out "Yes".

Right at the beginning of her reading, Shania interrupts and asks, "Do you know what 'hoarse' means?", thus implying that Elaysa and Anna do not know the word "hoarse". In doing so, Shania addresses herself as being competent and assumes that Elaysa and Anna may have no knowledge. The note that Shania gives further explanations indicates that Shania conceptualises herself as an "explanatory and knowledgeable person" and provides herself with specific expertise. In this, however, she does not seem to attract Anna's attention because while Shania is reading, Anna occupies herself with an additional task – she is meticulously measuring her own text. This corresponds with our previous interpretation that for Anna, her own amount of written text is obviously extremely relevant. She tries to profile herself as "someone who writes a lot", who not only fulfils the minimum class requirements but also achieves an exceptional performance by "writing a lot".

At the end of this scene, it becomes clear that Shania in turn is leading up to an end by passing over to Anna. However, before passing over to Anna, Shania leaves the desk for a short time and thus puts Anna "on hold".

Reading: "protecting the text"

Anna starts to read "The Mermaid Lili". Shania directly interrupts: "Oh, Anna, we can't make anything out". Elaysa also asks, "Yes, read a little more loudly". Shania asks Anna, "Shall I read or do you really want to?" Then Anna taps herself on her own chest and says "Me". She reads the heading again. Now she is interrupted by Elaysa: "Anna, please hold on for a short moment, Anna, please hold on for a short moment". Shania points out: "Look, we can't make anything out. You must read more loudly and more fluently". Elaysa now suggests that Shania should read: "Let her read". Shortly afterwards she tries to get the text from Anna, but Anna is not willing to give Elaysa her text. She holds her text firmly with both hands. Shania points out to her, "We will get it anyway later on in in order to correct it". Anna asks "Seriously?" and Elaysa and Shania reply in the affirmative. Elaysa then adds, "And then we will definitely change a lot". Shania gets up and calls the teacher.

Similar to the previous scene, there are again several interruptions during the reading, except that Anna, the one who is reading, does not cause these interruptions herself to give explanations to her audience. Instead, the interruptions are initiated externally by Shania and Elaysa. Here, it is particularly noticeable that Shania not only directly addresses Anna by name but also uses a "we" form. This implies that she feels authorised to speak on behalf of Elaysa. After Elaysa again affiliates with Shania's demands ("Yes, read a little more loudly"), Shania offers to "help" Anna with the reading. However, strictly speaking, this offer of help is not really one, as Anna did not ask for it. Thus, through this addressing, Anna is addressed as a school student subject who is "in need of help". However, Anna does not accept the "offer of help", which again underlines the fact that she does not see the offer as "real" help. Only shortly afterwards, Anna's reading is interrupted again. Once more the comments aim to stop Anna from reading her text: Through her addressing ("Let her read"), Elaysa now suggests that Shania should read Anna's text. Anna, however, bears up and does not give her text away. Instead, she "protects" it by holding on to it with both hands. This is followed by Elaysa's threatening comments that Anna's resistance is futile because Elaysa and Shania will receive the text anyway. This brings us back to the "protecting your text" from the first scene, indicating that this is a matter of a specific practice of re-addressing within the pedagogic context.

Conclusion

What are the implications of these remarks for the concept of "children as social actors"? Which possibilities and limitations are associated with this kind of practice theory perspective? This chapter aimed to provide ideas for opening up processes of addressing and subject constitution both empirically and theoretically at the level of elementary school student behaviour concerning the concept of addressing.

Taken together, from this praxeological perspective "agency" is not just naturally attached to the actor. Instead, it develops *in* as well as *through* practices of addressing. This praxeological approach goes against the idea of an actor who has always been *confident, autonomous* and *capable of acting* and who can be assumed to act independently of the specific conditions. From a practice theory perspective, it appears inappropriate for the actors to have this ontological status because a statement about the actors' agency is only possible if the actors' social and addressing practices have been considered. As Schatzki et al. (2001, p. 20) point out, "the status of human beings as 'subjects' (and 'agents') is bound to practices".

The case study reveals that within school practice, children are able to gain their agency through *calls to order*. With the help of these *calls to order*, the children "show" each other *how school works*. Therefore, these calls indicate a routine handling of school imperatives, but children do not only simply imitate the adult teacher. Instead, children's action can be described using the term "mimesis". This mimetic action is not only an identical "copy" of the adult teacher's action, but also a re-creating of the subject form of the "adult teacher", producing an "image" that makes visible something that does not necessarily conform with the "original" (in German, you could say "Vorbild").[4] Thus, via practices of addressing, children place themselves in the generational order (e.g. the "tidy school children", the "judging teacher"). These practices of addressing are not simple speech acts or words, but have to be performed *bodily* (e.g. attentive looks, "invasive" hands). Here, the case study illustrates that a "deviant" handling of the text reveals a norm of heteronomy. Thus, school-related agency seems to depend on practical knowledge in handling school artefacts and documents. This practical knowledge enables school actors to carry out certain practices of addressing that help them to constitute a (pedagogic) social order and make them visible and recognisable as school student subjects. "Right" and "wrong" practices can be checked and controlled not only by the adult teacher, but also by the peers. The peer group is often described as a counter-world ("anti-schoolculture") to school requirements. But the peer activities during a lesson in the classroom reveal that the peers constantly oscillate between the significance of their relationships among their peers on the one hand, and the significance of the school requirements on the other hand. Moreover, school is a public space and thus it may be true that there is a "hidden curriculum". According to Foucault (1979), there are similarities between his well-known *Panopticon* and the ways in which school works. But there are also differences, meaning that the children are not "docile bodies" (for example, see Anna's opposing behaviour). Although the adult teacher has been delegated the "guardianship" and thus the power of the teacher role over the children during the cooperative learning situation, the children still interact among their peers, which means that they have a claim to equality and reciprocity.

In this chapter, we present a practice theory perspective on children's agency that opens up the possibility for Childhood Studies not to reduce children's agency to characteristics or abilities ascribed to the individual child. Instead, it allows us to look at the social practice as an event of addressing in which children, through addressing, relate to one another, to others and to the (school) world (Ricken, 2013). However, this kind of praxeological approach not only provides opportunities but also entails risks: There is certainly a risk due to the stronger *decentration* of the actor to reduce the actor to his pure participation in social practice.[5] Thus, Caldwell (2012, p. 287) underlines the fact that "a practice theory of agency can be equally destabilizing; it can dissolve agency into practice". Furthermore, there is a risk of misjudging – believing that social practice is not constituted until the concrete performance or specific practice of addressing and the acquirement of artefacts *by the actors*. Therefore, practice theory also cannot do without a definition of the "actor", which remains to be created. In this context, the concepts of Childhood Studies might be helpful. For example, the concept of "differential contemporaneity" (Hengst, 2013) allows a reconstruction of the actor's and subject's formations beyond the dichotomy of the "adult-child". This concept is based on the assumption that within the concrete performance of social practices, children and adults are to some extent coequal as "differential contemporaries". Therefore, Hengst (2013) advocates a contemporary diagnostic and sensitised practice theory that is able to take a closer look at those subject formations of the "contemporary", which are carried out within social practices. For this, however, both the "relative absence of childhood in social theories" as well as the "partial abstinence from social theory in Childhood Studies" (Hengst, 2013, p. 16) must be overcome.

Notes

1 The English language distinguishes between other titles for a child such as "toddler", "infant" and "newborn".
2 All direct quotations of German texts were translated into English by the authors. We would like to thank Constanze Rickmeyer, who is part of the research project "FIRST STEPS"(an integration project for infants with a migrant background), for her continued support.
3 Erickson (2006, p. 572) points out that the "videotape itself is not data. It is a resource for data construction, an information source containing potential data out of which actual data must be defined and searched for". Moreover, Snell (2011) indicates that the 'richness of video data brings with it the problem of sensory overload'. Thus, the observer has to make a selection and interpret the video material. Therefore, video-based field notes are – like ethnographic field notes – highly selective and involve interpretation.
4 It should be noted, however, that children are both *producers* and *consumers* of these images; thus, they can be seen as *prosumers*.
5 The fact that we "decentre the subject" theoretically does not mean that we assume that there are no subjects or actors in social life.

References

Alkemeyer, T., Budde, G. & Freist, D. (2013). *Selbst-Bildungen: Soziale und kulturelle Praktiken der Subjektivierung* [*Self-making: Social and cultural practices of subjectivation*]. Bielefeld: transcript.

Althusser, L. (1971). *Lenin and Philosophy and Other Essays*. New York: Monthly Review Press.

Butler, J. (1997). *The Psychic Life of Power: Theories in Subjection*. Stanford: Stanford University Press.

Butler, J. (2001). *Psyche der Macht: Das Subjekt der Unterwerfung* [*The Psychic Life of Power: Theories in Subjection*]. Frankfurt/M.: Suhrkamp.

Bühler-Niederberger, D. (2011). *Lebensphase Kindheit: Theoretische Ansätze, Akteure und Handlungsräume* [*Life stage childhood: Theoretical approaches, actors and action areas*]. Weinheim: Juventa.

Caldwell, R. (2012). Reclaiming agency, recovering change? An exploration of the practice theory of Theodore Schatzki. *Journal for the Theory of Social Behaviour*, *42*(3), 284–303.

Castañeda, C. (2001). The child as a feminist figuration: toward a politics of privilege. *Feminist Theory*, *2*(1), 29–53.

Corsaro, W. A. (2014). *The Sociology of Childhood*. Los Angeles: Sage Publications.

De Graeve, K. (2015). Children's rights from a gender studies perspective: gender, intersectionality and the ethics of care. In W. Vandenhole, E. Desmet, D. Reynaert & S. Lambrechts (Eds.), *Routledge International Handbook of Children's Rights Studies* (pp. 147–164). New York: Routledge.

Esser, F. (2009). *Kinderwelten – Gegenwelten? Pädagogische Impulse aus der Kindheitsforschung* [*Children's Worlds – Counter Worlds? Pedagogic Stimuli from Childhood Studies*]. Baltmannsweiler: Schneider Hohengehren.

Elliott, A. (2014). Structuration theories: Giddens and Bourdieu. In A. Elliott (Ed.), *Routledge Handbook of Social and Cultural Theory* (pp. 56–74). Abingdon: Routledge.

Erickson, F. (1992). Ethnographic microanalysis of interaction. In M. D. Le Compte, W. L. Millroy & J. Preissle (Eds.), *The Handbook of Qualitative Research in Education* (pp. 201–225). London: Academic Press.

Erickson, F. (2006). Definition and analysis of data from videotape. Some research procedures and their rationales. In J. Green, G. Camilli & P. Elmore (Eds.), *Handbook of Complementary Methods in Education Research* (pp. 177–191). Mahwah: Lawrence Erlbaum Associates.

Foucault, M. (1979). *Discipline and Punish: The Birth of the Prison*. New York: Vintage.

Giddens, A. (1984). *The Constitution of Society: Outline of the Theory of Structuration*. Berkeley: University of California Press.

Heinzel, F. (2012). *Methoden der Kindheitsforschung: Ein Überblick über Forschungszugänge zur kindlichen Perspektive* [*Methods of Childhood Studies: An Overview of Research Approaches to Children's Perspective*]. Weinheim: Juventa.

Heinzel, F., Kruse, N., Lipowsky, F., Eckermann, T., Ludwig, M. & Reichardt, A. (2013). Kooperative Schülerrückmeldungen bei der Textüberarbeitung im Deutschunterricht der Grundschule (KoText) [Cooperative peer feedback during text revision in primary German classes]. *Schulpädagogik heute*, 7(4). Retrieved from: www.schulpaedagogik-heute.de/conimg/SH7_3a_2.pdf

Hengst, H. (2013). *Kindheit im 21. Jahrhundert: Differenzielle Zeitgenossenschaft* [*Childhood in the 21st Century: Differential Contemporaneity*]. Weinheim: Beltz Juventa.

Honig, M. -S., Lange, A. & Leu, H. -R. (1999). *Aus der Perspektive von Kindern? Zur Methodologie der Kindheitsforschung* [*From Children's Perspective? Toward a Methodology of Childhood Studies*]. Weinheim: Juventa.

James, A. & Prout, A. (1990/2003). *Constructing and Reconstructing Childhood*. London: Falmer press.

James, A., Jenks, C. & Prout, A. (1998). *Theorizing Childhood*. Oxford: Blackwell.

James, A. (2009). Agency. In J. Qvortrup, W. A. Corsaro & M. -S. Honig (Eds.), *The Palgrave Handbook of Childhood Studies* (pp. 34–46). Basingstoke: Palgrave Macmillan.

Kelle, H., & Breidenstein, G. (1996). Kinder als Akteure: Ethnographische Ansätze in der Kindheitsforschung [Children as actors: Ethnographic approaches in Childhood Studies]. *Zeitschrift für Sozialisationsforschung und Erziehungssoziologie*, 16(1), 47–67.

Magnus, K. (2006). The unaccountable subject: Judith Butler and the social conditions of intersubjective agency. *Hypatia. A Journal of Feminist Philosophy*, 21(1), 81–103.

McHoul, A. (1978). The organization of turns at formal talk in the classroom. *Language in Society*, 7(2), 183–213.

Robinson, K. H. (2013). *Innocence, Knowledge, and the Construction of Childhood: The Contradictory Nature of Sexuality and Censorship in Children's Contemporary Lives*. Abingdon: Routledge.

Reckwitz, A. (2010). *Das hybride Subjekt: Eine Theorie der Subjektkulturen von der bürgerlichen Moderne zur Postmoderne* [*The Hybrid Subject: A Theory of the Subject Cultures from the Civil Modern Society to the Postmodernism*]. Weilerswist: Vellbrück.

Reh, S., & Ricken, N. (2012). Das Konzept der Adressierung. Zu einer Methodologie einer qualitativ-empirischen Erforschung von Subjektivation [The Concept of Addressing. Towards a Methodology of a Qualitative-empirical Research of Subjectivation]. In I. Miethe, & H.-R. Müller (Eds.), *Qualitative Bildungsforschung und Bildungstheorie* [*Qualitative Theories of Learning and Learning Theory*] (pp. 35–56). Opladen: Budrich.

Reh, S. & Rabenstein, K. (2012). Normen der Anerkennbarkeit in pädagogischen Ordnungen: Empirische Explorationen zur Norm der Selbständigkeit [Norms of Recognition in Pedagogic Orders. Empirical Explorations to the Norm of Autonomy]. In N. Ricken, & N. Balzer (Eds.), *Judith Butler: Pädagogische Lektüren* [*Judith Butler: From the Perspective of Pedagogy*] (pp. 225–247). Wiesbaden: VS.

Ricken, N. (2013). Anerkennung als Adressierung: Über die Bedeutung von Anerkennung für Subjektivationsprozesse [Recognition as Addressing. On the Relevance of Recognition in the Subjectivation Process]. In T. Alkemeyer, G. Budde & D. Freist (Eds.), *Selbst-Bildungen: Soziale und kulturelle Praktiken der Subjektivierung* [*Educating the self: Social and cultural practices of subjectification*] (pp. 69–101). Bielefeld: transcript.

Schatzki, T. R., Knorr Cetina, K. & Savigny, E. (2001). *The Practice Turn in Contemporary Theory*. London: Routledge.

Schmidt, R. (2012). Soziologie der Praktiken: Konzeptionelle Studien und empirische Analysen [Sociology of social practices: Conceptual studies and empirical analysis]. Berlin: Suhrkamp.

Snell, J. (2011). Interrogating video data: Systematic quantitative analysis versus micro-ethnographic analysis. *International Journal of Social Research Methodology, 14*(3), 253–258.

Streeck, J. & Mehus, S. (2005). Microethnography: the study of practices. In K. Fitch & R. Sanders (Eds.), *Handbook of Language and Social Interaction* (pp. 381–404). Mahwah: Lawrence Erlbaum Associates.

Valentine, K. (2011). Accounting for agency. *Children & Society, 25*(5), 347–358.

Villa, P. -I. (2013). Subjekte und ihre Körper [Subjects and their bodies]. In J. Graf, K. Ideler & S. Klinger (Eds.), *Geschlecht zwischen Struktur und Subjekt. Theorie, Praxis, Perspektiven* [*Gender between structure and subject. Theory, praxis, perspectives*] (pp. 59–78). Opladen: Barbara Budrich.

Wenzel, T. (2010). Sich-Melden: Zur inhärenten Spannung zwischen individuellem Schülerinteresse und klassenöffentlichem Unterrichtsgespräch [Raise your hand: Towards the inherent tension between the individual pupils' interest and the classroom talk]. *Sozialer Sinn, 11*(1), 33–52.

Winterhager-Schmidt, L. (2002): Die Beschleunigung der Kindheit [The Acceleration of Childhood]. In W. Datler, A. Eggert-Schmid Noerr & L. Winterhager-Schmid (Eds.), *Das selbständige Kind* [*The autonomous child*] (pp. 15–31). Gießen: Psychosozial Verlag.

Whyness, M. (1999). Childhood, agency and educational reform. *Childhood, 6*(3), 353–368.

Chapter 18

Accounting for children's agency in research on educational inequality

The influence of children's own practices on their academic habitus in elementary school

Frederick de Moll and Tanja Betz

The role of children's agency in the socio-cultural reproduction of educational inequality is mostly overlooked by quantitative research in education. This is problematic because a potentially important source of variance in children's educational success is not included in the analyses. Childhood Studies offers different ways to conceptualise children's agency. To address the role of children's agency in educational inequality, the authors outline a conceptual framework that merges socio-cultural reproduction theory following Bourdieu with the idea of children's agency. Using quantitative data on elementary school children and their parents, the authors ask how children contribute to the reproduction of educational inequality. They explore the links between children's dispositions towards school, their out-of-school practices and social class, and they discuss the implications of their findings for investigating children's agency in both Childhood Studies and educational research.

This chapter aims to add to the continuing debate about a better understanding of educational inequalities. In Western societies, educational inequality refers to the fact that children's educational achievement depends largely on their parents' position in the social class system, aside from other important factors such as ethnicity, gender, race and factors related to the school system. Basically, children from the lower classes are less likely to succeed at school than children from the middle and upper classes, and these inequalities are most evident during the first years of school. This makes the elementary school an important gatekeeper for later academic success and for advantageous positions in society.

There have been numerous attempts in educational research to explain the nexus between children's social class and educational outcomes (Feinstein et al., 2004). One influential account of the underlying processes that lead to unequal opportunities of children from different social classes can be found in the idea of the intergenerational transmission of academically important skills within the family. This notion turns *parents* into the basic providers of educational opportunity, and how parents accomplish this task is closely linked to their position in the class system. Internationally, the mainstream of quantitative research on educational inequality concerns itself with the effects of family background and parenting practices on children's skill development and school performance (e.g. Baumert & Schümer, 2002; Lee & Bowen, 2006). Taken together, current research on those out-of-school factors highlights the role of parents, and thus of adults in the process of educational stratification, while children are mostly thought to copy their parents' ways of thinking and acting. However, there is no account of *children's own contributions* to their lives and to the (re-)production of educational inequality. Unlike Childhood Studies, educational research on inequality still has no clear understanding of children as social actors. Instead, children are looked at from a developmental perspective.

We argue that current efforts to model the effects on success in school often reduce the role of children to variables of educational outcomes, and the extent of agency in different settings in their lives is widely neglected. Therefore, this study aims to dispute the common conceptualisation of children as mere recipients of parenting and schooling by extending previous theoretical and empirical attempts at explaining and understanding educational inequality. The intention is to sensitise educational research to the role that children's agency plays in social reproduction and mobility. Consequently, we explore how children's agency adds to the traditional picture of social class and parenting effects on children's educational opportunities. Drawing inspiration from current accounts of children's agency within Childhood Studies, we seek to merge the concept with the classical theory of socio-cultural reproduction. Simultaneously, we believe that Childhood Studies can profit from inequality research. Within Childhood Studies, the social status of children is often stressed as opposed to adults (for a critique of this, see Esser in this volume), and the generational order is emphasised as being the most fundamental differentiation within society. However, it needs to be acknowledged that the social class hierarchy plays a significant role not only in shaping adulthood, but also in shaping children's lives and agency. Besides that, the self-restraint Childhood Studies displays with regard to qualitative research on children's agency needs to be overcome. Our goal is to show how Childhood Studies and educational inequality research can benefit from one another.

Our study puts children's agency into practice by analysing empirical data from children and their parents that include information on children's own and peer-related practices, on parenting and family background, as well as measures of children's dispositions toward school, their academic habitus. The following section provides a brief overview of current research on explaining educational inequalities. The third section lays out the theoretical background for our study, the Bourdieusian theory of socio-cultural reproduction and habitus and the concept of children's agency from the perspective of Childhood Studies. The fourth and fifth parts give quantitative empirical insights into children's out-of-school practices and academic habitus. The final section contains a discussion of the results and some thoughts on future research.

The current mainstream of research on educational inequalities

There is a vast body of quantitative research on educational inequalities that aims to explain the underlying processes of social class differences in children's school success. When it comes to out-of-school factors, research regularly focusses on parents and family processes, which are used to explain a portion of the variance in children's educational outcomes that is not accounted for by schooling processes such as instruction or the composition of the student body.

In a full discussion of contextual and family characteristics that might affect children's educational outcomes, Feinstein et al. (2004) outline a model of distal and proximal effects drawn on studies from various fields. In their comprehensive model of the intergenerational transmission of educational success, the authors include distal factors such as family structures and parents' income; family characteristics, such as parental cognition, parents' mental and physical health and the possession of resources; and proximal family processes, such as parenting style. Family factors and processes are only attributed to parents, with children completely out of the picture. It does not take long to notice that these models reduce the role of children to variables of educational outcomes. The authors do recognise that their model remains somewhat static as it neglects the agency of children, but they conceive of children's capacity to influence their own lives as something that mainly depends on age and maturity. The underlying logic of these approaches to educational inequality is essentially developmental. The consequence is that these approaches perpetuate the notion of children as "becomings" that is also common in child indicator research and educational policy (Betz, 2013).

Lately, Wohlkinger and Ditton (2012) have begun to question the assertion that parents and teachers are the main actors in processes of educational reproduction. Their research shows that children's aspirations exert a unique and equal influence on whether they enter the higher track of the school system after finishing elementary education. The findings raise the broader issue of how children participate in processes that shape their lives, and correspondingly how social class shapes children's ways of thinking and acting. Quantitative research has yet to explain the remaining variance in children's school success that is not accounted for by common variables such as schooling processes, the family or children's ability. This is where the debate in Childhood Studies about children's agency has much to offer educational research. Until now, the consequences of *children's (own) actions* for their academic success have not been adequately accounted for by educational research because most approaches do not explicitly theorise children's agency. Childhood Studies draws on a long tradition of counteracting the notion of children's incompleteness and of emphasising children as social agents (see Esser in this volume). This perspective is a prerequisite to overcome the idea that children have nothing more to contribute to their educational success than a certain level of intelligence or cognitive abilities.

Theoretical background

Socio-cultural reproduction and children's habitus

Socio-cultural reproduction theory (Bourdieu & Passeron, 1990; Bourdieu, 1986) offers a powerful conceptual repertoire to explain the persistent inequality of educational opportunities of children from different social classes. One of Bourdieu's goals was to overcome the dualism of structure and agency and to think of practice in a strictly relational manner (see Esser, Raithelhuber or Oswell in this volume for alternative relational approaches).

Simply stated, the socio-cultural reproduction theory suggests that the lasting relationship between children's social background and their educational attainment is fundamentally due to cultural differences in family processes that stem from the parents' social class. Cultural practices such as child-rearing and parental lifestyle provide children with skills and dispositions (a habitus) that are evaluated by teachers. The process of social stratification that allocates people to different social classes is seen as a reciprocal process of cultural transmission in the family and cultural recognition at school. People's social position is influenced by their structural resources, such as economic capital (e.g. income) and cultural capital (e.g. educational credentials, cultural goods and competencies). Basically, the combined capital defines someone's social position and corresponds with a particular habitus. This means that the family provides children with a habitus that regulates their performance in relation to school. A type of habitus that is highly compatible to school is reflected in someone's *cultural goodwill*, as Bourdieu calls it, which is displayed by hard work and seriousness, the dispositions that the conformist actor "offers to these institutions while putting himself entirely at their mercy" (Bourdieu, 1984, pp. 333, 337). Habitus can be understood as the children's dispositions towards school. How children think about school and how they interact with teachers and the learning materials matters for their school success: Children's academic habitus is acknowledged by teachers and schools.

In fact, research supports Bourdieu's theory: Dispositions, such as work habit, effort and educational aspiration, have been shown to be related to school performance (e.g. Farkas, 1996; Dumais, 2002). Such dispositions provide information about *how* children are oriented towards school. As a whole, they can best be understood as different aspects of a *habitus of cultural goodwill*.

In a vivid portrayal of how parents from different social classes approach child-rearing, Lareau (2011) describes the family processes in middle- and lower-class households that affect children's dispositions towards school when they are 7–10 years of age. Lareau's theoretical constructs have inspired much research, both qualitative and quantitative, which could show evidence of the positive correlation between social class, parenting practices and children's school performance (e.g. Cheadle, 2008). Drawing on her field work, Lareau proposes a framework to reconceptualise the role parenting practices play in social reproduction. *Concerted cultivation*, a specific type of middle-class parenting, is geared to the promotion of children's talents and academic success. Those parenting practices include frequent discussion between children and adults, children's participation in organised activities and parent-child activities with educational content. *Concerted cultivation* provides children with the cultural resources needed to succeed in school and thereby signifies the process through which life chances are transmitted from one generation to the next. Lareau (2011) argues that *concerted cultivation* affects children's dispositions and actions in out-of-family contexts, especially in educational institutions. Middle-class children develop a self-assured sense of entitlement that is fostered by participating in organised activities and by frequently taking part in reasoning and discussion with their parents. Clearly, what Lareau calls the sense of entitlement is closely related to Bourdieu's notion of cultural goodwill. Thus, their habitus provides children from the middle and upper class with a competitive advantage at school.

The parenting practices that are typically found in lower-class families are termed *accomplishment of natural growth* by Lareau (2011). Lower-class parents are mainly concerned with making sure of their children's physical well-being, and otherwise often leave children to themselves. As a result of this parenting style, there is a clear line between the generations in lower-class families, which also can be observed in parents' style of communicating with children, for example the use of directives. Lareau believes that *accomplishment of natural growth* parenting practices and growing up in economic hardship result in children being disadvantaged at school.

However, Lareau's work falls somewhat short of the role of children's agency. While we discover that working-class children spend more time with peers and kin than middle-class children, the reason for this pattern seems to lie within parents' style of child-rearing. There is no sign of children's opportunities to interact with resources and others in a way that alters the path laid out for them by their family's position in society. Lareau's perspective needs to be widened in order to appreciate the role of children's practices in shaping their (family) lives and therefore their opportunities at school. This brings attention not only to what children do whilst they are parented or educated at school, but also to their own and peer-related practices. At the same time, practice draws its meaning from the relations between actors who occupy similar or different social positions (Bourdieu, 1984). Whereas Childhood Studies often highlights the position of children as opposed to the position of adults within the generational order, inequality research following Bourdieu puts an emphasis on people's and therefore also children's position in the social class hierarchy. Drawing inspiration from both branches of research means combining both views and asking questions about how children from different social classes are positioned in school-home relations, and in interactions with adults from different social strata. This approach therefore involves classed relations between adults and children. From a Bourdieusian perspective, the social order is defined by power relations between social classes *and* generations (Mayall, 2015).

Children's agency

The shortcoming in the theory of socio-cultural reproduction has drawn criticism from Childhood Studies where the role of children's agency in social reproduction is studied. For example, James and James (2004, p. 38) raise concern over the fact that "in discussions of cultural reproduction, few social theorists have considered the status and position of children; and fewer still have examined *the potential of children themselves as the agents of social change*, their roles being usually cast as its victims or, less commonly, its beneficiaries" (emphasis added).

In Childhood Studies, children are conceptualised as social actors (James & James, 2004). This view implies that children must not be seen as products of parenting and schooling, but as active co-producers of childhood experiences and of society. Together with adults and peers, children participate as social actors in shaping their own childhood and the generational and social order. Whereas educational research has often overlooked children's active part in educational inequality, there has been a vital discussion in Childhood Studies about the role of children's agency in adult-dominated settings such as the school. The concept often implies that children's agency is something pre-social that unfolds in children's opposition to structures that have been established by adults. However, the social structure always precedes children's agency (Mayall, 2002). Children's agency then amounts to their ability to alter their daily lives, which are regularly controlled by adults, for example at school (see Mayall, 2015). Like other members of society, children can transform structures even if change is not necessarily what they have intended. In order to highlight the transformational actions that children take in the process of social (re-)production, Mayall (2002, p. 33) calls for researchers to focus "not only on the child and adult, but on the social position of student in relation to that of teacher and in relation to the sedimented education system". Bühler-Niederberger (2011) stresses that children need to be acknowledged as contributors to the perpetuation of the generational and social order. We might add that the same is true of social and educational inequality. The point is that children actively assist in upholding the social structure in their interactions with adults because both children and adults always occupy certain positions within the social space. This understanding of agency is useful for studying how children take part in the reproduction of society in a relatively conformist manner. When doing research on educational inequality, one can examine children's agency in terms of both defiance *and* conformity because both aspects of agency are important factors for children's opportunities for success in school. Defiance may impede children's successful participation in the classroom in terms of good grades, while conformity may give them an advantage. In the end, children from diverse social backgrounds have to conform to academic and behavioural norms that are represented by powerful adult teachers.

To sum up, children's agency calls for conceptualising children as social actors who have the agency both to reproduce and to transform the social structure. From our perspective, children could then – in a complex interplay with adults – either overcome or replicate educational inequalities. With regard to educational inequality, studying children's agency refers to how children as idiosyncratic actors contribute to their lives (at school and out of school) and how this contribution is reflected in children's orientation towards school. With respect to Childhood Studies, our research not only shows a way to integrate Bourdieusian thinking into research on children's agency (see also Alanen, Brooker, & Mayall, 2015), but also offers an example of using quantitative methods to capture children's agency and their perspective on out-of-school life as well as on schooling processes.

The EDUCARE study

Research questions

Two research questions are addressed in this study. The first is that of how children's out-of-school lives are shaped by their social class. That is, to what extent does social class influence not only parent-child activities but also children's own and peer-related practices that are not monitored by adults? The second question focuses on the relative effects of children's own and peer-related practices on children's academic habitus, on top of the effects of parenting practices.

Data

The current study is part of a larger research project, which is concerned with social inequality in early and middle childhood. The EDUCARE study ("Childhood education and care from the perspective of policy makers, professionals in kindergartens and elementary schools, parents and children")[1] involved the collection of data from third and fourth graders and their parents at 16 elementary schools in two major urban areas in West and East Germany. The data collection was carried out in 2012 and 2013, when n = 985 children (aged 7–12 years) and n = 503 of their parents completed questionnaires providing information on the school, family and peer-related attitudes, activities and numerous background variables. For the analyses, we used m = 20 multiply imputed datasets that included the completed information for all n = 1,069 parent-child cases.

Variables

Descriptive statistics for all variables that were used in the analyses are shown in Table 18.1. The following section contains a more detailed description of the variables.

   Children's academic habitus – cultural goodwill: A measure of children's habitus of *cultural goodwill* is used as the dependent variable in the multivariate analyses. In our understanding, this habitus refers to a set of dispositions that reflect children's enthusiasm to succeed and their commitment to excellence in school,

Table 18.1 Sample statistics for the entire set of analysed variables

Variable	M	SD	Range of Possible Values	
Children's academic habitus				
Cultural goodwill	3.03	.47	1	4
Family background				
Family structure	.78	.25	1	2
Social class: lower	.17		0	1
Social class: upper	.20		0	1
Parental habitus	−.08	.67	z-scores	
Immigrant status: non-German parents	.26		0	1
Children's resources				
Learning space	4.18	.64	1	3
No. of children's books	3.73	1.21	1	5
Concerted cultivation				
Use of dialogue	3.98	.57	1	5
Promoting a sense of entitlement	2.98	.72	1	5
Cultural parent-child activities	2.60	.64	1	5
Children's participation in adult-organised activities	1.39	.35	1	5
Accomplishment of natural growth				
Use of directives	3.70	.58	1	5
Involvement in adult activities	2.33	.46	1	5
Frequency of kin care	1.53	.61	1	5
Children's practices by themselves				
Media use	2.69	1.04	1	5
Literacy practices	2.32	.84	1	5
Outdoor activities	2.15	.83	1	5
School work and chores	2.60	1.17	1	5
Children's school performance				
Last annual GPA	2.00	.70	1	6
Children's demographic characteristics				
Children's age	8.90	.79	7	12
Children's gender: boy	.51		0	1
Regional context				
Place of residence: East-German	.44		0	1

Note. Sample statistics averaged over 20 multiply imputed data sets with n = 1,069; mean of dummy variables shows the percentage of participants in the given group.

both in terms of attitude and behaviour. Thus, the construct incorporates a wider understanding of dispositions, which are equally geared towards successful participation in school. In order to obtain a theoretically sound measurement of habitus, we chose to integrate four subscales that reflect children's *ambitiousness, self-regulation,* perceived *appreciation by teachers,* and children's *conformity to classroom rules* (see Table 18.2). A factor analysis revealed substantial loadings (between .41 and .64) of the four subscales on one common factor.

Table 18.2 Descriptive statistics for children's academic habitus

Construct	No. of Items	Example	Mean	SD	Cronbach's alpha
General scale Habitus of cultural goodwill			3.03	.47	.61
Subscales Ambitiousness	3	I work hard so that I always get good grades.	3.13	.69	.52
Self-regulation	3	It is easy for me to concentrate.	2.75	.74	.59
Appreciation by teachers	3	I think that I am important to my teacher.	2.88	.72	.48
Conformity to classroom norms	3	I always try to be quiet in class.	3.35	.62	.56

Note. n = 978 children with complete scores for the habitus scale.

Children's own and peer-related practices: Our operationalisation of children's practices reflects the fact that children's lives are not only supervised by adults or parents. Rather, the children were asked to provide information on how often they do various things alone and with friends, without adults present. All items were measured on a five-point scale (from 1 = never to 5 = every day). We constructed four scales, which allude to children's involvement in practices that differ by content, location and peers taking part: *Media use* alone or with peers is measured by four items, e.g. "I watch TV or video/DVD" (α = .75); children's *literacy practices* refer to five activities that are mostly done alone, with the exception of one item covering peer conversations about books; other items include "I write a diary" and "I listen to audiobooks" (α = .59). We also measured the time children spent with *school work and chores.* Our account of children's unsupervised involvement in school work and chores is inferred from two items "I practice for school, even after homework is done" and "I clean or tidy up" (α = .61). The final set of activities represents children's *outdoor activities* (α = .69). Children reported on how often they do things with friends outside. The scale consists of five items, e.g. "We explore the city or the neighbourhood"[2].

Family background: social class: In our analyses, we used two dummy variables to compare children from the lower and upper classes to middle-class offspring. Children were assigned to the lower class if their parents' combined income and average educational attainment was less than one standard deviation from the mean. Interviewees whose score lay above one standard deviation from the mean were coded as upper class. Accordingly, 17 per cent of the sample is coded as lower-class families, 63 per cent of the children are from middle-class families and 20 per cent are assigned to the upper class.

Parental habitus constitutes a theoretically important influencing factor for children's habitus. Our measure of parental habitus relates to the expressive dimension of a habitus of cultural goodwill. Since parental habitus and parents' volume of capital are highly correlated ($r = .63$, $p < .01$), parental habitus might inform children about their position in the social hierarchy, and therefore serve as a proxy for the visibility of social class. The variable was computed by averaging six standardised items that include information on how often parents read a daily newspaper and whether they possess classical literature ($\alpha = .73$).

In addition to social class and parental habitus, control variables for *immigrant status* (0 = at least one parent autochthonous, 1 = neither parent from Germany) and *family structure* were included in the multivariate analyses. Greater values of *family structure* indicate reduced parental daily presence.

Parenting practices: concerted cultivation and accomplishment of natural growth: Drawing on Lareau's (2011) work on parenting practices, we constructed three scales that are indicative of parents' *concerted cultivation* strategies: *use of dialogue* (3 items, $\alpha = .62$); *promoting a sense of entitlement* (4 items, $\alpha = .63$); and *cultural parent-child activities* (5 items, $\alpha = .61$). In addition, we computed an index on children's involvement in *adult-organised activities*, averaging children's information on participation in music lessons, club sports and dancing.

The *accomplishment of natural growth* practices are represented by two scales: *use of directives*, which are aimed at children's acceptance of the authority of adults (7 items, $\alpha = .73$); and *involvement in adult activities* (5 items, $\alpha = .54$). Moreover, we computed a variable on how often parents used relatives and friends as caregivers for their children (*kin care*). All items were measured on a five-point scale (from 1 = never to 5 = every day).

Further control variables: To control for the home opportunity structure, we included a variable for *children's home space* and a measure of the *number of children's books* in the home as a common proxy for children's objectified cultural resources. Children's school performance is closely linked to their dispositions towards school, which integrate former experiences at school. To control for prior academic success, we used children's *last annual grade point average*. Note that the German grading system goes from 1 = very good to 6 = deficient. In the multivariate analyses, we control for children's *age* and *gender* (0 = female, 1 = male). Public resources and the standard of living are still different in West and East Germany, which is why we control for children's *place of residence* (West = 0, East = 1).

Methods

Due to the cross-sectional character of the dataset, the analyses are essentially correlational. With regard to the first research goal, a broad description of children's out-of-school lives, we conducted a series of regression analyses to examine the extent to which children's involvement in various activities depends on social class membership. The standardised coefficients (beta weights) are interpreted as follows: If the independent variable is a scale variable (e.g. organised activities), the coefficient indicates the change in the dependent variable in standard deviation units for a standard deviation change in the predictor variable; if the predictor is a dummy variable (e.g. gender), the coefficient is interpreted as the change in the criterion (in the criterion's standard deviation units) when the predictor changes from zero to one. In the first set of analyses, the only predictor variables are the social class dummies.

In the second set of analyses, we examine the relative importance of various predictor variables for children's academic habitus, which is why we compute diverse measures of the effects on the dependent variable (Nathans, Oswald & Nimon, 2012). To put a figure on each predictor's isolated relationship with the criterion, we computed the zero-order correlations between the independent and dependent variables. To assess the predictive power of each independent variable while accounting for the variance contributions of the remaining predictors to the regression model, the standardised regression coefficients (beta weights) are shown in the regression tables. While there was no evidence of multicollinearity, there were some associations between independent variables. This makes it difficult to determine variable importance by comparing the beta weights. To bypass this problem, we used Pratt's (1987) product measure of relative variable importance. This measure allows for partitioning the variance explained by a model, even if some predictors are correlated. By dividing the product measure by the model's R^2, one obtains the relative Pratt index d_j. This index is interpreted as each predictor's contribution to the criterion's variance explained by the model. Thus, the index provides an easy way to evaluate each predictor's contribution to the regression effect.

There are two models to predict children's habitus of goodwill. The first model shows the effects of the family and parenting variables on children's academic habitus. The variables covering children's own practices were added in the second model. That way we are able to examine the "adult-free" activities of children as an additional effect on children's academic habitus, as well as how the other predictors' predictive power changes once the specific child effect is included in the model.

All analyses were done using Version 7 of the Mplus software package (Muthén & Muthén, 2012). To account for the nested data structure we used the type = complex option of Mplus, which tells the program to compute robust standard errors.

Results

Social class differences in children's activities

The graph (Figure 18.1) shows the standardised scores of children from the lower, middle and upper classes on various activities. Basically, one can look at two types of activities here: (1) activities carried out by children without adults; and (2) activities with adults involved, for example parent-child activities.

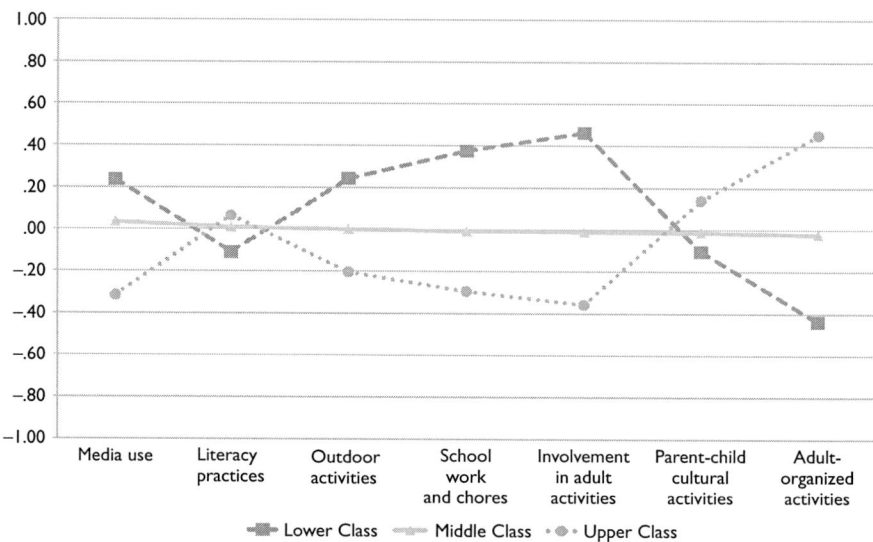

Figure 18.1 Social class differences in children's activities.

(1) Upper-class children take part in media activities significantly less often than lower-class (beta = −.55, p < .01) and middle-class children (beta = −.35, p < .01). While lower-class children do not engage in literacy practices as often as children from the middle and upper classes, this difference is not statistically meaningful. With regard to children's activities that are not monitored by adults, the biggest social class differences refer to outdoor activities and doing school work and chores. Lower-class children are significantly more often involved in outdoor activities with peers than middle-class and upper-class children (beta = .24, p = .03 and beta = .45, p < .01, respectively). There is also a significant difference between middle- and upper-class children; the latter less often hang out with peers (beta = −.20, p = .02). The same differences hold true for children's school and household work. In the after-school hours, lower-class children "work" considerably more than middle-class (beta = .39, p < .01) and upper-class (beta = .67, p < .01) children. Middle-class children "work" more than members of the upper class (beta = .28, p < .01).

(2) Upper-class children score about a quarter of a standard deviation above lower-class children on parent-child cultural activities. However, that difference is not statistically significant. Clearly, children's involvement in their parents' necessary day-to-day activities is a classed practice: Lower-class children differ significantly from middle-class (beta = .47, p < .01) and upper-class (beta = .82, p < .01) children, while middle-class children are involved in adult activities more often than are their upper-class peers (beta = .35, p < .01).

Upper-class children participate in organised activities more often than middle-class (beta = .48, p <.01) and lower-class (beta = .89, p < .01) children. Children from the lower class are also less frequently enrolled in organised activities than middle-class children (beta = −.41, p < .01).

Effects of children's own and peer-related practices on their academic habitus

In the final set of analyses, we examine two regression models for the dependent variable, i.e. children's habitus of *cultural goodwill* (Table 18.3). The *first model* checks the effects of family background and parenting variables on children's academic habitus without consideration of the contributions of children's own practices. Note that we used the middle class as a reference category for the class comparisons. The purpose of the *second model* is to test the effects of children's own practices, net of all other variables.

(1) The first model explains about 14 per cent of the variance in the criterion. Most noticeably, there is a counterintuitive negative relation between children's cultural goodwill and parental habitus (β = −.26, p < .01), and according to the Pratt index about 23 per cent of the R^2 value is accounted for by parental habitus. As a group of variables, *concerted cultivation* practices explain about 26.6 per cent of the R^2 value, with participation in organised activities being the strongest single predictor here (β = .14, p < .01). Children who do more organised activities tend to show higher *goodwill* at school.

(2) After adding children's unsupervised activities in the second model, one can observe a considerably enlarged R^2. The predictors now explain about 25 per cent of the variance in children's cultural goodwill and a large portion of that figure goes to children's own practices, mostly to children's school work and chores (d = .48). Predictors related to *concerted cultivation* now account for about 13.4 per cent of the variance explained, and thus remain important factors with regard to children's academic habitus. The same holds true for parental habitus, which still is a significant negative predictor of children's cultural goodwill (β = −.25, p < .01). The analyses reveal no effect of children's social class on their academic habitus.

Analyses not reported here show that literacy practices and outdoor activities do have a significant effect when children's school work and household chores are not included in the regression model. This is likely due to moderate correlations between these variables, whereas "work" has the strongest bivariate correlation with the criterion and therefore receives all the credit in a model with all variables included. Furthermore, the control variables, namely children's GPA and place of residence, account for approximately half of the variance explained.

Table 18.3 Multiple regression analyses predicting children's habitus of cultural goodwill

Effect	Model 1						Model 2				
	Zero-Order Correlation	Beta weight	S.E.	Est./S.E.	p-value	Relative Pratt Index d	Beta weight	S.E.	Est./S.E.	p-value	Relative Pratt Index d
Family background											
Family structure	.003	−.029	.059	−.482	.630	−.001	−.022	.050	−.445	.656	.000
Social class: lower	.004	−.099	.119	−.832	.405	−.001	−.173	.126	−1.369	.171	−.001
Social class: upper	−.031	−.067	.113	−.588	.557	.006	−.018	.111	−.163	.870	.003
Parental habitus	−.124***	−.258***	.063	−4.086	.000	.230+	−.247***	.062	−3.976	.000	.122+
Immigrant status: non-German parents	.113***	.087	.100	.876	.381	.031+	.009	.089	.098	.922	.017
Children's resources											
Children's space	.000	.019	.032	.596	.551	.000	.001	.032	.024	.981	.000
No. of children's books	−.075	−.018	.061	−.303	.762	.010	.020	.060	.339	.735	−.006
Concerted Cultivation											
Use of dialogue	.098*	.089	.064	1.392	.164	.063+	.133**	.057	2.344	.019	.052+
Promoting a sense of entitlement	.008	−.051	.050	−1.011	.312	−.003	−.040	.048	−.838	.402	−.001
Cultural parent-child activities	.081*	.114**	.047	2.451	.014	.066+	.092**	.045	2.034	.042	.030+
Child's participation in organized activities	.139***	.137***	.040	3.392	.001	.137+	.094***	.035	2.679	.007	.052+
Accomplishment of natural growth											
Use of directives	.049	.014	.053	.273	.785	.005	−.010	.050	−.206	.837	−.002
Involvement in adult activities	.022	−.013	.051	−.258	.796	−.002	−.032	.052	−.613	.540	−.003

Frequency of kin care	−.038	−.048	.048	−1.009	.313	.013	−.031	.044	−.689	.491	.005
Children's own and peer-related practices											
Media use	−.050						−.071**	.035	−2.028	.043	.014
Literary practices	.144***						−.012	.032	−.365	.715	−.007
Outdoor activities	.117***						.074**	.036	2.052	.040	.035+
School work and chores	.358***						.338***	.033	10.173	.000	.482+
Children's school performance											
Last annual GPA	−.136***	−.172***	.041	−4.197	.000	.168+	−.192***	.039	−4.976	.000	.104+
Children's demographic characteristics											
Children's age	−.066*	−.050	.035	−1.411	.158	.024	−.059	.034	−1.706	.088	.016
Children's gender: boy	−.075**	−.096	.061	−1.562	.118	.026	−.018	.061	−.300	.764	.014
Regional context											
Place of residence: East Germany	−.132***	−.284***	.100	−2.834	.005	.134+	−.227**	.091	−2.490	.013	.074+
R-Square		.139					.251				
Wald Test of Parameter Constraints		χ²(18) = 164.145, p = .000					χ²(22) = 351.851, p = .000				

Note. *p<.10, **p<.05, ***p<.01; +Relative Pratt Index > 1/(2 · no. of predictors) indicates a substantial contribution to the variance explained.

Summary and discussion

With regard to our first research question, our analyses reveal classed activity patterns in children's lives. Children's out-of-school lives are shaped by social class in several ways. For example, children's participation in outdoor peer activities displays a classed pattern similar to the one found by Lareau (2011). With regard to children's own practices, the differences are most profound in children's media use, outdoor activities and their school work and chores. Children's involvement in adult activities, e.g. doing grocery shopping, and participation in organised activities clearly indicate classed patterns of growing up. Lower-class children are more involved in their parents' daily routines than are middle- and upper-class children, while the latter show higher participation rates in organised activities.

Focussing on the second research question, we were able to show that children's academic habitus depends not only on activities that are part of a concerted cultivation parenting strategy, but also on children's own and peer-related practices. We see this as evidence of children's agency in a quantitative approach. Interestingly, children whose parents maintain a typical bourgeois lifestyle show less goodwill in the school setting. In the bivariate situation, there are only small correlations between parental habitus and children's academic habitus. We need to conduct further analyses to look into that finding more deeply. The result underscores the relevance of parental habitus for children's habitus, although the direction of this relationship would not be expected from theory. Yet one needs to consider the slight differences between parental habitus and children's cultural goodwill. The way we operationalised parental habitus hints at the cultural competence and ease that Bourdieu (1984) says is typically found in the bourgeoisie, while cultural goodwill would be more akin to a middle-class lifestyle. In other words, those who are not as familiar with high-status culture struggle more than others. Aside from that, since the connection between parental habitus and children's habitus is not as clear as one would think, the finding is by itself a hint at children's agency: Children have a say when it comes to their orientation toward school.

Remember that lower-class children engage more often with school work and chores, and that children's unsupervised work proves to be a strong predictor of academic habitus. Basically, this means that children who try to play by the rules in school are also relatively conformist in other settings. The findings give rise to another picture of lower-class childhood. There might even be two types of "disadvantaged childhoods": the accomplishment of natural growth and a variant of a culture of goodwill. Another explanation would be that disadvantaged children engage in more practices among themselves that are directly related to school, and thereby enhance their academic agency. At the same time, children from the middle and upper classes participate in organised activities that might only be remotely related to school, and yet these activities are also predictive of conformist dispositions toward school. When it comes to parenting effects on children's habitus, the results reveal positive relations between *concerted cultivation* and children's cultural goodwill.

Although following Lareau (2011), one would expect children exposed to *accomplishment of natural growth* strategies to feel less ambitious and behave less so at school, there is no evidence of negative effects of those parenting practices. This finding suggests that it is probably a lack of *concerted cultivation* practices that impedes children's positive orientation toward school. However, it is not the *accomplishment of natural growth* practices themselves that are related to disaffection from school. Furthermore, we did not find any direct effects of social class on children's habitus, which means that there is little room for assumptions about solid structural effects on children's habitus. Rather, it looks as if social class has an influence on various characteristics of children's lives, and these characteristics have a unique effect on children's academic habitus.

The results of our research have several implications for future research on social inequalities at the intersection of Childhood Studies and educational research.

With regard to educational research, more work needs to be done asking what lower-class children do to alter their own lives in the presence of limited resources. The fact that unsupervised activities, with the exception of frequent media use, are associated with children's agency at school shows that where children are granted room for their own practices, they also get the opportunity to be agentic in ways that help them thrive in adult-dominated contexts such as the school. To some extent, this contradicts the silent assumption that children's lives in disadvantaged homes are deficient per se. Yet our study is but a glimpse of how family processes and children's own and peer-related practices mutually affect academic habitus. Given the cross-sectional design of our study, future research should look further into how the habitus transforms over time with respect to the actions children take in order to alter their life course. It would be a valuable amplification of existing research to study how and in what way, theoretically and methodically, children themselves make a difference.

From the perspective of Childhood Studies, the results remind us of the fact that the influence of social class is ubiquitous in children's lives, no matter what part of their lives and which kinds of actions we observe. Our empirical data give reason to further develop the concept of agency from Childhood Studies combined with Bourdieu's relational approach (see also Alanen, Brooker & Mayall, 2015) in order to better explain and understand educational inequalities. Due to Bourdieu's focus on adult lives, a reconceptualisation of his concepts such as habitus is needed from a Childhood Studies perspective. As Childhood Studies favours qualitative approaches to children and childhood, there is little reference for a quantitative assessment of children's agency and habitus. Hence, there is still a long way to go to develop adequate and multi-faceted instruments for measuring children's agency and habitus.

Notes

1 This research project is funded by the Volkswagen Foundation. It has been carried out at Goethe University, Frankfurt, Germany, in the Faculty of Educational Sciences since 2010.
2 The fact that the study was done during the winter may in part explain why outdoor activities have the lowest mean of all unsupervised activities.

References

Alanen, L., Brooker. L., & Mayall, B. (2015). *Childhood with Bourdieu.* Basingstoke: Palgrave Macmillan.
Baumert, J. & Schümer, G. (2002). Familiäre Lebensverhältnisse, Bildungsbeteiligung und Kompetenzerwerb im nationalen Vergleich [Family background, educational participation and attainment in national comparison]. In Deutsches PISA-Konsortium (Ed.), *PISA 2000 – die Länder der Bundesrepublik Deutschland im Vergleich [PISA 2000 - the German Federal States in comparison]* (pp. 159–202). Opladen: Leske + Budrich.
Betz, T. (2013). Counting what counts. How children are represented in national and international reporting systems. *Child Indicators Research, 6*(4), 637–657.
Bourdieu, P. (1984). *Distinction: A Social Critique of the Judgment of Taste.* Cambridge: Harvard University Press.
Bourdieu, P. (1986). The forms of capital. In J. G. Richardson (Ed.), *Handbook of Theory and Research for the Sociology of Education* (pp. 241–260). New York: Greenwood.
Bourdieu, P. & Passeron, J. C. (1990). *Reproduction in Education, Society and Culture* (2nd ed.). London: Sage Publications.
Bühler-Niederberger, D. (2011). *Lebensphase Kindheit. Theoretische Ansätze, Akteure und Handlungsräume [The life phase of childhood. Theoretical approaches, actors and action areas].* Weinheim: Juventa.
Cheadle, J. E. (2008). Educational investment, family context, and children's math and reading growth from kindergarten through the third grade. *Sociology of Education, 81*(1), 1–31.
Dumais, S. A. (2002). Cultural capital, gender, and school success: the role of habitus. *Sociology of Education, 75*(1), 44–68.
Farkas, G. (1996). *Human Capital or Cultural Capital? Ethnicity and Poverty Groups in an Urban School District.* New York: A. de Gruyter.
Feinstein, L., Duckworth, K., & Sabates, R. (2004). *A Model of the Inter-generational Transmission of Educational Success* (Wider Benefits of Learning Research Report, Vol. 10). London: The Centre for Research on the Wider Benefits of Learning.
James, A. & James, A. L. (2004). *Constructing Childhood: Theory, Policy and Social Practice.* London: Palgrave Macmillan.
Lareau, A. (2011). *Unequal Childhoods: Class, race, and Family Life.* Berkeley: University of California Press.
Lee, J. -S. & Bowen, N. K. (2006). Parent involvement, cultural capital, and the achievement gap among elementary school children. *American Educational Research Journal, 43*, 193–218.
Mayall, B. (2002). *Towards a Sociology for Childhood: Thinking from Children's Lives.* Buckingham: Open University Press.
Mayall, B. (2015). Intergenerational relations: embodiment over time. In L. Alanen, L. Brooker & B. Mayall (Eds.), *Childhood with Bourdieu* (pp. 13–33). Basingstoke: Palgrave Macmillan.

Muthén, L. K. & Muthén, B. O. (2012). *Mplus: Statistical Analysis with Latent Variables.* User's Guide. Los Angeles: Muthén & Muthén.

Nathans, L. L., Oswald, F. L., & Nimon, K. (2012). Interpreting multiple linear regression: a guidebook of variable importance. *Practical Assessment, Research & Evaluation, 17*(9), 1–19.

Pratt, J. W. (1987). Dividing the indivisible: using simple symmetry to partition variance explained. In T. Pukkila & S. Puntanen (Eds.), *Proceedings of the Second International Conference in Statistics* (pp. 245–260). Tampere: University of Tampere.

Wohlkinger, F. & Ditton, H. (2012). Der Einfluss von Eltern, Lehrern und Kindern auf den Übergang nach der Grundschule [To what extent are students involved in decision-making? The role of parents, teachers and children in the transition from elementary school to the secondary level]. In R. Becker & H. Solga (Eds.), *Soziologische Bildungsforschung* [*Sociological Educational Research*] (pp. 44–63). Wiesbaden: Springer.

Conclusion

Potentials of a reconceptualised concept of agency

Florian Esser, Meike S. Baader, Tanja Betz and Beatrice Hungerland

After around 25 years as a key concept in Childhood Studies, agency is due for a thorough revision, and the reconceptualisation undertaken in this volume serves this purpose. This process has brought to light the wide-ranging theoretical and analytical potential that a critical and relational concept of agency still offers today. In the actual interdisciplinary research field of agency and childhood, we have identified five topics: (1) new paths in the theoretical conceptualisation of agency; (2) children as actors in research and their effects on research practice; (3) historical world; (4) transnational and majority world; and (5) institution-based approaches to childhood and agency.

One of the reasons why James and James (2012) refer to agency as an important topic is that it connects Childhood Studies as an interdisciplinary research field with other theoretical debates in the social sciences (p. 4). In particular, it prompts us to question, on various levels, explicit and implicit dichotomies between action and structure, micro-level and macro-level or childhood and adulthood.

The contributions to this volume make it clear how little childhood can be conceived without adulthood, though no straightforward contrast emerges. One crucial result of this volume shows that the concept of agency, as a former, actual and future key concept of Childhood Studies, is connected with a second important concept, that of "generational order". The discourse on generational order includes debate about breaking up and decentring the concept: There is talk of a plurality of unequal generational orders (Honig, 2009, p. 48), for example, or of different scripts for postmodern childhood, which allow or restrict different forms of childhood (Zinnecker, 2001, p. 15). Similarly, the concept of agency needs to be subjected to constant theoretical and empirical testing. This can be achieved – as it was shown in this volume – by asking what actor positions children can occupy in different institutional settings and social contexts, in specific sets of circumstances, and also what form child agency takes when children are among themselves. Here, childhood agency is also linked with key features of social differentiation and power relations, which include, but are not limited to, the generational order (see above; see also the Introduction). Some of the categories that become relevant here are sex, class, race and age, which may – but do not have to – have repercussions for agency (Thorne, 1993; Konstantoni, 2012).

Agency should not be conceived simply as individual action directed against *the* social structure. Against this background, the sharp differentiation between qualitative and quantitative research approaches in Childhood Studies also becomes questionable. Thanks to this differentiation, agency is still mainly investigated within the framework of qualitative research designs, while quantitative research deals with the "hard" structures. The essays brought together in this volume offer relevant theoretical possibilities and preliminary empirical approaches, and thus encourage a future strengthening of the connection between qualitative and quantitative techniques.

Such individualistic theories of action also become questionable in light of feminist and post-colonialist positions. These positions question established Western ideas of autonomous agency, according to which an autonomous (male) subject appropriates and subjugates the world (Haraway, 1989). Gender studies and queer studies have also underlined the existence of two different ways of looking at agency: one that tends to position agency substantively as an ability of the individual, and one that associates it with social relations and contexts (McClintock, 1999, p. 15; Engel, 2015, p. 193). This "decentred" idea of agency opens up new theoretical connections, for example to approaches based on theories of interdependence or theories of the subaltern. It also allows research questions that have previously been marginalised in the context of agency, including research with very young children (0–3 years), research on transcultural processes between minority and majority worlds, on political contexts (Renner, 2015, p. 304) and on race-class-gender differences (Bernstein, 2011). In this way, agency analyses can take into account the multiplicity of childhoods that exist globally and historically, and the diversity of the horizons of experience that arise in these childhoods.

Thus, the core question of (future) research on agency, from the perspective of Childhood Studies, is not "How can we use Childhood Studies to make children into agents?" This would only lead to a politically and pedagogically motivated normative short circuit: Children are supposed to have agency, therefore they must have agency, and this can and must be found in the course of the research (Oswell, 2013, p. 38; Kraftl, 2013). Instead agency gains its epistemic potential not as a clear-cut concept but as an "ambiguous" one (Bordonaro & Payne, 2012; Renner, 2015): "Children and young people's agency should certainly be a contested and scrutinised concept rather than one which is taken-for-granted, unproblematised or assumed inherently to be positive and desired by all children and young people" (Tisdall & Punch, 2013, p. 256). If we look at it in this way, the analytical question that presents itself is: What agency arises for children from the fact that they are children (Honig, 2013, p. 144) in different contexts, and what actor positions can they occupy as children?

References

Bernstein, R. (2011). *Racial Innocence: Performing American Childhood from Slavery to Civil Rights.* New York, London: New York University Press.

Bordonaro, L. I. & Payne, R. (2012). Ambiguous agency. Critical perspectives on social interventions with children and youth in Africa. *Children's Geographies, 10*(4), 365–372.

Engel, A. (2015). Queere Politik der Paradoxie: Widerstand unter Bedingungen neoliberaler Vereinnahmungen [Queer politics of the paradox: Resistance under the conditions of neoliberal appropriation]. In K. Walgenbach & A. Stach (Eds.), *Geschlecht in gesellschaftlichen Transformationsprozessen [Gender in social processes of transformation]* (pp. 191–204). Opladen, Berlin: Barbara Budrich.

Haraway, D. J. (1989). *Primate Visions: Gender, Race and Nature in the World of Modern Science.* New York: Routledge.

Honig, M. -S. (2013). Kindheiten [Childhoods]. In A. Scherr (Ed.), *Soziologische Basics. Eine Einführung für pädagogische und soziale Berufe [Sociological basics. An introduction for educational and social professions]* (2nd ed., pp. 143–148). Wiesbaden: Springer VS.

Honig, M. -S. (2009). Das Kind der Kindheitsforschung. Gegenstandskonstitution in den childhood studies [The Child in Childhood Studies. A Constitution of the Research Object]. In M. -S. Honig (Ed.), *Ordnungen der Kindheit: Problemstellungen und Perspektiven der Kindheitsforschung [Regimes of childhood: scientific problems and perspectives in childhood studies]* (pp. 25–52). Weinheim: Juventa.

James, A. & James, A. (2012). *Key Concepts in Childhood Studies* (2nd ed.). Los Angeles: Sage Publications.

Konstantoni, K. (2012). Children's peer relationships and social identities: exploring cases of young children's agency and complex interdependencies from the minority world. *Children's Geographies, 10*(3), 337–346.

Kraftl, P. (2013). Beyond "voice", beyond "agency", beyond "politics"? Hybrid childhoods and some critical reflections on children's emotional geographies. *Emotion, Space and Society, 9,* 13–23.

McClintock, A. (1995). *Imperial Leather: Race, Gender and Sexuality in the Colonial Contest.* London: Routledge.

Oswell, D. (2013). *The Agency of Children: From Family to Global Human Rights.* Cambridge: Cambridge University Press.

Renner, K. J. (2015). The ambiguous role of agency in Childhood Studies. *Child, special issue of WSQ, 43*(1/2), 304–307.

Thorne, B. (1993). *Gender Play: Girls and Boys in School.* Buckingham: Open University Press.

Tisdall, E. K. M. & Punch, S. (2013). Not so "new"? Looking critically at Childhood Studies. *Children's Geographies, 10*(3), 249–264.

Zinnecker, J. (2001). Children in young and aging societies: the order of generations and models of childhood in comparative perspective. In S. L. Hofferth & T. J. Owens (Eds.), *Children at the Millenium: Where Have We Come From? Where Are We Going?* (pp. 11–52). Amsterdam, London, New York: Elsevier Science.

Index

absence and presence 82–3
academic habitus 271–87
academic success 2–3, 271–80
actor-network theory 52–6
"addressing acts" 257–62
agency: actor-network theory and 52–6; analysis of 75–8; boundaries and 165–78; in Childhood Studies 1–12, 19–31, 48–51, 89–99, 290–1; child protection cases and 243–53; conceptualisations of 8–9, 35, 42, 48, 71, 90–1, 136, 151, 157, 184–90, 211, 243–53, 272, 290; conscious agency 86; critical realism and 12, 75–87; critiquing 185–7; cross-cultural learning and 192–3; effects on research 9–10; extending 89–99; feminist ethic of care and 61–72; historical approaches 10–11, 135–46, 290; human agency 11, 75–7, 85–90, 95, 99, 120; in India 197–208; individual agency 11, 76, 86–7, 94–8, 176; institution-based approaches to 10–12, 290; as key concept 1–12, 48–51, 290–1; meanings of 75–87; network theories and 51–8; new paths in 8–9, 290; ontology of 24–8, 30–1; parent guidebooks and 165–78; peer cultures and 42, 256–7; personal agency 86–7; perspectives of 51–8; practice theories and 34–45; pre-school children and 227–40; rational agency 86; re-aligning

19–31; reconceptualising 1–12, 48–58, 271–87; relational approaches to 95–9; relational perspectives of 51–8; relational theories and 51–8; relational understanding of 38, 48–9, 62–3; relativistic approaches to 95–9; research on 128–9, 271–87; social relationships and 53–6; in social theory 93–5; sociology of childhood and 61–72; structure and 8, 19–20, 34, 50–1, 62, 75–82, 93–5, 228–9, 258–9, 274; substantialist understanding of 9, 48–58; theoretical conceptualisation of 8–9, 290; theoretical perspectives on 19–31; "thick/thin" agency 48–58; transnational perspectives of 10–11, 183–94, 290; understanding of 48–58, 62–3, 75–87, 89–99, 183–94; world perspectives of 10–11, 183–94, 290; *see also* childhood agency
ambiguous voices 109–13; *see also* voice
artefacts, role of 34, 36–9

babies 44, 86, 167, 174; *see also* children
"back to nature" 171–4
being and thinking 81–2
boundaries for children 165–78; *see also* children

care theories 61–72; *see also* ethic of care
change and difference 83